CHILDREN'S MODERN F·I·R·S·T EDITIONS

CHILDREN'S

MODERN

F·I·R·S·T

EDITIONS

Their Value to Collectors
JOSEPH CONNOLLY

Macdonald Orbis

For

VICTORIA and CHARLES,

despite whose youthful enthusiasm
and voluble exuberance,
I finally managed to finish this book.

A Macdonald Orbis BOOK

© Joseph Connolly 1988

First published in Great Britain in 1988
by Macdonald & Co (Publishers) Ltd
London & Sydney

A member of Maxwell Pergamon Publishing
Corporation plc

British Library Cataloguing in Publication Data

Connolly, Joseph, *1950–*
    Children's modern first editions: their
    value to collectors.
    1. Children's literature in English. First
    editions, 1900–1987
    I. Title
    094´.4

    ISBN 0–356–15741–5

Filmset by August Filmsetting, Haydock, St Helens
Printed and bound in Great Britain by
Hazell Watson & Viney Limited,
Member of BPCC plc,
Aylesbury, Bucks

Editor: Jennifer Jones
Art Editor: Bobbie Colegate-Stone
Designers: Bill Mason and Sarah Scrutton
Photographer: Chris Linton
Indexer: Alexandra Corrin

Macdonald & Co (Publishers) Ltd
Greater London House
Hampstead Road
London NW1 7QX

CONTENTS

Introduction   6

Code of Values   13

Index of Authors   14

The Books   16

Index of Illustrators   332

Acknowledgements   336

INTRODUCTION

Ten or so years ago, I published a book called *Collecting Modern First Editions* which was a pioneering attempt to demonstrate to collectors (and, more to the point, *would-be* collectors) the range of (largely) contemporary books that was available, together with an indication of prices one might be expected to pay. The exercise was received tolerably well (although viewed with suspicion by the trade, for whom it was never primarily intended) but subsequent editions seem to have found a ready, and ever-growing market; indeed, over the past decade, the collecting of modern first editions has become the biggest growth area in the entire field of book collecting, and in the original edition were listed authors who were at the time quite neglected by both collectors and dealers alike, but who have since gone on to become the most avidly sought-after of all. It is hard to believe now that the inclusion of the likes of P.G. Wodehouse, Ian Fleming and Agatha Christie incurred a good deal of adverse criticism – the posh end of the market wouldn't even be seen to *touch* such people; now, of course, the very earliest work by these authors is *famous* for being hugely valuable, and at each notable auction those very up-market dealers who ten years ago rejected the stuff out of hand are to be seen frantically out-bidding each other in order to secure the prizes for their own – at least until they can be sold on to some rich collector in New York, Tokyo or (at a pinch) London.

The foregoing is no mere idle and protracted exercise in I-told-you-so-ing, but rather something to be borne in mind for the very near future: history might just be about to repeat itself. In the third and latest edition of *Modern First Editions: Their Value to Collectors* (Macdonald 1987) I included more children's writers than ever – the likes of Leon Garfield joining ranks with old favourites such as Anthony Buckeridge, Richmal Crompton, Frank Richards, Milne, Tolkien, Dahl and so on. But if Garfield, why not Alan Garner and Jane Gardam? What about Rosemary Sutcliff, Diana Wynne Jones, Philippa Pearce, John Rowe Townsend? Yes indeed – to say nothing of the giants such as Beatrix Potter, nor of the creators of Paddington, Rupert, The Wizard of Oz, Babar, Ameliaranne, Tintin, Asterix, Mary Poppins, the Moomins, Dr Dolittle, Orlando, Worzel Gummidge and, yes – little Noddy and Big Ears. But all that, I reasoned, would require a separate book – and such was the inspiration for this one. All these characters are here, along with authors as diverse as Edward Ardizzone, J.M. Barrie, Raymond Briggs, Ted Hughes, William Mayne, Arthur Ransome, Dr Seuss – well, have a glance at the Index of Authors, and you'll get the spirit of the thing.

Collecting children's modern first editions will prove to be enormous fun and not nearly as expensive as you might have imagined; perhaps more to the point, I believe it to be so undervalued and little explored a field as to be poised upon becoming the great growth area of book collecting into the 1990s.

As you will see from the values of much of the contemporary fiction (more about values later), a vast amount of first-rate and beautifully illustrated material (and more about *illustrators* later, as well) may be acquired at very low prices indeed. It is true that if you are hell-bent on possessing the first (privately printed) edition of *The Tale of Peter Rabbit* you will have to find about £3,000 to pay for it, but from these giddy heights prices descend pretty dramatically – the vast majority of the thousands of books listed here cost less than £20, and a great deal of them a quarter of that. This book, of course, will heighten people's awareness, but it should also serve to release on to the market a mass of previously unrated material, which will prove beneficial to both dealers and collectors alike.

By 'unrated' I mean *extremely* modern – for although of course there is nothing at all *new* about collecting children's books, attention given to contemporary writers is unjustly slight. I suppose that second to early chap-books and nursery rhymes, the field of Victorian illustrated classics is the most popular of all (illustrators such as Walter Crane, Arthur Rackham and Kate Greenaway continuing to hold sway) along with what are termed 'Boys' Stories' – those fat and highly ornately bound Hentys and similar, forever eager to spill out endless tales of derring-do, pluck and grit. Comics, annuals and Puffins also have their devotees, but the brief of this book is more mainstream: the word 'modern', with a very few important exceptions, means twentieth-century (thus, Henty doesn't qualify, and nor do all those sadistic nineteenth-century public school stories, but such as Percy Westerman and our very own Biggles, Bunter, William and Jennings, do).

The new concept I am putting forward is for children's books to be pursued not just for their age, illustrations, bindings and classic tales, but as an *extension* of modern first edition collecting, with the same criteria applied: the quest for fine copies in dust-wrapper (if applicable) of quality, lasting literature from the year 1900 right up to *now* (the listings are complete to January 1988) – together with an inordinate amount of downright *fun*, for children's books are all about entertainment, magic, wit and inspiration. Very many excellent contemporary children's writers are bought, endlessly borrowed from libraries, read and re-read by their adoring juvenile audience, and entirely overlooked by the book collector: this will change.

Collecting Modern Firsts

That said, a few words on the general subject of collecting modern firsts, before narrowing down to the specific brief of this book. The basic idea is to decide on what you *want* to collect (an author, a period, a genre) and then to set about seeking out the very best copies that your budget will allow. The more recent a book, the finer the condition should be – ideally in a state identical to that on publication day. If presented with the choice of a mint, dust-wrappered first or a so-so copy with either partial dust-wrapper or none at all, it is always folly to go for the latter – even though it may be a quarter of the price. The reason is simple – you will never be really content with it; at the back of your mind you will be wanting a perfect copy, and when you find it you will encounter difficulties offloading the scruffy number because everyone else is hunting for fine copies too. The traditional exceptions to this rule have always been in the cases of a book being impossibly scarce – in which case one is glad to possess any copy at all – or if the dust-wrapper (as opposed to the book itself) is virtually unknown, in which case the unadorned boards will serve. In the realms of children's books, however, one encounters additional irritations, wouldn't you know it – the most problematical being the truth that on first publication of some beautiful and highly collectable children's book or other, adults were very often foolish enough to entrust it to a *child*; do I have to draw pictures? No. Alas, many of the said children did just that – blue crayon, generally, all over the page. The colouring-in of line drawings (or *partial* colouring-in – children get bored easily) is another horror you will come across, along with endless records of ownership starting off 'This Book Belongs Too...' and culminating in '...The Wurld, The Universe, Outer Spaice!' Some see such youthful exuberance as charming, but it makes most people want to be sick.

Even in the world of adult modern first editions, truly mint copies are scarce, but one will always come across novels and slim volumes of poetry that clearly had been bought new, carefully read once, and shelved; with children's books, this is unknown – these books have been *loved* (often, to bits). So, a level of tolerance is required here, but still one shouldn't settle for utterly *repellent* copies – unless, of course, it truly isn't important to you (in which case, it quite simply isn't important).

The Dust-wrapper

Now I have already hinted at the relevance of the dust-wrapper; if you are at all serious about assembling a decent collection it is *extremely* important – not faddist – and I am sure will come to be seen as particularly so in the field of children's books. Firstly, why does the dust-wrapper matter at all? Basically because one is trying to gather books in their original condition, and the dust-wrapper formed a vital part of the whole on first publication. It is also true to say, however, that from an aesthetic point of view, the earlier the book, the less important the dust-wrapper. Beatrix Potters look much nicer without their rather dull dust-wrappers (which is just as well, as these rather dull dust-wrappers are prized on a par with gold dust) simply because during the early part of the century so much design attention was focused upon the boards and not upon the often drab and starkly utilitarian dust-wrapper, as will be seen further with, say, A.A. Milne, early Angela Brazil and Kipling. Although the *financial* value of any of these would be greatly enhanced by the presence of this all-important paper wraparound, the books look none the worse for their lack of it – and often, as I have implied, a good deal better. As we come forward in time, however, we find a situation where *all* of the design thinking has been lavished upon the dust-wrapper, the boards of the book bearing only the title and author on the spine, and nothing else whatever – except in the case of picture books for younger children, where often the dust-wrapper depiction is repeated on the hard covers. This exception apart, unwrappered copies of children's modern first editions of the 1940s onwards look singularly uninspiring; the very *essence* of stuff such as the 'William' series or the 'Biggles' books is conveyed in the spirited and colourful artwork of the dust-wrappers – and is quite often carried through with a frontispiece and illustrations throughout the text. This brings us to the other area of importance with regard to the dust-wrapper, together with one more factor vital to the business of collecting children's books: the illustrators.

The Illustrations
With straightforward modern firsts, it is the exception rather than the rule for the book to be illustrated; with *children's* modern firsts, the reverse is the case. I think it is true to say that the great majority of books listed here do have illustrations, and in each case I append the artist's name after the title (the illustrators' names are indexed separately at the end of the book). Very often, the illustrator will also be responsible for the dust-wrapper, and equally often the author him/herself is both illustrator *and* dust-wrapper artist, and in such cases the particular importance of the wrapper becomes self-evident. Although this book will be of some assistance to those collectors who are *primarily* interested in illustrators (regardless of what work they are illustrating) it is aimed much more at collectors of *writing*. Thus, every book *both* written *and* illustrated by, for instance, Charles Keeping is listed under his author entry; his illustrations for other authors are also indexed – but only if these authors appear in this book. So, Keeping is credited as the illustrator of, say, Alan Garner's *Elidor* in the Garner entry, as he is for various books in many other author entries – Bernard Ashley, Henry Treece and Nina Bawden, to name a few – but his body of work for things as various as *Beowulf* and *Les Misérables* does not appear here, because these titles do not come within the scope of this book. The value of a book *rises* if it is illustrated by an established and collectable artist, and declines *sharply* if any plate is damaged or missing – or if it lacks the dust-wrapper.

Values
Value: the very word is a minefield, but I shall try to make plain what I have

done. Each title in this book is followed by its date and British and American publishers (if both are applicable) in order of publication precedence. There is then a price code in the form of a letter ranging from **A** (the lowest – up to £5) to **U** (the top – up to £3,000); a table of these and all intermediary codes will be found at the very end of the book, and is interchangeable with that used in the companion volume *Modern First Editions: Their Value to Collectors*. These values translate as the price you could expect to pay for a fine first edition of the book in dust-wrapper (if issued) from a professional bookseller – but the very situation of the shop, the predilections of a dealer, and the amount he or she had to pay for a book (along with the weather and the time of day) are all factors that can cause variations. What might prove interesting and maybe surprising to both the established collector and to the novice, however, are the vast numbers of books in the **A** and **B** category – these low valuations in no way reflecting the often superb quality of the books, but rather underlining the truth that a great deal of good stuff is not yet seriously collected at all, and represents a golden and unplumbed opportunity.

Another encouraging factor is that even when *dizzy* prices are encountered, they reflect true scarcity and desirability, for despite the high incidence of illustration and handsome production already discussed, all the signed, artificially expensive limited-edition nonsense is virtually unknown in the realm of children's books, and so one will never be required to fork out hundreds of pounds simply because some publisher has elected to print only 250 copies of a book by a sought-after author (knowing the demand to be greater) and bind the whole in some outrageously kitsch material and stick it in a fur-lined box. Ninety-nine per cent of the books listed here are straightforward trade editions of books intended to be bought for and read by children and not collected at all – hence the vexing difficulty of finding good copies, the exciting and worthwhile pursuit of same, and the comfortable knowledge that one is unlikely to go bankrupt in the process.

Authors' Inscriptions

None of this is to suggest that authors' signatures are in themselves worthless – generally they add to the financial value of the book, and always to the romance of the thing, for a signature in a book is the ultimate authentication of the fact that its creator has handled that very copy; I agree not *very* romantic if the book is one of a stack of hundreds that the author has ploughed through like a robot during a signing session – but what of an inscribed *Peter Pan* or *The Wind in the Willows*? Heady stuff.

There is a class structure to the importance of autographs, and with children's books – because of the prominence of the illustrators – this is made rather more complicated and enticing. The raw signature of a living writer is not seen to be heart-stopping because of his or her relative accessibility (dead authors are known to sign nothing). Exceptions to this generalization arise in the cases of elderly modern masters who as a matter of policy never sign anything that isn't one of those aforementioned expensive limited things, or else a gift to a personal friend (in terms of this book, this probably comes down to Graham Greene). An inscription to yourself is better than just a plain signature, and an inscription to someone of greater renown is even better. One step up from that is a book inscribed to a person in some way associated with the author – a relative, colleague, the subject of the dedication or – maybe best of all – the illustrator; this can work the other way around too – the *illustrator's* inscription in the author's own copy. To obtain a personal inscription from both author *and* illustrator (assuming them not to be, as is often the case, one and the same person) is highly desirable – Roald Dahl and Quentin Blake, say. Sometimes, an ownership name of someone *other* than the author can be very attractive too – Alison Uttley's copy of a Beatrix Potter, for instance (she *must* have had them) or a 'Rupert' first edition bearing the signature of John Betjeman. Unless you are yourself slightly (or even *very*) famous or in some way associated with the book, it is best not to write in your own name, however; a bookplate is a somewhat grandiose but marginally more acceptable substitute, but no subsequent owner will thank you for it.

How to Recognize Firsts and Where to Find Them

Recognizing a first edition is not generally a problem – the verso (other side) of the title page (or, often in the case with heavily illustrated and picture books, the last page of text) will make plain the date of publication; if the book is a reprint, a reissue, a second or later impression or a new edition, this information is normally recorded. The more recent a book, the more straightforward the recognition; however, many rattling good tales by such as Bessie Marchant, Elinor Brent-Dyer, Percy Westerman and so on quite often make no mention at all of dates, and in such cases one has to be guided by hand-written and dated inscriptions on the endpaper (a dicey business) or rely on the research of a trusted and knowledgeable bookseller; comparison with a *known* first edition is another possibility, but sometimes – as with Beatrix Potter – the whole ritual of identification becomes such a nightmare that only direct comparison with copies in the British Museum is the answer – and as Beatrix Potter is exceptional in *every* way, in her case I go into all sorts of details for each and every title, as her entry will reveal.

And where to find all these mouth-watering goodies? All secondhand bookshops, obviously, but particularly the few that sell nothing *but* children's books as well as the many more 'private' dealers who also specialize. 'Private' means that there is no shop as such, but appointments may generally be made to view the stock, and very often catalogues are issued; look also at the trade advertisements at the rear of most book-related journals, notably the *Times Literary*

Supplement. The increasing number of book fairs up and down the country are also good quarry, and many of the private dealers exhibit there, together with the better known shops. That doughty old factory of dreams, the jumble sale, is maybe a better bet for children's books than for any other kind, as households frequently clear out loads of them – mainly, I think, in order to be able to regret ever having done any such thing, much in the same way as we all rue the day we got rid of our comics and Matchbox toys. Do not neglect *anywhere* where things are for sale: street markets, charity shops, garage and car-boot sales – they all have potential, and just one overlooked gem can compensate for weeks of fruitless searching as well as restoking the fire of acquisitiveness and renewing the thrill of the chase.

At this point, it seems apposite to append a chunk of all-purpose information for the collector, reprinted from *Modern First Editions*.

Care of Books

Understandably, if a collector has whacked out more than he anticipates earning during the coming quarter on a fine copy of some juicy rarity, he is fairly anxious to keep it that way. There is no special trick to this, and most of it is common sense, but a few guidelines are as follows:

* If the dust-wrapper is unlaminated, it can make good sense to cover it with *non-adhesive* transparent acetate such as Libra-Film. This improves the look (although it can make for irritating reflection) while proving resistant to the clamminess of collectors' (and – more to the point – others') fingers. It is also a good way of discouraging a slightly frayed or chipped dust-wrapper from becoming more so. Do not Sellotape the front *or* rear of a dust-wrapper. In time it becomes quite cancerously yellow, and drops off in disgust.
* Do not pack books too tightly in shelves. This in itself does not damage them, but it risks disfigurement every time you want to pull one out.
* Do not let books flop about, either. Pages sag, bindings warp, dust gets in – enough said.
* Avoid placing books directly opposite a sunny window – the spine colours will fade; particularly red and navy, for some reason or another.
* Glass-fronted bookcases are not a good idea. Books need air, or the pages go brown and smell like Venice.
* Steer clear of radiators – they dry the air, suck the natural moisture out of the books, with warped boards and foxing as a result. It is altogether more wholesome to freeze.
* Damp is the arch-enemy. Damp will rapidly render your desirables not.
* Try to avoid your house catching fire, as this does no good at all. And while your house is still intact, it is a sound idea to persuade all babies and animals to live elsewhere – and if you *really* value your books, only offer hospitality to

illiterates who won't persist in bloody *touching* them all the time. Mind you, you *will* have to tolerate them telling you you could open a shop with all these books (people have even suggested this to me – *in* the shop) and betting that you haven't read them all.

In this book you will find all the information necessary to form as fine a collection of children's modern first editions as luck, space, money and a gradually acquired 'feel' and expertise will allow. Here too, among the fashionably beleaguered and introspective young teenagers who populate the most recent fiction, you will discover or re-encounter all manner of wizards, witches, school bullies, adventurers, explorers, puppets, dolls, dragons, scarecrows, soldiers, cowboys, fairies, steam engines, dancers, detectives, eccentrics, knights in armour, swots and leprechauns – to say nothing of every single member of the animal kingdom you can think of, and quite a few more that your imagination wouldn't even run to. Throw caution to the winds and gather them all – remembering only to keep them well away from the arch-enemies heat, damp, dust – and particularly children. Just joking, kids! I think.

CODE OF VALUES USED THROUGHOUT THIS BOOK

A	up to £5	L	up to £200
B	up to £10	M	up to £250
C	up to £20	N	up to £300
D	up to £30	O	up to £400
E	up to £40	P	up to £500
F	up to £50	Q	up to £750
G	up to £60	R	up to £1,000
H	up to £80	S	up to £1,500
I	up to £100	T	up to £2,000
J	up to £125	U	up to £3,000
K	up to £150		

INDEX OF AUTHORS

ADAMS, Richard
AHLBERG, Allan
AIKEN, Joan
ARDIZZONE, Edward
ASHFORD, Daisy
ASHLEY, Bernard
AVERY, Gillian
AWDRY, The Rev. W.

BAGNOLD, Enid
BANNERMAN, Helen
BARRIE, J.M.
BAUM, L. Frank
BAWDEN, Nina
B.B.
BELLOC, Hilaire
BERESFORD, Elisabeth
BETJEMAN, John
BIRO, Val
BLAKE, Quentin
BLYTON, Enid
BOND, Michael
BOSTON, Lucy
BRAZIL, Angela
BRENT-DYER, Elinor M.
BRIGGS, Katharine M.
BRIGGS, Raymond
BRISLEY, Joyce Lankester
BRUNA, Dick
BUCKERIDGE, Anthony
BURNETT, Frances Hodgson
BURNINGHAM, John

CHRISTOPHER, John
CLARK, Leonard
COREN, Alan
CRADOCK, Mrs Henry
CRESSWELL, Helen
CROMPTON, Richmal
CUNLIFFE, John

DAHL, Roald
de BRUNHOFF, Jean
de la MARE, Walter
DICKINSON, Peter

ELIOT, T.S.
ENRIGHT, Elizabeth
ESTES, Eleanor

FARJEON, Eleanor
FLEMING, Ian
FOREMAN, Michael
FOREST, Antonia
FULLER, Roy

GARDAM, Jane
GARFIELD, Leon
GARNER, Alan
GARNETT, Eve
GODDEN, Rumer
GOSCINNY & UDERZO
GOUDGE, Elizabeth
GRAHAME, Kenneth
GREEN, Roger Lancelyn
GREENE, Graham
GRUELLE, Johnny

HALDANE, J.B.S.
HALE, Kathleen
HARRIS, Rosemary
HEINLEIN, Robert A.
HERGÉ
HEWARD, Constance
HILL, Eric
HOBAN, Russell
HUGHES, Richard
HUGHES, Ted
HUNTER, Norman
HUTCHINS, Pat

JANSSON, Tove
JARRELL, Randall
JOHNS, W.E.
JONES, Diana Wynne
JOYCE, James

KASTNER, Erich
KEEPING, Charles
KING, Clive
KING-SMITH, Dick
KIPLING, Rudyard

le GUIN, Ursula K.
LEWIS, C. Day
LEWIS, C.S.
LINGARD, Joan
LIVELY, Penelope
LOFTING, Hugh
LONDON, Jack

MANNING, Rosemary
MARCHANT, Bessie
MASEFIELD, John
MAYNE, William
MILLIGAN, Spike
MILNE, A.A.
MONTGOMERY, L.M.
MOORE, Dorothea
MURPHY, Jill

NAUGHTON, Bill
NEEDHAM, Violet
NESBIT, E.
NICOLL, Helen
NORTON, Mary
NYE, Robert

OXENHAM, Elsie J.

PARDOE, M.
PEAKE, Mervyn
PEARCE, Philippa

PIEŃKOWSKI, Jan
PORTER, Eleanor H.
PORTER, Gene Stratton
POTTER, Beatrix
PRØYSEN, Alf

RANSOME, Arthur
REEVES, James
RICHARDS, Frank
ROSS, Diana

SCARRY, Richard
SENDAK, Maurice
SEUSS, Dr.
SIMMONDS, Posy
SMITH, Dodie
STRANG, Herbert
STREATFEILD, Noel
SUTCLIFF, Rosemary
SYMONDS, John

THURBER, James
TODD, Barbara Euphan
TOLKIEN, J.R.R.
TOURTEL, Mary
TOWNSEND, John Rowe
TRAVERS, P.L.
TREASE, Geoffrey
TREECE, Henry

UTTLEY, Alison

WALSH, Jill Paton
WESTERMAN, Percy
WHITE, E.B.
WHITE, T.H.
WILDER, Laura Ingalls
WILLANS, Geoffrey
WILLARD, Barbara
WILLIAMSON, Henry
WODEHOUSE, P.G.

ADAMS, Richard

Born in Berkshire, 1920

Certainly Adams is a unique writer in that it is difficult to draw the line between what is and what is not expressly intended for children. Adams himself is reported as recognizing no such distinction, citing (with maybe just a tinge of arrogance) *Alice*. All such considerations aside, it is now clear, in my view, that while *Watership Down* is secure in terms of permanence as a children's classic, no such status may be accorded any of his other books. *Shardik* has its fans, it is true, but *The Plague Dogs* made a lot of Adams' admirers worried as to what he might come up with next.

There have been a couple of attractive stories – attractive largely because of the illustrations and the production – but lately Adams seems to have given himself over to rather cumbersome books that most decidedly *are* for adults, if they are for anyone (*The Girl in a Swing, Maia*).

In terms of collectability, *Watership Down* remains the only truly scarce and desirable item, as is reflected in the price. Below are listed what may generally be considered the *children's* books.

1	**Watership Down** (*novel*) *The first illustrated edition (illus. John Lawrence) was published in a slip-case by Penguin/Kestrel 1976.*	REX COLLINGS 1972 MACMILLAN NY 1974	**N** **E**
2	**Shardik** (*novel*)	LANE 1974 SIMON & SCHUSTER 1975	**B** **A**
3	**Nature Through the Seasons** (*non-fiction*)	KESTREL 1975 SIMON & SCHUSTER 1975	**A** **A**
4	**The Tyger Voyage** (*verse*) (*illus. Nicola Bayley*)	CAPE 1976 KNOPF 1976	**B** **A**
5	**The Ship's Cat** (*verse*) (*illus. Alan Aldridge*)	CAPE 1977 KNOPF 1977	**B** **A**
6	**The Plague Dogs** (*novel*)	LANE 1977 KNOPF 1978	**A** **A**
7	**Nature Day and Night** (*non-fiction*) *3 & 7 form a pair. Both were written with Max Hooper. 3 was illustrated by David Goddard & Adrian Williams, 7 by David Goddard & Stephen Lee.*	KESTREL 1978 VIKING 1978	**A** **A**

8	**The Watership Down Film Picture Book**	LANE 1978	**B**
		MACMILLAN NY 1978	**B**
	Based on the animated film by CIC, 1978.		
9	**The Iron Wolf and Other Stories**	LANE 1980	**A**
	(*illus. Yvonne Gilbert & Jennifer Campbell*)		
10	**The Unbroken Web**	CROWN US 1980	**A**
	Same as 9.		
11	**The Bureaucrats** (*story*)	VIKING KESTREL 1985	**A**
		VIKING US 1985	**A**

AHLBERG, Allan *British, born 1938*

Allan Ahlberg and his illustrator wife Janet are truly book-makers extraordinary; book-makers in no derogatory sense, it must be understood, for although they are undeniably prolific, there is never a sense of their cobbling up a book from not very much. On the contrary, the books seem jam-packed with ideas and inventiveness, the finished production having as much importance as the stories, verse and illustrations within. This is best exemplified by such delights as *Peepo!*, in which the cleverly positioned holes in the pages are integral to the book and the game being played, and *The Jolly Postman*, where each page is an envelope yielding all sorts of secrets when the letters are withdrawn. This book seems set to become an all-time classic, appealing so strongly as it does to a child's sense of discovery, to say nothing of nosiness.

1	**Brick Street Boys** (*stories*)	COLLINS 1975–6	**A**
	5 little volumes (*illus. Janet Ahlberg*): Here		**Each**
	are the Brick Street Boys; A Place to		
	Play; Sam the Referee; Fred's Dream;		
	The Great Marathon Football Match.		
2	**The Old Joke Book**	KESTREL 1976	**A**
		VIKING US 1977	**A**
3	**Burglar Bill** (*story*)	HEINEMANN 1977	**A**
	(*illus. Janet Ahlberg*)	GREENWILLOW US 1977	**A**
4	**Jeremiah in the Dark Woods** (*story*)	KESTREL 1977	**A**
	(*illus. Janet Ahlberg*)	VIKING US 1978	**A**
5	**The Vanishment of Thomas Tull**	BLACK 1977	**A**
	(*story*) (*illus. Janet Ahlberg*)	SCRIBNER 1977	**A**

6	**Cops and Robbers** (*verse*)	HEINEMANN 1978	**A**
	(*illus. Janet Ahlberg*)	GREENWILLOW 1978	**A**
7	**Each Peach Pear Plum** (*verse*)	KESTREL 1978	**A**
	(*illus. Janet Ahlberg*)	VIKING US 1979	**A**
8	**The One and Only Two Heads** (*story*)	COLLINS 1979	**A**
	(*illus. Janet Ahlberg*)		
9	**Son of a Gun** (*story*)	HEINEMANN 1979	**A**
	(*illus. Janet Ahlberg*)		
10	**The Little Worm Book** (*story*)	GRANADA 1979	**A**
	(*illus. Janet Ahlberg*)	VIKING US 1980	**A**
11	**Two Wheels, Two Heads** (*story*)	COLLINS 1979	**A**
	(*illus. Janet Ahlberg*)		
12	**Funnybones** (*story*)	HEINEMANN 1980	**A**
	(*illus. Janet Ahlberg*)	GREENWILLOW US 1981	**A**
13	**A Pair of Sinners** (*story*)	GRANADA 1980	**A**
	(*illus. John Lawrence*)		
14	**Mr Biff the Boxer** (*reader*)	KESTREL 1980	**A**
	This is the first in the series of 'readers' whose blanket title is Happy Families.	GOLDEN PRESS US 1982	**A**
15	**Mrs Plug the Plumber** (*reader*)	KESTREL 1980	**A**
	(*illus. Joe Wright*)	GOLDEN PRESS US 1982	**A**
16	**Mrs Wobble the Waitress** (*reader*)	KESTREL 1980	**A**
		GOLDEN PRESS US 1982	**A**
17	**Master Salt the Sailor's Son** (*reader*)	KESTREL 1980	**A**
	(*illus. André Amstutz*)	GOLDEN PRESS US 1982	**A**
18	**Miss Jump the Jockey** (*reader*)	KESTREL 1980	**A**
	(*illus. André Amstutz*)		
19	**Mr Cosmo the Conjurer** (*reader*)	KESTREL 1980	**A**
	(*illus. Joe Wright*)		
20	**Peepo!** (*verse*)	KESTREL 1981	**B**
	(*illus. Janet Ahlberg*)		
21	**Peek-a-boo!**	VIKING US 1981	**B**
	Same as 20.		

22	**Miss Brick the Builder's Baby** (*reader*) (*illus. Colin McNaughton*)	PENGUIN 1981 GOLDEN PRESS US 1982	**A** **A**
23	**Mr Buzz the Beeman** (*reader*) (*illus. Faith Jaques*)	PENGUIN 1981 GOLDEN PRESS US 1982	**A** **A**
24	**Mr and Mrs Hay the Horse** (*reader*) (*illus. Colin McNaughton*)	PENGUIN 1981 GOLDEN PRESS US 1982	**A** **A**
25	**Mrs Lather's Laundry** (*reader*) (*illus. André Amstutz*)	PENGUIN 1981 GOLDEN PRESS US 1982	**A** **A**
26	**Master Money the Millionaire** (*reader*) (*illus. André Amstutz*)	PENGUIN 1981	**A**
27	**Mr Tick the Teacher** (*reader*) (*illus. Faith Jaques*)	PENGUIN 1981	**A**
28	**The Ha Ha Bonk Book** (*jokes*)	KESTREL 1982	**A**
29	**Help Your Child to Read** *This is the blanket title for six individual* *publications*: Fast Frog; Silly Sheep; Double Ducks; Bad Bear; Poorly Pig; Rubber Rabbit. (*illus. Eric Hill*)	GRANADA 1982	**A** **Each**
30	**The Baby's Catalogue** (*story*) (*illus. Janet Ahlberg*)	KESTREL 1982	**A**
31	**Ten in a Bed** (*story*) (*illus. André Amstutz*)	GRANADA 1983	**A**
32	**Please, Mrs Butler** (*verse*) (*illus. Fritz Wegner*)	KESTREL 1983	**A**
33	**Daisychains** (*verse*) *This is the blanket title for a series of* *four*: That's My Baby; Summer Snowmen; Which Witch?; Ready Teddy Go.	HEINEMANN 1983	**A** **Each**
34	**Readers** (*illus. André Amstutz*) *Six individual titles*: Hip-Hippo Ray; King Kangaroo; Mister Wolf; Spider Spy; Tell-Tale Tiger; Travelling Moose.	GRANADA 1983	**A** **Each**
35	**Yum Yum** (*slot book*) (*illus. Janet Ahlberg*)	VIKING 1984	**A**

36 Playmates (*slot book*) (*illus. Janet Ahlberg*)	VIKING 1984	**A**
37 The One True Santa (*story*) (*illus. Janet Ahlberg*)	HEINEMANN 1985	**A**
38 Red Nose Readers (*illus. Colin McNaughton*) *Eight individual titles*: Bear's Birthday; Big Bad Pig; Fee Fi Fo Fum; Happy Worm; Help!; Jumping; Make a Face; So Can I.	WALKER 1985	**A** **Each**
39 Woof! (*story*) (*illus. Fritz Wegner*)	VIKING 1986	**A**
40 Yellow Nose Readers (*illus. Colin McNaughton*) *Four individual titles*: Me and My Friend; Shirley's Shops; Push the Dog; Crash! Bang! Wallop!	WALKER 1986	**A** **Each**
41 The Cinderella Show (*story*) (*illus. Janet Ahlberg*)	VIKING 1986	**A**
42 Blue Nose Readers (*illus. Colin McNaughton*) *Four individual titles*: One, Two, Flea; Tell Us a Story; Blow Me Down; Look Out for the Seals.	WALKER 1986	**A** **Each**
43 The Jolly Postman (*story*) (*illus. Janet Ahlberg*)	HEINEMANN 1986	**B**

AIKEN, Joan   *Born in Sussex, 1924*

For her sheer energy, humour and enthusiasm, Joan Aiken has been favoura-
bly compared with everyone from Leon Garfield to Dickens. To this may be
added an almost wild inventiveness and imagination (many of her novels are
'historical', except for the fact that they take place during a period that never
existed – the nineteenth-century reign of James III) and an output and
range that are little short of extraordinary. Her short stories tend to be not
quite fairytales, not quite supernatural – but certainly brimful of elements of
these; sheer *magic* comes closest, and some of them jolly scary to boot: you'll

have to read them to know what I mean – and if you *have* read them, then you already know.

In addition to the children's books listed below, Joan Aiken has published nearly twenty other works – mainly very stylish thrillers for adults. Her one work of non-fiction will be of interest to collectors: *The Way to Write for Children* (Elm Tree, 1982).

1	**All You've Ever Wanted and Other Stories** (*illus. Pat Marriott*)	CAPE 1953		**D**
2	**More Than You Bargained for and Other Stories** (*illus. Pat Marriott*)	CAPE 1955 ABELARD SCHUMAN 1957		**D** **B**
3	**The Kingdom and the Cave** (*fiction*) (*illus. Dick Hart*)	ABELARD SCHUMAN 1960		**C**
4	**The Wolves of Willoughby Chase** (*fiction*) (*illus. Pat Marriott*)	CAPE 1962 DOUBLEDAY 1963		**C** **B**
5	**Black Hearts in Battersea** (*fiction*) (*illus. Robin Jacques*)	DOUBLEDAY 1964 CAPE 1965		**C** **C**
6	**Nightbirds on Nantucket** (*fiction*) (*illus. Pat Marriott*)	CAPE 1966 DOUBLEDAY 1966		**C** **B**
7	**The Whispering Mountain** (*fiction*)	CAPE 1968 DOUBLEDAY 1969		**C** **B**
8	**A Necklace of Raindrops and Other Stories** (*illus. Jan Pienkowski*)	CAPE 1968 DOUBLEDAY 1968		**C** **C**
9	**Armitage, Armitage, Fly Away Home** (*fiction*) (*illus. Betty Fraser*)	DOUBLEDAY 1968		**B**
10	**A Small Pinch of Weather and Other Stories** (*illus. Pat Marriott*)	CAPE 1969		**B**
11	**Night Fall** (*fiction*)	MACMILLAN 1969 HOLT RINEHART 1971		**B** **B**
12	**Smoke From Cromwell's Time and Other Stories**	DOUBLEDAY 1970		**B**

13	**The Green Flash and Other Tales of Horror, Suspense and Fantasy**	HOLT RINEHART 1971	**B**
14	**The Cuckoo Tree** (*fiction*) (*illus. Pat Marriott*)	CAPE 1971 DOUBLEDAY 1971	**B** **B**
15	**The Kingdom Under the Sea and Other Stories**	CAPE 1971	**B**
16	**All and More** (*fiction*) (*illus. Pat Marriott*)	CAPE 1971	**B**
17	**A Harp of Fishbones and Other Stories** (*illus. Pat Marriott*)	CAPE 1972	**B**
18	**Arabel's Raven** (*fiction*) (*illus. Quentin Blake*) *This is the first collection of the BBC's* Jackanory *stories, featuring Arabel and her talking raven, Mortimer Jones.*	BBC 1972 DOUBLEDAY 1974	**C** **B**
19	**The Escaped Black Mamba** (*fiction*) (*illus. Quentin Blake*)	BBC 1973	**C**
20	**All But a Few** (*fiction*)	PENGUIN 1974	**A**
21	**The Bread Bin** (*fiction*) (*illus. Quentin Blake*)	BBC 1974	**C**
22	**Midnight is a Place** (*fiction*)		
23	**Not What You Expected: A Collection of Short Stories**	DOUBLEDAY 1974	**B**
24	**Mortimer's Tie** (*fiction*) (*illus. Quentin Blake*)	BBC 1976	**C**
25	**A Bundle of Nerves: Stories of Horror, Suspense and Fantasy**	GOLLANCZ 1976	**B**
26	**The Faithless Lollybird and Other Stories** (*illus. Pat Marriott*)	CAPE 1977 DOUBLEDAY 1978	**B** **A**
27	**The Far Forests: Tales of Romance, Fantasy and Suspense**	VIKING 1977	**B**

28	**Go Saddle the Sea** (*fiction*)	DOUBLEDAY 1977	B
	(*illus. Pat Marriott*)	CAPE 1978	B
29	**Tale of a One-way Street and Other Stories** (*illus. Jan Pienkowski*)	CAPE 1978	B
		DOUBLEDAY 1979	B
30	**Mice and Mendelson** (*fiction*)	CAPE 1978	B
	(*illus. Babette Cole. Music John Sebastian Brown*)		
31	**Mortimer and the Sword Excalibur** (*fiction*) (*illus. Quentin Blake*)	BBC 1979	B
32	**The Spiral Stair** (*fiction*) (*illus. Quentin Blake*)	BBC 1979	B
33	**A Touch of Chill: Stories of Horror, Suspense and Fantasy**	GOLLANCZ 1979	B
		DELACORTE 1980	A
34	**Arabel and Mortimer** (*fiction*) (*illus. Quentin Blake*) Contains 24, 31 & 32	CAPE 1980	B
		DOUBLEDAY 1981	B
35	**The Shadow Guests** (*fiction*)	CAPE 1980	B
		DELACORTE 1980	A
36	**Mortimer's Portrait on Glass** (*fiction*) (*illus. Quentin Blake*)	BBC 1980	B
37	**Mr Jones's Disappearing Taxi** (*fiction*) (*illus. Quentin Blake*)	BBC 1980	B
38	**The Stolen Lake** (*fiction*) (*illus. Pat Marriott*)	CAPE 1981	A
		DELACORTE 1981	A
39	**A Whisper in the Night: Stories of Horror, Suspense and Fantasy**	GOLLANCZ 1982	A
40	**Mortimer's Cross** (*fiction*) (*illus. Quentin Blake*)	CAPE 1983	B
		HARPER 1983	B
41	**Bridle the Wind** (*novel*) (*illus. Pat Marriott*) A sequel to 28.	CAPE 1983	A
		DELACORTE 1983	A
42	**The Kitchen Warriors** (*stories*)	BBC 1983	A
43	**Up the Chimney Down and Other Stories** (*illus. Pat Marriott*)	CAPE 1984	A
		HARPER 1984	A

44	**Mortimer Says Nothing** (*fiction*)	CAPE 1985	**B**
	(*illus. Quentin Blake*)	HARPER 1985	**B**
45	**Dido and Pa** (*fiction*)	CAPE 1986	**A**
	(*illus. Pat Marriott*)	DELACORTE 1987	**A**
46	**Past Eight O'Clock** (*fiction*)	CAPE 1986	**A**
	(*illus. Pat Marriott*)		

ARDIZZONE, Edward   *Born in China, 1900 Italian, British Citizen 1921.*
Died 1979

Still very much collected today, though maybe with not quite the enthusiasm of ten or fifteen years ago, Ardizzone is probably better known as an illustrator than as a *writer* of children's books – and this is hardly surprising when you consider that during his lifetime – in addition to the books listed below (written *and* illustrated by Ardizzone) he supplied the drawings for no less than 160 works by other hands – authors as diverse as Dickens, H.E. Bates, Walter de la Mare, Trollope, T.H. White, John Buchan and Eleanor Farjeon. Although I am *not* an Ardizzone addict, I do have a special fondness for his version of de la Mare's *Peacock Pie*, John Betjeman's *A Ring of Bells* and the 1970s reissue of Graham Greene's *The Little Fire Engine, The Little Train, The Little Steam Roller* and *The Little Horse Bus*.

Ardizzone's drawing style is more complex than at first it might appear, while retaining a child-like simplicity that matches his prose very well.

1	**Little Tim and the Brave Sea Captain**	OUP 1936	**K**
	A revised edition was published in 1955 by OUP and in America by Walck.		
2	**Lucy Brown and Mr Grimes**	OUP 1937	**J**
	A revised edition was published by Bodley Head in 1970, and in America by Walck in 1971.		
3	**Tim and Lucy Go to Sea**	OUP 1938	**I**
	A revised edition was published in 1958 by OUP and in America by Walck.		
4	**Nicholas and the Fast-moving diesel**	EYRE & SPOTTISWOODE 1947	**G**
		WALCK 1959	**B**

5	**Paul, the Hero of the Fire**	PENGUIN 1948	C
	A revised edition was published in 1962 by	HOUGHTON MIFFLIN 1949	B
	Constable and in 1963 in America by Walck.		
6	**Tim to the Rescue**	OUP 1949	E
7	**Tim and Charlotte**	OUP 1951	E
8	**Tim in Danger**	OUP 1953	E
9	**Tim All Alone**	OUP 1956	D
		WALCK 1961	B
10	**Johnny the Clockmaker**	OUP 1960	D
		WALCK 1960	C
11	**Tim's Friend Towser**	OUP 1962	D
		WALCK 1962	C
12	**Peter the Wanderer**	OUP 1963	D
		WALCK 1964	C
13	**Diana and Her Rhinoceros**	BODLEY HEAD 1964	D
		WALCK 1964	C
14	**Sarah and Simon and No Red Paint**	CONSTABLE 1965	D
		DELACORTE 1966	C
15	**Tim and Ginger**	OUP 1965	D
		WALCK 1965	C
16	**Tim to the Lighthouse**	OUP 1968	D
		WALCK 1968	C
17	**Johnny's Bad Day**	BODLEY HEAD 1970	C
18	**The Wrong Side of the Bed**	DOUBLEDAY 1970	B
	Same as 17.		
19	**Tim's Last Voyage**	BODLEY HEAD 1972	C
		WALCK 1973	B
20	**Ship's Cook Ginger**	BODLEY HEAD 1977	B
		MACMILLAN US 1978	B

Two autobiographical titles will be of interest to the collector:

The Young Ardizzone: An Autobiographical Fragment	STUDIO VISTA & MACMILLAN US 1970	C
Diary of a War Artist	BODLEY HEAD 1974	B

Also of interest:
GABRIEL WHITE: **Edward Ardizzone: Artist and Illustrator** (BODLEY HEAD 1979, SHOCKEN US 1980)

ASHFORD, Daisy   *Born in Sussex, 1881. Died 1972*

At the age of nine, Daisy Ashford wrote a little book, and forgot about it for nearly twenty years. No doubt herself intensely amused by the fantastically convoluted prose style, misspellings and outrageous syntax, she showed it to a friend who conveyed the manuscript to Chatto & Windus. They published in 1919 with a Preface by J.M. Barrie – popularly supposed by everyone to have written the thing himself – and between May and October had printed fifteen impressions. It is a truly *wonderful* book – one that can come along only once a century, if we are lucky. Impossible that it could have been written by an adult, for there is no 'cleverness' or selfconsciousness in the howlers. One could quote it endlessly, but try these for size:

'His friend gave a weary smile and swollowed a few drops of sherry wine. It is fairly decent he replied with a bashful glance at Ethel after our repast I will show you over the premisis. Many thanks said Mr. Salteena getting rarther flustered with his forks.'

Or: 'No no cried Bernard and taking the bull by the horns he kissed her violently on her dainty face.' Or even: 'The toilit set was white and mouve and there were some violets in a costly varse.' Priceless.

Here I will end my chapter.

The Young Visiters or Mr Salteena's Plan   CHATTO & WINDUS 1919   **H**

ASHLEY, Bernard   *Born in London, 1935*

A good example of the genre writer for older children, who draws upon his experience as a London headmaster to build more complex stories than usual, concerning problems and conflicts within a largely working-class and multi-racial urban environment. 'Realism' – sometimes harsh – abounds, but they read nowhere near so depressingly as I might have made them sound; the plotting is tight, and the language carries them along. The very nature of the bulk of Ashley's fiction *might* render it desirable in the future as a 'period piece', or else its relevance and power might become reduced by the events he describes becoming too commonplace. But I am sure that Bernard Ashley will move with the times.

Below is a complete listing of the fiction, which was preceded by half a dozen 'readers' and the like, intended for younger children, and not central to the Ashley *oeuvre*.

1	**The Trouble with Donovan Croft** (*illus. Fermin Rocker*)	OUP 1974	C
2	**Terry on the Fence** (*illus. Charles Keeping*)	OUP 1975 PHILLIPS 1977	C B
3	**All My Men**	OUP 1977 PHILLIPS 1978	B B
4	**A Kind of Wild Justice** (*illus. Charles Keeping*)	OUP 1978 PHILLIPS 1979	B B
5	**Break in the Sun** (*illus. Charles Keeping*)	OUP 1980 PHILLIPS 1980	B B
6	**Dinner Ladies Don't Count** (*illus. Janet Duchesne*)	MACRAE 1981	A
7	**I'm Trying to Tell You** (*illus. Lyn Jones*)	KESTREL 1981	A
8	**Dodgem**	MACRAE 1981 WATTS 1982	A A
9	**Linda's Lie** (*illus. Janet Duchesne*)	MACRAE 1982	A
10	**High Pavement Blues**	MACRAE 1983	A
11	**Janey**	MACRAE 1985	A
12	**Running Scared**	MACRAE 1986	A
13	**Clipper Street Stories:** (*illus. Jane Cope*) Calling for Sam; Taller Than Before.	ORCHARD 1987	A Each

---

AVERY, Gillian   *Born in Surrey, 1926*

A highly respected and a unique author who has successfully drawn upon her intimate knowledge and understanding of the Victorian age in order to set her children's fiction in the 1870s. The authenticity of the settings and Avery's skill as a storyteller ensure the life of these novels – in addition to

which she has published several books on the Victorian age and its literature,
as well as having edited new editions of many novels of the period by such as
Mrs Molesworth, Mrs Ewing and Charlotte Yonge.

1	**The Warden's Niece** (*illus. Dick Hart*)	COLLINS 1957	**D**
2	**Trespassers at Charlcote** (*illus. Dick Hart*)	COLLINS 1958	**D**
3	**James without Thomas** (*illus. John Verney*)	COLLINS 1959	**C**
4	**The Elephant War** (*illus. John Verney*)	COLLINS 1960 HOLT RINEHART 1971	**C** **A**
5	**To Tame a Sister** (*illus. John Verney*)	COLLINS 1961 VAN NOSTRAND 1964	**C** **A**
6	**The Greatest Gresham** (*illus. John Verney*)	COLLINS 1962	**C**
7	**The Peacock House** (*illus. John Verney*)	COLLINS 1963	**C**
8	**The Italian Spring** (*illus. John Verney*)	COLLINS 1964 HOLT RINEHART 1972	**C** **A**
9	**Call of the Valley** (*illus. Laszlo Acs*)	COLLINS 1966 HOLT RINEHART 1968	**B** **A**
10	**A Likely Lad** (*illus. Faith Jaques*)	COLLINS 1971 HOLT RINEHART 1971	**B** **A**
11	**Ellen's Birthday** (*illus. Krystyna Turska*)	HAMISH HAMILTON 1971	**B**
12	**Ellen and the Queen** (*illus. Krystyna Turska*)	HAMISH HAMILTON 1972 NELSON US 1974	**B** **A**
13	**Jemima and the Welsh Rabbit** (*illus. John Lawrence*)	HAMISH HAMILTON 1972	**B**
14	**Freddie's Feet** (*illus. Krystyna Turska*)	HAMISH HAMILTON 1976	**B**
15	**Huck and Her Time Machine**	COLLINS 1977	**B**
16	**Mouldy's Orphan** (*illus. Faith Jaques*)	COLLINS 1978	**B**

17 Sixpence!   COLLINS 1979   **B**
   (*illus. Antony Maitland*)

AWDRY, The Rev. W.   *Born in Hampshire, 1911*

Extremely popular with little boys (and bigger ones) for over forty years, not only does Awdry's splendid Railway series seemed to have not suffered a jot from the passing of the age of steam, but it seems to have blossomed into a truly permanent landmark in twentieth-century children's books. Of course, the television programmes and the *phenomenal* spin-off market have done no harm, but I doubt whether they were strictly necessary. Rather like Noddy, Thomas the Tank Engine has been puffing away quite contentedly since the 1940s, both characters (along with their friends) certain to enchant many generations to come. I should imagine that first editions of the earlier titles are damnably difficult to come across in a state where they have not been, shall we say, *loved* to death by their original owners – but, as usual, well worth the chase.

There follows a listing of the Tank Engine series:

1	**The Three Railway Engines**	WARD 1945	**E**
2	**Thomas, the Tank Engine**	WARD 1946	**F**
3	**James, the Red Engine**	WARD 1948	**C**
4	**Tank Engine Thomas, Again**	WARD 1949	**C**
5	**Troublesome Engines**	WARD 1950	**C**
6	**Henry, the Green Engine**	WARD 1951	**C**
7	**Toby, the Tram Engine**	WARD 1952	**C**
8	**Gordon, the Big Engine**	WARD 1953	**C**
9	**Edward, the Blue Engine**	WARD 1954	**C**
10	**Four Little Engines**	WARD 1955	**C**
11	**Percy, the Small Engine**	WARD 1956	**C**

   (*1–11 are illustrated by C. Reginald Dalby*)

12	**The Eight Famous Engines**	WARD 1957	**B**
13	**Duck and the Diesel Engine**	WARD 1958	**B**
14	**The Little Old Engine**	WARD 1959	**B**
15	**The Twin Engines**	WARD 1960	**B**

16	**Branch Line Engines**	WARD 1961	**B**
17	**Gallant Old Engine**	WARD 1962	**B**
	(12–17 are illustrated by John Kenney)		
18	**Stepney, the Bluebell Engine**	WARD 1963	**B**
19	**Mountain Engines**	WARD 1964	**A**
20	**Very Old Engines**	WARD 1965	**A**
21	**Main Line Engines**	WARD 1966	**A**
22	**Small Railway Engines**	KAYE & WARD 1967	**A**
23	**Enterprising Engines**	KAYE & WARD 1968	**A**
24	**Oliver, the Western Engine**	KAYE & WARD 1969	**A**
25	**Duke, the Lost Engine**	KAYE & WARD 1970	**A**
26	**Tramway Engines**	KAYE & WARD 1972	**A**
	(18–26 are illustrated by Gunvor & Peter Edwards)		

The original format of the little books has been retained for the Rev. Awdry's son Christopher's continuation of the series, and the numeration on the spine runs consecutively. This series could chug and chug!

27	**Really Useful Engines**	KAYE & WARD 1983	**A**
28	**James and the Diesel Engines**	KAYE & WARD 1984	**A**
29	**Great Little Engines**	KAYE & WARD 1986	**A**
30	**More About Thomas the Tank Engine**	KAYE & WARD 1986	**A**
31	**Gordon the High-speed Engine**	KAYE & WARD 1987	**A**

Also by the Rev. Awdry:

Belinda the Beetle *(illus. Ionicus)*	BROCKHAMPTON 1958	**C**
Railway Map of the Island of Sodor *(illus. C. Reginald Dalby)* *(Revised ed. Kaye & Ward 1971)*	WARD 1958	**C**
Belinda Beats the Band *(illus. John Kenney)*	BROCKHAMPTON 1961	**B**
Surprise Packet *(illus. Peter Edwards)*	KAYE & WARD 1972	**A**

BAGNOLD, Enid

Born in Kent, 1889. Died 1981

More of a popular playwright than a children's author – but nonetheless the creator of a classic that seems to live on for ever, despite the rather snooty disdain with which it is regarded by the *cognoscenti*. I suppose the reason for this attitude is that the book is seen to be just another of those things that are latched on to by pony-fixated schoolgirls, and that the film provided the vehicle for Elizabeth Taylor's vault to stardom; both of these factors are true, and I can't see that they affect the book either way. From a collector's point of view, the first edition of *National Velvet* is not easily come across, but because of the reasons outlined above, it is unlikely to be terribly expensive.

Enid Bagnold wrote only two children's books (as opposed to sixteen other works) and they are both listed below.

1	**Alice and Thomas and Jane** (*novel*)	HEINEMANN 1930	**B**
	(*illus. the author & Laurian Jones*)	KNOPF 1931	**A**
2	**National Velvet** (*novel*)	HEINEMANN 1935	**C**
	(*illus. Laurian Jones*)	MORROW 1935	**B**

BANNERMAN, Helen

Born in Edinburgh, 1862. Died 1946

The Story of Little Black Sambo is an intensely amusing and imaginative little story made up by Helen Bannerman in 1898 while she was living in India, and like many tales, its original intention was simply to divert her own children. Her rather attractive primary-coloured illustrations helped the book to become an immediate success, this in turn spawning the sequels. As is well known, the books have been attacked on grounds of racism, just as Billy Bunter has been denounced on grounds of fatism; all this is monstrously silly, and very boring; I fully expect these humourless dolts to ban Paddington Bear on grounds of duffle-coatism and I am *amazed* that the Mad Hatter's Tea Party has escaped castigation for deriving fun from those who are round the bend.

1	**The Story of Little Black Sambo**	GRANT RICHARDS 1899	**J**
		STOKES US 1900	**J**
2	**The Story of Little Black Mingo**	NISBET 1901	**H**
		STOKES US 1902	**H**
3	**The Story of Little Black Quibba**	NISBET 1902	**E**
		STOKES US 1903	**E**

4 **Little Degchie-Head: An Awful Warning to Bad Babas**	NISBET 1903	**E**
5 **The Story of Little Kettle-head** *Same as 4.*	STOKES US 1904	**E**
6 **Pat and the Spider: The Biter Bit**	NISBET 1904 STOKES US 1905	**D** **D**
7 **The Story of the Teasing Monkey**	NISBET 1906 STOKES US 1907	**D** **D**
8 **The Story of Little Black Quasha**	NISBET 1908 STOKES US 1908	**D** **D**
9 **The Story of Little Black Bobtail**	NISBET 1909 STOKES US 1909	**D** **D**
10 **The Story of Sambo and the Twins**	STOKES US 1936 NISBET 1937	**C** **C**
11 **The Story of Little White Squibba**	CHATTO & WINDUS 1966	**B**

(It should be noted that the 1899–1909 titles were published anonymously.)

Also of interest to collectors:

ELIZABETH HAY: **Sambo Sahib: The Story of Little Black Sambo and Helen Bannerman** (HARRIS [EDINBURGH] 1981)

BARRIE, J.M. *Born in Scotland, 1860. Died 1937*

Although Barrie is still best known for *Peter Pan* (despite the fact that he published around seventy books during his lifetime) it is not popularly realized that essentially this is his *only* work for children; there are, however, one or two relevant lead-up works, and a couple of important developments, as you will see below.

The saga began in 1897, when Barrie became captivated first by a beautiful woman named Sylvia Llewelyn Davies, who was married to a barrister, and then as an extension of this, by her three strikingly good-looking young sons – his 'lost boys'. These boys loved playing castaways, explorers and pirates and Barrie encouraged them in this and took photographs of their exploits. He had these published in book form in an edition of only two; one he kept himself, and the other he gave to the boys' father – who instantly 'lost' it. Arthur Llewelyn

'The Borrowers' quartet (1952–1961) all with artwork by Diana Stanley, together with the fifth and final volume, twenty years on, illustrated by Pauline Baynes.

Four corkers for girls – a late (*non*-chalet) Brent-Dyer and a representative Bessie
Marchant, together with one of the eleven 'Josephine' books (illustrated by Honor C.
Appleton) and the last of the nine 'Ameliaranne's, with artwork by S.B. Pearse.

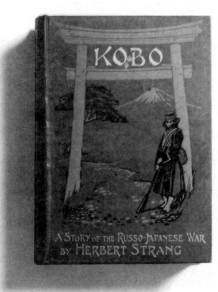

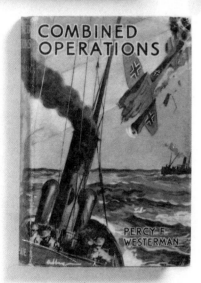

A quartet of humdingers for chaps with the right stuff and a leaning towards grit, pluck and derring-do.

An early B.B. (written and illustrated by D.J. Watkins-Pitchford), a Ransome (again illustrated by the author), a golden period 'Bunkle', and the classic *Mary Poppins* (1934) illustrated by E.H. Shepard's daughter, Mary.

Davies, not unnaturally, rather resented Barrie's intense influence upon his wife and children, although no impropriety was at the time suggested. There was no happy ending: Arthur died of cancer in 1907 – by which time there were four boys in the family; Barrie's own marriage came to an end in 1909, due to his wife's infidelity, and although Barrie hoped then to marry Sylvia, she died the following year. Of the boys, George – who had inspired *Peter Pan* – was killed in Flanders in 1915, and Michael, the second eldest, drowned at Oxford in 1921; it seems that Barrie's further interest in life died with him.

1 **The Boy Castaways of Black Lake Island**
This was the book of photographs taken by Barrie, and privately printed (by Constable) in an edition of only two.

2 **Peter Pan in Kensington Gardens**   HODDER & STOUGHTON   **N**
(fiction) (illus. Arthur Rackham)   1906
This was derived from Barrie's adult play The Little White Bird *(1902) and is a prose reworking for children. The play of Peter Pan had already been performed to huge acclaim, but was not published in script form until much later – see below.*

3 **Peter and Wendy** *(fiction)*   HODDER & STOUGHTON   **I**
(illus. F.D. Bedford)   1911
This was reissued by Hodder & Stoughton in 1921 as Peter Pan and Wendy.

4 **Peter Pan: or, the Boy Who Wouldn't Grow Up** *(play)*   HODDER & STOUGHTON   **C**
1928
This was published as a five-shilling volume in Barrie's Collected Plays.

5 **When Wendy Grew Up: An Afterthought** *(play)*   NELSON 1957   **C**
This play was first produced in 1908.

There have been several critical studies and biographies of Barrie; there follows a selection:
B.D. CUTLER: **Sir James M. Barrie: A Bibliography** (GREENBERG US 1931)
JANET DUNBAR: **J.M. Barrie: The Man Behind the Image** (COLLINS 1970)
ANDREW BIRKIN: **J.M. Barrie and The Lost Boys** (CONSTABLE 1979, POTTER 1979)

BAUM, L. Frank — *Born in New York, 1856. Died 1919*

Baum is hailed less as a stylist than the creator of the first truly enduring American fantasy. Certainly the MGM film of *The Wizard of Oz* forms most people's entire familiarity with Baum's work (if, indeed, they are aware it *is* Baum's work) and although this is perfectly reasonable, it should none the less be borne in mind that this film was made in 1939 – nearly forty years after first publication, by which time the book was securely established in the annals of American children's literature.

In America, Baum is an institution, but by no means all of his books (he published over seventy) made their way to Britain, which maybe in some way accounts for the fact that we are aware only of the Wizard, the Whole Wizard and Nothing But the Wizard. Admittedly, a lot of the later books were fairly simplistic reworkings of similar themes, but I list all the related 'Oz' books here, while omitting the loads of other things that he wrote under a sheaf of pseudonyms.

1	**A New Wonderland** (*fiction*) (*illus. Frank Berbeck*)	RUSSELL US 1900	**L**
2	**The Wonderful Wizard of Oz** (*fiction*) (*illus. W.W. Denslow*)	HILL US 1900 HODDER & STOUGHTON 1906	**Q** **I**
3	**Dot and Tot of Merryland** (*fiction*) (*illus. W.W. Denslow*)	HILL US 1901	**J**
4	**The Master Key: An Electrical Fairy Tale**	BOWEN MERRILL US 1901 STEVENS & BROWN 1902	**I** **H**
5	**The Life and Adventures of Santa Claus** (*fiction*) (*illus. Mary Cowles Clark*)	BOWEN MERRILL US 1902 STEVENS & BROWN 1902	**K** **J**
6	**The Enchanted Island of Yew** (*illus. Fanny Cory*)	BOBBS MERRILL US 1903	**I**
7	**The Marvelous Land of Oz** (*illus. John R. Neill*)	REILLY & BRITTON US 1904 REVELL UK 1904	**K** **I**
8	**Queen Zixi of Ix** (*illus. Frederick Richardson*)	CENTURY US 1905 HODDER & STOUGHTON 1906	**J** **I**
9	**The Woggle-Bug Book** (*illus. Ike Morgan*)	REILLY & BRITTON US 1905	**J**

10	**John Dough and the Cherub** (*illus. John R. Neill*)	REILLY & BRITTON US 1906	**J**
		CONSTABLE 1974	**B**
11	**Ozma of Oz** (*illus. John R. Neill*) *Reissued in Britain by Hutchinson in 1942 as* Princess Ozma of Oz.	REILLY & BRITTON US 1907	**H**
12	**Dorothy and the Wizard in Oz** (*illus. John R. Neill*)	REILLY & BRITTON US 1908	**I**
13	**The Road to Oz** (*illus. John R. Neill*)	REILLY & BRITTON US 1909	**H**
14	**The Emerald City of Oz** (*illus. John R. Neill*)	REILLY & BRITTON US 1910	**H**
15	**The Sea Fairies** (*illus. John R. Neill*)	REILLY & BRITTON US 1911	**H**
16	**Sky Island** (*illus. John R. Neill*)	REILLY & BRITTON US 1912	**H**
17	**The Patchwork Girl of Oz** (*illus. John R. Neill*)	REILLY & BRITTON US 1913	**H**
18	**Tik-Tok of Oz** (*illus. John R. Neill*)	REILLY & BRITTON US 1914	**H**
19	**The Scarecrow of Oz** (*illus. John R. Neill*)	REILLY & BRITTON US 1915	**H**
20	**Rinkitink in Oz** (*illus. John R. Neill*)	REILLY & BRITTON US 1916	**H**
21	**The Lost Princess of Oz** (*illus. John R. Neill*)	REILLY & BRITTON US 1917	**H**
22	**The Tin Woodman of Oz** (*illus. John R. Neill*)	REILLY & BRITTON US 1918	**H**
23	**The Magic of Oz** (*illus. John R. Neill*)	REILLY & LEE US 1919	**H**
24	**Glinda of Oz** (*illus. John R. Neill*)	REILLY & LEE US 1920	**H**

Also of interest:

FRANK JOSLYN BAUM & RUSSELL P. MACFALL: **To Please a Child: The Biography of L. Frank Baum, Royal Historian of Oz** (REILLY & LEE US 1961)

ALLEN EYLES: **The World of Oz** (VIKING 1985)

BAWDEN, Nina   ·   *Born in London, 1925*

Nina Bawden has written about twenty books for adults in addition to those for children listed here. Her reputation is equally high in both spheres, although I suspect that collectors have yet to wake up to her potential: she is well worth gathering *now*. She writes with power, and she certainly doesn't pull her punches. Some of her stuff – such as the highlight, *The Peppermint Pig* – adults might find a little hard to take, though children, I feel sure, would have no such qualms.

1	**Devil by the Sea** *(novel)*	COLLINS 1957	**D**
	Opinion seems divided upon whether or not this	LIPPINCOTT 1959	**B**
	novel was originally written for children.		
	Certainly an abridged *version appeared for*		
	children in 1976 from Gollancz and from		
	Lippincott US.		
2	**The Secret Passage** *(novel)*	GOLLANCZ 1963	**C**
3	**The House of Secrets**	LIPPINCOTT 1964	**B**
	Same as 2.		
4	**On the Run** *(novel)*	GOLLANCZ 1964	**C**
5	**Three on the Run**	LIPPINCOTT 1965	**B**
	Same as 4.		
6	**The White Horse Gang** *(novel)*	GOLLANCZ 1966	**C**
		LIPPINCOTT 1966	**B**
7	**The Witch's Daughter** *(novel)*	GOLLANCZ 1966	**C**
	(illus. Shirley Hughes)	LIPPINCOTT 1966	**B**
8	**A Handful of Thieves** *(novel)*	GOLLANCZ 1967	**B**
		LIPPINCOTT 1967	**A**
9	**The Runaway Summer** *(novel)*	GOLLANCZ 1969	**B**
		LIPPINCOTT 1969	**A**
10	**Squib** *(novel)*	GOLLANCZ 1971	**B**
	(illus. Shirley Hughes)	LIPPINCOTT 1971	**A**

11	**Carrie's War** (*novel*)	GOLLANCZ 1973	B
		LIPPINCOTT 1973	A
12	**The Peppermint Pig** (*novel*)	GOLLANCZ 1975	C
	(*illus. Alexy Pendle*)	LIPPINCOTT 1975	B
13	**Rebel on a Rock** (*novel*)	GOLLANCZ 1978	B
	Sequel to 11.	LIPPINCOTT 1978	A
14	**The Robbers** (*novel*)	GOLLANCZ 1979	B
	(*illus. Charles Keeping*)	LIPPINCOTT 1979	A
15	**William Tell** (*tale*)	CAPE 1981	B
	(*illus. Pascale Allamand*)	LOTHROP 1981	A
16	**Kept in the Dark** (*novel*)	GOLLANCZ 1982	B
		LOTHROP 1982	A
17	**The Finding** (*novel*)	GOLLANCZ 1985	B
		LOTHROP 1985	A
18	**Princess Alice** (*novel*)	DEUTSCH 1985	B
	(*illus. Phillida Gili*)	DEUTSCH US 1985	A

B.B. *Pseudonym of D.J. Watkins-Pitchford*
Born in Northamptonshire, 1905

I detect a great resurgence of interest in B.B. – although he has always been very much in favour among an élite. The draw of his books is the sheer authenticity of the rural setting, against which he sets his often extremely funny set pieces. He has written about twenty books for adults in addition to those listed below, which are all intended primarily for children, while continuing to exert a considerable pull for people of *all* ages. Quite simply, if you like B.B., then (rather as with W.H. Hudson and Richard Jeffries) you will like *all* of B.B. Strange – not to say unique – pseudonym; the first time I heard people talking of him, I thought they were rattling on about la Bardot: the two are somewhat different. All the following books are illustrated by the author.

1	**Wild Lone**	EYRE & SPOTTISWOODE 1938	J
		SCRIBNER 1938	H
2	**Sky Gypsy: The Story of a Wild Goose**	EYRE & SPOTTISWOODE 1939	I

3	**Manka, the Sky Gypsy**	SCRIBNER 1939	**H**
	Same as 2.		
4	**The Little Grey Men**	EYRE & SPOTTISWOODE 1942	**G**
		SCRIBNER 1949	**C**
5	**Brendon Chase**	HOLLIS & CARTER 1944	**F**
		SCRIBNER 1945	**D**
6	**Down the Bright Stream**	EYRE & SPOTTISWOODE 1948	**E**
7	**Meeting Hill: B.B.'s Fairy Book**	HOLLIS & CARTER 1948	**E**
8	**The Wind in the Wood**	HOLLIS & CARTER 1952	**D**
9	**The Forest of Boland Light Railway**	EYRE & SPOTTISWOODE 1955	**D**
10	**The Forest of the Railway**	DODD MEAD 1957	**C**
	Same as 9.		
11	**Monty Woodpig's Caravan**	WARD 1957	**D**
12	**Ben the Bullfinch**	HAMISH HAMILTON 1957	**D**
13	**Wandering Wind**	HAMISH HAMILTON 1957	**D**
	Reissued in 1981 by Methuen as Bill Badger and the Wandering Wind.		
14	**Alexander**	BLACKWELL 1957	**D**
15	**Monty Woodpig and His Bumblebuzz Car**	WARD 1958	**D**
16	**Mr Bumstead**	EYRE & SPOTTISWOODE 1958	**C**
17	**The Wizard of Boland**	WARD 1959	**C**
18	**Bill Badger's Winter Cruise**	HAMISH HAMILTON 1959	**C**
19	**Bill Badger and the Pirates**	HAMISH HAMILTON 1960	**C**
20	**Bill Badger's Finest Hour**	HAMISH HAMILTON 1961	**C**
21	**Bill Badger's Whispering Reeds Adventure**	HAMISH HAMILTON 1962	**C**
22	**Lepus, the Brown Hare**	BENN 1962	**C**

23 **Bill Badger's Big Mistake**	HAMISH HAMILTON 1963	**C**
24 **Bill Badger and the Big Store Robbery**	HAMISH HAMILTON 1967	**C**
25 **The Whopper**	BENN 1967	**C**
26 **At the Back o' Ben Dee**	BENN 1968	**C**
27 **Bill Badger's Voyage to the World's End**	KAYE & WARD 1969	**C**
28 **The Tyger Tray**	METHUEN 1971	**B**
29 **The Pool of the Black Witch**	METHUEN 1974	**B**
30 **Lord of the Forest**	METHUEN 1975	**B**
31 **Stories of the Wild** (*with A.L.E. Fenton & A. Windsor-Richards*)	BENN 1975	**B**
32 **More Stories of the Wild** (*with A. Windsor-Richards*)	BENN 1977	**B**

BELLOC, Hilaire   *Born in France, 1870. Died 1953*

Belloc wrote far more books than is seemly – *hundreds* of them – and far fewer for children than one might have expected. And even these aren't *really* for children (the archness and sophistication is pitched at an adult market), but children always seem to readily latch on to all the cautionary verses, and the books became set favourites rather like Lear's nonsense. This is a good thing.

The books listed below will not be easier to gather than all Belloc's adult work – on the contrary, they are the most avidly collected of the canon – but they are worth the hunt, and they are worth the money.

1 **The Bad Child's Book of Beasts: Verses** (*illus. Basil Blackwood*)	ALDEN PRESS 1896 DUTTON 1896	**J** **H**
2 **More Beasts (for Worse Children): Verses** (*illus. Basil Blackwood*)	ARNOLD 1897	**I**
3 **A Moral Alphabet** (*verse*) (*illus. Basil Blackwood*)	ARNOLD 1899	**I**

4	**Cautionary Tales for Children** (*verse*)	NASH 1907	**J**
	(*illus. Basil Blackwood*)	KNOPF 1922	**D**
5	**New Cautionary Tales: Verses**	DUCKWORTH 1930	**E**
	(*illus. Nicolas Bentley*)	HARPER 1931	**D**
6	**Cautionary Verses: The Collected Humorous Poems of Hilaire Belloc**	DUCKWORTH 1939	**C**
		KNOPF 1941	**C**

BERESFORD, Elisabeth · *British. Born in France*

A hugely prolific writer who – in addition to the long list that follows – has published over a dozen novels for adults. Of course – whether she likes it or not – she will be forever remembered as the creator of those strange things called Wombles (Beresford wrote *sixty* scripts for the TV series) about whom it is impossible to talk or write without that blasted song entering one's head, and refusing to leave: here it comes now. (For years I thought the creatures suffered from a class complex: I always used to hear the lyrics sung thus: 'Wombles of Wimbledon. Common are We.')

1	**The Television Mystery**	PARRISH 1957	**C**
2	**The Flying Doctor Mystery**	PARRISH 1958	**C**
3	**Trouble at Tullington Castle**	PARRISH 1958	**B**
4	**Cocky and the Missing Castle**	CONSTABLE 1959	**B**
	(*illus. Jennifer Miles*)		
5	**Gappy Goes West**	PARRISH 1959	**B**
6	**The Tullington Film-makers**	PARRISH 1960	**B**
7	**Two Gold Dolphins**	CONSTABLE 1961	**B**
	(*illus. Peggy Fortnum*)	BOBBS MERRILL 1964	**B**
8	**Danger on the Old Pull n' Push**	PARRISH 1962	**B**
9	**Strange Hiding Place**	PARRISH 1962	**B**
10	**Diana in Television**	COLLINS 1963	**B**
11	**The Missing Formula Mystery**	PARRISH 1963	**B**
12	**The Mulberry Street Team**	FRIDAY PRESS 1963	**B**
	(*illus. Juliet Pannett*)		

13	**Awkward Magic** (*illus. Judith Valpy*)	HART-DAVIS 1964	**B**
14	**The Magic World** Same as 13.	BOBBS MERRILL 1965	**A**
15	**The Flying Doctor to the Rescue**	PARRISH 1964	**B**
16	**Holiday For Slippy** (*illus. Pat Williams*)	FRIDAY PRESS 1965	**A**
17	**Game, Set and Match**	PARRISH 1965	**A**
18	**Knights of the Cardboard Castle** (*illus. C.R. Evans*)	METHUEN 1965	**A**
19	**Travelling Magic** (*illus. Judith Valpy*)	HART-DAVIS 1965	**A**
20	**The Vanishing Garden** Same as 19.	FUNK & WAGNALLS 1967	**A**
21	**The Hidden Mill**	BENN 1965 MEREDITH PRESS US 1967	**A** **A**
22	**Peter Climbs a Tree** (*illus. Margery Gill*)	BENN 1966	**A**
23	**Fashion Girl**	COLLINS 1967	**A**
24	**The Black Mountain Mystery**	PARRISH 1967	**A**
25	**Looking for a Friend** (*illus. Margery Gill*)	BENN 1967	**A**
26	**The Island Bus** (*illus. Robert Hodgson*)	METHUEN 1968	**A**
27	**Sea-green Magic** (*illus. Ann Tout*)	HART-DAVIS 1968	**A**
28	**The Wombles** (*illus. Margaret Gordon*)	BENN 1968 MEREDITH PRESS US 1969	**D** **B**
29	**David Goes Fishing** (*illus. Imre Hofbauer*)	BENN 1969	**A**
30	**Gordon's Go-kart** (*illus. Margery Gill*)	BENN 1970	**A**

31	**Stephen and the Shaggy Dog** (*illus. Robert Hales*)	METHUEN 1970	A
32	**Vanishing Magic** (*illus. Ann Tout*)	HART-DAVIS 1970	A
33	**The Wandering Wombles** (*illus. Oliver Chadwick*)	BENN 1970	B
34	**Dangerous Magic** (*illus. Oliver Chadwick*)	HART-DAVIS 1972	A
35	**The Invisible Womble and Other Stories** (*illus. Ivor Wood*)	BENN 1973	B
36	**The Secret Railway** (*illus. James Hunt*)	METHUEN 1973	A
37	**The Wombles in Danger**	BENN 1973	B
38	**The Wombles at Work** (*illus. Margaret Gordon*)	BENN 1973	B
39	**Invisible Magic** (*illus. Reg Gray*)	HART-DAVIS 1974	A
40	**The Wombles Go to the Seaside**	WORLD 1974	B
41	**The Wombles Gift Book** (*illus. Margaret Gordon*)	BENN 1975	B
42	**The Snow Womble** (*illus. Margaret Gordon*)	BENN 1975	B
43	**Snuffle to the Rescue** (*illus. Gunvor Edwards*)	KESTREL 1975	A
44	**Tomsk and the Tired Tree** (*illus. Margaret Gordon*)	BENN 1975	A
45	**Wellington and the Blue Balloon** (*illus. Margaret Gordon*)	BENN 1975	A
46	**Orinoco Runs Away** (*illus. Margaret Gordon*)	BENN 1975	A
47	**The Wombles Make a Clean Sweep** (*illus. Ivor Wood*)	BENN 1975	B

48   **The Wombles to the Rescue**   BENN 1975   **B**
       (*illus. Margaret Gordon*)

49   **The Macwomble's Pipe Band**   BENN 1976   **A**
       (*illus. Margaret Gordon*)

50   **Madame Cholet's Picnic Party**   BENN 1976   **A**
       (*illus. Margaret Gordon*)

51   **Bungo Knows Best**   BENN 1976   **A**
       (*illus. Margaret Gordon*)

52   **Tobermory's Big Surprise**   BENN 1976   **A**
       (*illus. Margaret Gordon*)

53   **The Wombles Go Round the World**   BENN 1976   **A**
       (*illus. Margaret Gordon*)

54   **The World of the Wombles**   WORLD 1976   **A**
       (*illus. Edgar Hodges*)

55   **Wombling Free**   BENN 1978   **A**
       (*illus. Edgar Hodges*)

56   **Toby's Luck**   METHUEN 1978   **A**
       (*illus. Doreen Caldwell*)

57   **Secret Magic**   HART-DAVIS 1978   **A**
       (*illus. Caroline Sharpe*)

58   **The Happy Ghost**   METHUEN 1979   **A**
       (*illus. Joanna Carey*)

59   **The Treasure Hunters**   METHUEN 1980   **A**
       (*illus. Joanna Carey*)   ELSEVIER NELSON US   **A**
              1980

60   **Curious Magic**   GRANADA 1980   **A**
       (*illus. Clare Upsdale-Jones*)   ELSEVIER NELSON US   **A**
              1980

61   **The Four of Us**   HUTCHINSON 1981   **A**
       (*illus. Trevor Stubley*)

62   **The Animals Nobody Wanted**   METHUEN 1982   **A**
       (*illus. Joanna Carey*)

63   **The Tovers**   METHUEN 1982   **A**
       (*illus. Geoffrey Beitz*)

64	**The Adventures of Poon** (*illus. Dinah Shedden*)	HUTCHINSON 1984	**A**
65	**The Mysterious Island** (*illus. Joanna Carey*)	METHUEN 1984	**A**
66	**One of the Family** (*illus. Barry Thorpe*)	HUTCHINSON 1985	**A**
67	**The Ghosts of Lupus Street School** (*illus. Oliver Chadwick*)	METHUEN 1986	**A**
68	**Strange Magic** (*illus. Judith Valpy*)	METHUEN 1986	**A**
69	**Once Upon a Time Stories** (*illus. Alice Englander*)	METHUEN 1986	**A**
70	**Emily and the Haunted Castle** (*illus. Kate Rogers*)	HUTCHINSON 1987	**A**

BETJEMAN, John *Born in London, 1906. Died 1984*

Of course the late, lovable Sir John Betjeman was *not* a children's writer, but the two items listed below rather make one wish he had done more in this field. A good idea to introduce children to these, and then (maybe via Betjeman's irresistible LPs) an interest might be kindled in his grown-up stuff – which, of course, was never so grown-up as to be incomprehensible, as was much written by his contemporaries.

1	**A Ring of Bells** (*memoirs*) (*illus. Irene Slade*) *Extracts from Betjeman's verse autobiography* Summoned by Bells, *Murray and* *Houghton Mifflin US 1960, intended for* *children. Although the book was charmingly* *illustrated by Irene Slade, the no less charming* *d/w is by Edward Ardizzone.*	MURRAY 1963 HOUGHTON MIFFLIN 1963	**C** **C**
2	**Archie and the Strict Baptists** (*story*) (*illus. Phillida Gili*) *Possibly a contender for the shortest short story* *ever, this is a delightful tribute to Betjeman's* *much-loved teddy bear.*	MURRAY 1977	**B**

BIRO, Val   *Born in Hungary, 1921*

Primarily an illustrator and dust-wrapper designer (he has done hundreds),
Biro none the less deserves a place here for his 'Gumdrop' books – fun stories
based upon the author's vintage car – a 1926 Austin. Below are listed all his
children's books (actually, he hasn't written any for adults), which – not too
surprisingly – are illustrated by Biro.

1	**Bumpy's Holiday**	SYLVAN PRESS 1943	F
		TRANSATLANTIC ARTS US 1945	C
2	**Gumdrop: The Adventures of a Vintage Car**	BROCKHAMPTON 1966	D
		FOLLETT 1967	B
3	**Gumdrop and the Farmer's Friend**	BROCKHAMPTON 1967	C
		FOLLETT 1968	B
4	**Gumdrop on the Rally**	BROCKHAMPTON 1968	C
		FOLLETT 1969	B
5	**Gumdrop on the Move**	BROCKHAMPTON 1969	C
		FOLLETT 1970	B
6	**Gumdrop Goes to London**	BROCKHAMPTON 1971	B
7	**Gumdrop Finds a Friend**	BROCKHAMPTON 1973	B
8	**Gumdrop in Double Trouble**	BROCKHAMPTON 1975	B
9	**Gumdrop and the Steamroller**	HODDER & STOUGHTON 1976	B
		CHILDREN'S PRESS US 1977	A
10	**Gumdrop Posts a Letter**	HODDER & STOUGHTON 1976	B
		CHILDREN'S PRESS US 1977	A
11	**Gumdrop on the Brighton Run**	HODDER & STOUGHTON 1976	B
12	**Gumdrop Has a Birthday**	HODDER & STOUGHTON 1977	A
13	**Gumdrop Gets His Wings**	HODDER & STOUGHTON 1979	A

14	**Gumdrop Finds a Ghost**	HODDER & STOUGHTON 1980	**A**
15	**Gumdrop and the Secret Switches**	HODDER & STOUGHTON 1981	**A**
16	**Gumdrop Makes a Start**	HODDER & STOUGHTON 1982	**A**
17	**Gumdrop and Horace**	HODDER & STOUGHTON 1982	**A**
18	**Gumdrop Races a Train**	HODDER & STOUGHTON 1982	**A**
19	**Gumdrop Goes to School**	HODDER & STOUGHTON 1983	**A**
20	**Gumdrop Gets a Lift**	HODDER & STOUGHTON 1983	**A**
21	**Gumdrop at the Zoo**	HODDER & STOUGHTON 1983	**A**
22	**Gumdrop in a Hurry**	HODDER & STOUGHTON 1983	**A**
23	**Gumdrop to the Rescue**	HODDER & STOUGHTON 1986	**A**

BLAKE, Quentin   *Born in Britain, 1932*

One of the greatest and most admired cartoonists and illustrators of the century – a Quentin Blake doodle (although they are nowhere near as simple as they first appear) immediately confers status and *fun*. Below are listed the books both written and illustrated by Blake, but his name pops up quite frequently throughout this book as the man who has brought a vital extra dimension to the writings of others.

1	**Patrick**	CAPE 1968	**C**
		WALCK 1969	**B**
2	**Jack and Nancy**	CAPE 1969	**C**
3	**Angelo**	CAPE 1970	**C**
4	**The Adventures of Lester**	BBC 1971	**C**

5	**Snuff**	CAPE 1973	**C**
		LIPPINCOTT 1973	**B**
6	**The Puffin Book of Improbable Records** (*with John Yeoman*)	PUFFIN 1975	**B**
7	**Mr Magnolia**	CAPE 1980	**C**
		SALEM HOUSE 1980	**B**
8	**Quentin Blake's Nursery Rhyme Book**	CAPE 1983	**B**
		HARPER 1984	**B**
9	**The Story of the Dancing Frog**	CAPE 1984	**B**
		KNOPF 1985	**B**
10	**Mrs Armitage on Wheels**	CAPE 1987	**B**

BLYTON, Enid   *Born in London, 1897. Died 1968*

What *can* one say? Blyton – probably one of the best-known and most read authors ever – made the likes of Frank Richards and Agatha Christie look positively slothful. Over six hundred books appeared in about forty-five years; in 1951 alone she published thirty-six. Not all were full-length works, of course, but nonetheless the output was phenomenal; it is difficult to discuss any aspect of Enid Blyton without this word *phenomenal* creeping in, for not only does she remain the writer most adored by children (*pace* Roald Dahl) but she is still vilified by more up-market parents, and still banned from the sillier sorts of bookshop and library. Why? Because, say her critics, her vocabulary was non-existent (if so, she must have been a woman of few words who used them incessantly), her grammar and syntax doubtful, her plots either over-simplistic or else out-and-out incredible, and her general attitude sexist, jingoistic and snobbish. None of which matters a hoot, of course, because the average Blyton reader would not have understood a word of the above, but can comprehend every word that Enid Blyton writes with ease. This is no bad thing – it makes books attractive to the very young, and almost always leads them on to higher things. I can vouch for this: in my young days I took the *Beano*, but now I take *The Times* as well.

The listing that follows is huge, but it does *not* contain all 600 titles because I thought I might die of old age before completing it. Instead, I have selected the most perennially popular series and listed them *as* series (so far as I know the first time this has been done), thus enabling Noddy addicts to get right to the heart of the matter, while leaving Famous Five-ists to drool over their desiderata.

Enid Blyton – I think because of all the censure previously alluded to – has been almost completely ignored, if not *spurned* by collectors. There is a whiff of change in the air, and very soon this will intensify into the pungent aroma of *enthusiasm*, so follow your nose.

ADVENTURES AND MYSTERIES:

1	**Adventures of the Wishing Chair** (*illus. Hilda McGavin*)	NEWNES 1937	**D**
2	**The Secret Island**	BLACKWELL 1938	**D**
3	**The Enchanted Wood** (*illus. Dorothy M. Wheeler*)	NEWNES 1939	**D**
4	**The Treasure Hunters** (*illus. E. Wilson & Joyce Davies*)	NEWNES 1940	**C**
5	**The Adventurous Four**	NEWNES 1941	**C**
6	**The Secret Mountain**	BLACKWELL 1941	**C**
7	**The Magic Faraway Tree** (*illus. Dorothy M. Wheeler*)	NEWNES 1943	**C**
8	**The Mystery of the Burnt Cottage** (*illus. J. Abbey*)	METHUEN 1943 McNAUGHTON US 1946	**C** **B**
9	**The Secret of Killimooin**	BLACKWELL 1943	**C**
10	**The Island of Adventure** (*illus. Stuart Tresilian*)	MACMILLAN 1944	**B**
11	**Mystery Island** *Same as 10.*	MACMILLAN US 1945	**B**
12	**The Mystery of the Secret Room**	METHUEN 1945 PARKWOOD PRESS US 1950	**B** **A**
13	**The Castle of Adventure** (*illus. Stuart Tresilian*)	MACMILLAN 1946 MACMILLAN US 1946	**B** **A**
14	**The Mystery of the Spiteful Letters** (*illus. J. Abbey*)	METHUEN 1946	**B**
15	**The Adventurous Four Again** (*illus. Jessie Land*)	NEWNES 1947	**B**
16	**The Mystery of the Missing Necklace**	METHUEN 1947	**B**

17	**The Valley of Adventure** (*illus. Stuart Tresilian*)	MACMILLAN 1947 MACMILLAN US 1947	**B** **A**
18	**The Mystery of the Hidden House** (*illus. J. Abbey*)	METHUEN 1948	**B**
19	**The Sea of Adventure** (*illus. Stuart Tresilian*)	MACMILLAN 1948 MACMILLAN US 1948	**B** **A**
20	**The Secret of the Old Mill** (*illus. Eileen A. Soper*)	BROCKHAMPTON 1948	**B**
21	**The Mountain of Adventure** (*illus. Stuart Tresilian*)	MACMILLAN 1949 MACMILLAN US 1949	**B** **A**
22	**The Mystery of the Pantomime Cat**	METHUEN 1949	**B**
23	**The Rockingdown Mystery** (*illus. Gilbert Dunlop*)	COLLINS 1949	**B**
24	**The Mystery of the Invisible Thief** (*illus. Treyer Evans*)	METHUEN 1950	**B**
25	**The Rilloby Fair Mystery** (*illus. Gilbert Dunlop*)	COLLINS 1950	**B**
26	**The Ship of Adventure** (*illus. Stuart Tresilian*)	MACMILLAN 1950 MACMILLAN US 1950	**B** **A**
27	**The Wishing Chair Again**	NEWNES 1950	**B**
28	**The Mystery of the Vanished Prince** (*illus. Treyer Evans*)	METHUEN 1951	**B**
29	**Up the Faraway Tree** (*illus. Dorothy M. Wheeler*)	NEWNES 1951	**B**
30	**The Circus of Adventure** (*illus. Stuart Tresilian*)	MACMILLAN 1952 ST MARTIN'S 1953	**B** **A**
31	**The Mystery of the Strange Bundle** (*illus. Treyer Evans*)	METHUEN 1952	**B**
32	**The Queer Mystery** (*illus. Norman Meredith*)	STAPLES PRESS 1952	**B**
33	**The Rubadub Mystery** (*illus. Gilbert Dunlop*)	COLLINS 1952	**B**

34	**The Mystery of Holly Lane** (*illus. Treyer Evans*)	METHUEN 1953	B
35	**The Secret of Moon Castle**	BLACKWELL 1953	B
36	**The Adventure of the Secret Necklace** (*illus. Isabel Veevers*)	LUTTERWORTH 1954	A
37	**The Mystery of Tally-Ho Cottage** (*illus. Treyer Evans*)	METHUEN 1954	A
38	**Ring o' Bells Mystery**	COLLINS 1955	A
39	**The River of Adventure** (*illus. Stuart Tresilian*)	MACMILLAN 1955 ST MARTIN'S 1955	A A
40	**The Mystery of the Missing Man** (*illus. Lilian Buchanan*)	METHUEN 1956	A
41	**The Rat-a-tat Mystery** (*illus. Anyon Cook*)	COLLINS 1956	A
42	**Mystery of the Strange Messages** (*illus. Lilian Buchanan*)	METHUEN 1957	A
43	**Ragamuffin Mystery**	COLLINS 1959	A
44	**Adventure of the Strange Ruby** (*illus. Roger Payne*)	BROCKHAMPTON 1960	A
45	**Adventure Stories**	COLLINS 1960	A
46	**Mystery Stories**	COLLINS 1960	A
47	**The Mystery of Banshee Towers** (*illus. Lilian Buchanan*)	METHUEN 1961	A
48	**The Mystery That Never Was** (*illus. Gilbert Dunlop*)	COLLINS 1961	A

THE FAMOUS FIVE:

1	**Five on a Treasure Island**	HODDER & STOUGHTON 1942 CROWELL 1950	C A
2	**Five Go Adventuring Again**	HODDER & STOUGHTON 1943 CROWELL 1951	B A

3	**Five Run Away Together** (*illus. Eileen A. Soper*)	HODDER & STOUGHTON 1944 REILLY & LEE 1960	**B** **A**
4	**Five Go to Smugglers' Top**	HODDER & STOUGHTON 1945 REILLY & LEE 1960	**B** **A**
5	**Five Go Off in a Caravan** (*illus. Eileen A. Soper*)	HODDER & STOUGHTON 1946	**B**
6	**Five on Kirrin Island Again**	HODDER & STOUGHTON 1947	**B**
7	**Five Go Off to Camp** *This was reissued in America by Atheneum in* *1972 as* Five on the Track of a Spook Train (**A**).	HODDER & STOUGHTON 1948	**B**
8	**Five Get into Trouble** (*illus. Eileen A. Soper*) *This was reissued in America by Atheneum in* *1972 as* Five Caught in a Treacherous Plot (**A**).	HODDER & STOUGHTON 1949	**B**
9	**Five Fall into Adventure** (*illus. Eileen A. Soper*)	HODDER & STOUGHTON 1950 ATHENEUM 1972	**B** **A**
10	**Five on a Hike Together** (*illus. Eileen A. Soper*)	HODDER & STOUGHTON 1951	**B**
11	**Five Have a Wonderful Time** (*illus. Eileen A. Soper*)	HODDER & STOUGHTON 1952	**B**
12	**Five Go Down to the Sea** (*illus. Eileen A. Soper*)	HODDER & STOUGHTON 1953 REILLY & LEE 1961	**B** **A**
13	**Five Go to Mystery Moor**	HODDER & STOUGHTON 1954 REILLY & LEE 1963	**B** **A**
14	**Five Have Plenty of Fun**	HODDER & STOUGHTON 1955	**B**
15	**Five on a Secret Trail** (*illus. Eileen A. Soper*)	HODDER & STOUGHTON 1956	**B**

16	**Five Go to Billycock Hill** (*illus. Eileen A. Soper*)	HODDER & STOUGHTON 1957	**B**
17	**Five Get into a Fix** (*illus. Eileen A. Soper*)	HODDER & STOUGHTON 1958	**B**
18	**Five on Finniston Farm** (*illus. Eileen A. Soper*)	HODDER & STOUGHTON 1960	**A**
19	**Five Go to Demon's Rocks** (*illus. Eileen A. Soper*)	HODDER & STOUGHTON 1961	**A**
20	**Five Have a Mystery to Solve** (*illus. Eileen A. Soper*)	HODDER & STOUGHTON 1962	**A**
21	**Five are Together Again** (*illus. Eileen A. Soper*)	HODDER & STOUGHTON 1963	**A**

THE SECRET SEVEN:

1	**The Secret Seven** . (*illus. George Brook*) *This was reissued in America by the Children's* *Press in 1972 as* The Secret Seven and The Mystery of the Empty House (**A**).	BROCKHAMPTON 1949	**C**
2	**Secret Seven Adventure** (*illus. George Brook*) *This was reissued in America by the Children's* *Press in 1972 as* The Secret Seven and The Circus Adventure (**A**).	BROCKHAMPTON 1950	**B**
3	**Well Done, Secret Seven** (*illus. George Brook*) *This was reissued in America by the Children's* *Press in 1972 as* The Secret Seven and The Tree House Adventure (**A**).	BROCKHAMPTON 1951	**B**
4	**Secret Seven on the Trail** (*illus. George Brook*) *This was reissued in America by the Children's* *Press in 1972 as* The Secret Seven and The Railroad Mystery (**A**).	BROCKHAMPTON 1952	**B**
5	**Go Ahead Secret Seven** (*illus. Bruno Kay*) *This was reissued in America by the Children's*	BROCKHAMPTON 1953	**B**

Press in 1972 as The Secret Seven Get
Their Man (**A**).

6 Good Work, Secret Seven! BROCKHAMPTON 1954 **B**
(*illus. Bruno Kay*)
*This was reissued in America by the Children's
Press in 1972 as* The Secret Seven and
The Case of the Stolen Car (**A**).

7 Secret Seven Win Through BROCKHAMPTON 1955 **B**
(*illus. Bruno Kay*)
*This was reissued in America by the Children's
Press in 1972 as* The Secret Seven and
The Hidden Cave Adventure (**A**).

8 Three Cheers Secret Seven BROCKHAMPTON 1956 **B**
(*illus. Burgess Sharrocks*)
*This was reissued in America by the Children's
Press in 1972 as* The Secret Seven and
The Grim Secret (**A**).

9 Secret Seven Mystery BROCKHAMPTON 1957 **B**
(*illus. Burgess Sharrocks*)
*This was reissued in America by the Children's
Press in 1972 as* The Secret Seven and
The Missing Girl Mystery (**A**).

10 Puzzle for the Secret Seven BROCKHAMPTON 1958 **B**
(*illus. Burgess Sharrocks*)
*This was reissued in America by the Children's
Press in 1972 as* The Secret Seven and
The Case of the Music Lover (**A**).

11 Secret Seven Fireworks BROCKHAMPTON 1959 **B**
(*illus. Burgess Sharrocks*)
*This was reissued in America by the Children's
Press in 1972 as* The Secret Seven and
The Bonfire Mystery (**A**).

12 Good Old Secret Seven BROCKHAMPTON 1960 **A**
(*illus. Burgess Sharrocks*)
*This was reissued in America by the Children's
Press in 1972 as* The Secret Seven and
The Old Fort Adventure (**A**).

13 **Shock for the Secret Seven**   BROCKHAMPTON 1961   **A**
(*illus. Burgess Sharrocks*)
This was reissued in America by the Children's
Press in 1972 as The Secret Seven and
The Case of the Dog Lover (**A**).

14 **Look Out Secret Seven**   BROCKHAMPTON 1962   **A**
(*illus. Burgess Sharrocks*)
This was reissued in America by the Children's
Press in 1972 as The Secret Seven and
The Case of the Missing Medals (**A**).

15 **Fun for the Secret Seven**   BROCKHAMPTON 1963   **A**
(*illus. Burgess Sharrocks*)
This was reissued in America by the Children's
Press in 1972 as The Secret Seven and
The Case of the Old Horse (**A**).

ST CLARE'S:
1 **Twins at St Clare's**   METHUEN 1941   **C**

2 **Summer Term at St Clare's**   METHUEN 1943   **B**

3 **Claudine at St Clare's**   METHUEN 1944   **B**

4 **The Second Form at St Clare's**   METHUEN 1944   **B**
(*illus. W. Lindsay Cable*)

5 **Fifth Formers at St Clare's**   METHUEN 1945   **B**
(*illus. W. Lindsay Cable*)

MALORY TOWERS:
1 **First Term at Malory Towers**   METHUEN 1946   **C**

2 **The Second Form at Malory Towers**   METHUEN 1947   **B**

3 **Third Year at Malory Towers**   METHUEN 1948   **B**

4 **The Upper Fourth at Malory Towers**   METHUEN 1949   **B**

5 **In the Fifth at Malory Towers**   METHUEN 1950   **B**
(*illus. Stanley Lloyd*)

6 **Last Term at Malory Towers**   METHUEN 1951   **B**
(*illus. Stanley Lloyd*)

NODDY:

Apart from the countless spin-off books since Enid Blyton's death, there were over seventy during her lifetime – but many of these were little more than a pamphlet, or else large-format rejiggings of old texts. Below is listed the accepted canon of twenty-four, all uniform, and very attractive too. The much-loved dust-wrappers and end-papers are credited to Harmsen van Beek, but it seems likely that only the first half-dozen or so volumes are actually illustrated by him, the remainder seeming rather diluted, and uncredited.

1	**Little Noddy Goes to Toyland**	SAMPSON LOW 1949	C
2	**Hurrah for Little Noddy**	SAMPSON LOW 1950	B
3	**Noddy and His Car**	SAMPSON LOW 1951	B
4	**Here Comes Noddy Again!**	SAMPSON LOW 1951	B
5	**Well Done, Noddy!**	SAMPSON LOW 1952	B
6	**Noddy Goes to School**	SAMPSON LOW 1952	B
7	**Noddy at the Seaside**	SAMPSON LOW 1953	B
8	**Noddy Gets into Trouble**	SAMPSON LOW 1954	B
9	**Noddy and the Magic Rubber**	SAMPSON LOW 1954	B
10	**You Funny Little Noddy!**	SAMPSON LOW 1955	B
11	**Noddy Meets Father Christmas**	SAMPSON LOW 1955	B
12	**Noddy and Tessie Bear**	SAMPSON LOW 1956	B
13	**Be Brave, Little Noddy!**	SAMPSON LOW 1956	B
14	**Noddy and the Bumpy Dog**	SAMPSON LOW 1957	B
15	**Do Look Out, Noddy!**	SAMPSON LOW 1957	B
16	**You're a Good Friend, Noddy!**	SAMPSON LOW 1958	B
17	**Noddy Has an Adventure**	SAMPSON LOW 1958	B
18	**Noddy Goes to Sea**	SAMPSON LOW 1959	B
19	**Noddy and the Bunkey**	SAMPSON LOW 1959	B
20	**Cheer Up, Little Noddy!**	SAMPSON LOW 1960	A
21	**Noddy Goes to the Fair**	SAMPSON LOW 1960	A

22	**Mr Plod and Little Noddy**	SAMPSON LOW 1961	A
23	**Noddy and the Tootles**	SAMPSON LOW 1962	A
24	**Noddy and the Aeroplane**	SAMPSON LOW 1964	A

BOND, Michael   *Born in Berkshire, 1926*

Creator of possibly the most famous and best-loved bear since Pooh (although I'm not getting into an argument about it), Michael Bond has proved to be a pretty prolific author, as the ensuing checklist demonstrates. Paddington is without question here to stay – indeed, for many years the boudoir of any *serious* child-at-heart has been seen to be quite unfurnished without the furry version, complete – of course – with duffle coat, wellies and sou'wester. But how many have preserved the 'Please Look After This Bear' luggage label?

In addition to the books listed below, there have been quite a number of games, puzzle and colouring books. I think that if you try to gather all these, you might well go mad, but please do so if at all you feel inclined.

1	**A Bear Called Paddington**	COLLINS 1958	G
	(*illus. Peggy Fortnum*)	HOUGHTON MIFFLIN 1960	C
2	**More About Paddington**	COLLINS 1959	D
	(*illus. Peggy Fortnum*)	HOUGHTON MIFFLIN 1961	B
3	**Paddington Helps Out**	COLLINS 1960	C
	(*illus. Peggy Fortnum*)	HOUGHTON MIFFLIN 1961	B
4	**Paddington Abroad**	COLLINS 1961	C
	(*illus. Peggy Fortnum*)	HOUGHTON MIFFLIN 1962	B
5	**Paddington at Large**	COLLINS 1962	C
	(*illus. Peggy Fortnum*)	HOUGHTON MIFFLIN 1963	B
6	**Paddington Marches On**	COLLINS 1964	C
	(*illus. Peggy Fortnum*)	HOUGHTON MIFFLIN 1965	B
7	**Here Comes Thursday**	HARRAP 1966	B
	(*illus. Daphne Rowles*)	LOTHROP 1967	A
8	**Paddington at Work**	COLLINS 1966	B
	(*illus. Peggy Fortnum*)	HOUGHTON MIFFLIN 1967	A
9	**Paddington Goes to Town**	COLLINS 1968	B
	(*illus. Peggy Fortnum*)	HOUGHTON MIFFLIN 1968	A

10	**Thursday Rides Again**	HARRAP 1968	A
	(*illus. Beryl Sanders*)	LOTHROP 1969	A
11	**Parsley's Good Deed**	BBC 1969	A
	(*illus. Esor*)		
12	**The Story of Parsley's Tail**	BBC 1969	A
	(*illus. Esor*)		
13	**Thursday Ahoy!**	HARRAP 1969	A
	(*illus. Leslie Wood*)	LOTHROP 1970	A
14	**Paddington Takes the Air**	COLLINS 1970	B
	(*illus. Peggy Fortnum*)	HOUGHTON MIFFLIN 1971	A
15	**Parsley's Last Stand**	BBC 1970	A
16	**Parsley's Problem Present**	BBC 1970	A
17	**Thursday in Paris**	HARRAP 1971	A
	(*illus. Leslie Wood*)		
18	**The Tales of Olga da Polga**	PENGUIN 1971	B
	(*illus. Hans Helweg*)	MACMILLAN 1973	B
19	**Parsley the Lion**	COLLINS 1972	A
	(*illus. Ivor Wood*)		
20	**Parsley Parade**	COLLINS 1972	A
	(*illus. Ivor Wood*)		
21	**Paddington Bear**	COLLINS 1972	B
	(*illus. Fred Banbery*)	RANDOM HOUSE 1973	A
22	**Paddington's Garden**	COLLINS 1972	B
	(*illus. Fred Banbery*)	RANDOM HOUSE 1973	A
23	**The Day the Animals Went on Strike**	STUDIO VISTA 1972	B
	(*illus. Jim Hodgson*)	HERITAGE PRESS 1973	B
24	**Olga Meets Her Match**	LONGMAN 1973	B
	(*illus. Hans Helweg*)	HASTINGS HOUSE 1975	A
25	**Paddington at the Circus**	COLLINS 1973	B
	(*illus. Fred Banbery*)	RANDOM HOUSE 1974	A
26	**Paddington Goes Shopping**	COLLINS 1973	B
	(*illus. Fred Banbery*)		

27	**Paddington's Lucky Day** *Same as 26.*	RANDOM HOUSE 1974	**A**
28	**Paddington on Top** (*illus. Peggy Fortnum*)	COLLINS 1974 HOUGHTON MIFFLIN 1975	**B** **A**
29	**Paddington's Blue Peter Story Book** (*illus. Ivor Wood*)	COLLINS 1974	**B**
30	**Paddington Takes to TV** *Same as 29.*	HOUGHTON MIFFLIN 1974	**A**
31	**Mr Cram's Magic Bubbles** (*illus. Gioia Fiammenghi*)	PENGUIN 1975	**A**
32	**Windmill** (*illus. Tony Cattaneo*)	STUDIO VISTA 1975	**B**
33	**Paddington at the Seaside** (*illus. Fred Banbery*)	COLLINS 1975 RANDOM HOUSE 1978	**B** **A**
34	**Paddington at the Tower** (*illus. Fred Banbery*)	COLLINS 1975 RANDOM HOUSE 1978	**B** **A**
35	**Olga Carries On** (*illus. Hans Helweg*)	KESTREL 1976 HASTINGS HOUSE 1977	**A** **A**
36	**Paddington at the Station** (*illus. Barry Wilkinson*)	COLLINS 1976	**B**
37	**Paddington Takes a Bath** (*illus. Barry Wilkinson*)	COLLINS 1976	**A**
38	**Paddington Goes to the Sales** (*illus. Barry Wilkinson*)	COLLINS 1976	**A**
39	**Paddington's New Room** (*illus. Barry Wilkinson*)	COLLINS 1976	**A**
40	**Paddington's Picture Book** (*anthology*) (*illus. Fred Banbery*)	COLLINS 1978	**A**
41	**Paddington Takes the Test** (*illus. Peggy Fortnum*)	COLLINS 1979 HOUGHTON MIFFLIN 1980	**A** **A**
42	**J.D. Polson and the Liberty Head Dime** (*illus. Roger Wade Walker*)	OCTOPUS 1980 MAYFLOWER 1980	**A** **A**
43	**Paddington at Home**	COLLINS 1980	**A**

44	**Paddington Goes Out**	COLLINS 1980	A
45	**J.D. Polson and the Dillogate Affair** (*illus. Roger Wade Walker*)	HODDER & STOUGHTON 1981	A
46	**Paddington on Screen: A Second Blue** **Peter Storybook** (*illus. Barry Macey*)	COLLINS 1981 HOUGHTON MIFFLIN 1982	A A
47	**J.D. Polson and the Great Unveiling** (*illus. Roger Wade Walker*)	HODDER & STOUGHTON 1982	A
48	**The Caravan Puppets** (*illus. Vanessa Julian-Ottie*)	COLLINS 1983	A
49	**The First Big Olga da Polga Book** (*illus. Hans Helweg*)	LONGMAN 1983	A
50	**The Second Big Olga da Polga Book** (*illus. Hans Helweg*)	LONGMAN 1983	A
51	**Paddington and the Knickerbocker** **Rainbow**	COLLINS 1984	A
52	**Paddington at the Zoo**	COLLINS 1984	A
53	**Paddington at the Fair**	COLLINS 1985	A
54	**Paddington's Painting Exhibition**	COLLINS 1985	A
55	**Paddington at the Palace**	COLLINS 1986	A
56	**Paddington Minds the House** *51–56 are billed collectively as* Paddington First Books, *and are illustrated by David* *McKee.*	COLLINS 1986	A
57	**Paddington's Bus Rides** (*with Karen Bond*)	HUTCHINSON 1986	A
58	**Paddington's Clock Book** (*with Karen Bond*)	HUTCHINSON 1986	A

BOSTON, Lucy   *Born in Lancashire, 1892*

A phenomenon in that she was 62 when she published her first book, Lucy
Boston is also somewhat difficult to define. Her 'Green Knowe' books are
certainly a landmark in children's literature, still much loved for their fan-

tasy and imagination, but possibly never achieved true greatness due to occasional weaknesses in the narrative – fantasy sometimes vying with sheer incredibility. That said, the books are full of adventure, highly entertaining – and surely of lasting value.

Included within the following complete listing of the 'Green Knowe' books are the few that Boston has published for younger readers.

1	**The Children of Green Knowe**	FABER 1954	**E**
	(*illus. Peter Boston*)	HARCOURT BRACE 1955	**C**
2	**The Chimneys of Green Knowe**	FABER 1958	**C**
	(*illus. Peter Boston*)		
3	**Treasure of Green Knowe**	HARCOURT BRACE 1958	**B**
	Same as 2.		
4	**The River at Green Knowe**	FABER 1959	**C**
	(*illus. Peter Boston*)	HARCOURT BRACE 1959	**B**
5	**A Stranger at Green Knowe**	FABER 1961	**C**
	(*illus. Peter Boston*)	HARCOURT BRACE 1961	**B**
6	**An Enemy at Green Knowe**	FABER 1964	**C**
	(*illus. Peter Boston*)	HARCOURT BRACE 1964	**B**
7	**The Castle of Yew**	BODLEY HEAD 1965	**B**
	(*illus. Margery Gill*)	HARCOURT BRACE 1965	**A**
8	**The Sea-Egg**	FABER 1967	**B**
	(*illus. Peter Boston*)	HARCOURT BRACE 1967	**A**
9	**The House That Grew**	FABER 1969	**B**
	(*illus. Caroline Hemming*)		
10	**Nothing Said**	FABER 1971	**B**
	(*Illus. Peter Boston*)	HARCOURT BRACE 1971	**A**
11	**Memory in a House**	BODLEY HEAD 1973	**B**
		MACMILLAN US 1974	**A**
12	**The Guardians of the House**	BODLEY HEAD 1974	**B**
	(*illus. Peter Boston*)	ATHENEUM 1975	**A**
13	**The Fossil Snake**	BODLEY HEAD 1975	**B**
	(*illus. Peter Boston*)	ATHENEUM 1976	**A**
14	**The Stones of Green Knowe**	BODLEY HEAD 1976	**B**
	(*illus. Peter Boston*)	ATHENEUM 1976	**A**

Also of interest:
JASPER ROSE: **Lucy Boston** (BODLEY HEAD 1965, WALCK US 1966)

BRAZIL, Angela   *Born in Lancashire, 1869. Died 1947*

Fearfully popular almost from the word go, and these days something of a cult, not to say an object of wonder (you could barely get away with a title like *Bosom Friends: A Seaside Story* today). Although associated with the school-girl slang of her period, teachers tended to want to ban Brazil's books on the grounds that the slang was her own invention that the girls tended to copy, and *not* a sincere reflection of the sort of language that was used in schools. Isn't it amazing that they could be bothered? Not really – whenever there is a book, or a style of writing that strays from the norm, there will always be someone in a position of authority who wishes to eradicate all traces of it from the face of the earth.

A lot of good stuff is contained in *You're a Brick, Angela!: A New Look at Girls' Fiction 1839–1975* (Mary Cadogan & Patricia Craig, Gollancz 1976). Oh yes – Angela liked her surname not to be pronounced like the country that the nuts come from, but rather as a rhyme for 'on the razzle'.

1	**A Terrible Tomboy** (*illus. Angela Brazil & Amy Brazil*)	GAY & BIRD 1904	K
2	**The Fortunes of Philippa**	BLACKIE 1906	I
3	**The Third Class at Miss Kaye's**	BLACKIE 1908	G
4	**The Nicest Girl in the School**	BLACKIE 1909 CALDWELL US 1911	G C
5	**Bosom Friends: A Seaside Story**	NELSON 1910	F
6	**The Manor House School** (*illus. F. Moorsom*)	BLACKIE 1910 CALDWELL US 1911	F C
7	**A Fourth Form Friendship**	BLACKIE 1911	E
8	**The New Girl at St Chad's**	BLACKIE 1911	E
9	**A Pair of Schoolgirls**	BLACKIE 1912	E
10	**The Leader of the Lower School**	BLACKIE 1913	E
11	**The Youngest Girl in the Fifth**	BLACKIE 1913	E
12	**The Girls of St Cyprian's**	BLACKIE 1914	E

13	**The School by the Sea**	BLACKIE 1914	**E**
14	**The Jolliest Term on Record** (*illus. Balliol Salmon*)	BLACKIE 1915	**D**
15	**For the Sake of the School**	BLACKIE 1915	**D**
16	**The Luckiest Girl in the School** (*illus. Balliol Salmon*)	BLACKIE 1916 STOKES 1916	**D** **C**
17	**The Madcap of the School** (*illus. Balliol Salmon*)	BLACKIE 1917 STOKES 1922	**C** **B**
18	**The Slap-bang Boys**	NELSON 1917	**C**
19	**A Patriotic Schoolgirl** (*illus. Balliol Salmon*)	BLACKIE 1918	**C**
20	**For the School Colours** (*illus. Balliol Salmon*)	BLACKIE 1918	**C**
21	**A Harum-scarum Schoolgirl** (*illus. John Campbell*)	BLACKIE 1919 STOKES 1920	**C** **B**
22	**The Head Girl at the Gables** (*illus. Balliol Salmon*)	BLACKIE 1919 STOKES 1920	**C** **B**
23	**Two Little Scamps and a Puppy** (*illus. E. Blampied*)	NELSON 1919	**C**
24	**A Gift from the Sea**	NELSON 1920	**C**
25	**A Popular Schoolgirl** (*illus. Balliol Salmon*)	BLACKIE 1920 STOKES 1921	**C** **B**
26	**The Princess of the School** (*illus. Frank Wiles*)	BLACKIE 1920 STOKES 1921	**C** **B**
27	**Loyal to the School** (*illus. Treyer Evans*)	BLACKIE 1921	**C**
28	**A Fortunate Term** (*illus. Treyer Evans*)	BLACKIE 1921	**C**
29	**Marjorie's Best Year** Same as 28.	STOKES 1923	**B**
30	**Monitress Merle** (*illus. Treyer Evans*)	BLACKIE 1922	**C**

31	**The School in the South** (*illus. W. Smithson Broadhead*)	BLACKIE 1922	C
32	**The Jolliest School of All** *Same as 31.*	STOKES 1923	B
33	**The Khaki Boys and Other Stories**	NELSON 1923	B
34	**Schoolgirl Kitty** (*illus. W.E. Wightman*)	BLACKIE 1923 STOKES 1924	B A
35	**Captain Peggie** (*illus. W.E. Wightman*)	BLACKIE 1924 STOKES 1924	B A
36	**My Own Schooldays** (*autobiography*)	BLACKIE 1925	C
37	**Joan's Best Chum** (*illus. W.E. Wightman*)	BLACKIE 1926 STOKES 1927	B A
38	**Queen of the Dormitory and Other Stories** (*illus. P.B. Hickling*)	CASSELL 1926	B
39	**Ruth of St Ronan's** (*illus. F. Oldham*)	BLACKIE 1927	B
40	**At School with Rachel** (*illus. W.E. Wightman*)	BLACKIE 1928	B
41	**St Catherine's College** (*illus. Frank Wiles*)	BLACKIE 1929	B
42	**The Little Green School** (*illus. Frank Wiles*)	BLACKIE 1931	B
43	**Nesta's New School** (*illus. J. Dewar Mills*)	BLACKIE 1932	B
44	**Jean's Golden Term**	BLACKIE 1934	B
45	**The School at the Turrets**	BLACKIE 1935	B
46	**An Exciting Term**	BLACKIE 1936	B
47	**Jill's Jolliest School**	BLACKIE 1937	B
48	**The School on the Cliff** (*illus. F.E. Hiley*)	BLACKIE 1938	B
49	**The School on the Moor** (*illus. Henry Coller*)	BLACKIE 1939	B

50	The New School at Scawdale (*illus. M. Mackinlay*)	BLACKIE 1940	A
51	Five Jolly Schoolgirls	BLACKIE 1941	A
52	The Mystery of the Moated Grange	BLACKIE 1942	A
53	The Secret of the Border Castle (*illus. Charles Willis*)	BLACKIE 1943	A
54	The School in the Forest (*illus. J. Dewar Mills*)	BLACKIE 1944	A
55	Three Terms at Uplands (*illus. D.L. Mays*)	BLACKIE 1945	A
56	The School on the Loch (*illus. W. Lindsay Cable*)	BLACKIE 1946	A

Also of interest:

GILLIAN FREEMAN: **The Schoolgirl Ethic: The Life and Work of Angela Brazil** (ALLEN LANE 1976)

BRENT-DYER, Elinor M.   *Born in Durham, 1894. Died 1969*

Although it is purely coincidental that Brent-Dyer follows on alphabetically from Angela Brazil, it really is quite apposite. They were the twin queens of schoolgirl fiction, and quite a deal of overlapping of style is evident. That said, Brent-Dyer will be seen to be the less inventive author, despite the fact that she hit on the very happy idea of setting her school in the Austrian Tirol – and in a chalet, fairly naturally. The international populace instantly becomes trilingual, the most awful scrapes and natural disasters occur, and the saga of the 'Chalet School' is spun out for 59 volumes. It is generally agreed that the earlier books are more eventful and relevant to the girl of the day, but I see all of these books living on – just as Enid Blyton's Famous Five will continue to do: the *idea* of a chalet school is so compelling, that I think even modern-day readers will forgive the blatant outdatedness – perhaps even seeing it as 'period charm'.

In addition to the 'Chalet School' books listed here, Brent-Dyer published about 50 others, but these tend not to have withstood the test of time quite so well.

| 1 | The School at the Chalet (*illus. Nina K. Brisley*) | CHAMBERS 1925 | I |

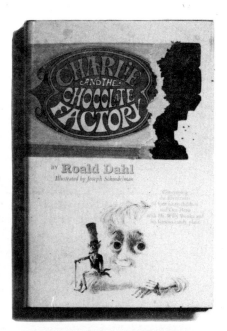

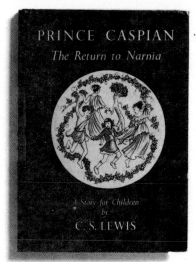

Four modern classics: *Watership Down* (1972), the original American edition of *Charlie* (1964 – three years before the British version), and the first two volumes of C.S. Lewis's seven-volume 'Chronicles of Narnia' illustrated by Pauline Paynes.

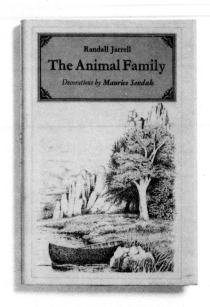

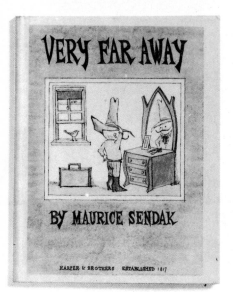

A quartet of books illustrated by Maurice Sendak – two by the American poet Randall Jarrell (1965, 1976), and two by the man himself (1957, 1967).

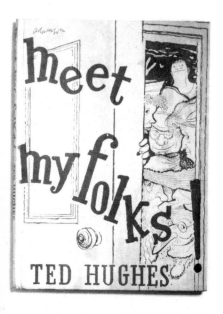

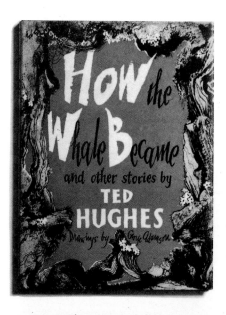

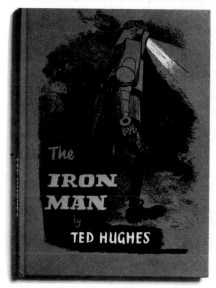

Four for children by the Poet Laureate – *Meet My Folks!*, *How the Whale Became* and *The Iron Man* illustrated by George Adamson, and *The Earth-owl* illustrated by R.A. Brandt.

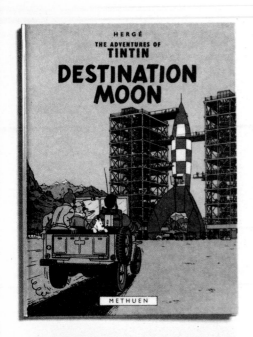

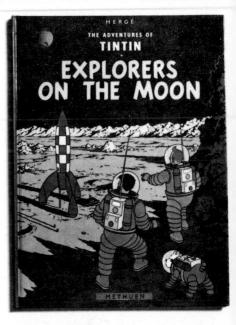

The inimitable reporters, Tintin and Snowy, together with those unconquerable Gauls (© 1988 Les Éditions Albert René/Goscinny and Uderzo) – a couple of representative examples of the two most revered comic-book series of all time.

2	**Jo of the Chalet School** (*illus. Nina K. Brisley*)	CHAMBERS 1926	G
3	**The Princess of the Chalet School** (*illus. Nina K. Brisley*)	CHAMBERS 1927	F
4	**The Head Girl of the Chalet School** (*illus. Nina K. Brisley*)	CHAMBERS 1928	E
5	**The Rivals of the Chalet School** (*illus. Nina K. Brisley*)	CHAMBERS 1929	E
6	**Eustacia Goes to the Chalet School**	CHAMBERS 1930	D
7	**The Chalet School and Jo** (*illus. Nina K. Brisley*)	CHAMBERS 1931	D
8	**The Chalet Girls in Camp**	CHAMBERS 1932	D
9	**The Exploits of the Chalet Girls** (*illus. Nina K. Brisley*)	CHAMBERS 1933	D
10	**The Chalet School and the Lintons** (*illus. Nina K. Brisley*)	CHAMBERS 1934	D
11	**The New House at the Chalet School**	CHAMBERS 1935	D
12	**Jo Returns to the Chalet School** (*illus. Nina K. Brisley*)	CHAMBERS 1936	D
13	**The New Chalet School** (*illus. Nina K. Brisley*)	CHAMBERS 1938	D
14	**The Chalet School in Exile**	CHAMBERS 1940	C
15	**The Chalet School Goes to It** (*illus. Nina K. Brisley*)	CHAMBERS 1941	C
16	**The Highland Twins at the Chalet School**	CHAMBERS 1942	C
17	**Lavender Laughs in the Chalet School**	CHAMBERS 1943	C
18	**Gay from China at the Chalet School**	CHAMBERS 1944	C
19	**Jo to the Rescue**	CHAMBERS 1945	C
20	**Three Go to the Chalet School**	CHAMBERS 1949	C
21	**Peggy of the Chalet School**	CHAMBERS 1950	C

22	The Chalet School and the Island	CHAMBERS 1950	C
23	The Chalet School and Rosalie	CHAMBERS 1951	C
24	Carola Storms the Chalet School	CHAMBERS 1951	C
25	The Chalet School in the Oberland	CHAMBERS 1952	C
26	The Wrong Chalet School	CHAMBERS 1952	C
27	Shocks for the Chalet School	CHAMBERS 1952	C
28	Bride Leads the Chalet School	CHAMBERS 1953	C
29	Changes for the Chalet School	CHAMBERS 1953	C
30	Joey Goes to the Oberland	CHAMBERS 1954	C
31	The Chalet School and Barbara	CHAMBERS 1954	C
32	A Chalet Girl from Kenya	CHAMBERS 1955	C
33	The Chalet School Does It Again	CHAMBERS 1955	C
34	Tom Tackles the Chalet School	CHAMBERS 1955	C
35	A Problem for the Chalet School	CHAMBERS 1956	C
36	Mary-Lou of the Chalet School	CHAMBERS 1956	C
37	A Genius at the Chalet School	CHAMBERS 1956	C
38	Excitements at the Chalet School	CHAMBERS 1957	B
39	The New Mistress at the Chalet School	CHAMBERS 1957	B
40	The Chalet School and Richenda	CHAMBERS 1958	B
41	The Coming-of-age at the Chalet School	CHAMBERS 1958	B
42	Theodora and the Chalet School	CHAMBERS 1959	B
43	Trials for the Chalet School	CHAMBERS 1959	B
44	Joey & Co in Tirol	CHAMBERS 1960	B
45	Ruey Richardson – Chaletian	CHAMBERS 1960	B
46	A Leader in the Chalet School	CHAMBERS 1961	B
47	The Chalet School Wins the Trick	CHAMBERS 1961	B
48	The Feud in the Chalet School	CHAMBERS 1962	B

49	**A Future Chalet School Girl**	CHAMBERS 1962	**B**
50	**The Chalet School Reunion**	CHAMBERS 1963	**B**
51	**The Chalet School Triplets**	CHAMBERS 1963	**B**
52	**Jane and the Chalet School**	CHAMBERS 1964	**B**
53	**Redheads at the Chalet School**	CHAMBERS 1964	**B**
54	**Summer Term at the Chalet School**	CHAMBERS 1965	**B**
55	**Adrienne and the Chalet School**	CHAMBERS 1965	**B**
56	**Challenge for the Chalet School**	CHAMBERS 1966	**B**
57	**Two Sams at the Chalet School**	CHAMBERS 1967	**B**
58	**Althea Joins the Chalet School**	CHAMBERS 1969	**B**
59	**Prefects of the Chalet School**	CHAMBERS 1970	**B**

You may care to know, or you may not, that in 1953 Chambers published Brent-Dyer's The Chalet Girls' Cook Book. (**C**)

BRIGGS, Katharine M.   *Born in London, 1898. Died 1980*

Although primarily known for her pioneering and ultimately definitive studies on folklore, fairies and the supernatural generally, Katharine Briggs has written a small body of work intended for children (although it is by no means an easy read, some fairy stories containing a distinctly callous element) which could be said to have sprung from her prodigious knowledge of her specialist subject. *Hobberdy Dick* and *Kate Crackernuts* have become classics of their kind, and will not be easy to locate in first edition – the earlier work being even tougher.

1	**The Legend of Maiden-Hair** (*fiction*)	STOCKWELL 1915	**J**
2	**The Witches' Ride** (*fiction*) (*illus. Winifred Briggs*)	CAPRICORNUS 1937	**I**
3	**The Prince, the Fox and the Dragon** (*fiction*) (*illus. Winifred Briggs*)	CAPRICORNUS 1938	**I**
4	**Mime for Guides and Brownies** (*non-fiction*)	GIRL GUIDES ASSOC. 1955	**F**

5	**Hobberdy Dick** (*fiction*)	EYRE & SPOTTISWOODE 1955	**E**
		GREENWILLOW US 1977	**B**
6	**Kate Crackernuts** (*fiction*)	ALDEN PRESS 1963	**E**
	A revised edition was published in 1979 by		**B**
	Kestrel, and by Greenwillow in America (**B**).		
7	**Abbey Lubbers, Banshees and**	KESTREL 1979	**B**
	Boggarts: A Who's Who of Fairies	PANTHEON 1979	**B**
	(*illus. Yvonne Gilbert*)		

BRIGGS, Raymond   *Born in London, 1934*

If Briggs had *only* created *The Snowman*, it seems certain that his name would live on – but of course he has done considerably more than that, some of it enchanting and some of it downright revolting. *Fungus* was nauseating enough, but I admit to finding *Unlucky Wally* . . . what shall we say? Less than palatable – that will do. It makes one wonder – after the chillingly brilliant *When the Wind Blows* and the frankly embarrassing *Tin Pot General* – what new ground he might break next. I have included these two – although they are clearly not intended for children – really just for completion's sake. All the following books are, of course, illustrated by the author.

1	**Midnight Adventure** (*fiction*)	HAMISH HAMILTON 1961	**F**
2	**The Strange House** (*fiction*)	HAMISH HAMILTON 1961	**F**
3	**Ring-a-ring o'Roses** (*verse*)	HAMISH HAMILTON 1962	**E**
		COWARD McCANN 1962	**C**
4	**Sledges to the Rescue** (*fiction*)	HAMISH HAMILTON 1963	**D**
5	**Jim and the Beanstalk** (*fiction*)	HAMISH HAMILTON 1970	**C**
		COWARD McCANN 1970	**B**
6	**Father Christmas** (*fiction*)	HAMISH HAMILTON 1973	**C**
		COWARD McCANN 1973	**B**
7	**Father Christmas Goes on Holiday** (*fiction*)	HAMISH HAMILTON 1975	**B**
8	**Fungus the Bogeyman** (*fiction*)	HAMISH HAMILTON 1977	**C**
9	**The Snowman** (*fiction*)	HAMISH HAMILTON 1978	**D**
		RANDOM HOUSE 1978	**C**

10	**Gentleman Jim** (*fiction*)	HAMISH HAMILTON 1980	**B**
11	**Fungus the Bogeyman Plop-up Book** (*pop-up*)	HAMISH HAMILTON 1982	**B**
12	**When the Wind Blows** (*adult*)	HAMISH HAMILTON 1982	**C**
		SHOCKEN 1982	**B**
13	**The Tin Pot General and the Old Iron Woman** (*adult*)	HAMISH HAMILTON 1984	**A**
14	**Building the Snowman** **Dressing Up** **Walking in the Air** **The Party** *Four small books based on* The Snowman.	HAMISH HAMILTON 1985	**A** **Each**
15	**The Snowman Pop-up Book**	HAMISH HAMILTON 1986	**B**
16	**Unlucky Wally** (*fiction*)	HAMISH HAMILTON 1987	**A**

BRISLEY, Joyce Lankester   *Born in Sussex, 1896. Died 1978*

Brisley will be remembered for the Milly-Molly-Mandy books. The simplicity of the illustrations (her own) and the prose endeared them to generations, and although out of favour recently, I see a rebirth of popularity as probable – particularly if this was occasioned by a handsome reissue. The name Milly-Molly-Mandy, incidentally, is a contraction of the less snappy Millicent Margaret Amanda.

1	**Milly-Molly-Mandy Stories**	HARRAP 1928	**H**
		McKAY 1977	**A**
2	**More of Milly-Molly-Mandy**	HARRAP 1929	**G**
		McKAY 1977	**A**
3	**Lambs'-tails and Suchlike: Verses and Sketches**	HARRAP 1930	**D**
		McKAY 1930	**C**
4	**Further Doings of Milly-Molly-Mandy**	HARRAP 1932	**E**
		McKAY 1932	**D**
5	**The Dawn Shops and Other Stories**	HARRAP 1933	**C**
		McKAY 1933	**B**
6	**Marigold in Godmother's House**	HARRAP 1934	**C**

7	**Bunchy**	HARRAP 1937	**C**
		McKAY 1937	**B**
8	**Three Little Milly-Molly-Mandy Plays**	HARRAP 1938	**C**

Comprises: Milly-Molly-Mandy Goes Errands; Milly-Molly-Mandy Keeps Shop; Milly-Molly-Mandy Meets Her Great Aunt.

9	**My Bible Book** (*non-fiction*)	HARRAP 1940	**C**
		McKAY 1940	**B**
10	**The Adventures of Purl and Plain**	HARRAP 1941	**C**
11	**Milly-Molly-Mandy Again**	HARRAP 1948	**C**
		McKAY 1977	**B**
12	**Another Bunchy Book**	HARRAP 1951	**B**
13	**Milly-Molly-Mandy & Co**	HARRAP 1955	**C**
		McKAY 1977	**B**
14	**Milly-Molly-Mandy and Billy Blunt**	HARRAP 1967	**B**
		McKAY 1977	**B**
15	**Children of Bible Days** (*non-fiction*)	HARRAP 1970	**A**
16	**The Joyce Lankester Brisley Book** (*anthology, edited by Frank Waters*)	HARRAP 1981	**A**

BRUNA, Dick   *Born in Holland, 1927*

Bruna – or, to invest him with his full nomenclature, Hendrik Magdalenus Bruna the Younger – is obviously not an author in whom collectors' (as opposed to children's) interest is terribly strong, and equally obviously, he is impossible to omit. Nonetheless, I list the whole lot here – partly because I believe that it has never before been done, but mainly so that collectors can be as selective or as dismissive as they choose. The books (all with illustrations and minimal texts by Bruna) were first published in Holland; below are listed the first English and American editions.

1	**The Little Bird**	METHUEN 1962	**B**
		TWO CONTINENTS 1975	**A**
2	**Tilly and Tessa**	METHUEN 1962	**A**
		FOLLETT 1963	**A**

3	The Fish	METHUEN 1962	A
		FOLLETT 1963	A
4	Circus	METHUEN 1963	A
		FOLLETT 1963	A
5	Little Bird Tweet	METHUEN 1963	A
		FOLLETT 1963	A
6	The Egg	METHUEN 1964	A
		FOLLETT 1968	A
7	The King	METHUEN 1964	A
		FOLLETT 1968	A
8	Miffy	METHUEN 1964	B
		FOLLETT 1970	A
9	Miffy at the Seaside	METHUEN 1964	A
		FOLLETT 1970	A
10	The Christmas Book	METHUEN 1964	A
		DOUBLEDAY 1969	A
11	Miffy in the Snow	METHUEN 1965	A
		FOLLETT 1970	A
12	Miffy at the Zoo	METHUEN 1965	A
		FOLLETT 1970	A
13	The Sailor	METHUEN 1966	A
		FOLLETT 1968	A
14	The School	METHUEN 1966	A
		FOLLETT 1968	A
15	The Apple	METHUEN 1966	A
16	Pussy Nell	METHUEN 1966	A
17	Little Red Riding Hood	FOLLETT 1966	A
		METHUEN 1967	A
18	Tom Thumb	FOLLETT 1966	A
		METHUEN 1967	A
19	Cinderella	FOLLETT 1966	A
		METHUEN 1968	A

20	**Snow White and the Seven Dwarfs**	FOLLETT 1966	**A**
		METHUEN 1968	**A**
21	**B is for Bear**	METHUEN 1967	**A**
22	**A Story to Tell**	METHUEN 1968	**A**
		TWO CONTINENTS 1975	**A**
23	**I Can Count**	METHUEN 1968	**A**
		TWO CONTINENTS 1975	**A**
24	**I Can Read**	METHUEN 1969	**A**
		TWO CONTINENTS 1975	**A**
25	**I Can Read More**	METHUEN 1969	**A**
		TWO CONTINENTS 1976	**A**
26	**Snuffy**	METHUEN 1970	**B**
		TWO CONTINENTS 1975	**A**
27	**Snuffy and the Fire**	METHUEN 1970	**A**
		TWO CONTINENTS 1975	**A**
28	**Miffy's Birthday**	METHUEN 1971	**A**
		TWO CONTINENTS 1976	**A**
29	**Miffy Goes Flying**	METHUEN 1971	**A**
		TWO CONTINENTS 1976	**A**
30	**ABC** (*frieze*)	METHUEN 1971	**A**
31	**My Vest is White**	METHUEN 1973	**A**
	Published in America by Two Continents in 1975 as My Shirt is White.		
32	**I Can Count More**	METHUEN 1973	**A**
		TWO CONTINENTS 1976	**A**
33	**123** (*frieze*)	METHUEN 1974	**A**
34	**Animal** (*frieze*)	METHUEN 1975	**A**
35	**Another Story to Tell**	METHUEN 1976	**A**
36	**Lisa and Lynn**	TWO CONTINENTS 1975	**A**
37	**Miffy at the Playground**	METHUEN 1976	**A**
		PRICE STERN 1984	**A**
38	**Dick Bruna's Animal Book**	METHUEN 1976	**A**
		TWO CONTINENTS 1976	**A**

39	**I am a Clown**	METHUEN 1976	**A**
40	**Miffy in Hospital**	METHUEN 1976	**A**
41	**I Can Read Difficult Words**	METHUEN 1977	**A**
42	**I Can Dress Myself**	METHUEN 1977	**A**
43	**Poppy Pig**	METHUEN 1978	**A**
44	**Poppy Pig's Garden**	METHUEN 1978	**A**
45	**Miffy's Dream**	METHUEN 1979	**A**
46	**My Toys**	METHUEN 1980	**A**
47	**Read with Miffy** (*frieze*)	METHUEN 1980	**A**
48	**Poppy Pig Goes to Market**	METHUEN 1981	**A**
49	**When I'm Big**	METHUEN 1981	**A**
50	**I Know About Numbers**	METHUEN 1981	**A**
51	**I Know More About Numbers**	METHUEN 1981	**A**
52	**Dick Bruna's Word Book**	METHUEN 1982	**A**
53	**Miffy's Bicycle**	METHUEN 1984	**A**
54	**Miffy at School**	METHUEN 1984	**A**
55	**I Know About Shapes**	METHUEN 1984	**A**
56	**I Can Make Music**	METHEUN 1984	**A**
57	**Farmer John**	METHUEN 1984	**A**
58	**The Lifeboat**	METHUEN 1984	**A**
59	**Find My Hat**	METHUEN 1984	**A**
60	**Back to Front**	METHUEN 1984	**A**
61	**My Sport Book**	METHUEN 1984	**A**
62	**Blue Boat** (*with Peter Jones*)	METHUEN 1984	**A**
63	**My House**	METHUEN 1984	**A**
64	**Playing in Winter**	METHUEN 1984	**A**
65	**My Playtime**	METHUEN 1985	**A**
66	**My Street**	METHUEN 1985	**A**

67	My Garden	METHUEN 1985	A
68	My Animals	METHUEN 1985	A
69	Miffy's Book of Colour	METHUEN 1986	A
70	Poppy Pig's Birthday	METHUEN 1987	A
71	Snuffy's Puppy	METHUEN 1987	A
72	Bear's Springtime	METHUEN 1987	A

BUCKERIDGE, Anthony *Born in London, 1912*

Creator of the funniest and best-written schoolboy books, bar none. Buckeridge is now enjoying a richly deserved revival following a dip in popularity during the 'seventies and early 'eighties – so much so that many of the Jennings books are being reissued. Of course, it is quite shameful (double ozard, indeed) that they ever went out of print in the first place – but the reissues are, I tremble to report, *revised*. This means, in effect, that all the glorious 'fifties prep school language has been updated by Buckeridge himself (I'm afraid I deplore this – did they update Shakespeare? Jane Austen? What has become of period *charm*?) and all references to Mr Carter and Mr Wilkins being pipe smokers have been deleted. I – I – Cor-Wumph!

Although the Jennings books were chronologically interspersed with the Rex Milligan books, I have split up the series for the convenience of collectors – who would be well advised to look sharp if they want to gather this lot: Buckeridge (largely my fault, I'm afraid) is *very* collected. Do stick out for copies in dust-wrapper, though – they are works of art (until the last few).

JENNINGS:

1	Jennings Goes to School	COLLINS 1950	F
2	Jennings Follows a Clue	COLLINS 1951	C
3	Jennings' Little Hut	COLLINS 1951	C
4	Jennings and Darbishire	COLLINS 1952	C
5	Jennings' Diary	COLLINS 1953	C
6	According to Jennings	COLLINS 1954	C
7	Our Friend Jennings	COLLINS 1955	C
8	Thanks to Jennings	COLLINS 1957	C

9	**Take Jennings, for Instance** (*illus. Mays*)	COLLINS 1958	C
10	**Jennings, as Usual** (*illus. Mays*)	COLLINS 1959	C
11	**The Trouble with Jennings** (*illus. Mays*)	COLLINS 1960	B
12	**Just Like Jennings**	COLLINS 1961	B
13	**Leave It to Jennings** (*illus. Mays*)	COLLINS 1963	B
14	**Jennings, Of Course!**	COLLINS 1964	B
15	**Especially Jennings!** (*illus. Mays*)	COLLINS 1965	B
16	**A Bookful of Jennings** (*anthology*) *A revised edition was published by Collins in 1972 as* The Best of Jennings.	COLLINS 1966	B
17	**Jennings Abounding** (*illus. Mays*)	COLLINS 1967	B
18	**Jennings in Particular** (*illus. Mays*)	COLLINS 1968	B
19	**Trust Jennings!** (*illus. Mays*)	COLLINS 1969	B
20	**The Jennings Report** (*illus. Mays*)	COLLINS 1970	B
21	**Typically Jennings!**	COLLINS 1971	B
22	**Speaking of Jennings**	COLLINS 1973	B
23	**Jennings at Large** (*a paperback original*)	ARMADA 1977	B

REX MILLIGAN:

1	**A Funny Thing Happened!**	LUTTERWORTH PRESS 1953	B
2	**Rex Milligan's Busy Term** (*illus. Mazure*)	LUTTERWORTH PRESS 1953	B

3 Rex Milligan Raises the Roof (*illus. Mazure*)	LUTTERWORTH PRESS 1955	**B**
4 Rex Milligan Holds Forth (*illus. Mazure*)	LUTTERWORTH PRESS 1955	**B**
5 Rex Milligan Reporting (*illus. Mazure*)	LUTTERWORTH PRESS 1961	**B**

BURNETT, Frances Hodgson *American. Born in England 1849. Died 1924*

Burnett was the respected author of nine adult novels when she came to write her first – and one of her two best-known – books for children, *Little Lord Fauntleroy*, in 1886. Although this doesn't come within the period brief of my book, I might mention that it was published by Scribner in America and by Warne in Britain – both editions being scarce and expensive. She went on to produce about two dozen more novels and volumes of short stories for adults and quite a few plays – as well as a score of children's books. Although a good many of these were published during the twentieth century, I list here the two best known – *The Secret Garden*, of course, having become an all-time classic. Robinson is an illustrator collected in his own right – one contributory factor to the high price of the elusive first edition.

1 A Little Princess, Being the Whole Story of Sara Crewe Now Told for the First Time *This is a largely rewritten – and generally held to be wholly superior – version of a children's book published by Unwin in 1887, and in America by Scribner in 1888, under the title* Sara Crewe; or, What Happened at Miss Michin's.	SCRIBNER 1905 WARNE 1905	**I** **G**
2 The Secret Garden (*illus. Charles Robinson*)	STOKES US 1911 HEINEMANN 1911	**M** **L**

Also of interest:
ANN THWAITE: **Waiting for the Party: The Life of Frances Hodgson Burnett 1849–1924** (SECKER & WARBURG 1974, SCRIBNER US 1974)

BURNINGHAM, John   *Born in Surrey, 1936*

A very stylish writer and illustrator indeed – conveying with minimum line and as few words as possible a true rapport with both his subject and his audience. Despite the delicacy of the drawing, the image and the message are strong – this in part due to the intense yet pallid colouring, and the variety of media. A good many of Burningham's books have scooped up prizes, and such as the Gumpy and Shirley books – and maybe the very attractive *Avocado Baby* – are well on the way to becoming classics of the future.

Burningham illustrated the three volumes of Ian Fleming's *Chitty-Chitty-Bang-Bang* (q.v.) and is – *en passant* – married to children's book illustrator Helen Oxenbury.

1	**Borka: The Adventures of a Goose with No Feathers**	CAPE 1963 RANDOM HOUSE 1964	**D** **B**
2	**Trubloff: The Mouse Who Wanted to Play the Balalaika**	CAPE 1964 RANDOM HOUSE 1965	**C** **B**
3	**ABC** (*illus. J.B. & Leigh Taylor*)	CAPE 1964 BOBBS MERRILL 1967	**B** **B**
4	**Humbert, Mister Firkin and the Lord Mayor of London**	CAPE 1965 BOBBS MERRILL 1967	**B** **B**
5	**Seasons**	CAPE 1969 BOBBS MERRILL 1971	**B** **B**
6	**Mr Gumpy's Outing**	CAPE 1970 HOLT RINEHART 1970	**B** **B**
7	**Mr Gumpy's Motor Car**	CAPE 1973 CROWELL 1976	**B** **B**
8	**Little Books** (*readers*) *A series of eight little books, comprising:* The Baby; The Rabbit; The School; The Snow; The Blanket; The Cupboard; The Dog; The Friend.	CAPE 1974–5 CROWELL 1975–6	**A** **A** **Each**
9	**Come Away from the Water, Shirley**	CAPE 1977 CROWELL 1977	**B** **A**
10	**Time to Get Out of the Bath, Shirley**	CAPE 1978 CROWELL 1978	**B** **A**
11	**Would You Rather...**	CAPE 1978 CROWELL 1978	**B** **A**

12	**The Shopping Basket**	CAPE 1980	**B**
		CROWELL 1980	**A**
13	**Avocado Baby**	CAPE 1982	**B**
		CROWELL 1982	**A**
14	**Concertina Board Books**	WALKER 1983	**A**

A series of six, comprising: Count Up; Read One; Ride Off; Pigs Plus; Five Down; Just Cats. **Each**

| 15 | **First Words:** | WALKER 1984 | **A** |

A series of six 'readers', comprising: Cluck Baa; Skip Trip; Slam Bang; Sniff Shout; Wobble Pop; Jangle Twang. **Each**

16	**Grandpa**	CAPE 1984	**B**
		CROWELL 1984	**B**
17	**Where's Julius?**	CAPE 1986	**A**
18	**John Patrick Norman McHennessy: The Boy Who was Always Late**	CAPE 1987	**A**

CHRISTOPHER, John

Pseudonym of Christopher S. Youd
Born in Lancashire, 1922

Author of about three dozen books for adults under various pseudonyms, John Christopher remains best known as the author who made children's science fiction *credible* – for if it is not credible, of course, it is just plain silly. He has been amply praised by contemporaries such as John Rowe Townsend, and his children's novels – and in particular his first three, which form a trilogy – seem set to stay. Christopher is still by no means yet in the mainstream of collectors' interest, but this situation might well soon change.

1	**The White Mountains**	HAMISH HAMILTON 1967	C
		MACMILLAN US 1967	B
2	**The City of Gold and Lead**	HAMISH HAMILTON 1967	C
		MACMILLAN US 1967	B
3	**The Pool of Fire**	HAMISH HAMILTON 1968	C
	1–3 form 'The Tripods Trilogy'.	MACMILLAN US 1968	B
4	**The Lotus Caves**	HAMISH HAMILTON 1969	B
		MACMILLAN US 1969	A
5	**The Guardians**	HAMISH HAMILTON 1970	B
		MACMILLAN US 1970	A
6	**The Prince in Waiting**	HAMISH HAMILTON 1970	B
		MACMILLAN US 1970	A
7	**Beyond the Burning Lands**	HAMISH HAMILTON 1971	B
		MACMILLAN US 1971	A
8	**The Sword of the Spirits**	HAMISH HAMILTON 1972	B
	6–8 form 'The Sword Trilogy'.	MACMILLAN US 1972	A
9	**In the Beginning** (*reader*)	LONGMAN 1972	A
10	**Dom and Va**	HAMISH HAMILTON 1973	A
	A revised edition of 9.	MACMILLAN US 1973	A
11	**A Figure in Grey**	WORLD'S WORK 1973	A
	(*Pseudonym Hilary Ford*)		
12	**Wild Jack**	HAMISH HAMILTON 1974	A
		MACMILLAN US 1974	A
13	**Empty World**	HAMISH HAMILTON 1977	A
		MACMILLAN US 1978	A

14	Fireball	GOLLANCZ 1981	B
		DUTTON 1981	A
15	New Found Land	GOLLANCZ 1983	B
16	Dragondance	VIKING KESTREL 1986	B

14–16 form a trilogy.

CLARK, Leonard *Born in Guernsey, 1905. Died 1981*

A prolific author, and editor of countless anthologies, Clark has been rather neglected lately – his volumes of verse for both children and adults having fallen by the wayside. There are very few poets who have worked specifically for children (de la Mare springs to mind, of course) and I include Clark chiefly for this reason; the poetry is gentle, and often displays insights that can be picked up by the young mind. He also wrote a few children's stories, and I list these too. Clark is not of great interest to collectors at present, and hence the low valuations.

1	**Daybreak: A First Book of Poems** (*illus. Selma Nankivell*)	HART-DAVIS 1963	B
2	**The Year Round: A Second Book of Poems** (*illus. Edward Ardizzone*)	HART-DAVIS 1966	C
3	**Fields and Territories** (*verse*)	TURRET 1967	B
4	**Good Company** (*verse*) (*illus. Jennie Corbett*)	DOBSON 1968	B
5	**Near and Far** (*verse*) (*illus. Kozo Kakimoto* et al)	HAMLYN 1968	A
6	**Here and There** (*verse*) (*illus. Kuniro Fukazawa*)	HAMLYN 1969	A
7	**Secret as Toads** (*verse*)	CHATTO & WINDUS 1972	A
8	**Singing in the Streets: Poems for Christmas**	DOBSON 1972	A
9	**The Broad Atlantic** (*verse*)	DOBSON 1974	A
10	**Mr Pettigrew's Harvest Festival** (*fiction*) (*illus. Toffee Sanders*)	THORNHILL 1974	B
11	**Mr Pettigrew's Train** (*fiction*) (*illus. Toffee Sanders*)	THORNHILL 1975	B

12	**Four Seasons** (*verse*) (*illus. Jennie Corbett*)	DOBSON 1975	**A**
13	**Collected Poems and Verses for Children**	DOBSON 1975	**A**
14	**Mr Pettigrew and the Bell-ringers** (*fiction*) (*illus. Toffee Sanders*)	THORNHILL 1976	**B**
15	**The Tale of Prince Igor** (*verse*) (*illus. Charles Keeping*)	DOBSON 1979	**A**
16	**Stranger Than Unicorns** (*verse*) (*illus. Jennie Corbett*)	DOBSON 1979	**A**
17	**The Singing Time: Poems and Verses for Children** (*illus. Doreen Caldwell*)	HODDER 1980	**A**
18	**The Corn Growing** (*verse*) (*illus. Lisa Kopper*)	HODDER 1982	**A**

COREN, Alan

Born in London, 1938

Until recently editor of *Punch*, and author of some of the wittiest and best journalism since the war, Alan Coren is by no means best known for the following clutch of children's books – but that is no reason why they should be overlooked: bright, intelligent, a touch sardonic, not at all patronizing – and most entertaining. Elusive, though, I should think. All the following are illustrated by John Astrop.

1	**The Lone Arthur**	ROBSON 1976	**B**
		LITTLE BROWN 1976	**A**
2	**Arthur the Kid**	ROBSON 1976	**B**
		LITTLE BROWN 1976	**A**
3	**Buffalo Arthur**	ROBSON 1976	**B**
		LITTLE BROWN 1976	**A**
4	**Arthur's Last Stand**	ROBSON 1977	**A**
		LITTLE BROWN 1977	**A**
5	**Railroad Arthur**	ROBSON 1977	**A**
		LITTLE BROWN 1977	**A**

6	**Klondike Arthur**	ROBSON 1977	**A**
		LITTLE BROWN 1977	**A**
7	**Arthur and the Great Detective**	ROBSON 1979	**A**
8	**Arthur and the Bellybutton Diamond**	ROBSON 1979	**A**
9	**Arthur and the Purple Panic**	ROBSON 1981	**A**
10	**Arthur v. the Rest**	ROBSON 1981	**A**

CRADOCK, Mrs Henry   *Born in Britain*

Nothing whatever seems to be known about Mrs Cradock, but her 'Josephine' books continue to be appreciated by collectors, and the theme of investing dolls with individual personalities seems certain to retain its attraction for young children. She wrote about twenty books in all, and below is the 'Josephine' series in its entirety. All are illustrated by Honor C. Appleton.

1	**Josephine and Her Dolls**	BLACKIE 1916	**H**
2	**Josephine's Happy Family**	BLACKIE 1917	**G**
3	**Josephine is Busy**	BLACKIE 1918	**G**
4	**Josephine's Birthday**	BLACKIE 1920	**F**
5	**Josephine, John and the Puppy**	BLACKIE 1920	**F**
6	**Josephine Keeps School**	BLACKIE 1925	**E**
7	**Josephine Goes Shopping**	BLACKIE 1926	**E**
8	**Josephine's Christmas Party**	BLACKIE 1927	**E**
9	**Josephine Keeps House**	BLACKIE 1931	**D**
10	**Josephine's Pantomime**	BLACKIE 1939	**D**
11	**Josephine Goes Travelling**	BLACKIE 1940	**D**

CRESSWELL, Helen   *Born in Nottinghamshire, 1934*

Helen Cresswell is undeniably prolific – as will be seen in the ensuing list – but the quality, and the comedy, remain. She is that rare thing – a children's writer who can marry the almost mandatory fantasy with a really very sophisticated humour; the humour is best appreciated neat, as in her

'Jumbo' books, and in the later 'Lizzie Dripping' series – all about a witch who is but a child's fantasy-figure: this series stemmed from a BBC *Jackanory* commission. A collector would maybe not want Cresswell's entire output (she tends to publish them faster than you can buy them) but key novels – such as *The Piemakers* and *The Night-watchmen* – together with representatives of her aforementioned series would be most desirable.

In addition to this listing, Cresswell has published around a dozen 'readers' which I do not see as integral to her main body of work.

1	**Sonya-by-the-Shore** (*illus. Robin Jane Wells*)	DENT 1960	E
2	**Jumbo Spencer** (*illus. Clixby Watson*)	BROCKHAMPTON PRESS 1963	C
		LIPPINCOTT 1966	B
3	**The White Sea Horse** (*illus. Robin Jacques*)	OLIVER & BOYD 1964	C
		LIPPINCOTT 1965	B
4	**Jumbo Back to Nature** (*illus. Leslie Wood*)	BROCKHAMPTON PRESS 1965	C
5	**Pietro and the Mule** (*illus. Maureen Eckersley*)	OLIVER & BOYD 1965	D
		BOBBS MERRILL 1965	B
6	**Jumbo Afloat** (*illus. Leslie Wood*)	BROCKHAMPTON PRESS 1966	C
7	**Where the Wind Blows** (*illus. Peggy Fortnum*)	FABER 1966	C
		FUNK & WAGNALLS 1968	B
8	**The Piemakers** (*illus. V.H. Drummond*)	FABER 1967	D
		LIPPINCOTT 1968	B
9	**A Day on Big O** (*illus. Shirley Hughes*)	BENN 1967	B
		FOLLETT 1968	A
10	**A Tide for the Captain** (*illus. Robin Jacques*)	OLIVER & BOYD 1967	C
11	**The Signposters** (*illus. Gareth Floyd*)	FABER 1968	B
12	**Jumbo and the Big Dig** (*illus. Leslie Wood*)	BROCKHAMPTON PRESS 1968	B
13	**The Barge Children** (*illus. Lynette Hemmant*)	HODDER & STOUGHTON 1968	B

14	**The Sea Piper** (*illus. Robin Jacques*)	OLIVER & BOYD 1968	**B**
15	**The Night-watchmen** (*illus. Gareth Floyd*)	FABER 1969 MACMILLAN US 1969	**C** **B**
16	**A Gift from Winklesea** (*illus. Janina Ede*)	BROCKHAMPTON PRESS 1969	**B**
17	**A Game of Catch** (*illus. Gareth Floyd*)	OLIVER & BOYD 1969 MACMILLAN US 1977	**B** **A**
18	**A House for Jones** (*illus. Margaret Gordon*)	BENN 1969	**B**
19	**The Outlanders** (*illus. Doreen Roberts*)	FABER 1970	**B**
20	**Rainbow Pavement** (*illus. Shirley Hughes*)	BENN 1970	**B**
21	**The Wilkeses** (*illus. Gareth Floyd*)	BBC 1970	**B**
22	**The Bird Fancier** (*illus. Renate Meyer*)	BENN 1971	**B**
23	**Up the Pier** (*illus. Gareth Floyd*)	FABER 1971 MACMILLAN US 1972	**B** **A**
24	**The Weather Cat** (*illus. Margery Gill*)	BENN 1971	**B**
25	**The Beachcombers** (*illus. Errol le Cain*)	FABER 1972 MACMILLAN US 1972	**B** **A**
26	**Bluebirds Over Pit Row** (*illus. Richard Kennedy*)	BENN 1972	**B**
27	**Jane's Policeman** (*illus. Margery Gill*)	BENN 1972	**B**
28	**The Long Day** (*illus. Margery Gill*)	BENN 1972	**B**
29	**Roof Fall!** (*illus. Richard Kennedy*)	BENN 1972	**B**
30	**Short Back and Sides** (*illus. Richard Kennedy*)	BENN 1972	**B**

31	**The Beetle Hunt** (*illus. Anne Knight*)	LONGMAN 1973	**B**
32	**The Bongleweed** (*illus. Ann Strugnell*)	FABER 1973 MACMILLAN US 1974	**B** **A**
33	**The Bower Birds** (*illus. Margery Gill*)	BENN 1973	**B**
34	**Lizzie Dripping** (*illus. Jenny Thorne*)	BBC 1973	**C**
35	**Lizzie Dripping by the Sea** (*illus. Faith Jaques*)	BBC 1974	**B**
36	**Lizzie Dripping and the Little Angel** (*illus. Faith Jaques*)	BBC 1974	**B**
37	**Lizzie Dripping Again** (*illus. Faith Jaques*)	BBC 1974	**B**
38	**Two Hoots** (*illus. Martine Blanc*) *Six volumes comprising:* Two Hoots; Two Hoots Go to Sea; Two Hoots in the Snow; Two Hoots and the Big Bad Bird; Two Hoots and the King; Two Hoots Play Hide-and-seek.	BENN 1974–77 CROWN US 1978	**A** **A** **Each**
39	**More Lizzie Dripping** (*illus. Faith Jaques*)	BBC 1974	**B**
40	**Butterfly Chase** (*illus. Margery Gill*)	KESTREL 1975	**A**
41	**The Winter of Birds**	FABER 1975 MACMILLAN US 1976	**A** **A**
42	**Ordinary Jack**	FABER 1977 MACMILLAN US 1977	**B** **A**
43	**Absolute Zero**	FABER 1978 MACMILLAN US 1978	**B** **A**
44	**Bagthorpes Unlimited**	FABER 1978 MACMILLAN US 1978	**B** **A**

45	**Bagthorpes v. the World**	FABER 1979	**B**
	42–45, illustrated by Jill Bennett, comprise	MACMILLAN US 1979	**A**
	'The Bagthorpe Saga'.		
46	**Donkey Days**	BENN 1977	**A**
	(*illus. Shirley Hughes*)		
47	**Awful Jack**	HODDER & STOUGHTON	**A**
	(*illus. Joanna Stubbs*)	1977	
48	**The Flyaway Kite**	KESTREL 1979	**A**
	(*illus. Bridget Clarke*)		
49	**My Aunt Polly by the Sea**	WHEATON 1980	**A**
	(*illus. Margaret Gordon*)		
50	**Dear Shrink**	FABER 1982	**A**
		MACMILLAN US 1982	**A**
51	**The Secret World of Polly Flint**	FABER 1982	**A**
	(*illus. Shirley Felts*)		
52	**Ellie and Hagwitch**	HARDY 1984	**A**
	(*illus. Jonathan Heap*)		
53	**Bagthorpes Abroad**	FABER 1984	**B**
	(*illus. Jill Bennett*)		
54	**Bagthorpes Haunted**	FABER 1985	**B**
	(*illus. Jill Bennett*)		
55	**Alice's Adventures in . . . Birmingham**	MALIN 1986	**A**
56	**Moondial**	FABER 1987	**A**
57	**Trouble**	GOLLANCZ 1987	**A**
	(*illus. Margaret Chamberlain*)		

CROMPTON, Richmal

*Full name Richmal Crompton Lamburn
Born in Lancashire, 1890. Died 1969*

No one has ever seemed terribly interested in Crompton's novels for adults – about *forty* of them – and it is indeed possible that if she had not written about a certain scruffy schoolboy, we might never have heard of her. As it is, William proves to be eternally popular – even with the new generation of readers – and good copies (and even *not* so good copies) have become ever scarcer and more sought-after. I see this situation changing not at all.

1	**Just William** (*illus. Thomas Henry*)	NEWNES 1922	**M**
2	**More William** (*illus. Thomas Henry*)	NEWNES 1922	**J**
3	**William Again** (*illus. Thomas Henry*)	NEWNES 1923	**I**
4	**William the Fourth** (*illus. Thomas Henry*)	NEWNES 1924	**I**
5	**Still William** (*illus. Thomas Henry*)	NEWNES 1925	**I**
6	**William the Conqueror** (*illus. Thomas Henry*)	NEWNES 1926	**G**
7	**William in Trouble** (*illus. Thomas Henry*)	NEWNES 1927	**G**
8	**William the Outlaw** (*illus. Thomas Henry*)	NEWNES 1927	**H**
9	**William the Good** (*illus. Thomas Henry*)	NEWNES 1928	**G**
10	**William** (*illus. Thomas Henry*)	NEWNES 1929	**G**
11	**William the Bad** (*illus. Thomas Henry*)	NEWNES 1930	**G**
12	**William's Happy Days** (*illus. Thomas Henry*)	NEWNES 1930	**G**
13	**William's Crowded Hours** (*illus. Thomas Henry*)	NEWNES 1931	**F**
14	**William the Pirate** (*illus. Thomas Henry*)	NEWNES 1932	**F**
15	**William the Rebel** (*illus. Thomas Henry*)	NEWNES 1933	**F**
16	**William the Gangster** (*illus. Thomas Henry*)	NEWNES 1934	**F**
17	**William the Detective** (*illus. Thomas Henry*)	NEWNES 1935	**F**

18	**Sweet William** (*illus. Thomas Henry*)	NEWNES 1936	**F**
19	**William the Showman** (*illus. Thomas Henry*)	NEWNES 1937	**F**
20	**William the Dictator** (*illus. Thomas Henry*)	NEWNES 1938	**F**
21	**William and A.R.P.** (*illus. Thomas Henry*) *Reissued in 1956 as* William's Bad Resolution.	NEWNES 1939	**F**
22	**William and the Evacuees** (*illus. Thomas Henry*) *Reissued in 1956 as* William the Film Star.	NEWNES 1940	**F**
23	**William Does His Bit** (*illus. Thomas Henry*)	NEWNES 1941	**F**
24	**William Carries On** (*illus. Thomas Henry*)	NEWNES 1942	**E**
25	**William and the Brains Trust** (*illus. Thomas Henry*) *Reissued in an abridged form by Collins in 1972 as* William The Hero.	NEWNES 1945	**E**
26	**Just William's Luck** (*illus. Thomas Henry*)	NEWNES 1948	**E**
27	**William the Bold** (*illus. Thomas Henry*)	NEWNES 1950	**E**
28	**William and the Tramp** (*illus. Thomas Henry*)	NEWNES 1952	**E**
29	**William and the Moon Rocket** (*illus. Thomas Henry*)	NEWNES 1954	**E**
30	**William and the Space Animal** (*illus. Thomas Henry*)	NEWNES 1956	**E**
31	**William's Television Show** (*illus. Thomas Henry*)	NEWNES 1958	**E**
32	**William the Explorer** (*illus. Thomas Henry*)	NEWNES 1960	**D**

33 **William's Treasure Trove** NEWNES 1962 **D**
    (*illus. Thomas Henry*)

34 **William and the Witch** NEWNES 1964 **D**
    (*illus. Thomas Henry & Henry Ford*)

35 **William and the Monster** ARMADA 1965 **B**
    (*illus. Peter Archer & Thomas Henry*)

36 **William the Ancient Briton** ARMADA 1965 **B**
    (*illus. Peter Archer & Thomas Henry*)

37 **William the Cannibal** ARMADA 1965 **B**
    (*illus. Peter Archer & Thomas Henry*)

38 **William the Globetrotter** ARMADA 1965 **B**
    (*illus. Peter Archer & Thomas Henry*)

39 **William and the Pop Singers** NEWNES 1965 **C**
    (*illus. Henry Ford*)

40 **William and the Masked Ranger** NEWNES 1966 **C**
    (*illus. Henry Ford*)

41 **William the Superman** NEWNES 1968 **C**
    (*illus. Henry Ford*)

42 **William the Lawless** NEWNES 1970 **C**
    (*illus. Henry Ford*)

Richmal Crompton also published for children:

43 **Jimmy** NEWNES 1949 **C**

44 **Jimmy Again** NEWNES 1951 **C**
    (*illus. Lunt Roberts*)

45 **Jimmy the Third** ARMADA 1965 **A**
    (*illus. Lunt Roberts*)

Also of interest:
MARY CADOGAN: **Richmal Crompton, The Woman Behind William**
   (ALLEN & UNWIN, 1986)

CUNLIFFE, John   *Born in Lancashire, 1933*

Although now famous for Postman Pat (impossible to believe that this character made his debut only in 1981), Cunliffe is the author of many attractive books – attractive chiefly on account of their simplicity and pace – and was quite well known for the 'Giant' and 'Farmer Barnes' stories before the ubiquitous Postman Pat engulfed them all. I rather like old Pat and his black and white cat, I must confess – and an improvement a million times over on British Telecom's last mascot, the totally horrendous Busby.

1	**Farmer Barnes Buys a Pig** (*illus. Carol Barker*)	DEUTSCH 1964 LION PRESS US 1968	C A
2	**Farmer Barnes and Bluebell** (*illus. Carol Barker*)	DEUTSCH 1966	B
3	**Farmer Barnes at the County Show** (*illus. Jill McDonald*)	DEUTSCH 1969	B
4	**Farmer Barnes at the County Fair** Same as 3.	LION PRESS US 1969	A
5	**The Adventures of Lord Pip** (*illus. Robert Hales*)	DEUTSCH 1970	A
6	**The Giant Who Stole the World** (*illus. Faith Jaques*)	DEUTSCH 1971	B
7	**Farmer Barnes and the Goats** (*illus. Jill McDonald*)	DEUTSCH 1971	A
8	**Riddles and Rhymes and Rigmaroles** (*illus. Alexy Pendle*)	DEUTSCH 1971	A
9	**The Giant Who Swallowed the Wind** (*illus. Faith Jaques*)	DEUTSCH 1972	A
10	**Farmer Barnes Goes Fishing** (*illus. Jill McDonald*)	DEUTSCH 1972	A
11	**Giant Kippernose and Other Stories** (*illus. Fritz Wegner*)	DEUTSCH 1972	A
12	**The King's Birthday Cake** (*illus. Faith Jaques*)	DEUTSCH 1973	A
13	**The Great Dragon Competition and Other Stories** (*illus. Alexy Pendle*)	DEUTSCH 1973	A

14	**The Farmer, the Rooks and the Cherry Tree** (*illus. Prudence Seward*)	DEUTSCH 1974	A
15	**Small Monkey Tales** (*illus. Gerry Downes*)	DEUTSCH 1974	A
16	**Farmer Barnes and the Snow Picnic** (*illus. Joan Hickson*)	DEUTSCH 1974	A
17	**Giant Brog and the Motorway** (*illus. Alexy Pendle*)	DEUTSCH 1976	A
18	**Farmer Barnes Fells a Tree** (*illus. Joan Hickson*)	DEUTSCH 1977	A
19	**Farmer Barnes and the Harvest Doll** (*illus. Joan Hickson*)	DEUTSCH 1977	A
20	**Mr Gosling and the Runaway Chair** (*illus. William Stobbs*)	DEUTSCH 1978	A
21	**Farmer Barnes' Guy Fawkes Day** (*illus. Joan Hickson*)	DEUTSCH 1978	A
22	**Mr Gosling and the Great Art Robbery** (*illus. William Stobbs*)	DEUTSCH 1979	A
23	**Sara's Giant and the Upside-down House** (*illus. Hilary Abrahams*)	DEUTSCH 1980	A
24	**Our Sam: The Daftest Dog in the World** (*illus. Maurice Wilson*)	DEUTSCH 1980	A
25	**Postman Pat and the Mystery Thief** (*illus. Celia Berridge*)	DEUTSCH 1981	C
26	**Postman Pat's Treasure Hunt** (*illus. Celia Berridge*)	DEUTSCH 1981	B
27	**Postman Pat's Secret** (*illus. Celia Berridge*)	DEUTSCH 1981	B
28	**Postman Pat's Rainy Day** (*illus. Celia Berridge*)	DEUTSCH 1982	A

29	**Postman Pat's Difficult Day** (*illus. Celia Berridge*)	DEUTSCH 1982	**A**
30	**Postman Pat's Foggy Day** (*illus. Celia Berridge*)	DEUTSCH 1982	**A**
31	**Postman Pat's Tractor Express** (*illus. Celia Berridge*)	DEUTSCH 1983	**A**
32	**Postman Pat Takes a Message** (*illus. Celia Berridge*)	DEUTSCH 1983	**A**
33	**Postman Pat's Thirsty Day** (*illus. Celia Berridge*)	DEUTSCH 1984	**A**
34	**Postman Pat Goes Sledging** (*illus. Celia Berridge*)	DEUTSCH 1984	**A**
35	**Baby Books** (*illus. Celia Berridge*) *Two individual titles:* A Day with Postman Pat; Postman Pat and the Summer Show.	DEUTSCH 1985	**A** **Each**
36	**Postman Pat's Letters on Ice** (*illus. Celia Berridge*)	DEUTSCH 1985	**A**
37	**Postman Pat's Breezy Day** (*illus. Celia Berridge*)	DEUTSCH 1985	**A**
38	**Beginners:** (*illus. Joan Hickson*) *Two individual titles*: Postman Pat's ABC Story; Postman Pat's 123 Story.	DEUTSCH 1986	**A** **Each**
39	**Easy Readers:** (*illus. Joan Hickson*) *Four individual titles:* Postman Pat's Wet Day; Postman Pat's Messy Day; Postman Pat Plays for Greendale; Postman Pat on Safari.	DEUTSCH 1986	**A** **Each**
40	**Postman Pat's Summer Storybook** (*illus. Celia Berridge*)	DEUTSCH 1987	**A**
41	**Postman Pat's Parcel of Fun** (*illus. Stuart Trotter*)	DEUTSCH 1987	**A**

42 **Standing on a Strawberry** (*verse*)   DEUTSCH 1987   **A**

43 **Postman Pat's Winter Storybook**   DEUTSCH 1987   **A**
    (*illus. Celia Berridge*)

44 **Easy Readers**
    (*illus. Joan Hickson*)   DEUTSCH 1987   **A**
    Two individual titles: Postman Pat and   **Each**
    the Greendale Ghost; Postman Pat and
    the Christmas Pudding

DAHL, Roald   *Born in South Wales, 1916*

Certainly the most popular living children's writer of all, and one of the most collected, Dahl seems to have made an art form of the rediscovery that children tend to warm to the sorts of horror that make lesser mortals (adults) squirm with displeasure. No matter that his more recent work becomes more and more slender – and increasingly dependent upon the gorgeous illustrations by Quentin Blake – the fans continue to lap it up. *Charlie and the Chocolate Factory* is already a great classic work – along with *Watership Down*, one of the most enduring post-war children's books – and I think we will not see its like again; but no matter – *anything* by Dahl is always received as something of a treat: he is undeniably special.

Below I list only the books intended for children – but I am including his autobiographical works because (as was intended) they can be read with pleasure by child and adult alike, and probably belong in a comprehensive collection.

1	**The Gremlins**	RANDOM HOUSE 1943	N
	(*illus. Walt Disney Studio*)	COLLINS 1944	M
2	**James and the Giant Peach**	KNOPF 1961	E
	(*illus. Nancy Ekholm Burkert*)	ALLEN & UNWIN 1967	C
3	**Charlie and the Chocolate Factory**	KNOPF 1964	H
	(*illus. Joseph Schindelman*)	ALLEN & UNWIN 1967	D
4	**The Magic Finger**	HARPER 1966	D
	(*illus. William Pène du Bois*)	ALLEN & UNWIN 1968	C
5	**Fantastic Mr Fox**	KNOPF 1970	C
	(*illus. Donald Chaffin*)	ALLEN & UNWIN 1970	C
6	**Charlie and the Great Glass Elevator**	KNOPF 1972	C
	(*illus. Joseph Schindelman*)	ALLEN & UNWIN 1973	C
7	**Danny, the Champion of the World**	CAPE 1975	B
	(*illus. Jill Bennett*)	KNOPF 1975	B
8	**The Wonderful Story of Henry Sugar**	CAPE 1977	B
		KNOPF 1977	B
9	**The Enormous Crocodile**	CAPE 1978	B
	(*illus. Quentin Blake*)	KNOPF 1978	B
10	**The Twits**	CAPE 1980	B
	(*illus. Quentin Blake*)	KNOPF 1981	B

11	George's Marvellous Medicine	CAPE 1981	B
	(*illus. Quentin Blake*)	KNOPF 1982	B
12	The BFG	CAPE 1982	B
	(*illus. Quentin Blake*)	FARRAR STRAUS 1982	B
13	Revolting Rhymes	CAPE 1983	B
	(*illus. Quentin Blake*)	KNOPF 1983	B
14	Dirty Beasts	CAPE 1983	B
	(*illus. Rosemary Fawcett*)	FARRAR STRAUS 1983	B
15	The Witches	CAPE 1983	B
	(*illus. Quentin Blake*)	FARRAR STRAUS 1983	B
16	Boy: Tales of Childhood (*memoir*)	CAPE 1984	B
		FARRAR STRAUS 1984	B
17	The Giraffe, the Pelly and Me	CAPE 1985	B
	(*illus. Quentin Blake*)	FARRAR STRAUS 1985	B
18	Going Solo (*memoir*)	CAPE 1986	B
		FARRAR STRAUS 1986	B

---

de BRUNHOFF, Jean   *Born in France, 1899. Died 1937*

Very stylish and desirable books, the design still as fresh and clear today as it was fifty years ago. The books were hand-written and illustrated by de Brunhoff and printed in colour in unusually large format. First editions in a decent state are not easy and nor – as the values below indicate – are they cheap. Difficult to shelve, maybe – but well worth the pursuit.

After Jean de Brunhoff's premature death, his son Laurent added a few more Babar titles to the list, but these are not perceived to be part of the purist's canon.

The following were first published in France by Editions du Jardin des Modes, Condé Nast, Paris.

1	Histoire de Babar, Le Petit Eléphant	1931	L
	The Story of Babar, the Little	SMITH & HAAS (US) 1933	J
	Elephant	METHUEN 1934	I
2	Le Voyage de Babar	1932	J
	The Travels of Babar	SMITH & HAAS (US) 1934	I
	Babar's Travels	METHUEN 1935	H

3	Le Roi Babar	1933	I
	Babar the King	SMITH & HAAS (US) 1935	H
		METHUEN 1936	G
4	ABC de Babar	1934	I
	ABC of Babar	RANDOM HOUSE 1936	H
	Babar's ABC	METHUEN 1937	H
5	Les Vacances de Zéphir	1936	H
	Zephir's Holidays	RANDOM HOUSE 1937	G
	(*Retitled the same year* Babar and Zephir)		
	Babar's Friend Zephir	METHUEN 1937	G
6	Babar en Famille	1938	H
	Babar and His Children	RANDOM HOUSE 1938	F
	Babar at Home	METHUEN 1938	F
7	Babar et le Père Noël	1940	G
	Babar and Father Christmas	RANDOM HOUSE 1940	F
		METHUEN 1940	F

de la MARE, Walter   *Born in Kent, 1873. Died 1956*

In addition to the very considerable list of children's prose and verse that follows, de la Mare also published about eighty books (prose and verse again) for adults. During his time a hugely vaunted author, winner of major literary prizes and various honours (including the Order of Merit), but now seen to be rather unfashionable and even *minor*. He might well be due for revival, but until that time provides ample quarry for the collector. Even if one isn't after de la Mare's entire output (and few are) there are quite a few classics in this listing that are worth hunting down – *Peacock Pie*, say, or *Broomsticks*, or *Stuff and Nonsense*, or *Bells and Grass* . . . well, you see what I mean.

1	**Songs of Childhood** (*verse*)	LONGMAN 1902	I
	(*Pseudonym Walter Ramal*)		
2	**The Three Mulla-Mulgars** (*fiction*)	DUCKWORTH 1910	H
	(*illus. Dorothy P. Lathrop*)	KNOPF 1919	C
3	**A Child's Day: A Book of Rhymes**	CONSTABLE 1912	E
	(*illus. Carine & Will Cadby*)	HOLT 1923	B
4	**Peacock Pie: A Book of Rhymes**	CONSTABLE 1913	G
		HOLT 1917	C

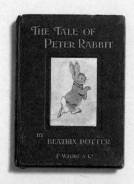
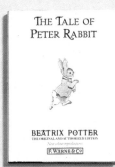

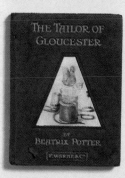

A clutch of first editions by the doyenne of twentieth-century children's literature. The
Peter Rabbit top centre is the first of the newly-originated edition (1987) and beneath it is
one of the rare concertina format books (1906). Illustrated too is the standard first edition
of *The Tailor of Gloucester*, together with the brocade-bound de luxe edition, published
simultaneously (1902).

The complete 'Noddy' saga, the first seven illustrated by the original artist Harmsen van Beek, the remainder uncredited (24 volumes 1949–1964).

HERE COMES NODDY AGAIN BY Enid Blyton

Pictures by Beek

"WELL DONE NODDY!" BY Enid Blyton

Pictures by Beek

NODDY GOES TO SCHOOL BY Enid Blyton

Pictures by Beek

YOU FUNNY LITTLE NODDY BY Enid Blyton

All Aboard for Toyland

NODDY MEETS FATHER CHRISTMAS BY Enid Blyton

All Aboard for Toyland

NODDY AND TESSIE BEAR BY Enid Blyton

All Aboard for Toyland

YOU'RE A GOOD FRIEND, NODDY! BY Enid Blyton

All Aboard for Toyland

NODDY HAS AN ADVENTURE BY Enid Blyton

All Aboard for Toyland

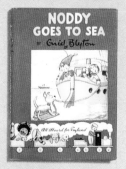

NODDY GOES TO SEA BY Enid Blyton

All Aboard for Toyland

MR. PLOD AND LITTLE NODDY BY Enid Blyton

All Aboard for Toyland

NODDY AND THE TOOTLES BY Enid Blyton

All Aboard for Toyland

NODDY AND THE AEROPLANE BY Enid Blyton

All Aboard for Toyland

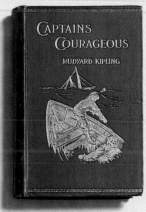

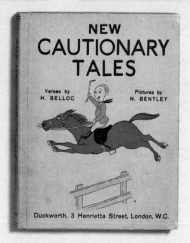

A couple of Kiplings (*Just So* with the author's own glorious artwork and cover design),
three written and illustrated by Hugh Lofting, a little-known Nesbit, and a classic Belloc
with pictures by Nicolas Bentley.

5	**Story and Rhyme: A Selection from the Writings of Walter de la Mare, Chosen by the Author**	DENT 1921 DUTTON 1921	C C
6	**Down-Adown-Derry: A Book of Fairy Poems** (*illus. Dorothy P. Lathrop*)	CONSTABLE 1922 HOLT 1922	D C
7	**Broomsticks and Other Tales** (*illus. Bold*)	CONSTABLE 1925 KNOPF 1925	E C
8	**Miss Jemima** (*fiction*)	BLACKWELL 1925 WRITERS & ARTISTS GUILD US 1935	C B
9	**Old Joe** (*fiction*) (*illus. C.T. Nightingale*)	BLACKWELL 1927	D
10	**Stuff and Nonsense and So on** (*verse*) (*illus. Bold*)	CONSTABLE 1927 HOLT 1927	E D
11	**Told Again: Traditional Tales** (*illus. A.H. Watson*)	BLACKWELL 1927	C
12	**Stories from The Bible** (*illus. Theodore Nadejen*)	FABER 1929 COSMOPOLITAN 1929	C B
13	**Poems for Children**	CONSTABLE 1930 HOLT 1930	C B
14	**The Dutch Cheese and the Lovely Myfanwy** (*fiction*) (*illus. Dorothy P. Lathrop*)	KNOPF 1931	D
15	**The Lord Fish and Other Tales** (*illus. Rex Whistler*)	FABER 1933	D
16	**This Year, Next Year** (*verse*) (*illus. Harold Jones*)	FABER 1937 HOLT 1937	C B
17	**Animal Stories, Chosen, Arranged and in Some Part Rewritten**	FABER 1939 SCRIBNER 1940	C B
18	**Bells and Grass: A Book of Rhymes** (*illus. Rowland Emett*)	FABER 1941 VIKING 1942	D B
19	**The Old Lion and Other Stories** (*illus. Irene Hawkins*)	FABER 1942	C

20	**Mr Bumps and His Monkey** (*illus. Dorothy P. Lathrop*)	WINSTON US 1942	**C**
21	**The Magic Jacket and Other Stories** (*illus. Irene Hawkins*)	FABER 1943	**C**
22	**Collected Rhymes and Verses** (*illus. Berthold Wolpe*)	FABER 1944	**C**
23	**The Scarecrow and Other Stories** (*illus. Irene Hawkins*)	FABER 1945	**C**
24	**The Dutch Cheese and Other Stories** (*illus. Irene Hawkins*)	FABER 1946	**C**
25	**Rhymes and Verses: Collected Poems for Children**	HOLT 1947	**B**
26	**Collected Stories for Children** (*illus. Irene Hawkins*)	FABER 1947	**B**
27	**A Penny a Day** (*fiction*) (*illus. Paul Kennedy*)	KNOPF 1960	**B**

Also of interest:

LEONARD CLARK: **Walter de la Mare** (BODLEY HEAD 1960, WALCK US 1961)
DORIS ROSS McCROSSON: **Walter de la Mare** (TWAYNE US 1966)

DICKINSON, Peter

Pseudonym of Malcolm de Brissac
British. Born in Zambia, 1927

Dickinson's early children's novels were hugely praised at the time, and are hardly less so now. The blend of normality and fantasy is almost always totally successful, and the power of Dickinson's writing is always to the fore; I admit to sometimes finding no great depth of emotion – which is singular, because the, as it were, 'feeling' of Dickinson's novels (particularly, it must be said again, the early ones) is all-encompassing. Recently, he has produced some rather ingenious fun books for younger children – ones in which the *production* of the book plays a large part (*à la* Ahlberg); all jolly nice, but not quite what the committed Dickinson fan is after.

In addition to the following complete listing of his children's books, Dickinson has produced about a dozen thrillers for adults.

1	**The Weathermonger**	GOLLANCZ 1968	**D**
		LITTLE BROWN 1969	**B**

2	**Heartsease**	GOLLANCZ 1969	**C**
	(*illus. Robert Hales*)	LITTLE BROWN 1969	**B**
3	**The Devil's Children**	GOLLANCZ 1970	**C**
	(*illus. Robert Hales*)	LITTLE BROWN 1970	**B**
	1–3 form a trilogy called 'The Changes'.		
4	**Emma Tupper's Diary**	GOLLANCZ 1971	**B**
		LITTLE BROWN 1971	**A**
5	**The Dancing Bear**	GOLLANCZ 1972	**B**
	(*illus. David Smee*)	LITTLE BROWN 1973	**A**
6	**The Iron Lion**	LITTLE BROWN 1972	**B**
	(*illus. Marc Brown*)	ALLEN & UNWIN 1973	**B**
7	**The Gift**	GOLLANCZ 1973	**B**
	(*illus. Gareth Floyd*)	LITTLE BROWN 1974	**A**
8	**Chance, Luck and Destiny** (*miscellany*)	GOLLANCZ 1975	**A**
	(*illus. David Smee & Victor Ambrus*)	LITTLE BROWN 1976	**A**
9	**The Blue Hawk**	GOLLANCZ 1976	**A**
	(*illus. David Smee*)	LITTLE BROWN 1976	**A**
10	**Annerton Pit**	GOLLANCZ 1977	**A**
		LITTLE BROWN 1977	**A**
11	**Hepzibah**	EEL PIE 1978	**A**
	(*illus. Sue Porter*)	GODINE 1980	**A**
12	**Tulku**	GOLLANCZ 1979	**A**
		DUTTON 1979	**A**
13	**City of Gold and Other Stories from**	GOLLANCZ 1980	**A**
	The Old Testament	PANTHEON 1980	**A**
	(*illus. Michael Foreman*)		
14	**The Seventh Raven**	GOLLANCZ 1981	**A**
		DUTTON 1981	**A**
15	**Healer**	GOLLANCZ 1983	**A**
		DUTTON 1983	**A**
16	**Giant Cold** (*illus. Alan Cober*)	GOLLANCZ 1984	**A**
		DUTTON 1984	**A**
17	**A Box of Nothing** (*illus. Ian Newsham*)	GOLLANCZ 1985	**A**
18	**Mole Hole** (*illus. Jean Claverie*)	BLACKIE 1987	**A**

ELIOT, T.S.   *British. Born in Missouri, 1888. Died 1965*

There are over seventy Eliot first editions for the buff to collect – but only one
that would remotely interest children. A classic from the day it was printed
and today – partly because of the irrepressible musical, *Cats* – one of the most
famous twentieth-century books of all. This one is a must – do you hear me? A
must.

1 **Old Possum's Book of Practical Cats**   FABER 1939   **M**
   This first edition bore a d/w by Eliot, but you   HARCOURT BRACE 1939   **K**
   should look out too for the 1940 edition from
   Faber which was illustrated by Nicholas
   Bentley – still the best illustrations to date.
   By far (**I**).

Also of interest:
PETER ACKROYD: **T.S. Eliot** (HAMISH HAMILTON 1984, SIMON & SCHUSTER US
   1984)

ENRIGHT, Elizabeth   *American. Born in Illinois, 1909. Died 1968*

It is rare for an American children's author to become as much liked in
Britain as in her native country, but such is the case with Elizabeth Enright.
It is her understanding of the child's mind, I think, that bestows upon the
books a realistic and enduring air (particularly with the 'Melendy' books)
and these days, of course, the evocation of small-town America during the
1930s is most attractive. Less known than they should be, these books could
well be overdue for re-evaluation.

1 **Kintu: A Congo Adventure**   FARRAR & RINEHART US   **D**
   (illus. author)   1935

2 **Thimble Summer**   FARRAR & RINEHART US   **C**
   (illus. author)   1938
                                    HEINEMANN 1939   **B**

3 **The Sea is All Around**   FARRAR & RINEHART US   **C**
   (illus. author)   1940
                                    HEINEMANN 1959   **A**

4 **The Saturdays**   FARRAR & RINEHART US   **C**
   (illus. author)   1941
                                    HEINEMANN 1955   **A**

5	**The Four-Story Mistake**	FARRAR & RINEHART US	**C**
	(*illus. author*)	1942	
		HEINEMANN 1955	**A**
6	**Then There Were Five**	FARRAR & RINEHART US	**C**
	(*illus. author*)	1944	
		HEINEMANN 1956	**A**
7	**The Melendy Family** (*anthology*)	FARRAR & RINEHART US	**B**
	Contains 4, 5, 6.	1947	
8	**A Christmas Tree for Lydia**	RINEHART US 1951	**B**
	(*illus. author*)		
9	**Spiderweb for Two: A Melendy Maze**	RINEHART US 1951	**B**
	(*illus. author*)	HEINEMANN 1956	**A**
10	**Gone-away Lake**	HARCOURT BRACE 1957	**B**
	(*illus. Beth & Joe Krush*)	HEINEMANN 1957	**B**
11	**Return to Gone-away**	HARCOURT BRACE 1961	**B**
	(*illus. Beth & Joe Krush*)	HEINEMANN 1962	**B**
12	**Tatsinda**	HARCOURT BRACE 1963	**B**
	(*illus. Irene Haas*)		
13	**ZEEE**	HARCOURT BRACE 1965	**A**
	(*illus. Irene Haas*)	HEINEMANN 1966	**A**

ESTES, Eleanor   *American. Born in Connecticut 1906*

Possibly rather dated now, but these books are still popular – particularly the 'Moffat' books, the first of which might prove damnably difficult to track down. There is much here for the confirmed nostalgic – the pleasures *and* the embarrassing pains of childhood are richly garnered.

1	**The Moffats**	HARCOURT BRACE 1941	**E**
	(*illus. Louis Slobodkin*)	BODLEY HEAD 1959	**B**
2	**The Middle Moffat**	HARCOURT BRACE 1942	**D**
	(*illus. Louis Slobodkin*)	BODLEY HEAD 1960	**B**
3	**Rufus M**	HARCOURT BRACE 1943	**C**
	(*illus. Louis Slobodkin*)	BODLEY HEAD 1960	**B**

4	**The Sun and the Wind and Mr Todd** (*illus. Louis Slobodkin*)	HARCOURT BRACE 1943	C
5	**The Hundred Dresses** (*illus. Louis Slobodkin*)	HARCOURT BRACE 1944	C
6	**The Sleeping Giant and Other Stories** (*illus. author*)	HARCOURT BRACE 1948	B
7	**Ginger Pye** (*illus. author*)	HARCOURT BRACE 1951	B
8	**A Little Oven** (*illus. author*)	HARCOURT BRACE 1955	B
9	**Pinky Pye** (*illus. Edward Ardizzone*)	HARCOURT BRACE 1958 CONSTABLE 1959	D C
10	**The Witch Family** (*illus. Edward Ardizzone*)	HARCOURT BRACE 1960 CONSTABLE 1962	D C
11	**The Alley** (*illus. Edward Ardizzone*)	HARCOURT BRACE 1964	C
12	**Miranda the Great** (*illus. Edward Ardizzone*)	HARCOURT BRACE 1967	C
13	**The Lollipop Princess: A Play for Paper Dolls** (*illus. author*)	HARCOURT BRACE 1967	B
14	**The Tunnel of Hugsy Goode** (*illus. Edward Ardizzone*)	HARCOURT BRACE 1971	C
15	**The Coat-hanger Christmas Tree** (*illus. Susanne Suba*)	ATHENEUM 1973 OUP 1976	B B
16	**The Lost Umbrella of Kim Chu** (*illus. Jacqueline Ayer*)	ATHENEUM 1978 OUP 1980	B B

FARJEON, Eleanor   *Born in London, 1881. Died 1965*

In addition to the vast list of works printed here, Eleanor Farjeon also published eight volumes of verse, seven works of non-fiction, and a dozen novels and short story collections for adults. It makes one wonder how the good lady ever had time to draw breath. Increasingly popular with collectors – I think because of both the scope and the quaint datedness of much of the stuff – though I should imagine almost totally neglected by children, these days.

1 **Nursery Rhymes of London Town**   DUCKWORTH 1916   **G**
(*illus. Macdonald Gill*)

2 **More Nursery Rhymes of London**   DUCKWORTH 1917   **G**
Town
(*illus. Macdonald Gill*)

3 **All the Way to Alfriston** (*verse*)   MORLAND PRESS 1918   **G**
(*illus. Robin Guthrie*)

4 **Singing Games for Children** (*verse*)   DENT 1919   **F**
(*illus. J. Littlejohns*)   DUTTON 1919   **D**

5 **A First Chapbook of Rounds** (*verse*)   DENT 1919   **D**
(*illus. John Garside*)   DUTTON 1919   **C**

6 **A Second Chapbook of Rounds** (*verse*)   DENT 1919   **D**
(*illus. John Garside*)   DUTTON 1919   **C**

7 **Martin Pippin in the Apple-orchard**   COLLINS 1921   **D**
(*novel*) (*illus. C.E. Brock*)   STOKES 1922   **B**

8 **Tunes of a Penny Piper** (*verse*)   SELWYN & BLOUNT 1922   **C**
(*illus. John Aveten*)

9 **Songs for Music and Lyrical Poems**   SELWYN & BLOUNT 1922   **C**
(*illus. John Aveten*)

10 **All the Year Round** (*verse*)   COLLINS 1923   **C**

11 **The Country Child's Alphabet** (*verse*)   POETRY BOOKSHOP 1924   **D**
(*illus. William Michael Rothenstein*)

12 **The Town Child's Alphabet** (*verse*)   POETRY BOOKSHOP 1924   **I**
(*illus. David Jones*)

13 **Mighty Men: Achilles to Julius**   BLACKWELL 1924   **C**
Caesar (*non-fiction*)   APPLETON 1924   **B**
(*illus. Hugh Chesterman*)

14	**Mighty Men: Beowulf to Harold** *(non-fiction)* *(illus. Hugh Chesterman)*	BLACKWELL 1925 APPLETON 1925	C B
15	**Songs from 'Punch' for Children** *(verse)*	SAVILLE 1925	C
16	**Young Folk and Old** *(verse)*	HIGH HOUSE PRESS 1925	C
17	**Tom Cobble** *(novel)* *(illus. M. Dobson)*	BLACKWELL 1925	D
18	**Nuts and May: A Medley for Children** *(illus. Rosalind Thorneycroft)*	COLLINS 1926	C
19	**Italian Peepshow and Other Tales** *(illus. Rosalind Thorneycroft)* *The Blackwell edition reads* Stories *instead of* Tales.	STOKES US 1926 BLACKWELL 1934	C B
20	**Joan's Door** *(verse)* *(illus. Will Townsend)*	COLLINS 1926 STOKES 1927	C B
21	**Singing Games from Arcady** *(verse)*	BLACKWELL 1926	C
22	**The Wonderful Knight** *(fiction)* *(illus. Doris Pailthorpe)*	OUP 1927	D
23	**The King's Barn; or, Joan's Tale** *(fiction)*	COLLINS 1927	C
24	**The Mill of Dreams; or, Jennifer's Tale** *(fiction)*	COLLINS 1927	C
25	**Young Gerard; or, Joyce's Tale** *(fiction)*	COLLINS 1927	C
26	**Come, Christmas** *(verse)* *(illus. Molly McArthur)*	COLLINS 1927 STOKES 1928	C B
27	**A Bad Day for Martha** *(fiction)* *(illus. Eugenie Richards)*	BLACKWELL 1928	C
28	**Kaleidoscope** *(fiction)*	COLLINS 1928 STOKES 1929	C B
29	**An Alphabet of Magic** *(verse)* *(illus. Margaret Tarrant)*	MEDICI SOCIETY 1928	C

30	**The Perfect Zoo** (*fiction*)	HARRAP 1929	C
		McKAY 1929	B
31	**The King's Daughter Cries for the**	BLACKWELL 1929	C
	Moon (*fiction*)		
	(*illus. May Smith*)		
32	**The Tale of Tom Tiddler** (*fiction*)	COLLINS 1929	C
	(*illus. Norman Tealby*)	STOKES 1930	B
33	**Westwoods** (*fiction*)	BLACKWELL 1930	C
	(*illus. May Smith*)	ARTISTS & WRITERS 1935	B
34	**Tales from Chaucer: The Canterbury**	MEDICI SOCIETY 1930	H
	Tales Done into Prose	CAPE & SMITH 1930	G
	(*illus. W. Russell Flint*)		
35	**The Old Nurse's Stocking Basket**	UNIVERSITY OF LONDON	C
	(*fiction*) (*illus. E. Herbert Whydale*)	1931	
		STOKES 1931	B
36	**Poems for Children**	LIPPINCOTT US 1931	B
37	**Perkin the Pedlar** (*fiction*)	FABER 1932	C
	(*illus. Clare Leighton*)		
38	**Katy Kruse at the Seaside; or, The**	HARRAP 1932	C
	Deserted Islanders (*fiction*)	McKAY 1932	B
39	**Kings and Queens** (*verse*)	GOLLANCZ 1932	B
	(*with Herbert Farjeon*)	DUTTON 1932	B
	(*illus. Rosalind Thorneycroft*)		
40	**Ameliaranne's Prize Packet** (*fiction*)	HARRAP 1933	D
	(*illus. S.B. Pearse*)		
41	**Ameliaranne and the Magic Ring**	McKAY 1933	C
	Same as 40.		
42	**Pannychis** (*fiction*)	HIGH HOUSE PRESS 1933	C
	(*illus. Clare Leighton*)		
43	**Heroes and Heroines** (*verse*)	GOLLANCZ 1933	B
	(*with Herbert Farjeon*)	DUTTON 1933	B
	(*illus. Rosalind Thorneycroft*)		
44	**Over the Garden Wall** (*verse*)	FABER 1933	E
	(*illus. Gwendolen Raverat*)	STOKES 1933	C

45	**Ameliaranne's Washing Day** (*fiction*)	HARRAP 1934	**D**
	(*illus. S.B. Pearse*)	McKAY 1934	**C**
46	**Jim at the Corner and Other Stories**	BLACKWELL 1934	**B**
	(*illus. Irene Mountfort*)		
47	**The Old Sailor's Yarn Box**	STOKES 1934	**B**
	Same as 46.		
48	**The Clumber Pup** (*fiction*)	BLACKWELL 1934	**B**
	(*illus. Irene Mountfort*)		
49	**And I Dance Mine Own Child** (*fiction*)	BLACKWELL 1935	**B**
	(*illus. Irene Mountfort*)		
50	**Jim and the Pirates** (*fiction*)	BLACKWELL 1936	**B**
	(*illus. Roger Naish*)		
51	**Ten Saints** (*non-fiction*)	OUP 1936	**B**
	(*illus. Helen Sewell*)		
52	**Lector Readings** (*reader*)	NELSON 1936	**B**
	(*illus. Ruth Westcott*)		
53	**Martin Pippin in the Daisy-field**	JOSEPH 1937	**B**
	(*fiction*) (*illus. Isobel & John Morton-Sale*)	STOKES 1938	**B**
54	**The Wonders of Herodotus** (*non-fiction*)	NELSON 1937	**B**
	(*illus. Edmund Nelson*)		
55	**Paladins in Spain** (*non-fiction*)	NELSON 1937	**B**
	(*illus. Katharine Tozer*)		
56	**Sing for Your Supper** (*verse*)	JOSEPH 1938	**B**
	(*illus. Isobel & John Morton-Sale*)	STOKES 1938	**B**
57	**Songs of Kings and Queens** (*verse*)	ARNOLD 1938	**B**
	(*with Herbert Farjeon*)		
58	**One Foot in Fairyland: Sixteen Tales**	JOSEPH 1938	**B**
	(*illus. Robert Lawson*)	STOKES 1938	**B**
59	**Grannie Gray: Children's Plays and Games with Music and without**	DENT 1939	**B**
	(*illus. Joan Jefferson Farjeon*)		
60	**A Sussex Alphabet** (*verse*)	PEAR TREE PRESS 1939	**C**
	(*illus. Sheila M. Thompson*)		

61	**The New Book of Days** (*non-fiction*) (*illus. Philip Gough & Meredith W. Hawes*)	OUP 1941	B
62	**Cherrystones** (*verse*) (*illus. Isobel & John Morton-Sale*)	JOSEPH 1942 LIPPINCOTT 1944	B B
63	**A Prayer for Little Things** (*verse*) (*illus. Elizabeth Orton Jones*)	MIFFLIN US 1945	B
64	**The Mulberry Bush** (*verse*) (*illus. Isobel & John Morton-Sale*)	JOSEPH 1945	B
65	**The Glass Slipper** (*play*) (*with Herbert Farjeon*) (*illus. Hugh Stevenson*)	WINGATE 1946	B
66	**The Starry Floor** (*verse*) (*illus. Isobel & John Morton-Sale*)	JOSEPH 1949	B
67	**Mrs Malone** (*verse*) (*illus. David Knight*)	JOSEPH 1950 WALCK US 1962	B A
68	**Silver Sand and Snow** (*verse*)	JOSEPH 1951	B
69	**The Silver Curlew: A Fairy Tale** (*play*)	FRENCH 1953	A
70	**The Silver Curlew** (*fiction*) (*illus. Ernest H. Shepard*)	OUP 1953 VIKING PRESS 1954	D C
71	**The Little Book-room** (*fiction*) (*illus. Edward Ardizzone*)	OUP 1955	D
72	**The Glass Slipper** (*fiction*) (*illus. Ernest H. Shepard*)	OUP 1955	D
73	**The Children's Bells: A Selection of Poems** (*illus. Peggy Fortnum*)	OUP 1957 WALCK 1960	C B
74	**Eleanor Farjeon's Book: Stories, Verses, Plays** (*illus. Edward Ardizzone*)	PENGUIN 1960	C
75	**My Garden** (*fiction*) (*illus. Jane Paton*)	HAMISH HAMILTON 1966 WALCK 1966	A A
76	**Morning Has Broken** (*verse*) (*illus. Gordon Stowell*)	MOWBRAY 1981	A

77 Invitation to a Mouse and Other   PELHAM 1981   **B**
     Poems
     (*ed. Annabel Farjeon*)
     (*illus. Antony Maitland*)

Also of interest:
THE ELEANOR FARJEON BOOK: **A Tribute to her Life and Work
1881–1965** (HAMISH HAMILTON 1966)
DENYS BLAKELOCK: **Eleanor: Portrait of a Farjeon** (GOLLANCZ 1966)

FLEMING, Ian   *Born in London, 1908. Died 1964*

Known primarily for having written about a certain secret agent, Fleming's
name is not one which springs readily to the mind when discussing *children's*
books, but the trilogy that he wrote (inspired by his passion for vintage motor
cars) has had a lasting impact, and has never been out of print. First editions
are very elusive because Fleming is one of the half-dozen most collected
authors in the field of modern first editions, and although these collector chaps
are mainly concerned with the intrepid 007, they are also completists – so you
have stiff and determined competition. All the following are illustrated by
John Burningham.

1 **Chitty-Chitty-Bang-Bang:**   CAPE 1964   **E**
   The Magical Car
   Adventure Number 1

2 **Chitty-Chitty-Bang-Bang:**   CAPE 1964   **E**
   The Magical Car
   Adventure Number 2

3 **Chitty-Chitty-Bang-Bang:**   CAPE 1965   **E**
   The Magical Car
   Adventure Number 3
   The three Adventures were published in one
   volume in America by Random House in 1964
   – this therefore preceding publication of the last
   *of the Cape editions (**E**).*

Also of interest:
JOHN PEARSON: **The Life of Ian Fleming** (CAPE 1966, McGRAW HILL US 1966)

FOREMAN, Michael   *Born in Suffolk, 1938*

Much admired and collected illustrator of dozens and dozens of books by other people, Foreman has also written quite a number himself. The illustrations, needless to say, are superb, and the stories themselves rather clever – in that their simplicity is immediately appealing, and yet there is often a satirical edge to be appreciated too. Already quite difficult to gather.

1	**The Perfect Present**	HAMISH HAMILTON 1967	**F**
		COWARD McCANN 1967	**D**
2	**The Two Giants**	BROCKHAMPTON PRESS 1967	**E**
		PANTHEON 1967	**D**
3	**The Great Sleigh Robbery**	HAMISH HAMILTON 1968	**D**
		PANTHEON 1969	**C**
4	**Horatio**	HAMISH HAMILTON 1970	**C**
5	**The Travels of Horatio**	PANTHEON 1970	**C**
	Same as 4.		
6	**Moose**	HAMISH HAMILTON 1971	**C**
		PANTHEON 1972	**B**
7	**Dinosaurs and All That Rubbish**	HAMISH HAMILTON 1972	**C**
		CROWELL 1973	**B**
8	**War and Peas**	HAMISH HAMILTON 1974	**C**
		CROWELL 1974	**B**
9	**All the King's Horses**	HAMISH HAMILTON 1976	**C**
		BRADBURY PRESS 1977	**B**
10	**Panda's Puzzle, and His Voyage of Discovery**	HAMISH HAMILTON 1977	**C**
		BRADBURY PRESS 1978	**B**
11	**Winter's Tales**	BENN 1979	**B**
	(illus. Freire White)		
12	**Trick a Tracker**	GOLLANCZ 1981	**B**
		PHILOMEL 1981	**B**
13	**Panda and the Odd Lion**	HAMISH HAMILTON 1981	**B**
14	**Land of Dreams**	ANDERSEN PRESS 1982	**B**
		HOLT RINEHART 1982	**A**

15	**Cat and Canary**	ANDERSEN PRESS 1984	A
		DIAL BOOKS 1985	A
16	**Panda and the Bunyips**	HAMISH HAMILTON 1984	B
		SCHOCKEN 1988	A
17	**Panda and the Bushfire**	HAMISH HAMILTON 1986	B
		PRENTICE HALL 1986	A
18	**Ben's Box**	METHUEN 1986	B
19	**Ben's Baby**	ANDERSEN PRESS 1987	A

FOREST, Antonia   *Born in London*

Author of school stories with a difference – the school is an upper-middle-class girls' boarding school, and many of the stories take place away from it, during the hols. The dialogue is particularly good – witty and authentic – and the reworking of traditional school-story plots can be ingenious. There is the unmistakable air of lasting quality about Antonia Forest's books, and collectors are slowly waking up to her collectability.

1	**Autumn Term** (*illus. Marjorie Owens*)	FABER 1948	D
2	**The Marlows and the Traitor** (*illus. Doritie Kettlewell*)	FABER 1953	C
3	**Falconer's Lure: The Story of a Summer Holiday** (*illus. Tasha Kallin*)	FABER 1957	B
4	**End of Term**	FABER 1959	B
5	**Peter's Room**	FABER 1961	B
6	**The Thursday Kidnapping**	FABER 1963	B
		COWARD McCANN 1965	A
7	**The Thuggery Affair**	FABER 1965	B
8	**The Ready-made Family**	FABER 1967	B
9	**The Player's Boy**	FABER 1979	B
10	**The Players and the Rebels**	FABER 1971	B
11	**The Cricket Term**	FABER 1974	B

| 12 | **The Attic Term** | FABER 1976 | B |
| 13 | **Run Away Home** | FABER 1982 | B |

FULLER, Roy   *Born in Lancashire, 1912*

Primarily a poet (although Fuller is the author of eight adult novels as well) his work does not attract much attention from collectors either of modern first editions or of children's books, but the fiction listed below is worthy – if at times just a shade pedantic – and carries the advantage of being not at all expensive. It remains to be seen whether Fuller will ever be seriously collected, but at the moment it rather looks not.

1	**Savage Gold** (*fiction*) (*illus. Robert Medley*)	LEHMANN 1946	B
2	**With My Little Eye** (*fiction*) (*illus. Alan Lindsay*)	LEHMANN 1948 MACMILLAN US 1957	B A
3	**Catspaw** (*fiction*) (*illus. David Gollins*)	ROSS 1966	B
4	**Seen Grandpa Lately?** (*verse*) (*illus. Joan Hickson*)	DEUTSCH 1972	A
5	**Poor Roy** (*verse*) (*illus. Nicolas Bentley*)	DEUTSCH 1977	B
6	**The Other Planet and Three Other Fables**	KEEPSAKE PRESS 1979	A
7	**More About Tompkins and Other Light Verse**	TRAGARA PRESS 1981	A

GARDAM, Jane   *Born in Yorkshire, 1928*

A small output, but a mighty reputation. Jane Gardam came to writing in
her forties, and was almost immediately perceived to be a superior thing
altogether. Her books (her earliest books, anyway) concern the business of
adolescence, but the vibrance, authenticity and sheer good writing render
them apart from the common run. If there has been any criticism of Gardam
at all, it has taken the form of carping about the middle class privilege
displayed in the books, or the elitism of the (usually literary) references: as
with all such carping, this will be seen to be nonsense.

Gardam is highly collectable, and one of the lasting names. In addition to
the following, she has published various novels and short stories for adults.

1	**A Few Fair Days**	HAMISH HAMILTON 1971	**E**
	(*illus. Peggy Fortnum*)	MACMILLAN US 1972	**D**
2	**A Long Way From Verona**	HAMISH HAMILTON 1971	**E**
		MACMILLAN US 1971	**D**
3	**The Summer After the Funeral**	HAMISH HAMILTON 1973	**D**
		MACMILLAN US 1973	**C**
4	**Bilgewater**	HAMISH HAMILTON 1976	**C**
		GREENWILLOW 1977	**B**
5	**The Hollow Land**	MACRAE 1981	**B**
	(*illus. Janet Rawlins*)	GREENWILLOW 1982	**A**
6	**Bridget and William**	MACRAE 1981	**B**
	(*illus. Janet Rawlins*)		
7	**Horse**	MACRAE 1982	**B**
	(*illus. Janet Rawlins*)		
8	**Kit**	MACRAE 1983	**B**
	(*illus. William Geldart*)		
9	**Kit in Boots**	MACRAE 1986	**A**
	(*illus. William Geldart*)		
10	**Through the Doll's House Door**	MACRAE 1987	**A**

GARFIELD, Leon   *Born in Brighton, 1921*

One of the most admired, collected – and prolific – of all. I put Garfield in the
last edition of my *Modern First Editions* because it is a brave soul who will

declare the novels and stories either for adults or for children; there are certainly elements of each, and this serves to make the books accessible to all – I should imagine that this skill alone will render Garfield's name indelible. Gather him while (if) you can.

1	**Jack Holborn**	CONSTABLE 1964	**F**
	(*illus. Antony Maitland*)	PANTHEON 1965	**C**
2	**Devil-in-the-Fog**	CONSTABLE 1966	**E**
	(*illus. Antony Maitland*)	PANTHEON 1966	**C**
3	**Smith**	CONSTABLE 1967	**D**
	(*illus. Antony Maitland*)	PANTHEON 1967	**C**
4	**Black Jack**	LONGMAN 1968	**C**
	(*illus. Antony Maitland*)	PANTHEON 1969	**B**
5	**Mister Corbett's Ghost**	PANTHEON 1968	**C**
	(*illus. Alan E. Cober*)		
6	**Mister Corbett's Ghost and Other Stories** (*illus. Antony Maitland*)	LONGMAN 1969	**C**
7	**The Drummer Boy**	PANTHEON 1969	**C**
	(*illus. Antony Maitland*)	LONGMAN 1970	**C**
8	**The Restless Ghost: Three Stories**	PANTHEON 1969	**C**
	(*illus. Saul Lambert*)		
9	**The Boy and the Monkey**	HEINEMANN 1969	**C**
	(*illus. Trevor Ridley*)	WATTS 1970	**B**
10	**The Strange Affair of Adelaide Harris**	LONGMAN 1971	**C**
	(*illus. Fritz Wegner*)	PANTHEON 1971	**B**
11	**The Captain's Watch**	- HEINEMANN 1972	**C**
	(*illus. Trevor Ridley*)		
12	**The Ghost Downstairs**	LONGMAN 1972	**C**
	(*illus. Antony Maitland*)	PANTHEON 1972	**B**
13	**Lucifer Wilkins**	HEINEMANN 1973	**C**
	(*illus. Trevor Ridley*)		
14	**The Sound of Coaches**	KESTREL 1974	**C**
	(*illus. John Lawrence*)	VIKING PRESS 1974	**C**

15	**The Prisoners of September**	KESTREL 1975	**C**
		VIKING PRESS 1975	**C**
16	**The Pleasure Garden**	KESTREL 1976	**C**
	(*illus. Fritz Wegner*)	VIKING PRESS 1976	**C**

The following twelve books comprise the series 'The Apprentices', *published later in one volume by Viking Press (US in 1978 and by Heinemann in 1982)*:

17	**The Lamplighter's Funeral**	HEINEMANN 1976	**B**
	(*illus. Antony Maitland*)		
18	**Mirror, Mirror**	HEINEMANN 1976	**B**
	(*illus. Antony Maitland*)		
19	**Moss and Blister**	HEINEMANN 1976	**B**
	(*illus. Faith Jaques*)		
20	**The Cloak**	HEINEMANN 1976	**B**
	(*illus. Faith Jaques*)		
21	**The Valentine**	HEINEMANN 1977	**B**
	(*illus. Faith Jaques*)		
22	**Labour in Vain**	HEINEMANN 1977	**B**
	(*illus. Faith Jaques*)		
23	**The Fool**	HEINEMANN 1977	**B**
	(*illus. Faith Jaques*)		
24	**Rosy Starling**	HEINEMANN 1977	**B**
	(*illus. Faith Jaques*)		
25	**The Dumb Cake**	HEINEMANN 1977	**B**
	(*illus. Faith Jaques*)		
26	**Tom Titmarsh's Devil**	HEINEMANN 1977	**B**
	(*illus. Faith Jaques*)		
27	**The Filthy Beast**	HEINEMANN 1978	**B**
	(*illus. Faith Jaques*)		
28	**The Enemy**	HEINEMANN 1978	**B**
	(*illus. Faith Jaques*)		

This concludes 'The Apprentices' *series.*

29	**An Adelaide Ghost**	WARD LOCK 1977	**C**

30	**The Confidence Man**	KESTREL 1978	**B**
		VIKING PRESS 1979	**B**
31	**Bostock and Harris; or, The Night of the Comet** (*illus. Martin Cottam*)	KESTREL 1979	**B**
32	**The Night of the Comet** *Same as 31.*	DELACORTE 1979	**B**
33	**John Diamond** (*illus. Antony Maitland*)	KESTREL 1980	**B**
34	**Footsteps** *Same as 33.*	DELACORTE 1980	**B**
35	**Fair's Fair** (*illus. Margaret Chamberlain*)	MACDONALD 1981	**B**
36	**King Nimrod's Tower** (*illus. Michael Bragg*)	METHUEN 1982	**B**
		LOTHROP 1982	**B**
37	**Writing on the Wall** (*illus. Michael Bragg*)	METHUEN 1983	**B**
		LOTHROP 1983	**B**
38	**King in the Garden** (*illus. Michael Bragg*)	METHUEN 1984	**B**
		LOTHROP 1984	**B**
39	**Guilt and Gingerbread** (*illus. Fritz Wegner*)	VIKING KESTREL 1984	**B**
40	**The Wedding Ghost** (*illus. Charles Keeping*)	OUP 1985	**B**
41	**Shakespeare Stories** (*illus. Michael Foreman*)	GOLLANCZ 1985	**B**
42	**The December Rose**	VIKING KESTREL 1986	**B**

In addition to this complete fictional oeuvre, *Garfield has published the following non-fiction for children:*

43	**The God Beneath the Sea** (*with Edward Blishen*) (*illus. Charles Keeping*)	LONGMAN 1970	**C**
		PANTHEON 1971	**B**
44	**Child o'War: The True Story of a Boy Sailor in Nelson's Navy** (*with David Proctor*) (*illus. Antony Maitland*)	COLLINS 1972	**C**
		HOLT RINEHART 1972	**B**

| 45 | **The Golden Shadow** (*with Edward Blishen*) (*illus. Charles Keeping*) | LONGMAN 1973 PANTHEON 1973 | **C** **B** |
| 46 | **The House of Hanover: England in the Eighteenth Century** | DEUTSCH 1976 SEABURY PRESS 1976 | **B** **B** |

GARNER, Alan   *Born in Cheshire, 1934*

Very much a writer's writer – although that is not to imply that Garner cannot be appreciated without an understanding of his craft, though such an understanding adds immeasurably to one's enjoyment. Novels such as *Red Shift* really turn all the conventions of juvenile writing on their heads – the fractured dialogue and almost ferocious energy ought really to add up to an unreadable disaster, but the power and sheer skill in its handling make it something very special indeed. He is very collected – and probably the most *discussed* contemporary children's writer ever: certainly a laster.

1	**The Weirdstone of Brisingamen: A Tale of Alderley** *A revised edition was published by Penguin in 1963, and in America by Walck in 1969.*	COLLINS 1960	**H**
2	**The Weirdstone** *Same as 1.*	WATTS 1961	**F**
3	**The Moon of Gomrath**	COLLINS 1963 WALCK 1967	**G** **C**
4	**Elidor** (*illus. Charles Keeping*)	COLLINS 1965 WALCK 1967	**F** **C**
5	**Holly from the Bongs: A Nativity Play** (*music by William Mayne*)	COLLINS 1966	**D**
6	**The Old Man of Mow**	COLLINS 1967 DOUBLEDAY 1970	**E** **C**
7	**The Owl Service**	COLLINS 1967 WALCK 1968	**E** **C**
8	**Red Shift**	COLLINS 1973 MACMILLAN US 1973	**E** **C**

9	**Potter Thompson** (*play*) (*music by Gordon Crosse*)	OUP 1975	**C**
10	**The Guizer: A Book of Fools**	HAMISH HAMILTON 1975 GREENWILLOW 1976	**C** **B**
11	**The Breadhorse** (*illus. Albin Trowski*)	COLLINS 1975	**C**
12	**The Stone Book** (*illus. Michael Foreman*)	COLLINS 1976	**C**
13	**Tom Fobble's Day** (*illus. Michael Foreman*)	COLLINS 1977	**B**
14	**Granny Reardun** (*illus. Michael Foreman*)	COLLINS 1977	**B**
15	**The Aimer Gate** (*illus. Michael Foreman*) *12–15 form* 'The Stone Book Quartet'.	COLLINS 1978	**B**
16	**Fairy Tales of Gold** (*illus. Michael Foreman*) *Four volumes comprising*: The Girl of the Golden Gate; The Golden Brothers; The Princess and the Golden Mane; The Three Golden Heads of the Well.	COLLINS 1979	**B** **Each**
17	**The Lad of the Gad** (*folktales*)	COLLINS 1980 PHILOMEL 1981	**B** **B**

Also of interest:

NEIL PHILIP: **A Fine Anger: A Critical Introduction to the Work of Alan Garner** (COLLINS 1981, PHILOMEL US 1981)

GARNETT, Eve   *Born in Worcestershire*

Author of a handful of very vigorous stories about the Ruggles family – working class, and combating the Depression. Gentle books, refreshing, and still very readable today – but a first edition of No 1 might be the very devil to locate.

All the books are illustrated by the author.

1	**The Family from One End Street and** **Some of Their Adventures**	MULLER 1937 VANGUARD PRESS 1939	**G** **D**

2	**In and Out and Roundabout: Stories of a Little Town**	MULLER 1948	**D**
3	**Further Adventures of the Family from One End Street**	HEINEMANN 1956 VANGUARD PRESS 1956	**E** **C**
4	**Holiday at the Dew Drop Inn: A One End Street Story**	HEINEMANN 1962 VANGUARD PRESS 1963	**C** **B**
5	**Lost and Found: Four Stories**	MULLER 1974	**B**
6	**First Affections** (*autobiography*)	MULLER 1982	**B**

GODDEN, Rumer   *Born in Sussex, 1907*

Rumer Godden seems set to be remembered for the well-made traditional children's story – as well as being the first writer to have tumbled to the fact that little girls who invent names, idiosyncrasies and dramas for their dolls would simply *adore* to read an author who did the same. It is probably Godden's 'Doll' books that will survive, but I list here all her work for children – in addition to which she has published about thirty books of fiction and non-fiction for adults.

1	**The Doll's House** (*illus. Dana Saintsbury*)	JOSEPH 1947 VIKING PRESS 1948	**C** **B**
2	**In Noah's Ark** (*verse*)	JOSEPH 1949 VIKING PRESS 1949	**B** **A**
3	**The Mousewife** (*illus. Dana Saintsbury*)	MACMILLAN 1951 VIKING PRESS 1951	**C** **B**
4	**Impunity Jane: The Story of a Pocket Doll** (*illus. Adrienne Adams*)	VIKING PRESS 1954 MACMILLAN 1955	**C** **C**
5	**The Fairy Doll** (*illus. Adrienne Adams*)	MACMILLAN 1956 VIKING PRESS 1956	**C** **B**
6	**Mouse House** (*illus. Adrienne Adams*)	VIKING PRESS 1957 MACMILLAN 1958	**C** **C**
7	**The Story of Holly and Ivy** (*illus. Adrienne Adams*)	MACMILLAN 1958 VIKING PRESS 1958	**B** **A**
8	**Candy Floss** (*illus. Adrienne Adams*)	MACMILLAN 1960 VIKING PRESS 1960	**B** **A**

9	**St Jerome and the Lion** (*verse*)	MACMILLAN 1961	**A**
	(*illus. Jean Primrose*)	VIKING PRESS 1961	**A**
10	**Miss Happiness and Miss Flower**	MACMILLAN 1961	**B**
	(*illus. Jean Primrose*)	VIKING PRESS 1961	**A**
11	**Little Plum**	MACMILLAN 1963	**B**
	(*illus. Jean Primrose*)	VIKING PRESS 1963	**A**
12	**Home is the Sailor**	MACMILLAN 1964	**B**
	(*illus. Jean Primrose*)	VIKING PRESS 1964	**A**
13	**The Kitchen Madonna**	MACMILLAN 1967	**B**
	(*illus. Carol Barker*)	VIKING PRESS 1967	**A**
14	**Operation Sippacik**	MACMILLAN 1969	**A**
	(*illus. James Bryan*)	VIKING PRESS 1969	**A**
15	**The Old Woman Who Lived in a Vinegar Bottle**	MACMILLAN 1972	**A**
		VIKING PRESS 1972	**A**
	(*illus. Mairi Hedderwick*)		
16	**The Diddakoi**	MACMILLAN 1972	**A**
	(*illus. Creina Glegg*)	VIKING PRESS 1972	**A**
17	**Mr McFadden's Hallowe'en**	MACMILLAN 1975	**A**
	(*illus. Ann Strugnell*)	VIKING PRESS 1975	**A**
18	**The Rocking Horse Secret**	MACMILLAN 1977	**A**
	(*illus. Juliet Stanwell Smith*)	VIKING PRESS 1978	**A**
19	**A Kindle of Kittens**	MACMILLAN 1978	**A**
	(*illus. Lynne Byrnes*)	VIKING PRESS 1979	**A**
20	**The Dragon of Og**	MACMILLAN 1981	**A**
	(*illus. Pauline Baynes*)	VIKING PRESS 1981	**A**
21	**The Valiant Chatti-maker**	MACMILLAN 1983	**A**
	(*illus. Jeroo Roy*)	VIKING PRESS 1983	**A**

Also of interest:

HASSELL A. SIMPSON: **Rumer Godden** (TWAYNE US 1973)

GOSCINNY AND UDERZO

Goscinny, René   *Born in Paris, 1926. Died 1977*
Uderzo, Albert   *Born in Paris, 1927*

The magnificent comic adventures of Asterix the Gaul and his dumbo side-kick Obelix will continue to lift the heart and gladden the eye for ever and ever and ever; I must calm down – a sedative from Getafix is the only answer. By the way – Goscinny wrote the text, Uderzo did the pictures.

1	**Asterix the Gaul**	BROCKHAMPTON PRESS 1969	C
		MORROW 1970	B
2	**Asterix and Cleopatra**	BROCKHAMPTON PRESS 1969	B
		MORROW 1970	B
3	**Asterix the Gladiator**	BROCKHAMPTON PRESS 1969	B
		BERKE 1979	A
4	**Asterix in Britain**	BROCKHAMPTON PRESS 1970	B
		BERKE 1979	A
5	**Asterix the Legionary**	BROCKHAMPTON PRESS 1970	B
		MORROW 1970	B
6	**Asterix in Spain**	BROCKHAMPTON PRESS 1971	B
		BERKE 1979	A
7	**Asterix and the Big Fight**	BROCKHAMPTON PRESS 1971	B
		BERKE 1979	A
8	**Asterix and the Roman Agent**	BROCKHAMPTON PRESS 1972	B
		BERKE 1979	A
9	**Asterix at the Olympic Games**	BROCKHAMPTON PRESS 1972	B
		BERKE 1979	A
10	**Asterix in Switzerland**	BROCKHAMPTON PRESS 1973	B
		BERKE 1979	A

11	**The Mansions of the Gods**	BROCKHAMPTON PRESS 1973	B
		BERKE 1979	A
12	**Asterix and the Laurel Wreath**	BROCKHAMPTON PRESS 1974	B
		BERKE 1979	A
13	**Asterix and the Goths**	BROCKHAMPTON PRESS 1974	B
		BERKE 1979	A
14	**Asterix and the Soothsayer**	BROCKHAMPTON PRESS 1975	B
		BERKE 1979	A
15	**Asterix and the Golden Sickle**	HODDER & STOUGHTON 1975	B
		BERKE 1979	A
16	**Asterix and the Great Crossing**	HODDER & STOUGHTON 1976	B
		BERKE 1979	A
17	**Asterix and the Cauldron**	HODDER & STOUGHTON 1976	B
		BERKE 1979	A
18	**Asterix and the Chieftain's Shield**	HODDER & STOUGHTON 1977	B
		BERKE 1979	A
19	**Asterix and Caesar's Gift**	HODDER & STOUGHTON 1977	B
		BERKE 1979	A
20	**Asterix and the Normans**	HODDER & STOUGHTON 1978	B
		BERKE 1979	A
21	**The Twelve Tasks of Asterix**	HODDER & STOUGHTON 1978	B
		BERKE 1978	B

The Hodder editions were paperback. There followed twelve little books, as follows,
which differed somewhat from the large ordinary edition:
The Race; The Javelin; The Judo Match; The Isle of Pleasure; The
Magician; The Chef; The Cave of the Beast; The Place That Sends You
Mad; The Crocodiles; The Old Man of the Mountains; The Legionnaires;
The Circus (**A**) each.

22	**Obelix and Co**	HODDER & STOUGHTON 1979	**B**
		BERKE 1979	**B**
23	**Asterix and the Banquet**	HODDER & STOUGHTON 1979	**B**
		BERKE 1979	**B**
24	**Asterix in Corsica**	HODDER & STOUGHTON 1979	**B**
		BERKE 1979	**B**
25	**Asterix in Belgium**	HODDER & STOUGHTON 1980	**B**
		DARGAUD (CANADA) 1980	**B**
26	**Asterix and the Great Divide**	HODDER & STOUGHTON 1981	**B**
27	**Asterix and the Black Gold**	HODDER & STOUGHTON 1982	**B**
28	**Asterix and Son**	HODDER & STOUGHTON 1983	**B**
29	**Asterix Versus Caesar**	HODDER & STOUGHTON 1986	**B**
30	**Asterix and the Magic Carpet**	HODDER & STOUGHTON 1988	**B**

GOUDGE, Elizabeth   *Born in Somerset, 1900*

Rather old-fashioned books – but in the realms of children's fiction, this is
rarely a severe criticism. Some might find the stuff a little sentimental, but
nonetheless the bulk of it will last – *The Little White Horse* will, anyway.

I was surprised to discover that in addition to the children's books listed
below, Elizabeth Goudge has published over thirty books for adults – mainly
novels.

1	**The Fairies' Baby and Other Stories**	MORLAND-FOYLE 1920	**G**
2	**Sister of the Angels: A Christmas Story** (*illus. C. Walter Hodges*)	DUCKWORTH 1939 COWARD McCANN 1939	**E** **C**
3	**Smoky-House** (*illus. C. Walter Hodges*)	DUCKWORTH 1940 COWARD McCANN 1940	**D** **C**
4	**The Well of the Star**	COWARD McCANN 1941	**C**
5	**Henrietta's House** (*illus. Lorna R. Steele*)	HODDER & STOUGHTON 1942	**D**
6	**The Blue Hills** Same as 5.	COWARD McCANN 1942	**C**
7	**The Little White Horse** (*illus. C. Walter Hodges*)	UNIVERSITY OF LONDON 1946 COWARD McCANN 1947	**D** **B**
8	**Make-believe** (*illus. C. Walter Hodges*)	DUCKWORTH 1949 BENTLEY 1953	**C** **B**
9	**God So Loved The World: A Life of Christ**	HODDER & STOUGHTON 1951 COWARD McCANN 1951	**B** **A**
10	**The Valley of Song** (*illus. Steven Spurrier*)	UNIVERSITY OF LONDON 1951 COWARD McCANN 1952	**C** **B**
11	**Linnets and Valerians** (*illus. Ian Ribbons*)	BROCKHAMPTON PRESS 1964 COWARD McCANN 1964	**C** **B**
12	**I Saw Three Ships** (*illus. Richard Kennedy*)	BROCKHAMPTON PRESS 1969 COWARD McCANN 1969	**B** **B**

GRAHAME, Kenneth

Born in Edinburgh, 1859. Died 1932

Author of surprisingly few books – but among them, one of the all-time most wonderful, stupendous (and so on) children's classics of fantasy and characterization. Toad, Rat and Mole live for ever – and quite right too. The first edition is scarce and expensive – and quite right too.

1 **The Golden Age**	LANE 1895	**E**
	STONE & KIMBALL 1895	**D**
2 **Dream Days**	LANE 1898	**E**
A revised edition was published by Lane in 1899.	LANE US 1898	**D**
3 **The Wind in the Willows**	METHUEN 1908	**R**
(*illus. Graham Robertson*)	SCRIBNER 1908	**O**
4 **First Whisper of 'The Wind in the Willows'**	METHUEN 1944	**C**
	LIPPINCOTT 1945	**B**
(*ed. Elspeth Grahame*)		

Also of interest:

PETER GREEN: **Kenneth Grahame 1959–1932: A Study of His Life, Work and Times** (MURRAY 1959, WORLD US 1959)

GREEN, Roger Lancelyn — *Born in Norfolk, 1918. Died 1987*

Roger Lancelyn Green is known primarily for his very long series of books retelling classical myths, and for his very valuable biographies of authors that should be of great interest to readers of this book – Andrew Lang, Lewis Carroll, J.M. Barrie, Mrs Molesworth, C.S. Lewis and Kipling. I list here just his little-known and somewhat neglected original children's fiction – there's not much of it, but it is well worth tracking down.

1 **The Wonderful Stranger: A Holiday Romance**	METHUEN 1950	**C**
(*illus. John Baynes*)		
2 **The Luck of the Lynns**	METHUEN 1952	**C**
(*illus. Sheila Macgregor*)		
3 **The Theft of the Golden Cat**	METHUEN 1955	**C**
(*illus. Edward McGrath*)		
4 **Mystery at Mycenae: An Adventure**	BODLEY HEAD 1957	**C**
(*illus. Margery Gill*)	BARNES 1959	**B**
5 **The Land Beyond the North**	BODLEY HEAD 1958	**B**
(*illus. Douglas Hall*)	WALCK 1959	**A**
6 **The Land of the Lord High Tiger**	BELL 1958	**B**
(*illus. John S. Goodall*)		

| 7 | **The Luck of Troy**
(*illus. Margery Gill*) | BODLEY HEAD 1961 | **B** |

GREENE, Graham   *Born in Hertfordshire, 1904*

One of the greatest writers of the century published only four children's books – a shame, as those four really do have 'classic' stamped all over them. Now Greene, if you don't already know, is one of the half-dozen most collected authors of all – and Greene collectors want *everything*. These children's books are both scarce and expensive – and you'll be vying with collectors who have not much interest in them *per se*, I'm afraid.

1	**The Little Train** (*illus. Dorothy Craigie*) *This was published anonymously, while Greene was a director at Eyre & Spottiswoode.*	EYRE & SPOTTISWOODE 1946 LOTHROP 1958	**M** **E**
2	**The Little Fire Engine** (*illus. Dorothy Craigie*)	PARRISH 1950	**I**
3	**The Little Red Fire Engine** Same as 2.	LOTHROP 1952	**E**
4	**The Little Horse Bus** (*illus. Dorothy Craigie*)	PARRISH 1952 LOTHROP 1954	**H** **E**
5	**The Little Steamroller** (*illus. Dorothy Craigie*)	PARRISH 1953 LOTHROP 1955	**H** **E**

GRUELLE, Johnny   *American. Born in Illinois, 1880. Died 1938*

Creator of that rather nice rag doll – and apparently able to go on writing about her for about forty years after his death. The truth is that a constant stream of 'Raggedy Ann' books have been pushed out under Gruelle's name that of course are not by him at all. I list the lot here – but be circumspect about anything much after 1940, if a purist. Until stated otherwise, all are illustrated by the author.

| 1 | **Mr Twee Deedle** | CUPPLES & LEON US 1913 | **J** |
| 2 | **Mr Twee Deedle's Further Adventures** | CUPPLES & LEON US 1914 | **H** |

3	**The Travels of Timmy Toodles**	MARINT US 1916	H
4	**My Very Own Fairy Stories**	VOLLAND US 1917	G
	Published in UK by Brentano's in 1923 as My Very Own Fairy Book.		
5	**The Funny Little Book**	VOLLAND US 1918	G
6	**Raggedy Ann Stories**	VOLLAND US 1918	I
		BRENTANO'S 1923	F
7	**Little Sunny Stories**	VOLLAND US 1919	F
8	**Friendly Fairies**	VOLLAND US 1919	F
		BRENTANO'S 1923	D
9	**Raggedy Andy Stories: Introducing the Little Rag Brother of Raggedy Ann**	VOLLAND US 1920	G
10	**The Little Brown Bear**	VOLLAND US 1920	F
11	**Orphan Annie Story Book**	BOBBS MERRILL 1921	F
12	**Eddie Elephant**	VOLLAND 1921	E
13	**Johnny Mouse and the Wishing Stick**	BOBBS MERRILL 1922	E
14	**The Magical Land of Noom**	VOLLAND 1922	E
15	**Raggedy Ann and Andy and the Camel with the Wrinkled Knees**	VOLLAND 1924	F
	Published in UK by Hutchinson in 1942 as The Camel with the Wrinkled Knees.		
16	**Raggedy Ann's Wishing Pebble**	VOLLAND 1925	F
17	**Raggedy Ann's Alphabet Book**	VOLLAND 1925	E
18	**The Paper Dragon: A Raggedy Ann Adventure**	VOLLAND 1926	E
19	**Beloved Belindy**	VOLLAND 1926	D
20	**Wooden Willie**	VOLLAND 1927	D
21	**Raggedy Ann's Magical Wishes**	VOLLAND 1928	E
22	**Raggedy Ann's Number Book**	VOLLAND 1928	D
23	**Marcella Stories**	VOLLAND 1929	D

24	**The Cheery Scarecrow**	VOLLAND 1929	**D**
25	**Raggedy Ann in the Deep Deep Woods**	VOLLAND 1930	**D**
26	**Raggedy Ann's Sunny Songs**	VOLLAND 1930	**C**
27	**Raggedy Ann in Cookie Land**	VOLLAND 1931	**D**
28	**Raggedy Ann's Lucky Pennies**	VOLLAND 1932	**D**
29	**Raggedy Ann and the Left-handed Safety Pin**	WHITMAN 1935	**D**
30	**Raggedy Ann in the Golden Meadow**	WHITMAN 1935	**D**
31	**Raggedy Ann's Joyful Songs**	MILLER 1937	**C**
32	**Raggedy Ann in the Magic Book** (*illus. Worth Gruelle*)	GRUELLE 1939	**C**
33	**Raggedy Ann and the Golden Butterfly**	GRUELLE 1940	**C**
34	**Raggedy Ann and the Hoppy Toad**	McLOUGHLIN 1940	**C**
35	**Raggedy Ann and the Laughing Brook**	McLOUGHLIN 1940 HUTCHINSON 1942	**C** **C**
36	**Raggedy Ann Helps Grandpa Hoppergrass**	McLOUGHLIN 1940 HUTCHINSON 1942	**C** **C**
37	**Raggedy Ann in the Garden**	McLOUGHLIN 1940	**C**
38	**Raggedy Ann Goes Sailing**	McLOUGHLIN 1941 HUTCHINSON 1942	**C** **C**
39	**Raggedy Ann and Andy and the Nice Fat Policeman** (*illus. Worth Gruelle*)	GRUELLE 1942	**B**
40	**Raggedy Ann and the Betsy Bonnet String**	GRUELLE 1943	**B**
41	**Raggedy Ann and Andy** (*illus. Julian Wehr*)	SAALFIELD 1944	**B**
42	**Raggedy Ann in the Snow White Castle** (*illus. Justin Gruelle*)	GRUELLE 1946	**B**

43	**Raggedy Ann and the Slippery Slide** (*illus. Ethel Hays*)	SAALFIELD 1947	B
44	**Raggedy Ann at the End of the Rainbow** (*illus. Ethel Hays*)	SAALFIELD 1947	B
45	**Raggedy Ann's Adventure** (*illus. Ethel Hays*)	SAALFIELD 1947	B
46	**Raggedy Ann's Mystery** (*illus. Ethel Hays*)	SAALFIELD 1947	B
47	**Stories About Raggedy Ann to Read Aloud** (*illus. Rachel Taft Dixon*)	SPRING UK 1960	A
48	**Raggedy Ann and the Golden Ring** (*illus. Worth Gruelle*)	BOBBS MERRILL 1961	B
49	**Raggedy Ann and the Happy Meadow** (*illus. Worth Gruelle*)	BOBBS MERRILL 1961	B
50	**Raggedy Ann and the Hobby Horse** (*illus. Worth Gruelle*)	BOBBS MERRILL 1961	B
51	**Raggedy Ann and the Wonderful Witch** (*illus. Worth Gruelle*)	BOBBS MERRILL 1961	B
52	**Raggedy Ann and Andy and the Kindly Ragman** (*illus. John Hopper*)	BOBBS MERRILL 1975	B
53	**Raggedy Ann and Andy and the Witchie Kissabye** (*illus. John Hopper*)	BOBBS MERRILL 1975	B
54	**More Raggedy Ann and Andy Stories** (*ed. Martin Williams*) (*illus. the author and Worth and Justin Gruelle*)	BOBBS MERRILL 1977	B

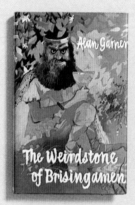

Three original Puffins (the pair of 'Orlando' books, and *Stig of the Dump* illustrated by Ardizzone) together with Alan Garner's first three books – the *Elidor* dust-wrapper by Charles Keeping – a late Rumer Godden, and one of Michael Bond's lesser-known characters.

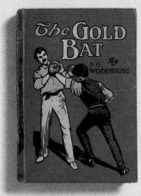

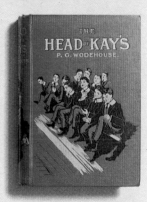

All of Wodehouse's school stories. The book bearing only a silver trophy is his first, *The Pothunters* (1902), while *Mike and Psmith* and *Mike at Wrykyn* (both 1953) are rewrites of the original *Mike* (1909).

A beautiful 'Rupert' surrounded by the first six volumes in the 'Jennings' saga, a later
'William' (illustrated by Thomas Henry), and a brace of 'Bunters'.

The complete 'Railway' saga by Rev W. Awdry – minus the very recent titles written by his son. The first eleven are illustrated by C. Reginald Dalby, numbers 12–17 by John Kenney, the remainder by Gunvor and Peter Edwards.

HALDANE, J.B.S.   *Born in Oxford, 1892. Died 1964*

In 1935 this eminent scientist published a book called *The Outlook of Science*; in 1938 he brought out *The Chemistry of the Individual* and *The Marxist Philosophy*. All very worthy stuff – but how fortunate we are that in *between* these books, Haldane saw fit to write his one and only children's book – and an all-time great it is, too. The magic and the wonder are unsurpassed – maybe they *had* to come from the mind of one who understood thoroughly just how strange were the workings of the *real* world.

1	**My Friend Mr Leakey**	CRESSET PRESS 1937	**I**
	(*illus. Leonard Rosoman*)	HARPER 1938	**F**

Also of interest (but don't expect too much about Mr Leakey in it):
RONALD W. CLARK: **J.B.S.: The Life and Work of J.B.S. Haldane** (HODDER & STOUGHTON 1968, COWARD McCANN US 1969)

HALE, Kathleen   *Born in Lanarkshire, 1898*

Writer and illustrator of the famous 'Orlando' series – great books to read out loud, with pictures immediate and colourful enough to appeal instantly. Certainly a collector should have at least a representation of this irrepressible ginger feline – who is, incidentally, nothing whatever to do with young Virginia Woolf's effort of the same name.

1	**Orlando, the Marmalade Cat: A Camping Holiday**	COUNTRY LIFE 1938 / SCRIBNER 1938	**J** / **H**
2	**Orlando's Evening Out**	PENGUIN 1941	**D**
3	**Orlando's Home Life**	PENGUIN 1942	**D**
4	**Orlando, the Marmalade Cat, Buys a Farm**	COUNTRY LIFE 1942	**H**
5	**Henrietta, the Faithful Hen**	TRANSATLANTIC ARTS 1943	**G**
6	**Orlando, the Marmalade Cat: His Silver Wedding**	COUNTRY LIFE 1944	**G**
7	**Orlando, the Marmalade Cat, Becomes a Doctor**	COUNTRY LIFE 1944	**G**
8	**Orlando's Invisible Pyjamas**	TRANSATLANTIC ARTS 1947	**G**

9	Orlando, the Marmalade Cat: A Trip Abroad	COUNTRY LIFE 1949	G
10	Orlando, the Marmalade Cat, Keeps a Dog	COUNTRY LIFE 1949	G
11	Orlando, the Judge	MURRAY 1950	E
12	Orlando's Country Life: A Peep-show Book	CHATTO & WINDUS 1950	F
13	Puss-in-Boots: A Peep-show Book	CHATTO & WINDUS 1951	F
14	Orlando, the Marmalade Cat: A Seaside Holiday	COUNTRY LIFE 1952	E
15	Manda	MURRAY 1952	D
		COWARD McCANN 1953	C
16	Orlando's Zoo	MURRAY 1954	D
17	Orlando, the Marmalade Cat: The Frisky Housewife	COUNTRY LIFE 1956	D
18	Orlando's Magic Carpet	MURRAY 1958	C
19	Orlando, the Marmalade Cat, Buys a Cottage	COUNTRY LIFE 1963	C
20	Orlando and the Three Graces	MURRAY 1965	C
21	Orlando, the Marmalade Cat, Goes to the Moon	MURRAY 1968	C
22	Orlando, the Marmalade Cat, and the Water Cats	CAPE 1972	C
23	Henrietta's Magic Egg	ALLEN & UNWIN 1973	C

HARRIS, Rosemary   *Born in London, 1923*

A writer of vivid, if rather pessimistic, stuff – hard, really, to classify them as children's books at all; certainly a young person who responded well to Rosemary Harris would make the full transition to adult literature with consummate ease, scarcely noticing the bump. One doesn't read these books for laughs, but some of the imagery is intensely memorable, as is the individuality of the style.

1	**The Moon in the Cloud**	FABER 1968	D
		MACMILLAN US 1969	B
2	**The Shadow on the Sun**	FABER 1970	C
		MACMILLAN US 1970	B
3	**The Seal-singing**	FABER 1971	C
		MACMILLAN US 1971	B
4	**The Child in the Bamboo Grove** *(legend)* *(illus. Errol le Cain)*	FABER 1971	C
		PHILLIPS 1972	B
5	**The Bright and Morning Star**	FABER 1972	C
		MACMILLAN US 1972	B
6	**The King's White Elephant** *(illus. Errol le Cain)*	FABER 1973	C
7	**The Lotus and the Grail: Legends from East to West** *(illus. Errol le Cain)*	FABER 1974	C
8	**Sea Magic and Other Stories of Enchantment** *Abridged version of 7.*	MACMILLAN US 1974	B
9	**The Flying Ship** *(illus. Errol le Cain)*	FABER 1975	C
10	**The Little Dog of Fo** *(legend)* *(illus. Errol le Cain)*	FABER 1976	C
11	**I Want to be a Fish** *(illus. Jill Bennett)*	KESTREL 1977	B
12	**A Quest for Orion**	FABER 1978	B
13	**Beauty and the Beast** *(legend)* *(illus. Errol le Cain)*	FABER 1979	C
		DOUBLEDAY 1980	B
14	**Green Finger House** *(illus. Juan Wijngaard)*	EEL PIE 1980	C
		KAMPMANN 1982	B
15	**Tower of the Stars**	FABER 1980	B
16	**The Enchanted Horse** *(illus. Pauline Baynes)*	KESTREL 1981	C

17 Janni's Stork *(illus. Juan Wijngaard)*	BLACKIE 1982	**B**
18 Zed	FABER 1982	**B**

HEINLEIN, Robert A. *American. Born in Missouri, 1907*

Now an acknowledged master of science fiction (and highly collectable, particularly in America), Heinlein's very first book was for children – and he followed it up with a good deal more, as will be seen below. Refreshingly different, these books seem to be jammed with all the pre-Moon-landing hokum of space travel books and glory in gadgetry while remaining totally plausible, great fun, and a gripping read.

In addition to these children's books, Heinlein has published upwards of thirty novels and collections of short stories for adults.

1 Rocket Ship Galileo	SCRIBNER 1947	**H**
(illus. Thomas Voter)	NEL 1971	**B**
2 Space Cadet	SCRIBNER 1948	**G**
(illus. Clifford Geary)	GOLLANCZ 1966	**B**
3 Red Planet	SCRIBNER 1949	**F**
(illus. Clifford Geary)	GOLLANCZ 1963	**B**
4 Farmer in the Sky	SCRIBNER 1950	**F**
(illus. Clifford Geary)	GOLLANCZ 1962	**B**
5 Between Planets	SCRIBNER 1951	**E**
(illus. Clifford Geary)	GOLLANCZ 1968	**B**
6 The Rolling Stones	SCRIBNER 1952	**E**
(illus. Clifford Geary) This was published in UK by NEL in 1971 as Space Family Stone – *the original title would have meant something else entirely by the 1970s.*		
7 Starman Jones	SCRIBNER 1953	**E**
(illus. Clifford Geary)	SIDGWICK & JACKSON 1954	**B**
8 The Star Beast	SCRIBNER 1954	**E**
(illus. Clifford Geary)	NEL 1971	**B**
9 Tunnel in the Sky	SCRIBNER 1955	**D**
	GOLLANCZ 1965	**B**

10	**Time for the Stars**	SCRIBNER 1956	**D**
		GOLLANCZ 1963	**B**
11	**Citizen of the Galaxy**	SCRIBNER 1957	**D**
		GOLLANCZ 1969	**B**
12	**Have Space Suit – Will Travel**	SCRIBNER 1958	**D**
		GOLLANCZ 1970	**B**
13	**Starship Troopers**	PUTNAM 1959	**D**
		NEL 1961	**B**
14	**Podkayne of Mars: Her Life and Times**	PUTNAM 1963	**C**
		NEL 1969	**B**

HERGÉ
Pseudonym of Georges Remi
Born in Belgium, 1907. Died 1983

Hergé is a pseudonym rather tortuously evolved by swapping around the author's initials (G.R.) and ending up with a sort of phonetic equivalent that I am sure works better in 'Belgian'. Anyway, creator of the deathless Tintin, Snowy, Captain Haddock (surely the model for Captain Birdseye) and the stereo Plod – Thompson and Thomson (or, in French, Dupont et Dupond). The densely packed coloured comic-strip pages are now familiar the world over – it is an underused format for children's books, the only other exponents, as far as I am aware, being Goscinny and Uderzo (q.v.). The books can stand endless re-readings, and the action never gives way to dull bits. I feel sure that Indiana Jones got some of his best ideas from the Tintin books.

The books started appearing in French in the 1930s, but below I list the English first editions.

1	**The Crab with the Golden Claws**	METHUEN 1958	**D**
		GOLDEN PRESS 1959	**C**
2	**King Ottokar's Sceptre**	METHUEN 1958	**C**
		GOLDEN PRESS 1959	**B**
3	**The Secret of the Unicorn**	METHUEN 1959	**C**
		GOLDEN PRESS 1959	**B**
4	**Destination Moon**	METHUEN 1959	**C**
		GOLDEN PRESS 1960	**B**
5	**Explorers on the Moon**	METHUEN 1959	**C**
		LITTLE BROWN 1976	**B**

6 Red Rackham's Treasure	METHUEN 1959	C
	GOLDEN PRESS 1959	B
7 The Calculus Affair	METHUEN 1960	C
	LITTLE BROWN 1976	A
8 The Red Sea Sharks	METHUEN 1960	C
	LITTLE BROWN 1975	A
9 The Shooting Star	METHUEN 1961	C
	LITTLE BROWN 1978	A
10 Tintin in Tibet	METHUEN 1962	C
	LITTLE BROWN 1975	A
11 The Seven Crystal Balls	METHUEN 1962	C
	LITTLE BROWN 1975	A
12 Prisoners of the Sun	METHUEN 1962	C
	LITTLE BROWN 1975	A
13 The Castafiore Emerald	METHUEN 1963	C
	LITTLE BROWN 1975	A
14 The Black Island	METHUEN 1966	B
	LITTLE BROWN 1975	A
15 Flight 714	METHUEN 1968	B
	LITTLE BROWN 1975	A
16 Cigars of the Pharaoh	METHUEN 1971	B
	LITTLE BROWN 1975	A
17 Land of Black Gold	METHUEN 1972	B
	LITTLE BROWN 1975	A
18 Tintin and the Lake of Sharks	METHUEN 1973	B
	LITTLE BROWN 1978	A
19 Tintin and the Broken Ear	METHUEN 1975	B
	LITTLE BROWN 1978	A
20 Tintin and the Picaros	METHUEN 1976	B
	LITTLE BROWN 1978	A
21 Tintin in America	METHUEN 1978	B
	LITTLE BROWN 1979	A
22 The Blue Lotus	METHUEN 1983	B
	LITTLE BROWN 1984	B

23 **The Adventures of Jo, Zette and
    Jocko:**

The Valley of the Cobras	METHUEN 1986	**B**
The Stratoship H22. Part One:	METHUEN 1987	**B**
Mr Pump's Legacy		
The Stratoship H22. Part Two:	METHUEN 1987	**B**
Destination New York		

Also of interest:
PHILIPPE GODDIN: **Hergé and Tintin, Reporters** (SUNDANCER, 1987)

HEWARD, Constance   *Born in Britain, 1884. Died 1968*

Although Constance Heward was the original creator of the lovably raggedy
Ameliaranne, about a dozen more books featuring the character were published by other hands – notably Eleanor Farjeon (q.v.). Heward wrote about
three dozen children's books, but as sole interest seems to be targeted upon
the Ameliaranne titles, it is these that I list below – all illustrated (as were
those *not* by Heward) by S.B. Pearse.

#	Title	Publisher	Grade
1	**Ameliaranne and the Green Umbrella**	HARRAP 1920	**G**
		JACOBS 1920	**D**
2	**Ameliaranne Keeps Shop**	HARRAP 1928	**C**
		McKAY 1928	**C**
3	**Ameliaranne, Cinema Star**	HARRAP 1929	**C**
4	**Ameliaranne and the Monkey**	McKAY 1929	**C**
5	**Ameliaranne at the Farm**	HARRAP 1937	**B**
		McKAY 1937	**B**
6	**Ameliaranne Gives a Christmas Party**	HARRAP 1938	**B**
		McKAY 1938	**B**
7	**Ameliaranne Camps Out**	HARRAP 1939	**B**
		McKAY 1939	**B**
8	**Ameliaranne Keeps School**	HARRAP 1940	**B**
		McKAY 1940	**B**
9	**Ameliaranne Goes Touring**	HARRAP 1941	**B**
		McKAY 1941	**B**

HILL, Eric   *Born in London, 1927*

A collector should probably have at least a representation of old Spot, if not the whole lot of Spot. Eric Hill has done other things too, but I confine this listing to Spot, the Whole Spot and Nothing But the Spot – although I omit those padded plastic numbers that are intended for bathtime and called, I hesitate to tell you, 'Soft Spots'. Enough of this – here's Spot (warts and all).

1	**Where's Spot?**	HEINEMANN 1980	**B**
		PUTNAM 1980	**A**
2	**Spot's First Walk**	HEINEMANN 1981	**A**
		PUTNAM 1981	**A**
3	**Spot's Birthday Party**	PUTNAM 1982	**A**
		HEINEMANN 1983	**A**
4	**Spot's First Christmas**	HEINEMANN 1983	**A**
		PUTNAM 1983	**A**
5	**Spot's Busy Year** (*colouring book*)	PUTNAM 1983	**A**
		HEINEMANN 1984	**A**
6	**Spot Tells the Time** (*colouring book*)	PUTNAM 1983	**A**
		HEINEMANN 1984	**A**
7	**Spot's Alphabet** (*colouring book*)	PUTNAM 1983	**A**
		HEINEMANN 1984	**A**
8	**Spot Learns to Count** (*colouring book*)	PUTNAM 1983	**A**
		HEINEMANN 1984	**A**
9	**Here's Spot**	HEINEMANN 1984	**A**
		PUTNAM 1984	**A**
10	**Spot Goes to School**	HEINEMANN 1984	**A**
		PUTNAM 1984	**A**
11	**Play with Spot**	HEINEMANN 1985	**A**
12	**Spot at Play**	PUTNAM 1985	**A**
	Same as 11.		
13	**Spot Goes to the Beach**	HEINEMANN 1985	**A**
		PUTNAM 1985	**A**
14	**Spot at the Fair**	HEINEMANN 1985	**A**
		PUTNAM 1985	**A**

15	**Spot at the Farm**	HEINEMANN 1985	A
		PUTNAM 1985	A
16	**Spot Goes on Holiday**	HEINEMANN 1985	A
		PUTNAM 1985	A
17	**Spot Goes to the Circus**	HEINEMANN 1986	A
		PUTNAM 1986	A
18	**Spot Looks at Colours**	HEINEMANN 1986	A
		PUTNAM 1986	A
19	**Spot Looks at Shapes**	HEINEMANN 1986	A
		PUTNAM 1986	A
20	**Spot's First Words**	HEINEMANN 1986	A
		PUTNAM 1986	A
21	**Spot Goes to the Farm**	HEINEMANN 1987	A
		PUTNAM 1987	A
22	**Spot's First Picnic**	HEINEMANN 1987	A
		PUTNAM 1987	A
23	**Spot's Hospital Visit**	HEINEMANN 1987	A
		PUTNAM 1987	A
24	**Spot's First Easter**	HEINEMANN 1988	A
		PUTNAM 1988	A

HOBAN, Russell   *American. Born in Pennsylvania, 1925*

Hugely prolific author of increasingly witty, shrewd and literary books for young people. Perhaps it was Hoban's growing sophistication that eventually led him towards adult fiction – a field in which he has very quickly aroused great acclaim. It will be fairly difficult (and space-consuming) to gather *all* Hoban's work, but a smattering would be no bad thing. The title he seems to be best remembered for is *The Mouse and His Child,* illustrated – as were many of his books – by his first wife, Lilian.

| 1 | **What Does It Do and How Does It Work? Power Shovel, Dump Truck, and Other Heavy Machines** | HARPER 1959 | C |
| | (*non-fiction*) | | |

2	**The Atomic Submarine: A Practice Combat Control Under the Sea** (*non-fiction*)	HARPER 1960	C
3	**Bedtime for Frances** (*illus. Garth Williams*)	HARPER 1960 FABER 1963	C C
4	**Herman the Loser** (*illus. Lilian Hoban*)	HARPER 1961 WORLD'S WORK 1972	C A
5	**The Song in My Drum** (*illus. Lilian Hoban*)	HARPER 1962	C
6	**London Men and English Men** (*illus. Lilian Hoban*)	HARPER 1962	C
7	**Some Snow Said Hello** (*illus. Lilian Hoban*)	HARPER 1963	C
8	**The Sorely Trying Day** (*illus. Lilian Hoban*)	HARPER 1964 WORLD'S WORK 1965	C B
9	**A Baby Sister for Frances** (*illus. Lilian Hoban*)	HARPER 1964 FABER 1965	B B
10	**Bread and Jam for Frances** (*illus. Lilian Hoban*)	HARPER 1964 FABER 1966	B B
11	**Nothing to Do** (*illus. Lilian Hoban*)	HARPER 1964	B
12	**Tom and the Two Handles** (*illus. Lilian Hoban*)	HARPER 1965 WORLD'S WORK 1969	B A
13	**The Story of Hester Mouse Who Became a Writer** (*illus. Lilian Hoban*)	NORTON 1965 WORLD'S WORK 1969	B A
14	**What Happened When Jack and Daisy Tried to Fool the Tooth Fairies**	FOUR WINDS PRESS 1965	C
15	**Goodnight** (*verse*) (*illus. Lilian Hoban*)	NORTON 1966 WORLD'S WORK 1969	B A
16	**Henry and the Monstrous Din** (*illus. Lilian Hoban*)	HARPER 1966 WORLD'S WORK 1967	B A
17	**The Little Brute Family** (*illus. Lilian Hoban*)	MACMILLAN US 1966	B

18	**Save My Place** (*illus. Lilian Hoban*)	NORTON 1967	B
19	**Charlie the Tramp** (*illus. Lilian Hoban*)	FOUR WINDS PRESS 1967	C
20	**The Mouse and His Child** (*illus. Lilian Hoban*)	HARPER 1967 FABER 1969	D C
21	**The Pedaling Man and Other Poems** (*illus. Lilian Hoban*)	NORTON 1968 WORLD'S WORK 1969	B A
22	**A Birthday for Frances** (*illus. Lilian Hoban*)	HARPER 1968 FABER 1970	B B
23	**The Stone Doll of Sister Brute** (*illus. Lilian Hoban*)	MACMILLAN 1968	B
24	**Harvey's Hideout** (*illus. Lilian Hoban*)	PARENTS' MAGAZINE PRESS 1969 CAPE 1973	B B
25	**Best Friends for Frances** (*illus. Lilian Hoban*)	HARPER 1969 FABER 1971	B B
26	**The Mole Family's Christmas** (*illus. Lilian Hoban*)	PARENTS' MAGAZINE PRESS 1969 CAPE 1973	B A
27	**Ugly Bird** (*illus. Lilian Hoban*)	MACMILLAN US 1969	B
28	**A Bargain for Frances** (*illus. Lilian Hoban*)	HARPER 1970 WORLD'S WORK 1971	B B
29	**Emmet Otter's Jug-band Christmas** (*illus. Lilian Hoban*)	PARENTS' MAGAZINE PRESS 1971 WORLD'S WORK 1971	B B
30	**Egg Thoughts and Other Frances Songs** (*illus. Lilian Hoban*)	HARPER 1972 FABER 1973	B B
31	**The Sea-thing Child** (*illus. Brom Hoban*)	HARPER 1972 GOLLANCZ 1972	B B
32	**Letitia Rabbit's String Song** (*illus. Mary Chalmers*)	COWARD McCANN 1973	B

33	**How Tom Beat Captain Najork and His Hired Sportsmen** (*illus. Quentin Blake*)	ATHENEUM 1974 CAPE 1974	C C
34	**Ten What? A Mystery Counting Book** (*illus. Sylvie Selig*)	CAPE 1974 SCRIBNER 1975	B B
35	**Dinner at Alberta's** (*illus. James Marshall*)	CROWELL 1975 CAPE 1977	B B
36	**Crocodile and Pierrot** (*illus. Sylvie Selig*)	CAPE 1975 SCRIBNER 1977	B B
37	**A Near Thing for Captain Najork** (*illus. Quentin Blake*)	CAPE 1975 ATHENEUM 1976	C C
38	**Arthur's New Power** (*illus. Byron Barton*)	CROWELL 1978 GOLLANCZ 1980	B B
39	**The Twenty-Elephant Restaurant** (*illus. Emily McCully*)	ATHENEUM 1978 CAPE 1980	B B
40	**The Dancing Tigers** (*illus. David Gentleman*)	CAPE 1979	C
41	**La Corona and the Tin Frog** (*illus. Nicola Bayley*)	CAPE 1979	B
42	**Flat Cat** (*illus. Clive Scruton*)	METHUEN 1980 PHILOMEL 1980	A A
43	**Ace Dragon Ltd** (*illus. Quentin Blake*)	CAPE 1980	B
44	**The Serpent Tower** (*illus. David Scott*)	METHUEN 1981	A
45	**The Great Fruit Gum Robbery** (*illus. Colin McNaughton*)	METHUEN 1981	A
46	**The Great Gumdrop Robbery** Same as 45.	PHILOMEL 1982	A
47	**They Came from Aargh!** (*illus. Colin McNaughton*)	METHUEN 1981 PHILOMEL 1981	A A
48	**The Battle of Zormla** (*illus. Colin McNaughton*)	METHUEN 1982 PHILOMEL 1982	A A

49	**The Flight of Bembel Rudzuk**	METHUEN 1982	A
	(*illus. Colin McNaughton*)	PHILOMEL 1982	A
50	**Ponders**	WALKER 1983	A
	(*all illus. Martin Baynton*):		**Each**
	Jim Frog; Big John Turkle; Charlie		
	Meadows; Lavinia Bat.		
51	**The Rain Door**	GOLLANCZ 1986	B
	(*illus. Quentin Blake*)		
52	**Marzipan Pig**	CAPE 1986	B
	(*illus. Quentin Blake*)		

HUGHES, Richard   *Born in Surrey, 1900. Died 1976*

A fine author, best known for his adult *High Wind in Jamaica*, and the sadly unfinished saga 'The Human Predicament'. His children's books, too, are elegant and excellent – and while *The Spider's Palace* is impossibly scarce, I think you would do well to forget all about the feasibility of acquiring No 1!

1	**Burial, and the Dark Child**	PRIVATELY PRINTED 1930	P
	(*verse and a story*)		
2	**The Spider's Palace and Other Stories**	CHATTO & WINDUS 1931	J
		HARPER 1932	G
	(*illus. George Charlton*)		
3	**Don't Blame Me! and Other Stories**	CHATTO & WINDUS 1940	G
	(*illus. Fritz Eichenberg*)	HARPER 1940	D
4	**Gertrude's Child**	HARLIN QUIST 1966	C
	(*illus. Rick Schreiter*)	ALLEN 1967	C
5	**The Wonder-dog: The Collected Children's Stories**	CHATTO & WINDUS 1977	B
		GREENWILLOW 1977	B
	(*illus. Antony Maitland*)		
6	**Gertrude and the Mermaid**	HARLIN QUIST 1979	B
	(*illus. Nicole Claveloux*)		

HUGHES, Ted   *Born in Yorkshire, 1930*

I think that many of the Poet Laureate's volumes for children are among his very best work – particularly *Meet My Folks!* and *The Iron Man*. Of course, you

don't need me to tell you how popular *and* collected Ted Hughes is – fine firsts
in dust-wrapper will be tough, but worth it.

In addition to the following, Hughes has published dozens and dozens of
books for adults – and more by the time you read this.

1	**Meet My Folks!** (*verse*)	FABER 1961	**F**
	(*illus. George Adamson*)	BOBBS MERRILL 1973	**B**
2	**How the Whale Became** (*fiction*)	FABER 1963	**G**
	(*illus. George Adamson*)	ATHENEUM 1964	**D**
3	**The Earth-Owl and Other Moon-People** (*verse*) (*illus. R.A. Brandt*)	FABER 1963	**E**
4	**Nessie the Mannerless Monster** (*verse*) (*illus. Gerald Rose*) *This was published in America by Bobbs Merrill in 1974 as* Nessie the Monster (**B**).	FABER 1964	**F**
5	**Poetry in the Making** (*non-fiction*) *An abridged version was published in 1970 by Doubleday US and entitled* Poetry Is (**D**).	FABER 1967	**E**
6	**The Iron Man** (*fiction*) (*illus. George Adamson*) *This was published in America by Harper in 1968 as* The Iron Giant (**D**).	FABER 1968	**F**
7	**Five Autumn Songs for Children's Voices** *500 copies for sale, as follows:*	GILBERTSON 1968	
	3–11: a verse in manuscript & a watercolour		**L**
	12–37: a verse in manuscript		**K**
	38–188: signed		**G**
	189–500: numbered		**C**
8	**The Coming of the Kings and Other Plays** *Includes*: The Tiger's Bones; Beauty and the Beast; Sean; The Fool; The Devil and the Cats.	FABER 1970	**C**
9	**The Tiger's Bones and Other Plays For Children** *As 8, with the addition of* Orpheus.	VIKING PRESS 1974	**B**

10 **Spring, Summer, Autumn, Winter** (*verse*) *140 copies, numbered and signed.*	RAINBOW PRESS 1974	**K**
11 **Season Songs** (*verse*) (*illus. Leonard Baskin*) First trade edition of 10.	VIKING PRESS 1975 FABER 1976	**B** **B**
12 **Earth-Moon** (*verse*) 226 signed and numbered copies, 200 for sale.	RAINBOW PRESS 1976	**J**
13 **Moon-Whales and Other Moon Poems** (*illus. Leonard Baskin*)	VIKING PRESS 1976	**B**
14 **Moon-Bells and Other Poems** (*illus. Leonard Baskin*)	CHATTO & WINDUS 1978	**B**
15 **Under the North Star** (*verse*) (*illus. Leonard Baskin*)	FABER 1981 VIKING PRESS 1981	**B** **B**
16 **What is the Truth?** (*illus. R.J. Lloyd*)	FABER 1984 HARPER 1984	**B** **B**
17 **Ffangs the Vampire Bat and the Kiss of Truth** (*illus. Chris Riddell*)	FABER 1986	**B**

HUNTER, Norman   *Born in Kent, 1899*

Exuberance, fun and invention – no message, a great deal of highly inventive twaddle and a stream of first-rate illustrators: it all adds up to Norman Hunter's irresistible Professor Branestawm. The author used to be a professional magician once, and it shows.

1 **The Bad Barons of Crashbania** (*illus. Eve Garnett*)	BLACKWELL 1932	**J**
2 **The Incredible Adventures of Professor Branestawm** (*illus. W. Heath Robinson*)	LANE 1933	**L**
3 **Professor Branestawm's Treasure Hunt and Other Incredible Adventures** (*illus. James Arnold*)	LANE 1937	**H**
4 **Larky Legends** (*illus. James Arnold*)	LANE 1938	**G**

5   **Stories of Professor Branestawm**   ARNOLD 1939   **J**
    (*illus. W. Heath Robinson*)

6   **Jingle Tales**   WARNE 1941   **F**

7   **Puffin Book of Magic**   PUFFIN 1968   **B**
    (*illus. Jill McDonald*)

8   **The Peculiar Triumph of Professor   BODLEY HEAD 1970   **D**
    Branestawm**
    (*illus. George Adamson*)

9   **The Home-made Dragon and Other   BODLEY HEAD 1971   **C**
    Incredible Stories**
    (*illus. Fritz Wegner*)

10 **Professor Branstawm Up the Pole**   BODLEY HEAD 1972   **C**
    (*illus. George Adamson*)

11 **The Frantic Phantom and Other   BODLEY HEAD 1973   **C**
    Incredible Stories**
    (*illus. Geraldine Spence*)

12 **Professor Branestawm's Dictionary**   BODLEY HEAD 1973   **C**
    (*illus. Derek Cousins*)

13 **Wizards are a Nuisance**   BBC 1973   **C**
    (*illus. Quentin Blake*)

14 **Professor Branestawm's Great   BODLEY HEAD 1974   **C**
    Revolution**
    (*illus. David Hughes*)

15 **Dust-up at the Royal Disco**   BODLEY HEAD 1975   **C**
    (*illus. Fritz Wegner*)

16 **Professor Branestawm's   BODLEY HEAD 1975   **C**
    Compendium of Conundrums,
    Riddles, Puzzles, Brain-Twisters
    and Dotty Descriptions**
    (*illus. Derek Cousins*)

17 **Professor Branestawm's Do-it-   BODLEY HEAD 1976   **C**
    yourself Handbook**
    (*illus. Jill McDonald*)

18 **Professor Branestawm 'Round the   BODLEY HEAD 1977   **C**
    Bend**
    (*illus. Derek Cousins*)

19	**Vanishing Ladies and Other Magic** (*illus. Jill McDonald*)	BODLEY HEAD 1978	**B**
20	**Count Bakwerdz on the Carpet** (*illus. Babette Cole*)	BODLEY HEAD 1979	**B**
21	**Professor Branestawm's Perilous Pudding** (*illus. Derek Cousins*)	BODLEY HEAD 1979	**C**
22	**Sneeze and be Slain and Other Incredible Stories** (*illus. Babette Cole*)	BODLEY HEAD 1980	**B**
23	**Professor Branestawm and the Wild Letters** (*illus. Gerald Rose*)	BODLEY HEAD 1981	**B**
24	**Professor Branestawm's Pocket Motor Car** (*illus. Gerald Rose*)	BODLEY HEAD 1981	**B**
25	**Professor Branestawm's Building Bust-up** (*illus. Gerald Rose*)	BODLEY HEAD 1982	**B**
26	**Professor Branestawm's Mouse War** (*illus. Gerald Rose*)	BODLEY HEAD 1982	**B**
27	**Professor Branestawm's Crunchy Cookery** (*illus. Gerald Rose*)	BODLEY HEAD 1983	**B**
28	**Professor Branestawm's Hair-raising Idea** (*illus. Gerald Rose*)	BODLEY HEAD 1983	**B**

HUTCHINS, Pat   *Born in Yorkshire, 1942*

Although it is still Pat Hutchins' first picture book that remains the desirable classic, the books that follow are very attractive in themselves, and should prove to be inexpensive quarry. Unless otherwise stated, the books are illustrated by the author – Laurence Hutchins, incidentally, is the husband.

1	**Rosie's Walk**	MACMILLAN US 1968	**D**
		BODLEY HEAD 1968	**D**

2   **Tom and Sam**   MACMILLAN US 1968   **C**
                                                    BODLEY HEAD 1969   **B**

3   **The Surprise Party**   MACMILLAN US 1969   **B**
                                                    BODLEY HEAD 1970   **B**

4   **Clocks and More Clocks**   MACMILLAN US 1970   **B**
                                                    BODLEY HEAD 1970   **B**

5   **Changes, Changes**   MACMILLAN US 1971   **A**
                                                    BODLEY HEAD 1971   **A**

6   **Titch**   MACMILLAN US 1971   **A**
                                                    BODLEY HEAD 1972   **A**

7   **Good Night, Owl**   MACMILLAN US 1972   **B**
                                                    BODLEY HEAD 1973   **B**

8   **The Silver Christmas Tree**   MACMILLAN US 1974   **A**
                                                    BODLEY HEAD 1974   **A**

9   **The Wind Blew** (*verse*)   MACMILLAN US 1974   **A**
                                                    BODLEY HEAD 1974   **A**

10 **The House That Sailed Away**   GREENWILLOW 1975   **A**
    (*illus. Laurence Hutchins*)   BODLEY HEAD 1976   **A**

11 **Don't Forget the Bacon!** (*verse*)   GREENWILLOW 1976   **A**
                                                    BODLEY HEAD 1976   **A**

12 **Follow That Bus!**   GREENWILLOW 1977   **A**
    (*illus. Laurence Hutchins*)   BODLEY HEAD 1977   **A**

13 **Happy Birthday, Sam**   GREENWILLOW 1978   **A**
                                                    BODLEY HEAD 1978   **A**

14 **The Best Train Set Ever**   GREENWILLOW 1978   **A**
                                                    BODLEY HEAD 1979   **A**

15 **One-eyed Jake**   GREENWILLOW 1979   **A**
                                                    BODLEY HEAD 1979   **A**

16 **The Tale of Thomas Mead** (*verse*)   GREENWILLOW 1980   **A**
                                                    BODLEY HEAD 1980   **A**

17 **The Mona Lisa Mystery**   GREENWILLOW 1981   **A**
    (*illus. Laurence Hutchins*)   BODLEY HEAD 1981   **A**

18 **1 Hunter**   GREENWILLOW 1982   **A**
                                                    BODLEY HEAD 1982   **A**

19 **The Curse of the Egyptian Mummy**   GREENWILLOW 1983   **A**
    (*illus. Laurence Hutchins*)   BODLEY HEAD 1983   **A**

20 **King Henry's Palace**   GREENWILLOW 1983   **A**
                                             BODLEY HEAD 1983   **A**

21 **You'll Soon Grow into Them, Titch**   GREENWILLOW 1983   **A**
                                             BODLEY HEAD 1983   **A**

22 **The Very Worst Monster**   GREENWILLOW 1985   **A**
                                             BODLEY HEAD 1985   **A**

23 **The Doorbell Rang**   GREENWILLOW 1986   **A**
                                             BODLEY HEAD 1986   **A**

JANSSON, Tove   *Born in Finland, 1914*

The much-loved 'Moomin' books seem set to soldier on for ever – though it would be interesting to know who coined the word. (Not the author, since the first in the series – *Comet in Moominland* – was first published in Finnish as *Kometjakten*; maybe the translator, Elizabeth Portch?). And, for the uninitiated, a moomin is a cross between one of your more approachable hippopotamuses, and one of the corpulent but lovable Muppets. Illustrations by the author.

1	**Finn Family Moomintroll**	BENN 1950	D

Actually the second *in the series – see 2 – but the first to be published in English. It was published in America in 1952 by Bobbs Merrill as* The Happy Moomins, *and reissued by Walck in 1965 under the original English title.*

2	**Comet in Moominland**	BENN 1951	D
		WALCK 1968	A

The first in the series – see above – and published in Finland in 1946.

3	**The Exploits of Moominpappa**	BENN 1952	C
		WALCK 1966	A
4	**Moomin, Mymble and Little My**	BENN 1953	C
5	**Moominsummer Madness**	BENN 1955	C
		WALCK 1961	A
6	**Moominland Midwinter**	BENN 1958	C
		WALCK 1962	A
7	**Who Will Comfort Toffle?**	BENN 1960	B
		WALCK 1969	A
8	**Tales from Moominvalley**	BENN 1963	B
		WALCK 1964	A
9	**Moominpappa at Sea**	BENN 1966	B
		WALCK 1967	B
10	**Moominvalley in November**	BENN 1971	B
		WALCK 1971	B

JARRELL, Randall   *American. Born in Tennessee, 1914. Died 1965*

Sensitive and intriguing books by one of America's leading poets, although I think that much of the fiction would not be immediately accessible to its intended audience. Jarrell is sought after (particularly, as you would expect, in America) and apart from the most recent one or two, none of the following will be easy to come by.

In addition to these children's books, Jarrell published about twenty for adults – very largely verse, but including one novel.

1	**The Rabbit Catcher and Other Fairy Tales of Ludwig Bechstein**	MACMILLAN US 1962 MACMILLAN UK 1962	H G
2	**The Golden Bird and Other Fairy Tales by the Brothers Grimm**	MACMILLAN US 1962 MACMILLAN UK 1962	G F
3	**The Gingerbread Rabbit** (*fiction*) (*illus. Garth Williams*)	MACMILLAN US 1964 MACMILLAN UK 1964	G F
4	**The Bat-Poet** (*fiction*) (*illus. Maurice Sendak*)	MACMILLAN US 1964 MACMILLAN UK 1966	H G
5	**The Animal Family** (*fiction*) (*illus. Maurice Sendak*)	PANTHEON 1965 HART-DAVIS 1967	G E
6	**Snow-White and the Seven Dwarfs: A Tale from the Brothers Grimm** (*illus. Nancy Ekholm Burkert*)	FARRAR STRAUS 1972 KESTREL 1974	C C
7	**The Juniper Tree and other Tales from Grimm** (*illus. Maurice Sendak*)	FARRAR STRAUSS 1973 BODLEY HEAD 1974	C C
8	**Fly by Night** (*fiction*) (*illus. Maurice Sendak*)	FARRAR STRAUS 1976 BODLEY HEAD 1977	C C
9	**A Bat is Born** (*verse*) (*illus. John Schoenherr*)	DOUBLEDAY 1978	B
10	**The Fisherman and His Wife** (*tale*) (*illus. Margot Zemach*)	FARRAR STRAUS 1980	B

Also of interest (though not dwelling on Jarrell's books for juveniles):
ED. ROBERT LOWELL, PETER TAYLOR & ROBERT PENN WARREN: **Randall Jarrell 1914–1965** (FARRAR STRAUS US 1967)

JOHNS, W.E. *Born in Hertfordshire, 1893. Died 1968*

And now for something completely different. It matters not that Johns' literary style is less than earth-shattering, nor must one give a jot for all the hysterical accusations of chauvinism, xenophobia and all the rest of it – simply because it doesn't matter whether or not they are true. This also applies to that other much-maligned author, Frank Richards; what both Johns and Richards did, of course, was to create deathless heroes that are still pursued today by youngsters of, shall we say, all ages. Collecting good dust-wrappered copies of even the most recent titles is not that easy any more – while the early ones have all but disappeared. However, as will be seen by the sheer volume of the ensuing listing, the scope is wide – and as I have gone to the considerable trouble of writing them all down for you, the very least you can do is attempt to collect them. Chocks away!

1	**The Camels are Coming**	JOHN HAMILTON 1932	**I**
2	**The Cruise of the Condor: A Biggles Story**	JOHN HAMILTON 1933	**I**
3	**Biggles of the Camel Squadron**	JOHN HAMILTON 1934	**I**
4	**Biggles Flies Again**	JOHN HAMILTON 1934	**H**
5	**Biggles Learns to Fly**	BOYS' FRIEND LIBRARY 1935	**F**
6	**Biggles Flies East** (*illus. Howard Leigh & Alfred Sindall*)	OUP 1935	**G**
7	**Biggles Hits the Trail** (*illus. Howard Leigh & Alfred Sindall*)	OUP 1935	**G**
8	**Biggles in France**	BOYS' FRIEND LIBRARY 1935	**F**
9	**The Black Peril: A Biggles Story** *This was reissued by Boys' Friend Library in 1938 as* Biggles Flies East, *but this is* not *the same as 6.*	HAMILTON 1935	**G**
10	**Biggles in Africa** (*illus. Howard Leigh & Alfred Sindall*)	OUP 1936	**F**
11	**Biggles & Co** (*illus. Howard Leigh & Alfred Sindall*)	OUP 1936	**F**

12	**Biggles – Air Commodore** (*illus. Howard Leigh & Alfred Sindall*)	OUP 1937	F
13	**Biggles Flies West** (*illus. Howard Leigh & Alfred Sindall*)	OUP 1937	F
14	**Biggles Flies South** (*illus. Howard Leigh & Jack Nicolle*)	OUP 1938	F
15	**Biggles Goes to War** (*illus. Howard Leigh & Martin Tyas*)	OUP 1938	F
16	**Champion of the Main** (*illus. H. Gooderman*)	OUP 1938	F
17	**Biggles Flies North** (*illus. Howard Leigh & Will Narraway*)	OUP 1939	F
18	**Biggles in Spain** (*illus. Howard Leigh & J. Abbey*)	OUP 1939	F
19	**The Rescue Flight: A Biggles Story** (*illus. Howard Leigh & Alfred Sindall*)	OUP 1939	F
20	**Biggles in the Baltic** (*illus. Howard Leigh & Alfred Sindall*)	OUP 1940	E
21	**Biggles in the South Seas** (*illus. Norman Howard*)	OUP 1940	E
22	**Biggles – Secret Agent** (*illus. Howard Leigh & Alfred Sindall*)	OUP 1940	E
23	**Worrals of the W.A.A.F.** (*illus. Leslie Stead*)	LUTTERWORTH PRESS 1941	D
24	**Spitfire Parade: Stories of Biggles in War-time** (*illus. Ratcliffe Wilson*)	OUP 1941	E
25	**Biggles Sees It Through** (*illus. Howard Leigh & Alfred Sindall*)	OUP 1941	E
26	**Biggles Defies the Swastika** (*illus. Howard Leigh & Alfred Sindall*)	OUP 1941	E
27	**Biggles in the Jungle** (*illus. Terence Cuneo*)	OUP 1942	E
28	**Sinister Service** (*illus. Stuart Tresilian*)	OUP 1942	E

29	**Biggles Sweeps the Desert** (*illus. Leslie Stead*)	HODDER & STOUGHTON 1942	C
30	**Worrals Flies Again** (*illus. Leslie Stead*)	HODDER & STOUGHTON 1942	C
31	**Worrals Carries On** (*illus. Leslie Stead*)	LUTTERWORTH PRESS 1942	C
32	**Worrals on the War-path** (*illus. Leslie Stead*)	HODDER & STOUGHTON 1943	C
33	**Biggles – Charter Pilot** (*illus. Mendoza*)	OUP 1943	C
34	**Biggles 'Fails to Return'** (*illus. Leslie Stead*)	HODDER & STOUGHTON 1943	C
35	**Biggles in Borneo** (*illus. Stuart Tresilian*)	OUP 1943	C
36	**King of the Commandos** (*illus. Leslie Stead*)	UNIVERSITY OF LONDON PRESS 1943	C
37	**Gimlet Goes Again** (*illus. Leslie Stead*)	UNIVERSITY OF LONDON PRESS 1943	C
38	**Worrals Goes West** (*illus. Leslie Stead*)	HODDER & STOUGHTON 1944	C

Unless otherwise stated, ALL the following books are illustrated by Leslie Stead:

39	**Biggles in the Orient**	HODDER & STOUGHTON 1945	C
40	**Worrals of the Islands:** **A Story of the War in the Pacific**	HODDER & STOUGHTON 1945	C
41	**Biggles Delivers the Goods**	HODDER & STOUGHTON 1946	C
42	**Gimlet Comes Home**	UNIVERSITY OF LONDON PRESS 1946	C
43	**Sergeant Bigglesworth CID**	HODDER & STOUGHTON 1947	C
44	**Comrades in Arms**	HODDER & STOUGHTON 1947	C

45	**Gimlet Mops Up**	BROCKHAMPTON PRESS 1947	C
46	**Worrals in the Wilds**	HODDER & STOUGHTON 1947	
47	**Biggles Hunts Big Game**	HODDER & STOUGHTON 1948	C
48	**Biggles' Second Case**	HODDER & STOUGHTON 1948	C
49	**Gimlet's Oriental Quest**	BROCKHAMPTON PRESS 1948	C
50	**The Rustlers of Rattlesnake Valley**	NELSON 1948	C
51	**Worrals Down Under**	LUTTERWORTH PRESS 1948	C
52	**Biggles Breaks the Silence**	HODDER & STOUGHTON 1949	C
53	**Biggles Takes a Holiday**	HODDER & STOUGHTON 1949	C
54	**Gimlet Lends a Hand**	BROCKHAMPTON PRESS 1949	C
55	**Worrals Goes Afoot**	LUTTERWORTH PRESS 1949	C
56	**Worrals in the Wastelands**	LUTTERWORTH PRESS 1949	C
57	**Worrals Investigates**	LUTTERWORTH PRESS 1950	C
58	**Biggles Gets His Men**	HODDER & STOUGHTON 1950	C
59	**Gimlet Bores In**	BROCKHAMPTON PRESS 1950	C
60	**Another Job for Biggles**	HODDER & STOUGHTON 1951	C
61	**Biggles Goes to School**	HODDER & STOUGHTON 1951	C

62 **Biggles Works It Out**   HODDER & STOUGHTON   C
                                                        1951

63 **Gimlet Off the Map**   BROCKHAMPTON PRESS   C
                                                        1951

64 **Biggles – Air Detective**   LATIMER 1952   C

65 **Biggles Follows On**   HODDER & STOUGHTON   C
                                                        1952

66 **Biggles Takes the Case**   HODDER & STOUGHTON   C
                                                        1952

67 **Gimlet Gets the Answer**   BROCKHAMPTON PRESS   C
                                                        1952

68 **Biggles and the Black Raider**   HODDER & STOUGHTON
                                                        1953

69 **Biggles in the Blue**   BROCKHAMPTON PRESS   C
                                                        1953

70 **Biggles in the Gobi**   HODDER & STOUGHTON   C
                                                        1953

71 **Biggles of the Special Air Police**   THAMES 1953   C

72 **Biggles and the Pirate Treasure and   BROCKHAMPTON PRESS   C
    other Biggles Adventures**   1954

73 **Biggles Cuts It Fine**   HODDER & STOUGHTON   C
                                                        1954

74 **Biggles, Foreign Legionnaire**   HODDER & STOUGHTON   C
                                                        1954

75 **Biggles, Pioneer Airfighter**   THAMES 1954   C

76 **Gimlet Takes a Job**   BROCKHAMPTON PRESS   C
                                                        1954

77 **Kings of Space**   HODDER & STOUGHTON
                                                        1954

78 **Adventure Bound**   NELSON 1955   C
    (*illus. Douglas Relf*)

79 **Biggles' Chinese Puzzle and Other   BROCKHAMPTON PRESS   C
    Biggles Adventures**   1955

80	**Biggles in Australia**	HODDER & STOUGHTON 1955	C
81	**Return to Mars**	HODDER & STOUGHTON 1955	C
82	**Biggles of 266**	THAMES 1956	C
83	**Biggles Takes Charge**	BROCKHAMPTON PRESS 1956	C
84	**No Rest for Biggles**	HODDER & STOUGHTON 1956	C
85	**Now to the Stars**	HODDER & STOUGHTON 1956	C
86	**Biggles Makes Ends Meet**	HODDER & STOUGHTON 1957	C
87	**Adventure Unlimited** (*illus. Douglas Relf*)	NELSON 1957	C
88	**Biggles of the Interpol**	BROCKHAMPTON PRESS 1957	C
89	**Biggles on the Home Front**	HODDER & STOUGHTON 1957	C
90	**The Outer Space**	HODDER & STOUGHTON 1957	C
91	**Biggles Buries a Hatchet**	BROCKHAMPTON PRESS 1958	C
92	**Biggles on Mystery Island**	HODDER & STOUGHTON 1958	C
93	**Biggles Presses On**	BROCKHAMPTON PRESS 1958	C
94	**The Edge of Beyond**	HODDER & STOUGHTON 1958	C
95	**Biggles at World's End**	BROCKHAMPTON PRESS 1959	C
96	**Biggles' Combined Operation**	HODDER & STOUGHTON 1959	C

97	Biggles in Mexico	BROCKHAMPTON PRESS 1959	C
98	The Death Rays of Ardilla	HODDER & STOUGHTON 1959	C
99	Adventures of the Junior Detection Club	PARRISH 1960	C
100	Biggles and the Leopards of Zinn	BROCKHAMPTON PRESS 1960	B
101	Biggles Goes Home	HODDER & STOUGHTON 1960	B
102	To Worlds Unknown	HODDER & STOUGHTON 1960	B
103	Where the Golden Eagle Soars (*illus. Colin Gibson*)	HODDER & STOUGHTON 1960	B
104	The Quest for the Perfect Planet	HODDER & STOUGHTON 1961	B
105	Biggles and the Missing Millionaire	BROCKHAMPTON PRESS 1961	B
106	Biggles and the Poor Rich Boy	BROCKHAMPTON PRESS 1961	B
107	Biggles Forms a Syndicate	HODDER & STOUGHTON 1961	B
108	Biggles Goes Alone	HODDER & STOUGHTON 1962	B
109	Biggles Sets a Trap	HODDER & STOUGHTON 1962	B
110	Orchids for Biggles	BROCKHAMPTON PRESS 1962	B
111	Worlds of Wonder: More Adventures in Space	HODDER & STOUGHTON 1962	B
112	Biggles and the Plane That Disappeared	HODDER & STOUGHTON 1963	B
113	Biggles Flies to Work	DEAN 1963	B

114 **Biggles' Special Case** — BROCKHAMPTON PRESS 1963 — B

115 **Biggles Takes a Hand** — HODDER & STOUGHTON 1963 — B

116 **Biggles Takes It Rough** — BROCKHAMPTON PRESS 1963 — B

117 **The Man Who Vanished into Space** — HODDER & STOUGHTON 1963 — B

118 **Biggles and the Black Mask** — HODDER & STOUGHTON 1964 — B

119 **Biggles and the Lost Sovereigns** — BROCKHAMPTON PRESS 1964 — B

120 **Biggles Investigates, and Other Stories of the Air Police** — BROCKHAMPTON PRESS 1965 — B

121 **Biggles and the Blue Moon** — BROCKHAMPTON PRESS 1965 — B

122 **Biggles and the Plot That Failed** — BROCKHAMPTON PRESS 1965 — B

123 **Biggles Looks Back** — HODDER & STOUGHTON 1965 — B

124 **Biggles Scores a Bull** — HODDER & STOUGHTON 1965 — B

125 **Biggles in the Terai** — BROCKHAMPTON PRESS 1966 — B

126 **Biggles and the Gun Runners** — BROCKHAMPTON PRESS 1966 — B

127 **Biggles and the Penitent Thief** — BROCKHAMPTON PRESS 1967 — B

128 **Biggles Sorts It Out** — BROCKHAMPTON PRESS 1967 — B

129 **Biggles and the Dark Intruder** — KNIGHT 1967 — A

130 **Biggles in the Underworld** — BROCKHAMPTON PRESS 1968 — B

131	The Boy Biggles	DEAN 1968	A
132	Biggles and the Deep Blue Sea	BROCKHAMPTON PRESS 1968	B
133	Biggles and the Little Green God	BROCKHAMPTON PRESS 1969	B
134	Biggles and the Noble Lord	BROCKHAMPTON PRESS 1969	B
135	Biggles Sees Too Much	BROCKHAMPTON PRESS 1970	B

Also of interest:

JOHN PEARSON: **Biggles: The Authorised Biography** (SIDGWICK & JACKSON 1979)

PETER BERRESFORD ELLIS & PIERS WILLIAMS: **By Jove, Biggles: The Life of Captain W.E. Johns** (W.H. ALLEN, 1981)

JONES, Diana Wynne   *Born in London, 1934*

This somewhat remarkable writer has produced eighteen full-length works in just fifteen years, and such is her skill in unleashing fantasy of a quite extraordinary kind, and allowing us to see the magic work within ordinary and quite often sad and troubled young lives, that her reputation was made almost instantly. She clearly intends to be prolific, so one ought to set about gathering her *oeuvre* fairly soon – already a task easier said than done.

1	**Wilkins' Tooth** (*illus. Julia Rodber*)	MACMILLAN 1973	D
2	**Witch's Business** *Same as 1.*	DUTTON 1974	B
3	**The Ogre Downstairs**	MACMILLAN 1974	C
		DUTTON 1975	B
4	**Eight Days of Luke**	MACMILLAN 1975	C
5	**Cart and Cwidder**	MACMILLAN 1975	C
		ATHENEUM 1977	B
6	**Dogsbody**	MACMILLAN 1975	C
		GREENWILLOW 1977	B

7	**Power of Three**	MACMILLAN 1976	B
		GREENWILLOW 1977	A
8	**Charmed Life**	MACMILLAN 1977	B
		GREENWILLOW 1977	A
9	**Drowned Amnet**	MACMILLAN 1977	B
		ATHENEUM 1978	A
10	**Who Got Rid of Angus Flint?** (*illus. John Sewell*)	EVANS 1978	B
11	**The Spellcoats**	MACMILLAN 1979	B
		ATHENEUM 1979	A
12	**The Magicians of Caprona**	MACMILLAN 1980	B
		GREENWILLOW 1980	A
13	**The Four Grannies** (*illus. Thelma Lambert*)	HAMISH HAMILTON 1980	B
14	**The Homeward Bounders**	MACMILLAN 1981	B
		GREENWILLOW 1981	A
15	**The Time of the Ghost**	MACMILLAN 1981	B
16	**Witch Week**	MACMILLAN 1982	B
		GREENWILLOW 1982	A
17	**Archer's Goon**	METHUEN 1984	B
		GREENWILLOW 1984	A
18	**Fire and Hemlock**	METHUEN 1985	B
		GREENWILLOW 1985	A
19	**A Tale of the City**	METHUEN 1987	B

JOYCE, James   *Born in Ireland, 1882. Died 1941*

Admittedly not the first name one would think of when discussing children's books, but the one posthumously published item listed below is rather charming. It was actually a short letter written to Joyce's grandson, the postscript of which informs us that the Devil – like Joyce himself – had a language all of his own: Bellsybabble.

| 1 | **The Cat and the Devil**
 (*illus. Gerald Rose*) | FABER 1965 | E |

KASTNER, Erich *Born in Germany, 1899. Died 1974*

Although a translation, a children's classic, and one that seems to be remembered by all with great fondness. Kastner wrote other books, and the character Emil appears again, but none captures the great appeal of the following:

1	**Emil and the Detectives**	CAPE 1930	**E**
	(*illus. the author*)	DOUBLEDAY 1930	**D**
	Introduction by Walter de la Mare. The book		
	was first published in Germany in 1929 as		
	Emil und die Detektive.		

KEEPING, Charles *Born in London, 1924. Died 1988*

Although – as will be seen throughout this book – Keeping was primarily an illustrator of other people's work, his own books are really very attractive, although I can see children warming much more readily to the pictures than to the words. The narratives are less than stupendous, it must be said, but the illustrations come across very forcibly – largely, I imagine, because they were inspired by the author's own thoughts.

1	**Black Dolly**	BROCKHAMPTON PRESS 1966	**D**
2	**Molly o' the Moors** *Same as 1.*	WORLD US 1966	**C**
3	**Shaun and the Cart-horse**	OUP 1966 WATTS 1966	**D** **C**
4	**Charley, Charlotte and the Golden Canary**	OUP 1967 WATTS 1967	**C** **C**
5	**Alfie and the Ferry Boat**	OUP 1968	**C**
6	**Alfie Finds the Other Side of the World** *Same as 5.*	WATTS 1968	**C**
7	**Joseph's Yard**	OUP 1969 WATTS 1969	**C** **B**
8	**Through the Window**	OUP 1970 WATTS 1970	**C** **B**

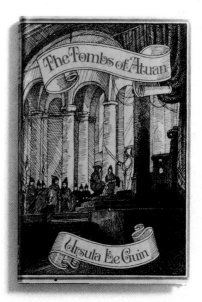

Ursula le Guin's highly respected 'Earthsea' trilogy.

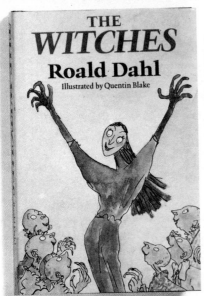
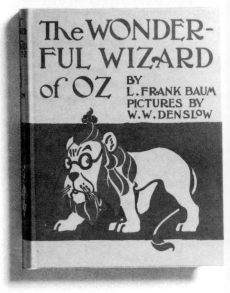

A mischievous bevy of witches and wizards, with artwork by W.W. Denslow, Jill Murphy herself, and Quentin Blake.

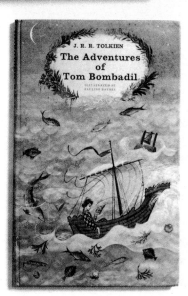

The classic Peake trilogy, with artwork by the author, together with some lively verses by
Tolkien illustrated by Pauline Baynes.

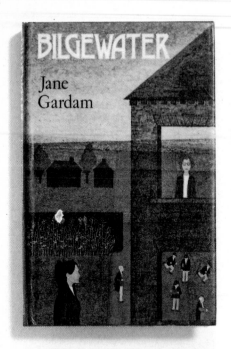
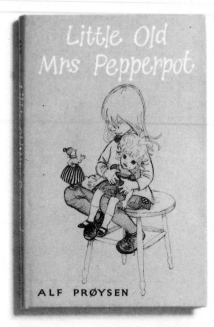
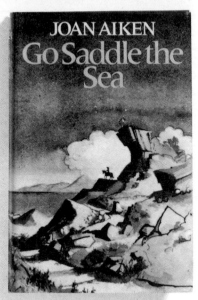

Three by three of the most liked and respected contemporary women children's writers, together with the perhaps incongruously placed but underrated *Mrs Pepperpot*.

9	The Garden Shed	OUP 1971	C
10	The Spider's Web	OUP 1972	C
11	The Nanny Goat and the Fierce Dog	ABELARD SCHUMAN 1973	C
		PHILLIPS 1974	C
12	Richard	OUP 1973	C
13	The Railway Passage	OUP 1974	B
14	Wasteground Circus	OUP 1975	B
15	Inter-city	OUP 1977	B
16	Miss Emily and the Bird of Make-believe	HUTCHINSON 1978	B
17	Willie's Fire-engine	OUP 1980	B
18	Sammy Streetsinger	OUP 1984	B
19	Charles Keeping's Book of Classic Ghost Stories	BLACKIE 1986	B
20	Charles Keeping's Tales of the Macabre	BLACKIE 1987	B

KING, Clive *Born in Surrey, 1924*

A very inventive writer, quite rightly best known for the Ardizzone illustrated *Stig of the Dump*, originally published – unusually – by Penguin. King is known and read, of course, but he is not yet a 'big name' with collectors, and so it might be perfectly possible to gather them all without *too* much fuss and expense.

1	Hamid of Aleppo (*illus. Giovanetti*)	MACMILLAN US 1958	C
2	The Town That Went South (*illus. Maurice Bartlett*)	MACMILLAN US 1959	C
		PENGUIN 1961	B
3	Stig of the Dump (*illus. Edward Ardizzone*)	PENGUIN 1963	C
4	The Twenty Two Letters (*illus. Richard Kennedy*)	HAMISH HAMILTON 1966	C
		COWARD McCANN 1967	B

5	**The Night the Water Came** (*illus. Mark Peppe*)	LONGMAN 1973 CROWELL 1982	**B** **A**
6	**Snakes and Ladders** (*illus. Richard Kennedy*)	KESTREL 1975	**B**
7	**Me and My Million**	KESTREL 1976 CROWELL 1979	**B** **A**
8	**Readers:** High Jacks, Low Jacks; First Day Out; Accident; The Secret. (*illus. Jacqueline Atkinson*)	BENN 1976	**A** **Each**
9	**The Devil's Cut** (*illus. Val Biro*)	HODDER & STOUGHTON 1978	**B**
10	**The Birds from Africa** (*illus. Diana Groves*)	MACDONALD 1980	**B**
11	**Ninny's Boat** (*illus. Ian Newsham*)	KESTREL 1980 MACMILLAN US 1981	**B** **B**
12	**The Sound of Propellers** (*illus. David Parkins*)	VIKING KESTREL 1986	**B**

KING-SMITH, Dick   *Born in Gloucestershire, 1922*

There is something of a cult-following for Dick King-Smith, but collectors take note because a lot of the humour (and there is a *lot* of humour) appeals to an audience rather more mature than that for which it is primarily intended. The author's farming background holds him in good stead when it comes to the animals who – can one say *people*? – his books, while the pace and ability to tell a good and exciting tale seem to come naturally and without effort, though this is probably not the case at all.

1	**The Fox Busters** (*illus. Jon Miller*)	GOLLANCZ 1978	**C**
2	**Daggie Dogfoot** (*illus. Mary Rayner*) *This was published in US by Viking Press in* *1982 as* Pigs Might Fly (**A**).	GOLLANCZ 1980	**C**
3	**The Mouse Butcher** (*illus. Wendy Smith*)	GOLLANCZ 1981 VIKING PRESS 1982	**B** **A**

4	**Magnus Powermouse** (*illus. Mary Rayner*)	GOLLANCZ 1982	B
5	**The Queen's Nose** (*illus. Jill Bennett*)	GOLLANCZ 1983	B
6	**The Sheep-Pig** (*illus. Mary Rayner*)	GOLLANCZ 1983	B
7	**Harry's Mad** (*illus. Jill Bennett*)	GOLLANCZ 1984	B
8	**Lightning Fred** (*illus. Michael Bragg*)	HEINEMANN 1985	B
9	**Saddlebottom** (*illus. Alice Englander*)	GOLLANCZ 1985	B
10	**E.S.P.**	MALIN 1986	B
11	**H. Prince** (*illus. Martin Honeysett*)	WALKER 1986	A
12	**Dumpling** (*illus. Jo Davies*)	HAMISH HAMILTON 1986	B
13	**Noah's Brother** (*illus. Ian Newsham*)	GOLLANCZ 1986	B
14	**Yob** (*illus. Abigail Pizer*)	HEINEMANN 1986	B
15	**The Hodgeheg** (*illus. Linda Birch*)	HAMISH HAMILTON 1987	B
16	**Tumbleweed** (*illus. Ian Newsham*)	GOLLANCZ 1987	B
17	**Cuckoobush Farm** (*illus. Kazuko*)	ORCHARD 1987	A
18	**Friends and Brothers** (*illus. Susan Hellard*)	HEINEMANN 1987	B

KIPLING, Rudyard   *British. Born in India, 1865. Died 1936*

Writing for children was just one of Kipling's formidable talents, and yet if he had done nothing else at all his name would live on for ever. As will be seen below, some of his greatest stuff is not *quite* twentieth century, but it seems daft to leave them out – consequently, there follows a complete listing of his books primarily intended for children (of all ages up to and beyond 101) in addition to which Kipling published well over a hundred other works.

1	**The Jungle Book**	MACMILLAN 1894	**M**
	(*illus. J. Lockwood Kipling* et al)	CENTURY 1894	**I**
2	**The Second Jungle Book**	MACMILLAN 1895	**G**
	(*illus. J. Lockwood Kipling*)	CENTURY 1895	**E**
3	**'Captains Courageous':**	MACMILLAN 1897	**C**
	A Story of the Grand Banks	CENTURY 1897	**C**
	(*illus. I.W. Taber*)		
4	**Stalky & Co**	MACMILLAN 1899	**I**
	A revised edition was published in 1929 by	DOUBLEDAY 1899	**G**
	Macmillan and in 1930 by Doubleday under		
	the title The Complete Stalky & Co.		
5	**Kim**	DOUBLEDAY 1901	**F**
	(*illus. J. Lockwood Kipling*)	MACMILLAN 1901	**D**
6	**Just So Stories for Little Children**	MACMILLAN 1902	**K**
	(*illus. the author*)	DOUBLEDAY 1902	**I**
7	**Puck of Pook's Hill**	MACMILLAN 1906	**C**
	(*illus. H.R. Millar*)	DOUBLEDAY 1906	**B**
8	**Kipling Stories and Poems Every**	DOUBLEDAY 1909	**C**
	Child Should Know		
	(*illus. Charles Livingston Bull* et al)		
9	**Rewards and Fairies**	MACMILLAN 1910	**C**
	(*illus. Frank Craig*)	DOUBLEDAY 1910	**B**
10	**Land and Sea Tales for Scouts and**	MACMILLAN 1923	**C**
	Guides	DOUBLEDAY 1923	**B**
11	**Ham the Porcupine**	DOUBLEDAY 1935	**C**

Also of interest:

ROSEMARY SUTCLIFF: **Rudyard Kipling** (BODLEY HEAD 1960)

J.I.M. STEWART: **Rudyard Kipling** (GOLLANZ 1966, DODD MEAD US 1966)

KINGLSEY AMIS: **Kipling and His World** (THAMES & HUDSON 1975, SCRIBNER US 1976)

ANGUS WILSON: **The Strange Ride of Rudyard Kipling: His Life and Works** (SECKER & WARBURG 1977, VIKING PRESS US 1978)

le GUIN, Ursula K. *American. Born in California, 1929*

Still best known, I suppose, for her adult fiction – but Ursula le Guin's reputation in the field of children's literature is growing all the time, while the fantasy trilogy *Earthsea* is well on its way to becoming a minor modern classic.

1	**A Wizard of Earthsea**	PARNASSUS PRESS US 1967	**C**
	(*illus. Gail Garraty*)	GOLLANCZ 1971	**C**
2	**The Tombs of Atuan**	ATHENEUM 1971	**B**
	(*illus. Gail Garraty*)	GOLLANCZ 1972	**B**
3	**The Farthest Shore**	ATHENEUM 1972	**B**
	(*illus. Gail Garranty*)	GOLLANCZ 1973	**B**

1–3 form a trilogy. This was published in one volume as Earthsea *by Gollancz in 1977.*

4	**Very Far Away from Anywhere Else**	ATHENEUM 1976	**B**
5	**A Very Long Way from Anywhere Else**	GOLLANCZ 1976	**B**

Same as 4.

6	**Leese Webster**	ATHENEUM 1979	**B**
	(*illus. James Brunsman*)	GOLLANCZ 1981	**B**
7	**The Beginning Place**	HARPER 1980	**B**
8	**Threshold**	GOLLANCZ 1980	**B**

Same as 7.

LEWIS, C. Day *Born in Ireland, 1904. Died 1972*

Although the recipient of countless awards for poetry (culminating in the Laureateship itself), C. Day Lewis is of most interest to collectors for his detective novels, written under the pseudonym Nicholas Blake. His very few children's books are notable too, however – particularly *The Otterbury Incident*, which is something of a classic.

1	**Dick Willoughby**	BLACKWELL 1933	**D**
		RANDOM HOUSE 1938	**C**
2	**Poetry for You: A Book for Boys and Girls on the Enjoyment of Poetry**	BLACKWELL 1944	**C**
		OUP US 1947	**B**

3	**The Otterbury Incident**	PUTNAM 1948	**G**
	(*illus. Edward Ardizzone*)	VIKING PRESS 1949	**E**

Also of interest:
SEAN DAY LEWIS: **C. Day Lewis: An English Literary Life** (WEIDENFELD & NICOLSON 1980)

LEWIS, C.S. *Born in Northern Ireland, 1898. Died 1963*

A hugely prolific writer in almost every field imaginable: philosophy, religion, literary criticism, science fiction, poetry – and a series of books for children that rank among the great classics of the century. Adored by children and academics alike, these books are *extremely* collectable, sought-after, scarce – and pricey. And worth every penny.

The following are known collectively as 'The Chronicles of Narnia'. All are illustrated by Pauline Baynes.

1	**The Lion, the Witch and the Wardrobe**	BLES 1950 MACMILLAN US 1950	**K** **H**
2	**Prince Caspian: The Return to Narnia**	BLES 1951 MACMILLAN US 1951	**G** **E**
3	**The Voyage of the 'Dawn Treader'**	BLES 1952 MACMILLAN US 1952	**F** **D**
4	**The Silver Chair**	BLES 1953 MACMILLAN US 1953	**F** **D**
5	**The Horse and His Boy**	BLES 1954 MACMILLAN US 1954	**F** **D**
6	**The Magician's Nephew**	BODLEY HEAD 1955 MACMILLAN US 1955	**F** **D**
7	**The Last Battle**	BODLEY HEAD 1956 MACMILLAN US 1956	**E** **C**

Also of interest:
ROGER LANCELYN GREEN: **C.S. Lewis** (BODLEY HEAD 1963, WALCK US 1963)
PAUL F. FORD: **Companion to Narnia** (HARPER US 1980)

LINGARD, Joan   *Born in Edinburgh*

Joan Lingard had published six novels for adults before turning to children's fiction, but these are pretty adult too. They tend to be set in Ulster during the 'troubles', and the problems connected with sex, violence and so on are never ducked. Rather daunting, it may sound – and it can be. But there is a vigour in the writing, an honesty, and a compulsive readability that together have earned Lingard a strong and growing following.

1	**The Twelfth Day of July**	HAMISH HAMILTON 1970	C
		NELSON US 1972	B
2	**Across the Barricades**	HAMISH HAMILTON 1972	C
		NELSON US 1973	B
3	**Into Exile**	HAMISH HAMILTON 1973	C
		NELSON US 1973	B
4	**Frying as Usual** *(illus. Priscilla Clive)*	HAMISH HAMILTON 1973	C
5	**The Clearance**	HAMISH HAMILTON 1974	B
		NELSON US 1974	A
6	**The Resettling**	HAMISH HAMILTON 1975	B
		NELSON US 1975	A
7	**A Proper Place**	HAMISH HAMILTON 1975	B
		NELSON US 1975	A
8	**The Pilgrimage**	HAMISH HAMILTON 1976	B
		NELSON US 1977	A
9	**Hostages to Fortune**	HAMISH HAMILTON 1976	B
		NELSON US 1977	A
10	**The Reunion** *5, 6, 8 & 10 collectively form the* 'Maggie' *series, televised during 1981 and 1982.*	HAMISH HAMILTON 1977 NELSON US 1978	B A
11	**Snake Among the Sunflowers**	HAMISH HAMILTON 1977	B
		NELSON US 1977	A
12	**The Gooseberry**	HAMISH HAMILTON 1978	B
13	**Odd Girl Out** *Same as 12.*	ELSEVIER NELSON US 1979	A

14	**The File on Fraulein Berg**	MACRAE 1980	**B**
		ELSEVIER NELSON US 1980	**A**
15	**Strangers in the House**	HAMISH HAMILTON 1981	**B**
16	**The Freedom Machine**	HAMISH HAMILTON 1986	**B**
17	**The Guilty Party**	HAMISH HAMILTON 1987	**B**

LIVELY, Penelope   *British. Born in Egypt, 1933*

In the last ten or so years, Penelope Lively has published half a dozen works for adults (three of which have been short-listed for the Booker Prize and one of which won it) but it is still very much for her children's writing that she is best known and collected. Her earliest work has been criticized for being derivative and a little predictable (although it maintains its hold on the children for whom it was intended), but later and more accomplished novels – notably *The Ghost of Thomas Kempe* – are praised to the skies by just about everyone. Lively is very popular and collected already, but it might still be possible to gather the lot without *too* much expense.

1	**Astercote**	HEINEMANN 1970	**D**
	(*illus. Antony Maitland*)	DUTTON 1971	**C**
2	**The Whispering Knights**	HEINEMANN 1971	**C**
	(*illus. Gareth Floyd*)	DUTTON 1976	**B**
3	**The Wild Hunt of Hagworthy**	HEINEMANN 1971	**C**
	(*illus. Juliet Mozley*)		
4	**The Wild Hunt of the Ghost Hounds**	DUTTON 1972	**B**
	Same as 3.		
5	**The Driftway**	HEINEMANN 1972	**C**
		DUTTON 1973	**B**
6	**The Ghost of Thomas Kempe**	HEINEMANN 1973	**C**
	(*illus. Antony Maitland*)	DUTTON 1973	**B**
7	**The House in Norham Gardens**	HEINEMANN 1974	**C**
		DUTTON 1974	**B**
8	**Going Back**	HEINEMANN 1975	**B**
		DUTTON 1975	**A**

9	**Boy Without a Name** (*illus. Ann Dalton*)	HEINEMANN 1975 PARNASSUS PRESS 1975	**B** **A**
10	**A Stitch in Time**	HEINEMANN 1976 DUTTON 1976	**B** **A**
11	**The Stained Glass Window** (*illus. Michael Pollard*)	ABELARD SCHUMAN 1976	**B**
12	**Fanny's Sister** (*illus. John Lawrence*)	HEINEMANN 1976 DUTTON 1980	**B** **A**
13	**The Voyage of QV66** (*illus. Harold Jones*)	HEINEMANN 1978 DUTTON 1979	**B** **A**
14	**Fanny and the Monsters** (*illus. John Lawrence*)	HEINEMANN 1979	**B**
15	**Fanny and the Battle of Potter's Piece** (*illus. John Lawrence*)	HEINEMANN 1980	**B**
16	**The Revenge of Samuel Stokes**	HEINEMANN 1981 DUTTON 1981	**B** **A**
17	**Uninvited Ghosts and Other Stories for Children** (*illus. John Lawrence*)	HEINEMANN 1984 DUTTON 1984	**B** **A**
18	**A House Inside Out** (*illus. David Parkins*)	DEUTSCH 1987	**B**

LOFTING, Hugh
Born in Berkshire, 1886. Died 1947

Creator of the most famous vet of all time (*pace* James Herriot) – and what a wonderfully sane loony Dr Dolittle is. The books are absolutely irresistible and deathless – as well as being immensely stylish, due to Lofting's fantastic illustrations and dust-wrapper designs. Very much collected, as is right and proper.

1	**The Story of Dr Dolittle, Being the History of His Peculiar Life and Astonishing Adventures in Foreign Parts**	STOKES 1920	**K**
2	**Doctor Dolittle** *Same as 1.*	CAPE 1922	**I**

3	**The Voyages of Dr Dolittle**	STOKES 1922	**J**
		CAPE 1923	**I**
4	**Dr Dolittle's Post Office**	STOKES 1923	**I**
		CAPE 1924	**H**
5	**The Story of Mrs Tubbs**	STOKES 1923	**G**
		CAPE 1924	**G**
6	**Dr Dolittle's Circus**	STOKES 1924	**I**
		CAPE 1925	**H**
7	**Dr Dolittle's Zoo**	STOKES 1925	**H**
		CAPE 1926	**G**
8	**Dr Dolittle's Caravan**	STOKES 1926	**H**
		CAPE 1927	**G**
9	**Dr Dolittle's Garden**	STOKES 1927	**G**
		CAPE 1928	**D**
10	**Dr Dolittle in the Moon**	STOKES 1928	**E**
		CAPE 1929	**F**
11	**Noisy Nora**	STOKES 1929	**D**
		CAPE 1929	**C**
12	**The Twilight of Magic** (*illus. Lois Lenski*)	STOKES 1930	**E**
		CAPE 1931	**D**
13	**Gub Gub's Book: An Encyclopedia of Food**	STOKES 1932	**E**
		CAPE 1932	**D**
14	**Dr Dolittle's Return**	STOKES 1933	**E**
		CAPE 1933	**D**
15	**Tommy, Tilly and Mrs Tubbs**	STOKES 1936	**D**
		CAPE 1937	**C**
16	**Dr Dolittle and the Secret Lake**	LIPPINCOTT 1948	**D**
		CAPE 1949	**D**
17	**Dr Dolittle and the Green Canary**	LIPPINCOTT 1950	**D**
		CAPE 1951	**D**
18	**Dr Dolittle's Puddleby Adventures**	LIPPINCOTT 1952	**D**
		CAPE 1953	**D**

Also of interest:

EDWARD BLISHEN: **Hugh Lofting** *(included in* Three Bodley Head Monographs,
  BODLEY HEAD 1968)

LONDON, Jack   *American. Born in San Francisco 1876. Died 1916*

The author of many macho and sometimes rather depressing novels, but
notable in this work for having produced two enduring tales for older
children, each with a dog as its central theme.

1	**The Call of the Wild**	MACMILLAN US 1903	**I**
	(illus. Philip R. Goodwin & Charles	HEINEMANN 1903	**H**
	Livingston Bull)		
2	**White Fang**	MACMILLAN US 1906	**G**
	(illus. Anon)	METHUEN 1907	**F**

For details of London's other works see:

H.C. WOODBRIDGE: **Jack London: A Bibliography** (TALISMAN PRESS US 1966)

Also of interest:

JOAN LONDON: **Jack London: His Life and Times** (UNIVERSITY OF
  WASHINGTON PRESS US 1968)

MANNING, Rosemary · *Born in Dorset, 1911*

A bit of a sleeper, as far as collectors are concerned – neither her children's books nor her work for adults are particularly enthusiastically sought after, but this may well be due to underestimation – certainly her charming stories concerning Sue and R. Dragon seem set to stay.

1	**Green Smoke**	CONSTABLE 1957	C
	(*illus. Constance Marshall*)	DOUBLEDAY 1957	B
2	**Dragon in Danger**	CONSTABLE 1959	C
	(*illus. Constance Marshall*)	DOUBLEDAY 1960	B
3	**The Dragon's Quest**	CONSTABLE 1961	C
	(*illus. Constance Marshall*)	DOUBLEDAY 1962	B
4	**Arripay**	CONSTABLE 1963	B
	(*illus. Victor Ambrus*)	FARRAR STRAUS 1964	B
5	**Boney was a Warrior**	HAMISH HAMILTON 1966	B
	(*illus. Lynette Hemmant*)		
6	**Heraldry** (*non-fiction*)	BLACK 1966	B
	(*illus. Janet Price*)		
7	**The Rocking Horse**	HAMISH HAMILTON 1970	B
	(*illus. Lynette Hemmant*)		
8	**Railways and Railwaymen** (*non-fiction*)	KESTREL 1977	B
9	**Dragon in the Harbour**	KESTREL 1980	B
	(*illus. Peter Rush*)		

MARCHANT, Bessie · *Born in Kent, 1862. Died 1941*

You may or may not be wondering why I append the enormous list that follows – and, no doubt, by the time I get it typed, I might be wondering the same. But I feel that if one is a fan of the sort of good, clean family adventure that Bessie Marchant offered, then one would probably appreciate all the books, and not just a few. None of them will be wildly expensive – but No. 6 might well have acquired a curiosity value, none of Bessie's making.

1	**The Old House by the Water**	RTS 1894	D
2	**In the Cradle of the North Wind**	NIMMO 1896	C
3	**Weasel Tim**	CULLEY 1897	C

4	**Among the Torches of the Andes**	NIMMO 1898	C
5	**The Bonded Three** (*illus. William Rainey*)	BLACKIE 1898	C
6	**Yuppie**	CULLEY 1898	C
7	**The Girl Captives** (*illus. William Rainey*)	BLACKIE 1899	C
8	**The Humbling of Mark Lester**	MARSHALL 1899	C
9	**Winning His Way**	GALL & INGLIS 1899	C
10	**The Rajah's Daughter; or, The Half-moon Girl**	PARTRIDGE 1899	C
11	**Tell-Tale-Tit**	CULLEY 1899	C
12	**The Ghost of Rock Range**	SPCK 1900	B
13	**Held at Ransom**	BLACKIE 1900	B
14	**Cicely Frome, the Captain's Daughter**	NIMMO 1900	B
15	**In the Toils of the Tribesmen**	GALL & INGLIS 1900	B
16	**From the Scourge of the Tongue**	MELROSE 1900	B
17	**Among Hostile Hordes**	GALL & INGLIS 1901	B
18	**The Fun o' the Fair**	CULLEY 1901	B
19	**In Perilous Times**	GALL & INGLIS 1901	B
20	**That Dreadful Boy!**	CULLEY 1901	B
21	**Three Girls on a Ranch** **Three Girls in Morocco** **Three Girls in Mexico** (*illus. William Rainey*)	BLACKIE 1901–11	B Each
22	**Tommy's Trek**	BLACKIE 1901	B
23	**The Bertrams of Ladywell** (*illus. John Jellicoe*)	WELLS GARDNER 1902	B
24	**A Brave Little Cousin**	SPCK 1902	B
25	**Fleckie**	BLACKIE 1902	B
26	**The House at Brambling Minster**	SPCK 1902	B

27	**Leonard's Temptation**	CULLEY 1902	**B**
28	**The Secret of the Everglades**	BLACKIE 1902	**B**
		MERSHON 1915	**A**
29	**A Heroine of the Sea**	BLACKIE 1903	**B**
30	**Lost on the Saguenay**	COLLINS 1903	**B**
31	**The Owner of Rushcote**	CULLEY 1903	**B**
32	**The Captives of the Kaid**	COLLINS 1904	**B**
33	**Chupsie**	CULLEY 1904	**B**
34	**The Girls of Wakenside**	COLLINS 1904	**B**
35	**Hope's Tryst**	BLACKIE 1904	**B**
36	**Yew Tree Farm**	SPCK 1904	**B**
37	**Caspar's Find**	CULLEY 1905	**B**
38	**A Daughter of the Ranges** (*illus. A.A. Dixon*)	BLACKIE 1905	**B**
39	**The Debt of the Damerals**	CLARKE 1905	**B**
40	**The Mysterious City** (*illus. W.S. Stacey*)	SPCK 1905	**B**
41	**The Queen of Shindy Flat** (*illus. Charles Sheldon*)	WELLS GARDNER 1905	**B**
42	**Athabasca Bill**	SPCK 1906	**B**
43	**A Girl of the Fortunate Isles** (*illus. Paul Hardy*)	BLACKIE 1906	**B**
44	**Kenealy's Ride**	GALL & INGLIS 1906	**B**
45	**Maisie's Discovery** (*illus. R. Tod*)	COLLINS 1906	**B**
46	**Uncle Greg's Man Hunt**	CULLEY 1906	**B**
47	**Darling of Sandy Point** (*illus. Harold Piffard*)	SPCK 1907	**B**
48	**Juliette, the Mail Carrier** (*illus. R. Tod*)	COLLINS 1907	**B**
49	**The Mystery of the Silver Run**	WELLS GARDNER 1907	**B**

50	**No Ordinary Girl**	BLACKIE 1907	**B**
	(*illus. Frances Ewan*)	CALDWELL 1911	**A**
51	**Sisters of Silver Creek**	BLACKIE 1907	**B**
	(*illus. Robert Hope*)		
52	**The Apple Lady**	COLLINS 1908	**B**
	(*illus. G. Soper*)		
53	**A Courageous Girl**	BLACKIE 1908	**B**
	(*illus. William Rainey*)		
54	**Daughters of the Dominion**	BLACKIE 1908	**B**
55	**Rolf the Rebel**	SPCK 1908	**B**
	(*illus. W.S. Stacey*)		
56	**An Island Heroine**	COLLINS 1909	**B**
	(*illus. W.H. Margetson*)		
57	**Jenny's Adventure**	BUTCHER 1909	**B**
58	**The Adventures of Phyllis**	CASSELL 1910	**B**
	(*illus. F. Whiting*)		
59	**The Black Cockatoo**	RTS 1910	**B**
	(*illus. Lancelot Speed*)		
60	**A Countess from Canada**	BLACKIE 1910	**B**
	(*illus. Cyrus Cuneo*)		
61	**Greta's Domain**	BLACKIE 1910	**B**
	(*illus. William Rainey*)		
62	**Molly of One Tree Bend**	BUTCHER 1910	**B**
63	**The Deputy Boss**	SPCK 1910	**B**
	(*illus. Oscar Wilson*)		
64	**The Ferry House Girls**	BLACKIE 1911	**B**
	(*illus. W.R.S. Scott*)		
65	**A Girl of Distinction**	BLACKIE 1911	**B**
	(*illus. William Rainey*)		
66	**Redwood Ranch**	SPCK 1911	**B**
	(*illus. Harold Piffard*)		
67	**A Girl of the Northland**	HODDER & STOUGHTON 1912	**B**
	(*illus. N. Tenison*)		

68	**His Great Surrender** (*illus. Gordon Browne*)	SPCK 1912	**B**
69	**A Princess of Servia** (*illus. William Rainey*)	BLACKIE 1912	**B**
70	**The Sibyl of St Pierre** (*illus. William Rainey*)	WELLS GARDNER 1912	**B**
71	**The Western Scout** (*illus. W.S. Stacey*)	SPCK 1912	**B**
72	**The Youngest Sister** (*illus. William Rainey*)	BLACKIE 1912	**B**
73	**The Adventurous Seven** (*illus. W.R.S. Stott*)	BLACKIE 1913	**B**
74	**The Heroine of the Ranch** (*illus. Cyrus Cuneo*)	BLACKIE 1913	**B**
75	**Denver Wilson's Double** (*illus. W. Douglas Almond*)	BLACKIE 1914	**B**
76	**Helen of the Black Mountain**	BLACKIE 1914	**B**
77	**The Loyalty of Hester Hope** (*illus. William Rainey*)	BLACKIE 1914	**B**
78	**A Mysterious Inheritance**	BLACKIE 1914	**B**
79	**A Girl and a Caravan**	BLACKIE 1915	**B**
80	**Joyce Harrington's Trust**	BLACKIE 1915	**B**
81	**Molly Angel's Adventures**	BLACKIE 1915	**B**
82	**A Canadian Farm Mystery; or, Pam The Pioneer**	BLACKIE 1916	**B**
83	**A Girl Munition Worker**	BLACKIE 1916	**B**
84	**The Unknown Island**	BLACKIE 1916	**B**
85	**The Gold-marked Charm**	BLACKIE 1917	**B**
86	**Lois in Charge; or, A Girl of Grit** (*illus. Cyrus Cuneo*)	BLACKIE 1917	**B**
87	**A V.A.D. in Salonica**	BLACKIE 1917	**B**

88	**Cynthia Wins** (*illus. John E. Sutcliffe*)	BLACKIE 1918	B
89	**A Dangerous Mission** (*illus. Wal Paget*)	BLACKIE 1918	B
90	**Norah to the Rescue** (*illus. W.R.S. Stott*)	BLACKIE 1919	B
91	**A Transport Girl in France**	BLACKIE 1919	B
92	**Sally Makes Good** (*illus. Leo Bates*)	BLACKIE 1920	B
93	**The Girl of the Pampas**	BLACKIE 1921	B
94	**Island Born** (*illus. Leo Bates*)	BLACKIE 1921	B
95	**The Mistress of Purity Gap**	CASSELL 1921 FUNK & WAGNALLS 1922	B B
96	**Harriet Goes A-roaming**	BLACKIE 1922	B
97	**The Fortunes of Prue**	WARD LOCK 1923	B
98	**Rachel Out West** (*illus. Henry Coller*)	BLACKIE 1923	B
99	**A Bid for Safety**	WARD LOCK 1924	B
100	**Diana Carries On**	NELSON 1924	B
101	**The Most Popular Girl in the School**	PARTRIDGE 1924	B
102	**Sylvia's Secret** (*illus. W.E. Wightman*)	BLACKIE 1924	B
103	**By Honour Bound**	NELSON 1925	B
104	**Her Own Kin**	BLACKIE 1925	B
105	**To Save Her School** (*illus. H.L. Bacon*)	PARTRIDGE 1925	B
106	**Delmayne's Adventures**	COLLINS 1925	B
107	**Cousin Peter's Money**	SHELDON 1926	B
108	**Di the Dauntless** (*illus. W.E. Wightman*)	BLACKIE 1926	B

109 Millicent Gwent, Schoolgirl   WARNE 1926   **B**

110 Molly in the West   BLACKIE 1927   **B**
(*illus. F.E. Hiley*)

111 The Two New Girls   WARNE 1927   **B**

112 Glenallan's Daughters   NELSON 1928   **A**

113 Lucie's Luck   BLACKIE 1928   **A**
(*illus. F.E. Hiley*)

114 The Bannister Twins   NELSON 1929   **A**
(*illus. E. Brier*)

115 Hilda Holds On   BLACKIE 1929   **A**
(*illus. F.E. Hiley*)

116 How Nell Scored   NELSON 1929   **A**

117 Laurel the Leader   BLACKIE 1930   **A**

118 Cuckoo of the Log Raft   NEWNES 1931   **A**

119 Two on Their Own   BLACKIE 1931   **A**
(*illus. F.E. Hiley*)

120 The Homesteader Girl   NELSON 1932   **A**
(*illus. V. Cooley*)

121 Jane Fills the Breach   BLACKIE 1932   **A**
(*illus. F.E. Hiley*)

122 Silla the Seventh   NEWNES 1932   **A**

123 Deborah's Find   BLACKIE 1933   **A**
(*illus. Henry Coller*)

124 The Courage of Katrine   WARNE 1934   **A**

125 Erica's Ranch   BLACKIE 1934   **A**

126 Lesbia's Little Blunder   WARNE 1934   **A**

127 Hosea's Girl   HUTCHINSON 1934   **A**

128 Anne of Tenterford   BLACKIE 1935   **A**
(*illus. F.E. Hiley*)

129 Felicity's Fortune   BLACKIE 1936   **A**

130 Nancy Afloat   NELSON 1936   **A**

131 A Daughter of the Desert	BLACKIE 1937	A
132 Miss Wilmer's Gang (*illus. J.A. May*)	BLACKIE 1938	A
133 Waifs of Woollamoo	WARNE 1938	A
134 A Girl Undaunted; or, The Honey Queen (*illus. J.A. May*)	BLACKIE 1939	A
135 Marta the Mainstay	BLACKIE 1940	A
136 Two of a Kind	BLACKIE 1941	A
137 The Triumphs of Three	BLACKIE 1942	A

MASEFIELD, John *Born in Hertfordshire, 1878. Died 1967*

Although Poet Laureate and, in his time, quite one of the most read and revered authors of all, Masefield is almost not at all collected in the field of modern first editions – with the notable exception of his scarce and expensive inaugural volume of poems *Salt-Water Ballads*, containing the endlessly anthologized 'Sea Fever'. His children's books, however – rather fewer than one might have expected – continue to exert their draw, and in particular the wondrous *The Box of Delights*, and *Jim Davis* – a great adventure.

1	**A Book of Discoveries** (*illus. Gordon Browne*)	WELLS GARDNER 1910 STOKES 1910	E D
2	**Lost Endeavour**	NELSON 1910 MACMILLAN US 1917	D C
3	**Martin Hyde,** **The Duke's Messenger** (*illus. T.C. Dugdale*)	WELLS GARDNER 1910 LITTLE BROWN 1910	D C
4	**Jim Davis; or, The Captive of** **Smugglers**	WELLS GARDNER 1911 STOKES 1912	G D
5	**The Midnight Folk**	HEINEMANN 1927 MACMILLAN US 1927	C B
6	**The Bird of Dawning; or, The** **Fortune of the Sea**	HEINEMANN 1933 MACMILLAN US 1933	C B
7	**The Box of Delights; or, When the** **Wolves Were Running**	HEINEMANN 1935 MACMILLAN US 1935	I G

| 8 | **Dead Ned: The Autobiography of a Corpse** | HEINEMANN 1938
MACMILLAN US 1938 | **D**
C |
| 9 | **Live and Kicking Ned** | HEINEMANN 1939
MACMILLAN US 1939 | **D**
C |

MAYNE, William   *Born in Yorkshire, 1928*

I suspect that Mayne – an author of tremendous output, and endless unconventionality – will become avidly collected largely because his work has always appealed more to adults (and critics) than to children – to many of whom Mayne remains, as it were, a closed book. This is not in any way to suggest that Mayne pitches his writing above his intended audience, but rather that his chosen method of revealing characters or situations is to employ either very elegant – sometimes quirky – dialogue, or else to allow the revelation to be relentlessly gradual. Much of Mayne's output is really superb, although one cannot point to any one highlight; the sheer *number* of books, however, offers tremendous scope to the collector – and it's virtually impossible to buy a dud.

1	**Follow the Footprints** (*illus. Shirley Hughes*)	OUP 1953	**G**
2	**The World Upside Down** (*illus. Shirley Hughes*)	OUP 1954	**F**
3	**A Swarm in May** (*illus. C. Walter Hodges*)	OUP 1955 BOBBS MERRILL 1957	**E** **D**
4	**The Member for the Marsh** (*illus. Lynton Lamb*)	OUP 1956	**E**
5	**Choristers' Cake** (*illus. C. Walter Hodges*)	OUP 1956 BOBBS MERRILL 1958	**E** **D**
6	**The Blue Boat** (*illus. Geraldine Spence*)	OUP 1957 DUTTON 1960	**D** **B**
7	**A Grass Rope** (*illus. Lynton Lamb*)	OUP 1957 DUTTON 1962	**D** **B**
8	**The Long Night** (*illus. D.J. Watkins-Pitchford*)	BLACKWELL 1958	**E**
9	**Underground Alley** (*illus. Marcia Lane Foster*)	OUP 1958 DUTTON 1961	**C** **B**

10 **The Gobbling Billy** GOLLANCZ 1959 **E**
   Co-written with Dick Caesar, this was
   published under the pseudonym Dynely James.
   Published under Mayne's own name in 1969 by
   Brockhampton Press.

11 **The Thumbstick** OUP 1959 **C**
   (*illus. Tessa Theobald*)

12 **Thirteen o'Clock** BLACKWELL 1960 **D**
   (*illus. D.J. Watkins-Pitchford*)

13 **The Rolling Season** OUP 1960 **C**
   (*illus. Christopher Brooker*)

14 **Cathedral Wednesday** OUP 1960 **C**
   (*illus. C. Walter Hodges*)

15 **The Fishing Party** HAMISH HAMILTON 1960 **C**
   (*illus. Christopher Brooker*)

16 **Summer Visitors** OUP 1961 **C**
   (*illus. William Stobbs*)

17 **The Changeling** OUP 1961 **C**
   (*illus. Victor Ambrus*) DUTTON 1963 **B**

18 **The Glass Ball** HAMISH HAMILTON 1961 **C**
   (*illus. Janet Duchesne*) DUTTON 1962 **B**

19 **The Last Bus** HAMISH HAMILTON 1962 **C**
   (*illus. Margery Gill*)

20 **The Twelve Dancers** HAMISH HAMILTON 1962 **C**
   (*illus. Lynton Lamb*)

21 **The Man from the North Pole** HAMISH HAMILTON 1963 **C**
   (*illus. Prudence Seward*)

22 **On the Stepping Stones** HAMISH HAMILTON 1963 **C**
   (*illus. Prudence Seward*)

23 **Words and Music** HAMISH HAMILTON 1963 **C**
   (*illus. Lynton Lamb*)

24 **Plot Night** HAMISH HAMILTON 1963 **C**
   (*illus. Janet Duchesne*) DUTTON 1968 **B**

| 25 | **A Parcel of Trees** (*illus. Margery Gill*) | PENGUIN 1963 | **B** |

| 26 | **Water Boatman** (*illus. Anne Linton*) | HAMISH HAMILTON 1964 | **C** |

| 27 | **Whistling Rufus** (*illus. Raymond Briggs*) | HAMISH HAMILTON 1964 DUTTON 1965 | **C** **B** |

| 28 | **Sand** (*illus. Margery Gill*) | HAMISH HAMILTON 1964 DUTTON 1965 | **C** **B** |

| 29 | **A Day without Wind** (*illus. Margery Gill*) | HAMISH HAMILTON 1964 DUTTON 1964 | **C** **B** |

| 30 | **The Big Wheel and the Little Wheel** (*illus. Janet Duchesne*) | HAMISH HAMILTON 1965 | **C** |

| 31 | **Pig in the Middle** (*illus. Mary Russon*) | HAMISH HAMILTON 1965 DUTTON 1966 | **C** **B** |

| 32 | **No More School** (*illus. Peter Warner*) | HAMISH HAMILTON 1965 | **C** |

| 33 | **Dormouse Tales** (*illus. Leslie Wood*) | HAMISH HAMILTON 1966 | **A** **Each** |

5 volumes comprising: The Lost Thimble; The Steam Roller; The Picnic; The Football; The Tea Party. *Published under the pseudonym Charles Molin.*

| 34 | **Earthfasts** | HAMISH HAMILTON 1966 DUTTON 1967 | **B** **A** |

| 35 | **Rooftops** (*illus. Mary Russon*) | HAMISH HAMILTON 1966 | **B** |

| 36 | **The Old Zion** (*illus. Margery Gill*) | HAMISH HAMILTON 1966 DUTTON 1967 | **B** **A** |

| 37 | **The Battlefield** (*illus. Mary Russon*) | HAMISH HAMILTON 1967 DUTTON 1967 | **B** **A** |

| 38 | **The Big Egg** (*illus. Margery Gill*) | HAMISH HAMILTON 1967 | **B** |

| 39 | **The Toffee Join** (*illus. Shirley Hughes*) | HAMISH HAMILTON 1968 | **B** |

40	**Over the Hills and Far Away**	HAMISH HAMILTON 1968	B
41	**The Hill Road** *Same as 40.*	DUTTON 1969	A
42	**The Yellow Aeroplane** *(illus. Trevor Stubley)*	HAMISH HAMILTON 1968 NELSON US 1974	B A
43	**The House on Fairmount** *(illus. Fritz Wegner)*	HAMISH HAMILTON 1968 DUTTON 1968	B A
44	**Ravensgill**	HAMISH HAMILTON 1970 DUTTON 1970	B A
45	**Royal Harry**	HAMISH HAMILTON 1971 DUTTON 1972	B A
46	**A Game of Dark**	HAMISH HAMILTON 1971 DUTTON 1971	B A
47	**The Incline** *(illus. Trevor Stubley)*	HAMISH HAMILTON 1972 DUTTON 1972	B A
48	**The Swallows** *(Pseudonym Martin Cobalt)*	HEINEMANN 1972 NELSON US 1974	B A
49	**Robin's Real Engine** *(illus. Mary Dinsdale)*	HAMISH HAMILTON 1972	B
50	**Skiffy** *(illus. Nicholas Fisk)*	HAMISH HAMILTON 1972	B
51	**The Jersey Shore**	HAMISH HAMILTON 1973 DUTTON 1973	B A
52	**A Year and a Day** *(illus. Krystyna Turska)*	HAMISH HAMILTON 1976 DUTTON 1976	B A
53	**Party Pants** *(illus. Joanna Stubbs)*	KNIGHT 1977	A
54	**Max's Dream** *(illus. Laszlo Acs)*	HAMISH HAMILTON 1977 GREENWILLOW 1977	B A
55	**It**	HAMISH HAMILTON 1977 GREENWILLOW 1978	B A
56	**While the Bells Ring** *(illus. Janet Rawlins)*	HAMISH HAMILTON 1979	B

57	**Salt River Times**	HAMISH HAMILTON 1980	**B**
	(*illus. Elizabeth Honey*)	GREENWILLOW 1981	**A**
58	**The Mouse and the Egg**	MACRAE 1980	**B**
	(*illus. Krystyna Turska*)	GREENWILLOW 1981	**A**
59	**The Patchwork Cat**	CAPE 1981	**B**
	(*illus. Nicola Bayley*)	KNOPF 1981	**A**
60	**All the King's Men**	CAPE 1982	**B**
61	**Winter Quarters**	CAPE 1982	**B**
62	**Skiffy and the Twin Planets**	HAMISH HAMILTON 1982	**B**
63	**A Small Puddding for Wee Gowrie**	MACMILLAN 1983	**B**
64	**The Mouldy**	CAPE 1983	**B**
	(*illus. Nicola Bayley*)		

65 **The Red Book of Hob Stories**   WALKER 1984   **A**
   The Green Book of Hob Stories   **Each**
   The Yellow Book of Hob Stories
   The Blue Book of Hob Stories
   (*illus. Patrick Benson*)

66	**Drift**	CAPE 1985	**B**

67 **Animal Library** (*4 vols*):   WALKER 1986   **A**
   Barnabas Walks (*illus. Barbara Firth*)   **Each**
   Come, Come To My Corner
   (*illus. Kenneth Lilly*)
   Tibber (*illus. Jonathan Heale*)
   Corbie (*illus. Peter Visscher*)

68	**Gideon Ahoy!**	VIKING KESTREL 1987	**B**
69	**Kelpie**	CAPE 1987	**B**

MILLIGAN, Spike   *British. Born in India, 1918*

Milligan's anarchic humour is very addictive and – although patchy – rather memorable. Most of his output could be enjoyed by children (except his latest, *The Looney* – very funny, but too many rude bits) but I list here the books that (I *think*) were intended for children. Not easy to find excellent copies because these books tend to be read, re-read, borrowed and stolen.

1	**Silly Verse for Kids** (*illus. the author*)	DOBSON 1959	**B**
2	**A Dustbin of Milligan** (*illus. the author*)	DOBSON 1961	**B**
3	**Puckoon** (*novel*) *Not* really *a children's book – but it* can't *be* omitted.	BLOND 1963	**C**
4	**A Book of Bits** (*illus. the author*)	DOBSON 1965	**B**
5	**The Little Pot Boiler** (*illus. the author*)	DOBSON 1965	**B**
6	**Milliganimals** (*illus. the author*)	DOBSON 1968	**B**
7	**The Bedside Milligan** (*illus. the author*)	DOBSON 1968	**B**
8	**The Bald Twit Lion** (*illus. the author*)	DOBSON 1970	**B**
9	**Milligan's Ark** (*illus. the author*)	JOSEPH 1971	**B**
10	**Badjelly The Witch**	JOSEPH 1973 MEMMACK 1973	**B** **A**
11	**Dip the Puppy**	JOSEPH 1974	**A**
12	**Goblins** (*verse*) (*illus. W. Heath Robinson*)	HUTCHINSON 1978	**B**
13	**Unspun Socks from a Chicken's** **Laundry** (*illus. the author – and occasionally Jane &* *Laura*)	JOSEPH 1981	**A**
14	**The 101 Best and Only Limericks of** **Spike Milligan**	JOSEPH 1982	**A**
15	**Sir Nobonk and the Terrible, Awful,** **Dreadful, Naughty, Nasty Dragon**	JOSEPH 1982	**A**

MILNE, A.A.   *Born in London, 1882. Died 1956*

Although known today only for the wonderful Christopher Robin and Pooh books, Milne was in his day an extremely prolific (and popular) playwright, novelist and essayist. Pooh very quickly took over in the public's esteem, however, and for the last thirty years of his life it was Pooh, Pooh and only Pooh that anyone had any time for – much to the resentment of the author. Conan Doyle felt the same about Holmes, of course, but we should not feel *too* sorry for the creators of these deathless characters – so total a reaction from the literary establishment as well as from the general reading public is, in fact, a tremendous mark of respect – truly the ultimate accolade that can be accorded an author.

    Pooh continues to sell and be read like no other children's books this century – with the possible exception of Peter Rabbit. If this great little bear and his inimitable chums can survive Disney, they can survive anything – and go on to make everyone concerned pots of munny.

1	**Once on a Time** (*fiction*) (*illus. H.M. Brock*)	HODDER & STOUGHTON 1917	G
		PUTNAM 1922	C
2	**The Man in the Bowler Hat: A Terribly Exciting Affair** (*play*)	FRENCH 1923	B
3	**When We Were Very Young** (*verse*)	METHUEN 1924	L
		DUTTON 1924	I
4	**A Gallery of Children** (*fiction*) (*illus. Saida*)	STANLEY PAUL 1925	D
		McKAY 1925	C
5	**Winnie-the-Pooh** (*fiction*) (*illus. Ernest Shepard*)	METHUEN 1926	K
		DUTTON 1926	H
6	**Now We are Six** (*verse*)	METHUEN 1927	J
		DUTTON 1927	F
7	**The House at Pooh Corner** (*fiction*) (*illus. Ernest Shepard*)	METHUEN 1928	I
		DUTTON 1928	F
8	**Toad of Toad Hall** (*play*) Adaptation of Kenneth Grahame's The Wind in The Willows, *music by H. Fraser-Simson.*	METHUEN 1929	F
		SCRIBNER 1929	D
9	**The Ugly Duckling** (*play*)	FRENCH 1941	B

10	**Prince Rabbit, and the Princess Who Could Not Laugh** (*fiction*) (*illus. Mary Shepard*)	WARD 1966	**B**
		DUTTON 1966	**B**

Also of interest:

CHRISTOPHER MILNE: **The Enchanted Places** (EYRE METHUEN 1974, DUTTON US 1975)

MONTGOMERY, L.M.　　*Canadian. Born Prince Edward Island, 1874.*
Died 1942

Fans of Lucy Maud Montgomery's first book *Anne of Green Gables* – and there are many – may or may not be aware of the number of sequels, but might be pleasantly surprised to discover that there are quite a few more neglected books to the author's credit, as the following list shows. Not what you would call common, but undervalued at present.

1	**Anne of Green Gables** (*illus. M.A. & W.A. Claus*)	PAGE 1908	**I**
		PITMAN 1908	**H**
2	**Anne of Avonlea**	PAGE 1909	**H**
		PITMAN 1909	**G**
3	**Kilmeny of the Orchard** (*illus. George Gibbs*)	PAGE 1910	**E**
		PITMAN 1910	**D**
4	**The Story Girl**	PAGE 1911	**D**
		PITMAN 1911	**C**
5	**Chronicles of Avonlea**	PAGE 1912	**E**
		SAMPSON LOW 1912	**E**
6	**The Golden Road**	PAGE 1913	**D**
		CASSELL 1914	**C**
7	**Anne of the Island**	PAGE 1915	**D**
		PITMAN 1915	**C**
8	**Anne's House of Dreams**	STOKES 1917	**D**
		CONSTABLE 1917	**C**
9	**Rainbow Valley**	McCLELLAND & STEWART (CANADA) 1919	**C**
		STOKES 1919	**C**
		CONSTABLE 1920	**B**

10	Further Chronicles of Avonlea...	PAGE 1920	D
	(illus. John Goss)	HARRAP 1953	C
11	Rilla of Ingleside	McCLELLAND & STEWART (CANADA) 1921	C
		STOKES 1921	C
		HODDER & STOUGHTON 1921	B
12	Emily of New Moon	STOKES 1923	C
		HODDER & STOUGHTON 1923	B
13	Emily Climbs	STOKES 1925	C
		HODDER & STOUGHTON 1925	B
14	The Blue Castle	McCLELLAND & STEWART (CANADA) 1926	C
		STOKES 1926	C
		HODDER & STOUGHTON 1926	B
15	Emily's Quest	STOKES 1927	C
		HODDER & STOUGHTON 1927	B
16	Magic for Marigold	McCLELLAND & STEWART (CANADA) 1929	C
		STOKES 1929	C
		HODDER & STOUGHTON 1929	B
17	A Tangled Web	STOKES 1931	C
18	Aunt Becky Began It	HODDER & STOUGHTON 1931	C
	Same as 17.		
19	Pat of Silver Bush	STOKES 1933	C
		HODDER & STOUGHTON 1933	B
20	Mistress Pat: A Novel of Silver Bush	STOKES 1935	C
		HARRAP 1935	B
21	Anne of Windy Poplars	STOKES 1936	C
22	Anne of Windy Willows	HARRAP 1936	C
	Same as 21.		

23	**Jane of Lantern Hill**	McCLELLAND & STEWART	C
		(CANADA) 1937	
		STOKES 1937	C
		HARRAP 1937	B
24	**Anne of Ingleside**	STOKES 1939	C
		HARRAP 1939	C
25	**The Road to Yesterday**	McGRAW HILL RYERSON	B
		(CANADA) 1974	
		ANGUS & ROBERTSON	B
		1975	
26	**The Doctor's Sweetheart and Other Stories**	McGRAW HILL RYERSON	B
		(CANADA) 1979	
		HARRAP 1979	B

Also of interest:

MOLLIE GILLEN: **The Wheel of Things: A Biography of L.M. Montgomery**
(FITZHENRY & WHITESIDE, CANADA 1975, HARRAP 1976)

MOORE, Dorothea
Born in London. Died 1933

Ripping-ish girls' school yarns for lovers of this sort of thing: Angela Brazil, with a healthy dose of Famous Five. The Girl Guide novels are the best known, but here I list the complete *oeuvre*.

1	**Mistress Dorothy**	NATIONAL SOCIETY 1902	C
2	**Evelyn**	NELSON 1904	B
3	**God's Bairn**	BLACKIE 1904	B
4	**Brown**	NISBET 1905	B
		EATON & MAINS 1905	B
5	**Sydney Lisle**	PARTRIDGE 1905	B
	(illus. Wal Paget)	McKAY 1910	B
6	**Jepthah's Ass**	PARTRIDGE 1907	B
7	**Elizabeth's Angel and Other Stories**	NATIONAL SOCIETY 1907	B
8	**Knights of the Red Cross**	NELSON 1907	B
9	**Pamela's Hero**	BLACKIE 1907	B
	(illus. A.A. Dixon)		

10   **A Plucky School-girl**   NISBET 1908   **B**

11   **The Christmas Children**   PARTRIDGE 1909   **B**

12   **The Luck of Ledge Point**   BLACKIE 1909   **B**
       (*illus. C. Horrell*)

13   **A Lady of Mettle**   PARTRIDGE 1910   **B**

14   **The Making of Ursula**   PARTRIDGE 1910   **B**

15   **The Lucas Girls**   PARTRIDGE 1911   **B**
       (*illus. Tom Peddie*)

16   **Under the Wolf's Fell**   PARTRIDGE 1911   **B**

17   **Nadia to the Rescue**   NISBET 1912   **B**

18   **A Runaway Princess**   PARTRIDGE 1912   **B**

19   **Terry the Girl-guide**   NISBET 1912   **B**
       (*illus. A.A. Dixon*)

20   **A Brave Little Royalist**   NISBET 1913   **B**
       (*illus. John Campbell*)

21   **Only a Girl**   PARTRIDGE 1913   **B**

22   **Rosemary the Rebel**   PARTRIDGE 1913   **B**

23   **Captain Nancy**   NISBET 1914   **B**

24   **Cecily's Highwayman**   NISBET 1914   **B**
       (*illus. John Campbell*)

25   **Septima, Schoolgirl**   CASSELL 1915   **B**

26   **Wanted, an English Girl: The**   PARTRIDGE 1916   **B**
       Adventures of an English
       Schoolgirl in Germany

27   **The New Girl**   NISBET 1917   **B**

28   **The Head Girl's Sister**   NISBET 1918   **B**

29   **Tam of Tiffany's**   PARTRIDGE 1918   **B**

30   **Her Schoolgirl Majesty**   PARTRIDGE 1918   **B**

31   **Head of the Lower School**   NISBET 1919   **B**
                                         PUTNAM 1920   **B**

32	**A Nest of Malignants**	SPCK 1919	B
		MACMILLAN US 1920	B
33	**The Right Kind of Girl**	NISBET 1920	B
34	**The New Prefect**	NISBET 1921	B
35	**An Adventurous Schoolgirl**	CASSELL 1921	B
	(*illus. Archibald Webb*)	FUNK & WAGNALLS 1922	B
36	**Greta of the Guides**	PARTRIDGE 1921	B
37	**Guide Gilly, Adventurer**	NISBET 1922	B
38	**The New Girl at Pen-y-Gant**	NISBET 1922	B
39	**The Only Day Girl**	NISBET 1923	B
40	**A Young Pretender**	NISBET 1924	B
41	**Fen's First Term**	CASSELL 1924	B
42	**In the Reign of the Red Cap**	SHELDON PRESS 1924	B
	(*illus. Archibald Webb*)		
43	**Smuggler's Way**	CASSELL 1924	B
	(*illus. H.M. Brock*)		
44	**A Rough Night**	PARTRIDGE 1925	B
45	**'Z' House**	NISBET 1925	B
46	**My Lady Venturesome**	SHELDON PRESS 1926	B
47	**Perdita, Prisoner of War**	CASSELL 1926	B
48	**A Schoolgirl Adventurer**	BLACK 1927	B
49	**Tenth at Trinder's**	CASSELL 1927	B
50	**Adventurers All!**	PARTRIDGE 1927	B
	(*illus. P. Walford*)		
51	**Brenda of Beech House**	NISBET 1927	B
52	**Seraphine-Di Goes to School**	RTS 1927	B
53	**Darry the Dauntless**	CASSELL 1928	B
54	**A Rebel of the Third**	NISBET 1929	B
55	**Adventurers Two**	SHELDON PRESS 1929	B
56	**The Wrenford Tradition**	NISBET 1929	B

57	Judy, Patrol Leader	COLLINS 1930	A
58	Judy Lends a Hand	COLLINS 1932	A
59	Nicky of Nine Schools	OUP 1932	A
60	Sara to the Rescue	NISBET 1932	A
61	At Friendship's Call	OUP 1932	A
62	Dick of the Day-girls	NISBET 1933	A
63	Queens for Choice	OUP 1934	A
64	Babs Goes to Court	SHELDON PRESS 1936	A
65	The Crooked Headstone	PEARSON 1939	A

MURPHY, Jill   *Born in London, 1949*

Very much an author to watch. Her 'Worst Witch' books are, of course, the highlights – and we hope for many more. Young Mildred Hubble has the makings of a classic.

All the following are (delightfully) illustrated by the author.

1	The Worst Witch	ALLISON & BUSBY 1974	C
2	The Worst Witch Strikes Again	ALLISON & BUSBY 1980	B
3	Peace at Last	MACMILLAN 1980	B
		DIAL PRESS 1980	B
4	A Bad Spell for the Worst Witch	KESTREL 1982	B
5	On the Way Home	MACMILLAN 1982	B
6	Whatever Next?	MACMILLAN 1983	B
7	Geoffrey Strangeways	VIKING KESTREL 1985	B
8	Five Minutes Peace	WALKER 1986	A

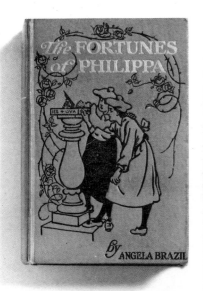

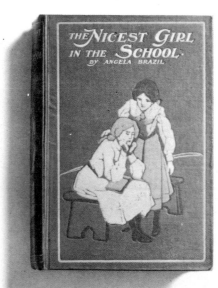

Three ripping yarns for gels by the leader in the field. Note the original *A Pair of Schoolgirls* (1912) and the sartorial adjustments to the 1930s reissue. You're a brick, Angela!

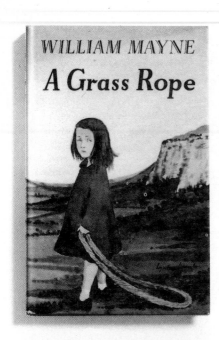

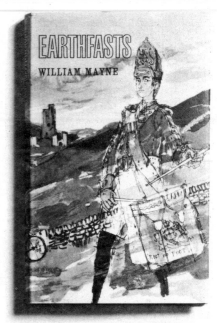

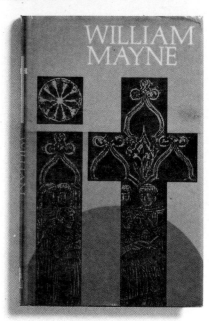

A quartet from the prolific and rather splendid William Mayne, including *It* (not for those of a nervous disposition).

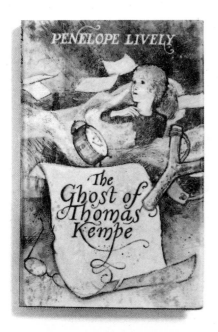

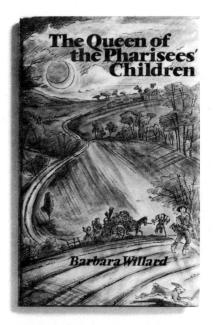

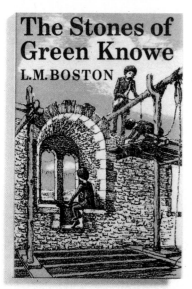

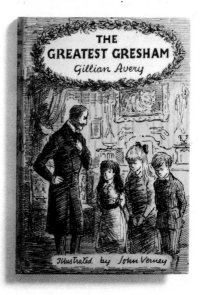

Booker Prize winner Penelope Lively in her original role as children's writer, together with three more popular and highly regarded ladies.

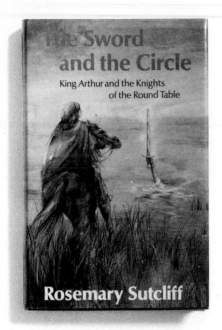

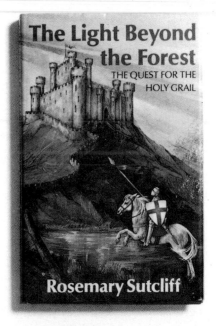

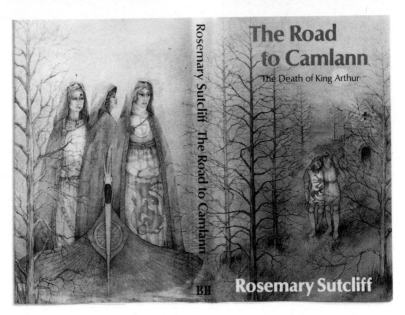

Rosemary Sutcliff's Arthurian trilogy, with wraparound dust-wrappers and illustrations by Shirley Felts.

NAUGHTON, Bill   *Born in Ireland, 1910*

Really very good working-class stuff from the author of *Alfie*. It is the dialogue
that is so convincing – but then, Naughton is primarily a playwright. The
children's books listed below will not be too easy to track down, but prices are
low at the moment.

1	**Pony Boy**	PILOT PRESS 1946	**C**
2	**The Goalkeeper's Revenge and Other Stories** (*illus. Dick de Wilde*)	HARRAP 1961	**B**
3	**The Goalkeeper's Revenge and Spit Nolan** (*illus. Trevor Stubley*)	MACMILLAN 1974	**B**
4	**A Dog Called Nelson** (*illus. Charles Mozley*)	DENT 1976	**B**
5	**My Pal Spadger** (*illus. Charles Mozley*)	DENT 1977	**B**

Also of interest:
AUTOBIOGRAPHY: **On the Pig's Back** (OUP 1987)

NEEDHAM, Violet   *Born in London, 1876. Died 1967*

Violet Needham was in her sixties when she published her first book, which
may go some way in explaining why she was always somewhat out of step
with her contemporaries – eschewing realism in favour of out-and-out (and
often rather stagey) fantasy, set in mythical Ruritarian empires. Very much
sought after by people who almost immediately became addicted to the stuff
as it was published, but rather less pursued by children themselves, these
days.

1	**The Black Riders** (*illus. Anne Bullen*)	COLLINS 1939	**D**
2	**The Emerald Crown** (*illus. Anne Bullen*)	COLLINS 1940	**C**
3	**The Stormy Petrel** (*illus. Joyce Bruce*)	COLLINS 1942	**C**

4   **The Horn of Merlyns**   COLLINS 1943   C
    (*illus. Joyce Bruce*)

5   **The Woods of Windri**   COLLINS 1944   C
    (*illus. Joyce Bruce*)

6   **The House of the Paladin**   COLLINS 1945   C
    (*illus. Joyce Bruce*)

7   **The Changeling of Monte Lucio** COLLINS 1946   B
    (*illus. Joyce Bruce*)

8   **The Bell of the Four Evangelists** COLLINS 1947   B
    (*illus. Joyce Bruce*)

9   **The Boy in Red**   COLLINS 1948   B
    (*illus. Joyce Bruce*)

10 **The Betrayer**   COLLINS 1950   B
    (*illus. Joyce Bruce*)

11 **Pandora of Parham Royal**   COLLINS 1951   B
    (*illus. Joyce Bruce*)

12 **The Avenue**   COLLINS 1952   B
    (*illus. Joyce Bruce*)

13 **How Many Miles to Babylon?**   COLLINS 1953   B
    (*illus. Joyce Bruce*)

14 **Adventures at Hampton Court**   LUTTERWORTH PRESS   B
    (*illus. Will Nickless*)   1954

15 **Richard and the Golden Horse Shoe** COLLINS 1954   B
    (*illus. Joyce Bruce*)

16 **The Great House of Estraville** COLLINS 1955   B
    (*illus. Joyce Bruce*)

17 **The Secret of the White Peacock** COLLINS 1956   B
    (*illus. Joyce Bruce*)

18 **The Red Rose of Ruvina**   COLLINS 1957   B
    (*illus. Richard Kennedy*)

19 **Adventures at Windsor Castle**   LUTTERWORTH PRESS   B
    (*illus. David Walsh*)   1957

NESBIT, E. — *Born in London, 1858. Died 1924*

In addition to the following lengthy listing of children's books, Edith Nesbit wrote over forty for adults – about half of them verse – and these are quite unregarded today. It is for the wonderful children's writing that Nesbit will always be remembered and collected – *The Railway Children* remaining the highlight, and a veritable classic.

1	**Songs of Two Seasons** (*verse*) (*illus. J. MacIntyre*)	TUCK 1890	**L**
2	**The Voyage of Columbus, 1492: The Discovery of America** (*verse*) (*illus. Will & Frances Brundage*)	TUCK 1892	**K**
3	**Our Friends and All About Them** (*verse*)	TUCK 1893	**I**
4	**Listen Long and Listen Well** (*fiction*) (*with others*)	TUCK 1893	**H**
5	**Sunny Tales for Snowy Days** (*fiction*) (*with others*)	TUCK 1893	**H**
6	**Told by Sunbeams and Me** (*fiction*) (*with others*)	TUCK 1893	**H**
7	**Fur and Feathers: Tales for All Weathers** (*fiction*) (*with others*)	TUCK 1894	**H**
8	**Lads and Lassies** (*fiction*) (*with others*)	TUCK 1894	**H**
9	**Tales That are True, for Brown Eyes and Blue** (*fiction*) (*with others*) (*illus. M. Goodman*)	TUCK 1894	**H**
10	**Tales to Delight, from Morning Till Night** (*fiction*) (*with others*) (*illus. M. Goodman*)	TUCK 1894	**H**
11	**Hours in Many Lands: Stories and Poems** (*with others*) (*illus. Frances Brundage*)	TUCK 1894	**H**
12	**Doggy Tales** (*fiction*) (*illus. Lucy Kemp-Welch*)	WARD 1895	**I**

13	**Pussy Tales** (*fiction*) (*illus. Lucy Kemp-Welch*)	WARD 1895	**I**
14	**Tales of the Clock** (*fiction*) (*illus. Helen Jackson*)	TUCK 1895	**K**
15	**Dulcie's Lantern and Other Stories** (*with others*)	FARRAN 1895	**G**
16	**Treasures from Storyland** (*fiction*) (*with others*)	TUCK 1895	**G**
17	**As Happy as a King** (*verse*) (*illus. S. Rosamund Praeger*)	WARD 1896	**H**
18	**Tales Told in Twilight: A Volume of Very Short Stories**	NISTER 1897	**K**
19	**Dinna Forget** (*verse*) (*with G.C. Bingham*)	NISTER 1897 DUTTON 1898	**G** **E**
20	**Dog Tales, and Other Tales** (*fiction*) (*with others*) (*illus. R.K. Mounsey*)	TUCK 1898	**G**
21	**The Story of the Treasure Seekers, Being the Adventures of the Bastable Children in Search of a Fortune** (*fiction*) (*illus. Gordon Browne & Lewis Baumer*)	UNWIN 1899 STOKES 1899	**L** **J**
22	**The Book of Dragons** (*fiction*) (*illus. H.R. Millar*)	HARPER 1900	**K**
23	**To Wish You Every Joy** (*verse*)	TUCK 1901	**G**
24	**Nine Unlikely Tales for Children** (*illus. H.R. Millar & Claude Shepperson*)	UNWIN 1901 DUTTON 1901	**J** **G**
25	**The Wouldbegoods, Being the Further Adventures of the Treasure Seekers** (*illus. Arthur H. Buckland & John Hassell*)	UNWIN 1901 HARPER 1902	**J** **G**
26	**Five Children and It** (*fiction*) (*illus. H.R. Millar*)	UNWIN 1902 DODD MEAD 1905	**J** **G**
27	**The Revolt of the Toys and What Comes of Quarrelling** (*fiction*) (*illus. Ambrose Dudley*)	NISTERE 1902 DUTTON 1902	**J** **G**

28	**Playtime Stories**	TUCK 1903	**H**
29	**The Rainbow Queen and Other Stories**	TUCK 1903	**H**
30	**The Phoenix and the Carpet** (*fiction*) (*illus. H.R. Millar*)	NEWNES 1904 MACMILLAN 1904	**I** **F**
31	**The Story of the Five Rebellious Dolls** (*fiction*)	NISTER 1904	**H**
32	**The New Treasure Seekers** (*fiction*) (*illus. Gordon Browne & Lewis Baumer*)	UNWIN 1904 STOKES 1904	**I** **F**
33	**Cat Tales** (*with Rosamund Bland*) (*illus. Isabel Watkin*)	NISTER 1904 DUTTON 1904	**E** **C**
34	**Pug Peter: King of Mouseland, Marquis of Barkshire, D.O.G., P.C. 1906, Knight of the Order of the Gold Dog Collar, Author of Doggerel Lays and Days...** (*illus. Harry Rountree*)	COOKE 1905	**J**
35	**Oswald Bastable and Others** (*fiction*) (*illus. C.E. Brock & H.R. Millar*)	GARDNER 1905 COWARD McCANN 1960	**H** **B**
36	**The Story of the Amulet** (*fiction*) (*illus. H.R. Millar*)	UNWIN 1906 DUTTON 1906	**I** **G**
37	**The Railway Children** (*fiction*) (*illus. C.E. Brock*)	GARDNER 1906 MACMILLAN 1906	**M** **I**
38	**The Enchanted Castle** (*fiction*) (*illus. H.R. Millar*)	UNWIN 1907 HARPER 1908	**H** **D**
39	**The House of Arden** (*fiction*) (*illus. H.R. Millar*)	UNWIN 1908 DUTTON 1909	**H** **D**
40	**Harding's Luck** (*fiction*) (*illus. H.R. Millar*)	HODDER & STOUGHTON 1909 STOKES 1910	**H** **D**
41	**The Magic City** (*fiction*) (*illus. H.R. Millar*)	MACMILLAN 1910 COWARD McCANN 1958	**G** **B**
42	**The Wonderful Garden; or, The Three C's** (*fiction*) (*illus. H.R. Millar*)	MACMILLAN 1911 COWARD McCANN 1935	**H** **C**

43	**The Magic World** (*fiction*) (*illus. H.R. Millar & Spencer Pryse*)	MACMILLAN 1912	**G**
44	**Wet Magic** (*fiction*) (*illus. H.R. Millar*)	LAURIE 1913 COWARD McCANN 1937	**F** **B**
45	**Our New Story Book** (*with others*) (*illus. Elsie Wood & Louis Wain*)	NISTER 1913 DUTTON 1913	**J** **H**
46	**Five of Us – and Madeleine** (*fiction*) (*illus. Nora S. Unwin*)	UNWIN 1925 ADELPHI 1926	**F** **D**
47	**Fairy Stories** (*illus. Brian Robb*)	BENN 1977	**C**

Also of interest:
DORIS LANGLEY MOORE: **E. Nesbit: A Biography** (BENN 1933, *Revised ed.* 1967)
NOEL STREATFIELD: **Magic and the Magician: E. Nesbit and Her Children's Books** (BENN 1958, ABELARD SCHUMAN US 1958)
JULIA BRIGGS: **E. Nesbit** (HUTCHINSON 1987)

NICOLL, Helen   *Born in Cumbria*

The combination of Helen Nicoll's text and Jan Pieńkowski's fabulously colourful illustrations makes an immediate and lasting impact. Children seem to have decided that the Meg and Mog books are lasters, and so collectors may as well fall in line: children are pretty good at nosing out winners.

1	**Meg and Mog**	HEINEMANN 1972 ATHENEUM 1973	**C** **B**
2	**Meg's Eggs**	HEINEMANN 1972 ATHENEUM 1973	**B** **A**
3	**Meg at Sea**	HEINEMANN 1973 HARVEY HOUSE 1976	**B** **A**
4	**Meg on the Moon**	HEINEMANN 1973 HARVEY HOUSE 1976	**B** **A**
5	**Meg's Car**	HEINEMANN 1975	**B**
6	**Meg's Castle**	HEINEMANN 1975	**B**

7	**Meg's Veg**	HEINEMANN 1976	B
8	**Mog's Mumps**	HEINEMANN 1976	B
9	**Quest for the Gloop:** **The Exploits of Murfy and Phix**	HEINEMANN 1980	B
10	**Mog at the Zoo**	HEINEMANN 1982	B
11	**Mog's Box**	HEINEMANN 1987	B

NORTON, Mary   *Born in London, 1903*

The Borrowers really is a marvellous read – on whatever level you choose: witty, observant and highly amusing children's fantasy, or a parable about all those who have no rightful place: the refugees who never quite *belong*. No matter – it's deathless stuff, and increasingly sought-after by collectors.

1	**The Magic Bed-knob; or, How to** **Become a Witch in Ten Easy** **Lessons** (*illus. Waldo Peirce*)	HYPERION PRESS US 1943	G
2	**The Magic Bed-knob** (*illus. Joan Kiddell-Monroe*)	DENT 1945	F
3	**Bonfires and Broomsticks** (*illus. Mary Adshead*)	DENT 1947	C
4	**The Borrowers** (*illus. Diana Stanley*)	DENT 1952 HARCOURT BRACE 1953	E B
5	**The Borrowers Afield** (*illus. Diana Stanley*)	DENT 1955 HARCOURT BRACE 1955	C B
6	**Bedknob and Broomstick** (*illus. Erik Blegvad*) *Revised edition of 2 & 3.*	DENT 1957 HARCOURT BRACE 1957	B B
7	**The Borrowers Afloat** (*illus. Diana Stanley*)	DENT 1959 HARCOURT BRACE 1959	C B
8	**The Borrowers Aloft** (*illus. Diana Stanley*)	DENT 1961 HARCOURT BRACE 1961	C B
9	**Poor Stainless** (*illus. Diana Stanley*)	DENT 1971 HARCOURT BRACE 1971	B A

10	**Are All the Giants Dead?**	DENT 1975	**B**
	(*illus. Brian Froud*)	HARCOURT BRACE 1975	**A**
11	**The Borrowers Avenged**	KESTREL 1982	**B**
	(*illus. Pauline Baynes*)	HARCOURT BRACE 1982	**A**

NYE, Robert   *Born in London, 1939*

Large-scale heroics characterize the rumbustious tales that Nye has spun for children – good, hearty stuff. At the moment, Robert Nye's work for both children and adults is collected only by a rather informed élite, but this situation may well change.

1	**March Has Horse's Ears**	FABER 1966	**C**
	(*illus. Sheila Hawkins*)	HILL & WANG 1967	**B**
2	**Taliesin**	FABER 1966	**C**
	(*illus. Sheila Hawkins*)	HILL & WANG 1967	**B**
3	**Bee Hunter: Adventures of Beowulf**	FABER 1968	**B**
	(*illus. Aileen Campbell*)		
4	**Beowulf: A New Telling**	HILL & WANG 1968	**B**
	Same as 3.		
5	**Wishing Gold**	MACMILLAN 1970	**B**
	(*illus. Helen Craig*)	HILL & WANG 1971	**B**
6	**Poor Pumpkin**	MACMILLAN 1971	**B**
	(*illus. Derek Collard*)		
7	**The Mathematical Princess and Other Stories**	HILL & WANG 1972	**B**
	Same as 6.		
8	**Cricket: Three Stories**	BOBBS MERRILL 1975	**B**
	(*illus. Shelley Freshman*)		
9	**Once Upon Three Times**	BENN 1978	**B**
	Same as 8.		
10	**Out of the World and Back Again**	COLLINS 1977	**B**
	(*illus. Joanna Troughton*)	BOBBS MERRILL 1978	**B**
11	**The Bird of the Golden Land**	HAMISH HAMILTON 1980	**B**
	(*illus. Krystyna Turska*)		
12	**Harry Pay the Pirate**	HAMISH HAMILTON 1981	**B**

OXENHAM, Elsie J.   *Born in Britain. Died 1960*

Another great exponent of the traditional 'girls' stories', the most enduring of which form the 'Abbey' series – but there are some really wonderful titles in the *You're a Brick, Angela* vein: I particularly like *The Tuck-shop Girl* and *'Tickles'; or, The School That Was Different.*

1	**Goblin Island** (*illus. T. Heath Robinson*)	COLLINS 1907	L
2	**A Princess in Tatters**	COLLINS 1908	I
3	**The Conquest of Christina** (*illus. G.B. Foyster*)	COLLINS 1909	H
4	**The Girl Who Wouldn't Make Friends**	NELSON 1909	H
5	**Mistress Nanciebel** (*illus. James Durden*)	HODDER & STOUGHTON 1909	G
6	**A Holiday Queen** (*illus. E.A. Overnell*)	COLLINS 1910	G
7	**Rosaly's New School** (*illus. T.J. Overnell*)	CHAMBERS 1913	G
8	**Girls of the Hamlet Club**	CHAMBERS 1914	F
9	**Schoolgirls and Scouts** (*illus. A.A. Dixon*)	COLLINS 1914	I
10	**At School with the Roundheads** (*illus. H.C. Earnshaw*)	CHAMBERS 1915	F
11	**Finding Her Family**	SPCK 1915	E
12	**The Tuck-shop Girl**	CHAMBERS 1916	F
13	**A School Camp Fire**	CHAMBERS 1917	F
14	**The School of Ups and Downs** (*illus. H.C. Earnshaw*)	CHAMBERS 1918	F
15	**A Go-ahead Schoolgirl** (*illus. H.C. Earnshaw*)	CHAMBERS 1919	E
16	**Expelled from School** (*illus. Victor Prout*)	COLLINS 1919	E

17	**The Abbey Girls** (*illus. A.A. Dixon*)	COLLINS 1920	**H**
18	**The School Torment** (*illus. H.C. Earnshaw*)	CHAMBERS 1920	**E**
19	**The Twins of Castle Charming**	SWARTHMORE PRESS 1920	**E**
20	**The Girls of the Abbey School** (*illus. Elsie Wood*)	COLLINS 1921	**F**
21	**The Two Form-Captains** (*illus. Percy Tarrant*)	CHAMBERS 1921	**E**
22	**The Abbey Girls Go Back to School** (*illus. Elsie Wood*)	COLLINS 1922	**F**
23	**The Captain of the Fifth** (*illus. Percy Tarrant*)	CHAMBERS 1922	**E**
24	**Patience Joan, Outsider**	CASSELL 1922 FUNK & WAGNALLS 1923	**E** **C**
25	**The Junior Captain**	CHAMBERS 1923	**E**
26	**The New Abbey Girls** (*illus. Elsie Wood*)	CHAMBERS 1923	**F**
27	**The Abbey Girls Again**	COLLINS 1924	**F**
28	**The Girls of Gwynfa**	WARNE 1924	**E**
29	**The School Without a Name** (*illus. Nina K. Brisley*)	CHAMBERS 1924	**E**
30	**'Tickles'; or, The School That was Different**	PARTRIDGE 1924	**E**
31	**The Testing of the Torment** (*illus. P.B. Hickling*)	CASSELL 1925	**E**
32	**Ven at Gregory's** (*illus. Nina K. Brisley*)	CHAMBERS 1925	**E**
33	**The Abbey Girls in Town** (*illus. Rosa Petherick*)	COLLINS 1926	**E**
34	**The Camp Fire Torment** (*illus. Nina Browne*)	CHAMBERS 1926	**E**

35	**Queen of the Abbey Girls** (*illus. E.J. Kealey*)	COLLINS 1926	F
36	**The Troubles of Tazy** (*illus. Percy Tarrant*)	CHAMBERS 1926	E
37	**Jen of the Abbey School** (*illus. F. Meyerheim*)	COLLINS 1927	F
38	**Patience and Her Problems** (*illus. Molly Benatar*)	CHAMBERS 1927	E
39	**Peggy Makes Good!** (*illus. H.L. Bacon*)	PARTRIDGE 1927	F
40	**The Abbey Girls Win Through**	COLLINS 1928	F
41	**The Abbey School**	COLLINS 1928	F
42	**The Crisis in Camp Keema** (*illus. Percy Tarrant*)	CHAMBERS 1928	D
43	**Deb at School** (*illus. Nina K. Brisley*)	CHAMBERS 1929	D
44	**The Girls of Rocklands School**	COLLINS 1929	C
45	**The Abbey Girls at Home** (*illus. I. Burns*)	COLLINS 1930	D
46	**The Abbey Girls Play Up**	COLLINS 1930	D
47	**Dorothy's Dilemma** (*illus. Nina K. Brisley*)	CHAMBERS 1930	C
48	**The Second Term at Rocklands**	COLLINS 1930	C
49	**The Abbey Girls on Trial**	COLLINS 1931	D
50	**Deb of Sea House** (*illus. Nina K. Brisley*)	CHAMBERS 1931	C
51	**The Third Term at Rocklands**	COLLINS 1931	C
52	**Biddy's Secret**	CHAMBERS 1932	C
53	**The Camp Mystery**	COLLINS 1932	C
54	**The Girls of Squirrel House**	COLLINS 1932	C
55	**The Reformation of Jinty**	CHAMBERS 1933	C
56	**Rosamund's Victory**	HARRAP 1933	C

57 **The Call of the Abbey School**   COLLINS 1934   **D**

58 **Jinty's Patrol**   NEWNES 1934   **C**

59 **Maidlin to the Rescue**   CHAMBERS 1934   **C**
    (*illus. R. Cloke*)

60 **Joy's New Adventure**   CHAMBERS 1935   **C**

61 **Peggy and the Brotherhood**   RTS 1936   **D**

62 **Rosamund's Tuck Shop**   RTS 1937   **D**

63 **Sylvia of Sarn**   WARNE 1937   **C**

64 **Damaris at Dorothy's**   SHELDON PRESS 1937   **C**

65 **Maidlin Bears the Torch**   RTS 1937   **C**

66 **Schooldays at the Abbey**   COLLINS 1938   **D**

67 **Rosamund's Castle**   RTS 1938   **C**

68 **Secrets of the Abbey**   COLLINS 1939   **D**
    (*illus. Heade*)

69 **Stowaways in the Abbey**   COLLINS 1940   **C**

70 **Damaris Dances**   OUP 1940   **C**

71 **Patch and a Pawn**   WARNE 1940   **C**

72 **Adventure for Two**   OUP 1941   **C**
    (*illus. Margaret Horder*)

73 **Jandy Mac Comes Back**   COLLINS 1941   **C**

74 **Pernel Wins**   MULLER 1942   **C**
    (*illus. Margaret Horder*)

75 **Maid of the Abbey**   COLLINS 1943   **C**
    (*illus. Heade*)

76 **Elsa Puts Things Right**   MULLER 1944   **B**
    (*illus. Margaret Horder*)

77 **Two Joans at the Abbey**   COLLINS 1945   **B**
    (*illus. Margaret Horder*)

78 **Daring Doranne**   MULLER 1945   **B**

79 **An Abbey Champion**   MULLER 1946   **B**
    (*illus. Margaret Horder*)

80	**Robins in the Abbey**	COLLINS 1947	**B**
81	**The Secrets of Vairy** (*illus. Margaret Horder*)	MULLER 1947	**B**
82	**Margery Meets the Roses**	LUTTERWORTH PRESS 1947	**B**
83	**A Fiddler for the Abbey** (*illus. Margaret Horder*)	MULLER 1948	**B**
84	**Guardians of the Abbey** (*illus. Margaret Horder*)	MULLER 1950	**B**
85	**Schoolgirl Jen at the Abbey**	COLLINS 1950	**B**
86	**Selma at the Abbey**	COLLINS 1952	**B**
87	**Rachel in the Abbey** (*illus. M.D. Neilson*)	MULLER 1952	**B**
88	**A Dancer from the Abbey**	COLLINS 1953	**B**
89	**The Song of the Abbey**	COLLINS 1954	**B**
90	**The Girls at Wood End**	BLACKIE 1957	**B**
91	**Tomboys at the Abbey**	COLLINS 1957	**B**
92	**Two Queens at the Abbey**	COLLINS 1959	**B**
93	**Strangers at the Abbey**	COLLINS 1963	**B**

PARDOE, M. *Born in London, 1902*

Author of generally very good adventures – but best known and loved for the character Bunkle, a schoolboy so named by his chums because he talks a lot of bunk: great stuff.

1	**The Far Island** (*illus. R.M. Turvey*)	ROUTLEDGE 1936	D
2	**Four Plus Bunkle** (*illus. J.D. Evans*)	ROUTLEDGE 1939	F
3	**Bunkle Began It** (*illus. Julie Neild*)	ROUTLEDGE 1942	C
4	**Bunkle Butts In** (*illus. Julie Neild*)	ROUTLEDGE 1943	C
5	**Bunkle Bought It** (*illus. Julie Neild*)	ROUTLEDGE 1944	C
6	**Bunkle Breaks Away** (*illus. Julie Neild*)	ROUTLEDGE 1945	C
7	**Bunkle and Belinda** (*illus. Julie Neild*)	ROUTLEDGE 1947	B
8	**Bunkle Baffles Them** (*illus. Julie Neild*)	ROUTLEDGE 1949	B
9	**Bunkle Went for Six** (*illus. Julie Neild*)	ROUTLEDGE 1950	B
10	**Bunkle Gets Busy** (*illus. Julie Neild*)	ROUTLEDGE 1951	B
11	**The Ghost Boat** (*with Howard Biggs*) (*illus. Webster Murray*)	HODDER & STOUGHTON 1951	B
12	**Bunkle's Brainwave** (*illus. Mary Smith*)	ROUTLEDGE 1952	B
13	**Bunkle Scents a Clue** (*illus. Pamela Kemp*)	ROUTLEDGE 1953	B
14	**The Boat Seekers** (*illus. B. Kay*)	HODDER & STOUGHTON 1953	B

15 Charles Arriving *(illus. Leslie Atkinson)*	ROUTLEDGE 1954	**B**
16 The Dutch Boat *(illus. Leslie Atkinson)*	HODDER & STOUGHTON 1955	**B**
17 May Madrigal *(illus. Leslie Atkinson)*	ROUTLEDGE 1955	**B**
18 Argle's Mist *(illus. Leslie Atkinson)*	ROUTLEDGE 1956	**B**
19 Curtain of Mist *Same as 18.*	FUNK & WAGNALLS US 1957	**B**
20 The Nameless Boat *(illus. Leslie Atkinson)*	HODDER & STOUGHTON 1957	**B**
21 Argle's Causeway *(illus. Leslie Atkinson)*	ROUTLEDGE 1958	**B**
22 Argle's Oracle *(illus. Audrey Fawley)*	ROUTLEDGE 1959	**B**
23 The Greek Boat Mystery	HODDER & STOUGHTON 1960	**B**
24 Bunkle Brings It Off *(illus. Audrey Fawley)*	ROUTLEDGE 1961	**B**

PEAKE, Mervyn   *British. Born in China, 1911. Died 1968*

Although the cult status of the 'Titus' trilogy is not quite so huge as it was in the 1960s, there is still a tremendous following for what is, after all, a unique work of art. In addition to the children's books listed below (you can make up your own minds as to whether the 'Titus' books are primarily intended for children or not, but I'm putting them in anyway) Peake published about half a dozen other works, largely verse, as well as illustrating some of the great children's classics: *Alice, Grimm, Swiss Family Robinson* and *Treasure Island*.

1 Captain Slaughterboard Drops Anchor	COUNTRY LIFE 1939 MACMILLAN US 1967	**P** **C**
2 Titus Groan	EYRE & SPOTTISWOODE 1946 REYNAL & HITCHCOCK 1946	**K** **H**

3	**Letters from a Lost Uncle from Polar Regions** (*stories*)	EYRE & SPOTTISWOODE 1948	**L**
4	**Gormenghast**	EYRE & SPOTTISWOODE 1950	**H**
		WEYBRIGHT & TALLEY 1967	**C**
5	**Titus Alone** *2, 4 & 5 form a trilogy. A revised edition of* Titus Alone *was published by Eyre & Spottiswoode in 1970.*	EYRE & SPOTTISWOODE 1959	**F**
		WEYBRIGHT & TALLEY 1967	**C**

Also of interest:
JOHN WATNEY: **Mervyn Peake** (MICHAEL JOSEPH 1976)

PEARCE, Philippa   *Born in Cambridgeshire, 1920*

One of the most respected of all contemporary children's writers, *Tom's Midnight Garden* having established itself as a post-war classic. Her later writing has been both praised and criticized for its sometimes almost austere control, but the control and restraint are treated with so sure a hand that it seems to me to be wholly successful. Philippa Pearce has become increasingly prolific (three new publications in 1987) but her first few books will not be easy to track down.

1	**Minnow on the Say** (*illus. Edward Ardizzone*)	OUP 1955	**E**
2	**The Minnow Leads to Treasure** *Same as 1.*	WORLD US 1958	**C**
3	**Tom's Midnight Garden** (*illus. Susan Einzig*)	OUP 1958	**E**
		LIPPINCOTT 1958	**D**
4	**Still Jim and Silent Jim**	BLACKWELL 1960	**C**
5	**Mrs Cockle's Cat** (*illus. Antony Maitland*)	CONSTABLE 1961	**C**
		LIPPINCOTT 1962	**B**
6	**A Dog So Small** (*illus. Antony Maitland*)	CONSTABLE 1962	**C**
		LIPPINCOTT 1963	**B**
7	**The Strange Sunflower** (*illus. Kathleen Williams*)	NELSON 1966	**C**

8	**The Children of the House**	LONGMAN 1968	**C**
	(*with Brian Fairfax-Lucy*)	LIPPINCOTT 1968	**B**
	(*illus. John Sergeant*)		
9	**The Elm Street Lot**	BBC 1969	**C**
	(*illus. Mina Martinez*)		
	An augmented edition was published by Kestrel		
	in 1979.		
10	**The Squirrel Wife**	LONGMAN 1971	**B**
	(*illus. Derek Collard*)	CROWELL 1972	**A**
11	**What the Neighbours Did and Other**	LONGMAN 1972	**B**
	Stories	CROWELL 1973	**A**
	(*illus. Faith Jaques*)		
12	**The Shadow-cage and Other Tales of**	KESTREL 1977	**B**
	the Supernatural	CROWELL 1977	**A**
	(*illus. Janet Archer*)		
13	**The Battle of Bubble and Squeak**	DEUTSCH 1978	**B**
	(*illus. Alan Barker*)		
14	**Wings of Courage**	KESTREL 1982	**B**
	(*illus. Hilary Abrahams*)		
15	**The Way to Sattin Shore**	KESTREL 1983	**B**
16	**Lion at School and Other Stories**	KESTREL 1985	**B**
	(*illus. Caroline Sharpe*)		
17	**Who's Afraid?** (*stories*)	KESTREL 1986	**B**
	(*illus. Peter Melnyczuk*)		
18	**Emily's Own Elephant**	MACRAE 1987	**B**
	(*illus. John Lawrence*)		
19	**The Tooth Ball**	DEUTSCH 1987	**B**
	(*illus. Helen Ganly*)		
20	**Portland Bill's Treasure Trove**	DEUTSCH 1987	**B**
	(*illus. David Armitage*)		

PIEŃKOWSKI, Jan *Born in Warsaw, 1936*

Unmistakable and stunning, Pieńkowski's illustrations render children's books more immediate and compelling than any other – particularly in the case of the 'Meg and Mog' books by Helen Nicoll (q.v.). Below are listed all the books in which Pieńkowski is responsible for both the text and the illustrations – including the classic post-war pop-up, *Haunted House*.

1	**Shapes**	HEINEMANN 1974	**B**
		SIMON & SCHUSTER 1981	**B**
2	**Sizes**	HEINEMANN 1974	**B**
		SIMON & SCHUSTER 1983	**B**
3	**Colours**	HEINEMANN 1974	**B**
	Published as Colors *by Simon & Schuster in 1981* (**A**).		
4	**Numbers**	HEINEMANN 1974	**B**
		SIMON & SCHUSTER 1981	**B**
5	**The Fairy Tale Library** (*six titles, available individually or in a boxed set*): Jack and the Beanstalk; Cinderella; Hansel and Gretel; Puss-in-Boots; Snow White; The Sleeping Beauty.	HEINEMANN 1977	**B** **Set**
6	**Home**	HEINEMANN 1979	**B**
		SIMON & SCHUSTER 1983	**B**
7	**Haunted House** (*pop-up*)	HEINEMANN 1979	**C**
		DUTTON 1979	**C**
8	**Weather**	HEINEMANN 1979	**B**
		SIMON & SCHUSTER 1983	**B**
9	**ABC**	HEINEMANN 1980	**B**
		SIMON & SCHUSTER 1981	**B**
10	**Time**	HEINEMANN 1980	**B**
		SIMON & SCHUSTER 1983	**B**
11	**Dinnertime** (*pop-up*)	GALLERY FIVE 1981	**C**
		PRICE STERN 1981	**C**
12	**Robert**	HEINEMANN 1981	**B**
		DELACORTE 1981	**B**

13	**ABC Colouring Book**	PUFFIN 1984	**A**
14	**123 Colouring Book**	PUFFIN 1984	**A**
15	**Christmas**	HEINEMANN 1984	**B**
		KNOPF 1984	**B**
16	**Farm: Colouring Book**	PUFFIN 1985	**A**
17	**Farm: Nursery Book**	HEINEMANN 1985	**A**
18	**Zoo: Colouring Book**	PUFFIN 1985	**A**
19	**Zoo: Nursery Book**	HEINEMANN 1985	**A**
20	**I'm...**	WALKER 1985	**A**
	Four titles, as follows: I'm Cat; I'm Frog;	SIMON & SCHUSTER 1985	**A**
	I'm Mouse; I'm Panda.		**Each**
21	**Food**	HEINEMANN 1986	**A**
22	**Little Monsters** (*pop-up*)	ORCHARD 1986	**B**
		PRICE STERN 1986	**B**
23	**Small Talk** (*pop-up*)	ORCHARD 1987	**B**

PORTER, Eleanor H.   *American. Born in New Hampshire, 1868. Died 1920*

Eleanor H. Porter wrote many more books for adults than for children, but none of them is remembered. Indeed, even within the context of her children's work, only *Pollyanna* is sought out today – probably one of the most famous twentieth-century titles.

1	**Cross Currents**	WILDE 1907	**F**
	(*illus. William Stecher*)	HARRAP 1928	**C**
2	**The Turn of the Tide**	WILDE 1908	**F**
	(*illus. Frank Merrill*)	HARRAP 1928	**C**
3	**The Sunbridge Girls at Six Star Ranch**	PAGE 1913	**E**
	(*illus. Frank Murch*)		
	Published under the pseudonym Eleanor Stuart.		
	Reissued as Six Star Ranch *by Page in 1916 and Stanley Paul UK.*		
4	**Pollyanna**	PAGE 1913	**I**
	(*illus. Stockton Mulford*)	PITMAN 1913	**H**

| 5 | **Pollyanna Grows Up** | PAGE 1915 | **F** |
| | (*illus. H. Weston Taylor*) | PITMAN 1915 | **E** |

PORTER, Gene Stratton   *American. Born in Indiana, 1863. Died 1924*

Hopelessly out of date and sentimental, cry the critics; but here lies the very charm for *aficionados* of the genre – and that is why such as *A Girl of the Limberlost* will live on, and be a tricky book to find, to boot.

1	**Freckles**	DOUBLEDAY 1904	**G**
	(*illus. E. Stetson Crawford*)	MURRAY 1905	**E**
2	**A Girl of the Limberlost**	DOUBLEDAY 1909	**I**
	(*illus. Wladyslaw T. Benda*)	HODDER & STOUGHTON 1911	**G**
3	**Morning Face** (*verse*)	DOUBLEDAY 1916	**D**
	(*illus. the author*)	MURRAY 1916	**C**
4	**The Magic Garden**	DOUBLEDAY 1927	**C**
	(*illus. Lee Thayer*)	HUTCHINSON 1927	**C**

Also of interest:

JEANETTE PORTER MEEHAN: **The Lady of the Limberlost: The Life and Letters of Gene Stratton Porter** (DOUBLEDAY US 1928, HUTCHINSON 1928)

POTTER, Beatrix   *Born in London, 1866. Died 1943*

You would think that by now everyone in the world must possess a copy of *Peter Rabbit*, wouldn't you? And yet, every year Warne sells between 75,000 and 100,000 copies – even more now in the new (1987) and brilliantly reoriginated edition. Beatrix Potter must be the most written-about and best loved author of twentieth-century children's books – and quite right too. Naturally enough, she is very eagerly collected – interest (and prices) rising all the time. And equally naturally, first editions of her little books are notoriously difficult to identify, sometimes a straight comparison with copies in the British Museum being the only means of positive classification. Fortunately, there are two books to help us through the minefield: *A History of the Writings of Beatrix Potter* by Leslie Linder (Warne 1971); and *Beatrix Potter: A Bibliographical Check List* by Jane Quinby (Privately Printed 1954 in an edition of 250 copies, and reissued in an edition of 450 by Ian Hodgkins & Co, 1983). In the checklist below, I draw on both of these, and append the barest issue points, but for all variations and issue details, I urge you to consult these two books in tandem. A further selection of books concerning Beatrix Potter in one way or another appears at the end of the checklist.

1 **The Tale of Peter Rabbit**   PRIVATELY PRINTED 1901   **U**
  No date appears on the book. Olive green
  boards printed in black. Flat *spine. Colour*
  frontispiece, black and white line drawings.
  White endpapers. 250 copies.

2 **The Tale of Peter Rabbit**   PRIVATELY PRINTED 1902   **T**
  'February 1902' printed on title page. Olive
  green boards printed in black. Rounded
  spine. Colour frontispiece, black and white line
  drawings. White endpapers. 200 copies.

3 **The Tale of Peter Rabbit**   WARNE 1902   **O**
  Dark brown boards stamped in white with
  rectangular coloured printed label. Colour
  illustrations. Grey leaf pattern endpapers.
  Glazed d/w with the price '1/–'. 8000 copies.
  A variant grey binding is known, but green
  boards denote a reprint of the same year as the 1st.

4 **The Tailor of Gloucester**   PRIVATELY PRINTED 1902   **T**
  Pink boards printed in black. Rounded *spine.*
  Colour frontispiece and illustrations. White
  endpapers with chain marks across the page.
  500 copies.

5 **The Tailor of Gloucester**   WARNE 1903   **L**
  Dark green boards (a maroon variant is
  known) printed in white, with rhomboid
  coloured printed label. Colour illustrations.
  Endpapers decorated with vignettes of Peter
  Rabbit, mice, a squirrel, a cat and an owl.
  20,000 copies. The 2nd printing also bears the
  date 1903.

6 **The Tale of Squirrel Nutkin**   WARNE 1903   **L**
  Dark grey or dark blue boards, printed in
  white, with circular coloured printed label.
  Colour illustrations. Endpapers as in 5. 10,000
  copies. The first three printings all bear the
  date 1903.

7 **The Tale of Benjamin Bunny** WARNE 1904 **K**
*Lavender, grey or tan boards, gilt
stamped, with oval coloured printed
label. Colour illustrations. Endpapers a
redrawn version of those in 5 and 6.
20,000 copies. Reprint of 10,000 copies
thought to be identical.*

8 **The Tale of Two Bad Mice** WARNE 1904 **L**
*Grey or maroon boards, stamped in white, with
rectangular coloured printed label. Colour
illustrations. Endpapers as in 7. 20,000 copies.
Reprint of 10,000 copies thought to be
identical.*

9 **The Tale of Mrs Tiggy-Winkle** WARNE 1905 **L**
*Green or brown boards, stamped in white, with
rectangular coloured printed label. Colour
illustrations. Endpapers as in 7. 20,000 copies.
Reprint of 10,000 copies thought to be
identical.*

10 **The Pie and the Patty-Pan** WARNE 1905 **J**
*Maroon, brown or light blue cloth, stamped in
white with circular coloured printed label.
Colour illustrations. Mottled light blue
endpapers. Larger format: just over $7 \times 5\frac{1}{2}$
inches. 17,500 copies. First edition title page
bears the date.*

11 **The Tale of Mr Jeremy Fisher** WARNE 1906 **K**
*Red or grey boards, stamped in white, with
oval coloured printed label. Colour illustrations.
Endpapers as in 7. 20,000 copies. Reprint of
5,000 copies thought to be identical.*

12 **The Story of a Fierce Bad Rabbit** WARNE 1906 **M**
*In wallet (panoramic) form, grey-green cloth
bearing rectangular illustration and lettered in
white. Colour illustrations. 10,000 copies.
Printed in book form 1916.*

13 **The Story of Miss Moppet** WARNE 1906 **L**
*In wallet (panoramic) form, grey cloth bearing
rectangular illustration and lettered in white.*

Colour illustrations. 10,000 copies. Printed in book form 1916.

14 The Tale of Tom Kitten   WARNE 1907   **K**

Green-grey or beige boards, stamped in white, with rectangular coloured printed label. Colour illustrations. Endpapers a new variation of those in 7. 20,000 copies. Reprints of 5,000 and 7,500 copies in the same year are thought to be identical to the 1st.

15 The Tale of Jemima Puddle-Duck   WARNE 1908   **K**

Grey or green boards, stamped in white with rectangular coloured printed label. Colour illustrations. Endpapers a third variation on those in 7. 20,000 copies. Two reprints in the same year of 5,000 copies each are thought to be identical with the 1st.

16 The Roly-Poly Pudding   WARNE 1908   **K**

Dark red cloth with bevelled edges, stamped in green and gilt with rectangular coloured printed label. Endpapers depict mice in and around sack. Title page of first printing bears the words 'All rights reserved.' 7,500 copies.

17 The Tale of the Flopsy Bunnies   WARNE 1909   **K**

Green or brown boards, stamped in white, with triangular coloured printed label. Colour illustrations. Endpapers a fourth variation on those in 7. 20,000 copies.

18 Ginger and Pickles   WARNE 1909   **J**

Tan or mid-green boards, stamped in green or white, with rectangular coloured printed label. Colour illustrations. Endpapers are four new illustrations, the two at the front depicting mice and a bottle, and those at the rear mice, a frog and a tortoise with weighing scales. 15,000 copies. Reprint of 10,875 copies thought to be identical.

19 The Tale of Mrs Tittlemouse WARNE 1910 J

Blue or cream boards, stamped in gilt, with hexagonal coloured printed label. Colour illustrations. Endpapers a fifth variation on those in 7. 25,000 copies. Reprint of 10,000 copies thought to be identical.

20 Peter Rabbit's Painting Book WARNE 1911 N

Green limp cloth, with twelve colour illustrations and twelve outline drawings. 20,000 copies.

21 The Tale of Timmy Tiptoes WARNE 1911 J

Dark green or brown boards, stamped in white, with arched coloured printed label. Colour illustrations. Endpapers as in 19. 25,000 copies. Reprint of 10,000 copies thought to be identical.

22 The Tale of Mr Tod WARNE 1912 K

Tan boards (rounded spine) stamped in brown, with rectangular coloured printed label. Colour illustrations. Endpapers are a new double spread illustration depicting many Potter characters clustered around a hoarding advertising the books. 25,000 copies. Reprint of 10,000 copies thought to be identical.

23 The Tale of Pigling Bland WARNE 1913 L

Maroon or green boards (rounded spine) stamped in white with rectangular coloured printed label. Colour illustrations. Endpapers as in 22. 25,000 copies. Reprint of 10,000 copies thought to be identical.

24 Appley-Dapply's Nursery Rhymes WARNE 1917 I

Green boards stamped in dark green, with rectangular coloured printed label. Colour illustrations. Endpapers a simplified variation of those in 22. 20,000 copies. No date appears on the title page, therefore indistinguishable from the reprint of 15,000 copies.

25 **Tom Kitten's Painting Book**   WARNE 1917   **M**
Brown limp cloth, with eight colour
illustrations and eight outline drawings.
5,000 copies.

26 **The Tale of Johnny Town-Mouse**   WARNE 1918   **K**
Brown or grey boards, stamped in white with
irregularly shaped coloured printed label.
Colour illustrations. Endpapers a sixth
variation of those in 7. 30,000 copies. The 1st
bears no date, but the 'n' of London is missing
in the imprint.

27 **Cecily Parsley's Nursery Rhymes**   WARNE 1922   **I**
Red boards, stamped in white with rectangular
coloured printed label. Colour illustrations.
Endpapers slight variation on those in 24.
20,000 copies. No date on the title page.

28 **Jemima Puddle-Duck's Painting**   WARNE 1925   **L**
Book
Limp grey cloth with eight coloured
illustrations and eight line drawings. 10,350
copies.

29 **Peter Rabbit's Almanac for 1929**   WARNE 1928   **I**
Tan boards, stamped in brown with egg-
shaped coloured printed label. Endpapers depict
a lettuce bordered by rabbits. 15,000 copies.

30 **The Fairy Caravan**   McKAY US 1929   **N**
Green boards stamped in dark green.
Frontispiece and five coloured illustrations. An
oddity, about which no one seems to know much
– including the number of copies printed. A
limited edition of 100 copies was put out in the
same year in grey boards and deckle-edged
paper. The first trade edition was published by
Warne in 1952 (7,500 copies) (**D**)*.*

31 **The Tale of Little Pig Robinson**   WARNE 1930   **I**
Blue boards stamped in gilt and brown, with
coloured vignette. Endpapers with brown and
white vignettes. 5,000 copies.

32 The Tale of Little Pig Robinson   McKAY US 1930   J
*Green cloth with light green label. Cream
endpapers with green vignettes as in 31. This
edition has more illustrations than the Warne
edition.*

33 Sister Anne   McKAY US 1932   J
*Blue cloth stamped in gilt and bearing vignette.
White endpapers. Unknown quantity printed.*

34 Wag-by-Wall   WARNE 1944   N
*Light green cloth. Limited to 100 numbered
copies. An American edition was published
during the same year by The Horn Book Inc,
unlimited, and with decorations by J.J.
Lankes. Tan buckram, stamped in red (**F**).*

35 The Tale of the Faithful Dove   WARNE 1955   K
*(illus. Marie Angel)
Light green cloth. Limited to 100 numbered
copies. A trade edition was published the
following year – 2,500 copies UK, 1,500
copies US (**E**).*

36 The Tailor of Gloucester: Facsimile   WARNE 1968   G
**of the Original Manuscript and
Illustrations**
*Black cloth, boxed. Limited to 1,500 numbered
copies, and sold at eight guineas.*

37 The Tailor of Gloucester from the   WARNE 1968   E
Original Manuscript
*Based on 36, first published in US (12,000
copies) and in UK in 1969 (5,000 copies).*

38 The Sly Old Cat   WARNE 1971   C

39 The Tale of Tuppenny   WARNE 1973   B
(illus. Marie Angel)

*It should be noted that nearly all of the 'little books' were issued simultaneously in a more
decorative binding, and at a slightly higher price.*

Also of interest:
ED. LESLIE LINDER & W.A. HERRING: **The Art of Beatrix Potter** (WARNE 1955,
revised ed. 1972)

LESLIE LINDER: **The Journal of Beatrix Potter from 1881 to 1897, Transcribed from Her Code Writing** (WARNE 1966)
MARGARET LANE: **The Tale of Beatrix Potter: A Biography** (WARNE 1946, *revised ed.* 1968)
The History of 'The Tale of Peter Rabbit' (WARNE, 1976)
JUDY TAYLOR: **That Naughty Rabbit!: Beatrix Potter and Peter Rabbit** (WARNE, 1987)

PRØYSEN, Alf   *Born in Norway, 1914. Died 1970*

Creator of the rather charming Mrs Pepperpot, who was often given to shrinking to the size of same. Prøysen wrote a few other things too, but I list here just the English and American editions of the Mrs Pepperpot series, all of which were illustrated by Bjorn Berg.

1	**Little Old Mrs Pepperpot and Other Stories**	HUTCHINSON 1959	C
		McDOWELL OBOLENSKY 1960	B
2	**Mrs Pepperpot Again and Other Stories**	HUTCHINSON 1960	B
		McDOWELL OBOLENSKSY 1961	B
3	**Mrs Pepperpot to the Rescue and Other Stories**	HUTCHINSON 1963	B
		PANTHEON 1964	A
4	**Mrs Pepperpot in the Magic Wood and Other Stories**	HUTCHINSON 1968	B
		PANTHEON 1968	A
5	**Mrs Pepperpot's Busy Day**	HUTCHINSON 1970	B
6	**Mrs Pepperpot's Outing**	HUTCHINSON 1971	B
		PANTHEON 1971	A
7	**Mrs Pepperpot's Christmas**	HUTCHINSON 1972	B
8	**Mrs Pepperpot's Year**	HUTCHINSON 1973	B

RANSOME, Arthur — *Born in Yorkshire, 1884. Died 1967*

Author of the hugely influential, much loved (and copied) *Swallows and Amazons*, Ransome remains popular with collectors today, although children themselves might feel that they have progressed from jolly holiday stories – until, of course, they read *Swallows and Amazons*, whereupon they are generally hooked. In addition to his children's books, Ransome published one adult novel and nearly twenty works of non-fiction as diverse as critical studies on Edgar Allan Poe and Oscar Wilde as well as several books on fishing.

1	**The Child's Book of the Seasons**	TREHERNE 1906	I
2	**The Things in Our Garden**	TREHERNE 1906	G
3	**Pond and Stream**	TREHERNE 1906	G
4	**Highways and Byways in Fairyland**	RIVERS 1906	H
		McBRIDE 1909	D
5	**The Imp and the Elf and the Ogre**	NISBET 1910	G
6	**Old Peter's Russian Tales**	JACK 1916	F
	(*illus. Dmitri Mitrokhin*)	STOKES 1917	D
7	**Aladdin and His Wonderful Lamp**	NISBET 1919	H
	(*verse*) (*illus. Mackenzie*)	BRENTANO'S 1920	F
8	**The Soldier and Death:**	WILSON 1920	E
	A Russian Folk Tale Told in	HUEBSCH 1922	C
	English		
9	**Swallows and Amazons**	CAPE 1930	I
	(*illus. Helene Carter*)	LIPPINCOTT 1931	F
10	**Swallowdale**	CAPE 1931	F
	(*illus. Clifford Webb*)	LIPPINCOTT 1932	D
11	**Peter Duck**	CAPE 1932	D
	(*illus. the author*)	LIPPINCOTT 1933	B
12	**Winter Holiday**	CAPE 1933	D
	(*illus. the author*)	LIPPINCOTT 1934	B
13	**Coot Club**	CAPE 1934	D
	(*illus. the author & Helene Carter*)	LIPPINCOTT 1935	B
14	**Pigeon Post**	CAPE 1936	D
	(*illus. the author*)	LIPPINCOTT 1937	B
15	**We Didn't Mean to Go to Sea**	CAPE 1937	D
	(*illus. the author*)	MACMILLAN 1938	B

16	**Secret Water**	CAPE 1939	**D**
	(*illus. the author*)	MACMILLAN 1940	**B**
17	**The Big Six**	CAPE 1940	**C**
	(*illus. the author*)	MACMILLAN 1941	**B**
18	**Missee Lee**	CAPE 1941	**C**
	(*illus. the author*)	MACMILLAN 1942	**B**
19	**The Picts and the Martyrs; or, No Welcome at All**	CAPE 1943	**C**
		MACMILLAN 1943	**B**
	(*illus. the author*)		
20	**Great Northern?**	CAPE 1947	**B**
		MACMILLAN 1948	**A**

New editions of Swallows and Amazons *and* Swallowdale *were published in 1938, with illustrations by the author.*

Also of interest:
HUGH BROGAN: **Arthur Ransome** (CAPE 1984)

REEVES, James *Born in London, 1909. Died 1978*

An author with a tremendous output, largely neglected by collectors – perhaps because of this very diversity and the sheer number of books for both children and adults that bear his name (including *dozens* of works edited by him). Reeves' writing is elegant and attractive, however, and a re-evaluation might be timely. I list here all the children's work.

1	**The Wandering Moon** (*verse*)	HEINEMANN 1950	**B**
	(*illus. Evadne Rowan*)	DUTTON 1960	**A**
2	**Mulcaster Market: Three Plays for Young People**	HEINEMANN 1951	**B**
		DUTTON 1963	**A**
	(*illus. Dudley Cutler*)		
	Includes: Mulcaster Market, The Pedlar's Dream *and* The Stolen Boy.		
3	**The Blackbird in the Lilac: Verses**	OUP 1952	**F**
	(*illus. Edward Ardizzone*)	DUTTON 1959	**C**
4	**The King Who Took Sunshine** (*play*)	HEINEMANN 1954	**A**
5	**Pigeons and Princesses** (*fiction*)	HEINEMANN 1956	**E**
	(*illus. Edward Ardizzone*)		

6	**A Health to John Patch: A Ballad Operetta**	BOOSEY 1957	**B**
7	**Prefabulous Animiles** (*verse*) (*illus. Edward Ardizzone*)	HEINEMANN 1957 DUTTON 1960	**E** **C**
8	**Mulbridge Manor** (*fiction*) (*illus. Geraldine Spence*)	HEINEMANN 1958	**B**
9	**Titus in Trouble** (*fiction*) (*illus. Edward Ardizzone*)	BODLEY HEAD 1959 WALCK 1960	**D** **B**
10	**Ragged Robin** (*verse*) (*illus. Jane Paton*)	HEINEMANN 1961 DUTTON 1961	**B** **A**
11	**Hurdy-Gurdy: Selected Poems for Children** (*illus. Edward Ardizzone*)	HEINEMANN 1961	**D**
12	**Sailor Rumbelow and Britannia** (*fiction*) (*illus. Edward Ardizzone*)	HEINEMANN 1962	**D**
13	**Sailor Rumbelow and Other Stories** (*illus. Edward Ardizzone*) *Contains 12 and 5.*	DUTTON 1962	**C**
14	**The Strange Light** (*fiction*) (*illus. Lynton Lamb*)	HEINEMANN 1964 RAND McNALLY 1966	**B** **A**
15	**The Story of Jackie Thimble** (*verse*) (*illus. Edward Ardizzone*)	DUTTON 1964 CHATTO & WINDUS 1965	**C** **C**
16	**The Pillar-box Thieves** (*fiction*) (*illus. Dick Hart*)	NELSON 1965	**B**
17	**Rhyming Will** (*fiction*) (*illus. Edward Ardizzone*)	HAMISH HAMILTON 1967 McGRAW HILL 1968	**C** **C**
18	**Mr Horrox and the Gratch** (*illus. Quentin Blake*)	ABELARD SCHUMAN 1969	**C**
19	**The Path of Gold** (*fiction*) (*illus. Krystyna Turska*)	HAMISH HAMILTON 1972	**B**
20	**Complete Poems For Children** (*illus. Edward Ardizzone*)	HEINEMANN 1973	**C**
21	**The Lion That Flew** (*fiction*) (*illus. Edward Ardizzone*)	CHATTO & WINDUS 1974	**C**

22	**More Prefabulous Animiles** (*verse*) (*illus. Edward Ardizzone*)	HEINEMANN 1975	C
23	**The Clever Mouse** (*illus. Barbara Swiderska*)	CHATTO & WINDUS 1976	B
24	**Eggtime Stories** (*fiction*) (*illus. Colin McNaughton*)	BLACKIE 1978	A
25	**The James Reeves Storybook** (*illus. Edward Ardizzone*)	HEINEMANN 1978	C
26	**A Prince in Danger** (*fiction*) (*illus. Gareth Floyd*)	KAYE & WARD 1979	A

In addition to the above gorgeously illustrated fiction and verse, Reeves also published the following gorgeously illustrated retellings, fables and the like:

27	**English Fables and Fairy Stories, Retold** (*illus. Joan Kiddell-Monroe*)	OUP 1954	B
28	**Exploits of Don Quixote, Retold** (*illus. Edward Ardizzone*)	BLACKIE 1959 WALCK 1960	D C
29	**Fables from Aesop, Retold** (*illus. Maurice Wilson*)	BLACKIE 1961 WALCK 1962	B B
30	**Three Tall Tales, Chosen from Traditional Sources** (*illus. Edward Ardizzone*)	ABELARD SCHUMAN 1964	C
31	**The Road to a Kingdom: Stories from the Old and New Testaments** (*illus. Richard Kennedy*)	HEINEMANN 1965	B
32	**The Secret Shoemakers and Other Stories** (*illus. Edward Ardizzone*)	ABELARD SCHUMAN 1966	C
33	**The Cold Flame, Based on a Tale from the Collection of the Brothers Grimm** (*illus. Charles Keeping*)	HAMISH HAMILTON 1967 MEREDITH PRESS 1969	C B
34	**The Trojan Horse** (*illus. Krystyna Turska*)	HAMISH HAMILTON 1968 WATTS 1969	B B

35	**Heroes and Monsters: Legends of Ancient Greece Retold: 1. Gods and Voyagers** (*illus. Sarah Nechamkin*)	BLACKIE 1969	**B**
36	**Heroes and Monsters: Legends of Ancient Greece Retold: 2. Islands and Palaces** (*illus. Sarah Nechamkin*)	BLACKIE 1971	**B**
37	**The Angel and the Donkey** (*illus. Edward Ardizzone*)	HAMISH HAMILTON 1969 McGRAW HILL 1970	**C** **B**
38	**Maildun the Voyager** (*illus. John Lawrence*)	HAMISH HAMILTON 1971 WALCK 1972	**B** **B**
39	**How The Moon Began** (*illus. Edward Ardizzone*)	ABELARD SCHUMAN 1971	**C**
40	**The Forbidden Forest and Other Stories** (*illus. Raymond Briggs*)	HEINEMANN 1973	**C**
41	**The Voyage of Odysseus: Homer's Odyssey Retold**	BLACKIE 1973	**B**
42	**Two Greedy Bears** (*illus. Gareth Floyd*)	HAMISH HAMILTON 1974	**B**
43	**Quest and Conquest: Pilgrim's Progress Retold** (*illus. Joanna Troughton*)	BLACKIE 1976	**B**
44	**Snow-White and Rose-Red** (*illus. Jenny Rodwell*)	ANDERSEN PRESS 1979	**A**

RICHARDS, Frank

Pseudonym of Charles Hamilton
Born in Middlesex, 1876. Died 1961

I say, you chaps: what more is there to say about the – oh, one *has* to say – 'phenomenon' that was Charles Hamilton, alias (among other things) Frank Richards? Author of millions and millions of words of pure and utter joy that will be read and re-read as long as civilization exists. As is well known, Richards single-handedly wrote the boys' papers *The Gem* and *The Magnet* during the early part of this century, and so were born Greyfriars and St Jim's – to say nothing of Harry Wharton, Bob Cherry, Frank Nugent, Johnny Bull

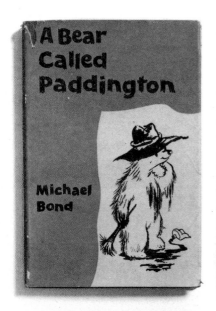

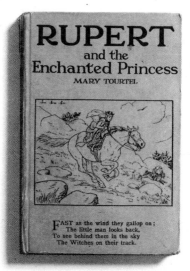

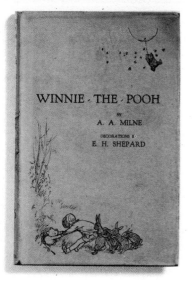

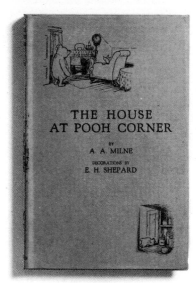

The three most famous bears in the world, with artwork by Peggy Fortnum, Mary Tourtel (the original creator of 'Rupert' in this the first of the little yellow books), and Ernest H. Shepard.

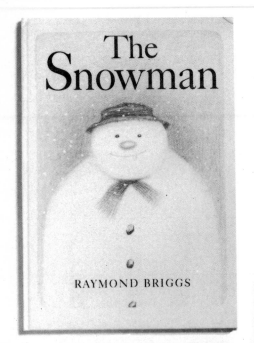

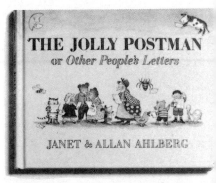

Four for the tinies, all illustrated by their authors. *The Snowman* and *The Jolly Postman* seem to be certain classics of the very near future.

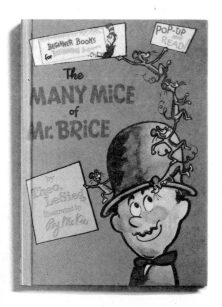

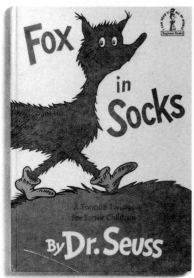

Four more guaranteed to delight the younger set, as well as to educate. Whether or not Dr. Seuss or Dick Bruna will be taken up by collectors largely remains to be seen.

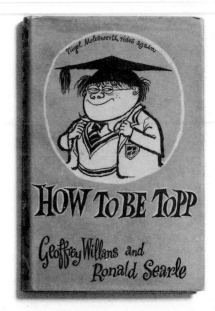

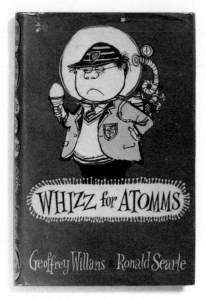

Nigel Molesworth lives for ever! This is guaranteed by the evergreen and achingly funny prose of Willans, and the brilliant illustrations by Ronald Searle.

and Hurree Jamset Ram Singh. And there was another one – name escapes me for a minute. Below are listed all Richards' book publications – firstly the stories written under pseudonyms other than Richards, as well as the non-Greyfriars stuff, and these are followed by a complete listing of the Bunter books; *that's* the name, Billy Bunter: I knew I'd get it in the end. I hope one day to complete my own collection – financed by a postal order that I am expecting any minute now.

AS FRANK RICHARDS (non-Bunter):

#	Title	Publisher	
1	**The Secret of the School**	MERRETT 1946	B
2	**The Black Sheep of Sparshott**	MERRETT 1946	B
3	**First Man In**	MERRETT 1946	B
4	**Looking After Lamb**	MERRETT 1946	B
5	**The Hero of Sparshott**	MERRETT 1946	B
6	**Pluck Will Tell**	MERRETT 1946	B
7	**Top Study at Topham**	MATTHEW 1947	B
8	**Bunny Binks on the Warpath**	MATTHEW 1947	B
9	**The Dandy of Topham**	MATTHEW 1947	B
10	**Sent to Coventry**	MATTHEW 1947	B
11	**Jack of All Trades**	MANDEVILLE 1950	B
12	**The Lone Texan**	ATLANTIC 1954	B

AS HILDA RICHARDS:

#	Title	Publisher	
1	**Winifred on the Warpath**	MERRETT 1946	C
2	**The Girls of Headland House**	MERRETT 1946	C
3	**Under Becky's Thumb**	MERRETT 1946	C
4	**Pamela of St Olive's**	MATTHEW 1947	C
5	**The Stranded Schoolgirls**	MATTHEW 1947	C
6	**The Jape of the Term**	MATTHEW 1947	C
7	**Bessie Bunter of Cliff House School** (*illus. R.J. Macdonald*)	SKILTON 1949	E

AS MARTIN CLIFFORD:

#	Title	Publisher	
1	**The Secret of the Study**	MANDEVILLE 1949	B

2	Tom Merry and Co of St Jim's	MANDEVILLE 1949	B
3	Rallying Round Gussie	MANDEVILLE 1950	B
4	The Scapegrace of St Jim's	MANDEVILLE 1951	B
5	Talbot's Secret	MANDEVILLE 1951	B
6	Tom Merry's Secret	HAMILTON 1952	B
7	Tom Merry's Rival	HAMILTON 1952	B
8	The Man from the Past	HAMILTON 1952	B
9	Who Ragged Railton?	HAMILTON 1952	B
10	Skimpole's Snapshot	HAMILTON 1952	B
11	Trouble for Trimble	HAMILTON 1952	B
12	D'Arcy in Danger	HAMILTON 1952	B
13	D'Arcy on the Warpath	HAMILTON 1952	B
14	D'Arcy's Disappearance	HAMILTON 1952	B
15	D'Arcy the Reformer	HAMILTON 1952	B
16	D'Arcy's Day Off	HAMILTON 1952	B
17	A Strange Secret	OLD BOYS' BOOK CLUB 1968	B

BILLY BUNTER BY FRANK RICHARDS:

1	**Billy Bunter of Greyfriars School** (*illus. R.J. Macdonald*)	SKILTON 1947	H
2	**Billy Bunter's Barring-out** (*illus. R.J. Macdonald*)	SKILTON 1948	E
3	**Billy Bunter's Banknote**	SKILTON 1948	E
4	**Billy Bunter in Brazil**	SKILTON 1949	E
5	**Billy Bunter's Christmas Party** (*illus. R.J. Macdonald*)	SKILTON 1949	E
6	**Billy Bunter Among the Cannibals** (*illus. R.J. Macdonald*)	SKILTON 1950	D
7	**Billy Bunter's Benefit** (*illus. R.J. Macdonald*)	SKILTON 1950	D

8	**Billy Bunter Butts In** (*illus. R.J. Macdonald*)	SKILTON 1951	**D**
9	**Billy Bunter's Postal Order** (*illus. R.J. Macdonald*)	SKILTON 1951	**D**
10	**Billy Bunter and the Blue Mauritius** (*illus. R.J. Macdonald*)	SKILTON 1952	**D**
11	**Billy Bunter's Beanfeast** (*illus. R.J. Macdonald*)	CASSELL 1952	**D**
12	**Billy Bunter's Brain-wave** (*illus. R.J. Macdonald*)	CASSELL 1953	**D**
13	**Billy Bunter's First Case** (*illus. R.J. Macdonald*)	CASSELL 1953	**D**
14	**Billy Bunter the Bold** (*illus. R.J. Macdonald*)	CASSELL 1954	**D**
15	**Bunter Does His Best** (*illus. R.J. Macdonald*)	CASSELL 1954	**D**
16	**Backing Up Billy Bunter** (*illus. C.H. Chapman*)	CASSELL 1955	**C**
17	**Billy Bunter's Double** (*illus. R.J. Macdonald*)	CASSELL 1955	**C**
18	**The Banishing of Billy Bunter** (*illus. C.H. Chapman*)	CASSELL 1956	**C**
19	**Lord Billy Bunter**	CASSELL 1956	**C**
20	**Billy Bunter Afloat** (*illus. C.H. Chapman*)	CASSELL 1957	**C**
21	**Billy Bunter's Bolt** (*illus. C.H. Chapman*)	CASSELL 1957	**C**
22	**Billy Bunter the Hiker** (*illus. C.H. Chapman*)	CASSELL 1958	**C**
23	**Billy Bunter's Bargain** (*illus. C.H. Chapman*)	CASSELL 1958	**C**
24	**Bunter Comes for Christmas** (*illus. C.H. Chapman*)	CASSELL 1959	**C**

25 **Bunter Out of Bounds**   CASSELL 1959   C
    (*illus. C.H. Chapman*)

26 **Bunter Keeps It Dark**   CASSELL 1960   C
    (*illus. C.H. Chapman*)

27 **Bunter the Bad Lad**   CASSELL 1960   C

28 **Billy Bunter at Butlin's**   CASSELL 1961   C
    (*illus. C.H. Chapman*)

29 **Billy Bunter's Treasure Hunt** CASSELL 1961   C
    (*illus. C.H. Chapman*)

30 **Bunter the Ventriloquist**   CASSELL 1961   C
    (*illus. C.H. Chapman*)

31 **Billy Bunter's Bodyguard**   CASSELL 1962   C
    (*illus. C.H. Chapman*)

32 **Bunter the Caravanner**   CASSELL 1962   C
    (*illus. C.H. Chapman*)

33 **Just Like Bunter**   CASSELL 1963   C
    (*illus. C.H. Chapman*)

34 **Big Chief Bunter**   CASSELL 1963   C
    (*illus. C.H. Chapman*)

35 **Bunter the Stowaway**   CASSELL 1964   C
    (*illus. C.H. Chapman*)

36 **Thanks to Bunter**   CASSELL 1964   C
    (*illus. C.H. Chapman*)

37 **Bunter and the Phantom of the   ARMADA 1965   B
    Towers**

38 **Bunter the Racketeer**   ARMADA 1965   B

39 **Bunter the Sportsman**   CASSELL 1965   C
    (*illus. C.H. Chapman*)

40 **Bunter the Tough Guy of Greyfriars** ARMADA 1965 B

41 **Bunter's Holiday Cruise**   ARMADA 1965   B

42 **Bunter's Last Fling**   CASSELL 1965   C
    (*illus. C.H. Chapman*)

43	**Billy Bunter and the Man from South America**	HAMLYN 1967	**B**
44	**Billy Bunter and the School Rebellion**	HAMLYN 1967	**B**
45	**Billy Bunter and the Secret Enemy**	HAMLYN 1967	**B**
46	**Billy Bunter's Big Top**	HAMLYN 1967	**B**
47	**Billy Bunter and the Bank Robber**	HAMLYN 1968	**B**
48	**Billy Bunter, Sportsman**	HAMLYN 1968	**B**
49	**Billy Bunter and the Crooked Captain**	HAMLYN 1968	**B**
50	**Billy Bunter's Convict**	HAMLYN 1968	**B**

Also of interest:
The Autobiography of Frank Richards (SKILTON 1952)
W.O.G. LOFTS & DEREK J. ADLEY: **The World of Frank Richards** (BAKER 1975)

ROSS, Diana   *British. Born in Malta, 1910*

An author with a loyal band of enthusiasts, despite her lack of production in recent years. Perhaps rather less known now than she was during the 'forties and 'fifties, when her 'Little Red Engine' series began to appear – incidentally predating Awdry's *Thomas the Tank Engine*. The illustrator 'Gri' who appears several times in the ensuing listing is none other than Diana Ross herself.

1	**The World at Work: Getting You Things** (*non-fiction*)	COUNTRY LIFE 1939	**D**
2	**The World at Work: Making You Things** (*non-fiction*)	COUNTRY LIFE 1939	**D**
3	**The Story of the Beetle Who Lived Alone** (*illus. Margaret Kaye*)	FABER 1941	**C**
4	**Uncle Anty's Album** (*illus. Antony Denny*)	FABER 1942	**C**
5	**The Golden Hen and Other Stories** (*illus. Gri*)	FABER 1942	**C**

6 **The Little Red Engine Gets a Name** FABER 1942 C
  (*illus. George Lewitt-Him*)

7 **The Wild Cherry** FABER 1943 C
  (*illus. Gri*)

8 **Nursery Tales** FABER 1944 C
  (*illus. Nancy Innes*)

9 **The Story of Louisa** PENGUIN 1945 B
  (*illus. Margaret Kaye*)

10 **Little Red Engine Series:**
  (*illus Leslie Wood*)
  The Story of the Little Red Engine FABER 1945 C
  The Little Red Engine Goes to FABER 1946–7 B
  Market Each
  The Little Red Engine Goes to Town
  The Little Red Engine Goes Travelling
  The Little Red Engine and the Rocket
  The Little Red Engine Goes Home
  The Little Red Engine Goes to be Mended
  The Little Red Engine and the Taddlecome Outing
  The Little Red Engine Goes Carolling

11 **Whoo, Whoo, the Wind Blew** FABER 1946 B
  (*illus. Leslie Wood*)

12 **The Tooter and Other Nursery Tales** FABER 1951 B
  (*illus. Irene Hawkins*)

13 **The Enormous Apple Pie and Other Miss Pussy Tales** LUTTERWORTH PRESS 1951 C
  (*illus. Peggy Fortnum*)

14 **Ebenezer the Big Balloon** FABER 1952 B
  (*illus. Leslie Wood*)

15 **The Bridal Gown and Other Stories** FABER 1952 B
  (*illus. Gri*)

16 **The Bran Tub** LUTTERWORTH PRESS 1954 B
  (*illus. Gri*)

17	**William and the Lorry** (*illus. Shirley Hughes*)	FABER 1956	B
18	**Child of Air** (*illus. Gri*)	LUTTERWORTH PRESS 1957	B
19	**The Dreadful Boy** (*illus. Prudence Seward*)	HAMISH HAMILTON 1959	B
20	**The Merry-go-round** (*illus. Shirley Hughes*)	LUTTERWORTH PRESS 1963	B
21	**Old Perisher** (*illus. Edward Ardizzone*)	FABER 1965	C
22	**Nothing to Do** (*illus. Constance Marshall*)	HAMISH HAMILTON 1966	B
23	**I Love My Life with an A: Where is He?** (*illus. Leslie Wood*)	FABER 1972	B

SCARRY, Richard
American. Born in Boston, 1919

Although Scarry is far too important a figure to omit (his international following is colossal) I did agonize a fair bit over whether or not to include the whole lot, because I do not imagine that collectors will be seriously interested in gathering them all (and especially not the unshelvable *huge* ones). But such is the policy of this book, wherever possible, so here goes:

1	**The Great Big Car and Truck Book**	SIMON & SCHUSTER 1951	**C**
2	**Rabbit and His Friends**	SIMON & SCHUSTER 1953	**C**
		MULLER 1954	**C**
3	**Nursery Tales**	SIMON & SCHUSTER 1958	**B**
4	**Naughty Bunny**	GOLDEN PRESS 1959	**B**
		MULLER 1959	**B**
5	**Tinker and Tanker**	DOUBLEDAY 1960	**B**
		HAMLYN 1969	**A**
6	**Tinker and Tanker Out West**	DOUBLEDAY 1961	**B**
		HAMLYN 1969	**A**
7	**Tinker and Tanker and the Pirates**	DOUBLEDAY 1961	**B**
8	**Tinker and Tanker and Their Space Ship**	DOUBLEDAY 1961	**B**
9	**Manners**	GOLDEN PRESS 1962	**B**
10	**Tinker and Tanker, Knights of the Round Table**	DOUBLEDAY 1963	**B**
		HAMLYN 1969	**A**
11	**Tinker and Tanker in Africa**	DOUBLEDAY 1963	**B**
		HAMLYN 1969	**A**
12	**Best Word Book Ever**	GOLDEN PRESS 1963	**B**
		HAMLYN 1964	**B**
13	**What Animals Do**	GOLDEN PRESS 1963	**B**
14	**A Tinker and Tanker Coloring Book**	DOUBLEDAY 1963	**A**
15	**The Rooster Struts**	GOLDEN PRESS 1963	**B**
	Reissued in 1964 by Golden Press as The Golden Happy Book of Animals *and in the same year by Hamlyn as* Animals.		
16	**Polite Elephant**	GOLDEN PRESS 1964	**B**

17	**Is This the House of Mistress Mouse?**	GOLDEN PRESS 1964	**B**
18	**Animal Mother Goose**	GOLDEN PRESS 1964	**B**
		HAMLYN 1965	**A**
19	**Best Nursery Rhymes Ever**	GOLDEN PRESS 1964	**B**
		HAMLYN 1971	**A**
20	**Teeny Tiny Tales**	GOLDEN PRESS 1965	**B**
		HAMLYN 1970	**A**
21	**The Santa Claus Book**	GOLDEN PRESS 1965	**B**
22	**The Bunny Book**	GOLDEN PRESS 1965	**B**
		HAMLYN 1966	**A**
23	**Busy Busy World**	GOLDEN PRESS 1965	**B**
		HAMLYN 1966	**A**
24	**Storybook Dictionary**	RANDOM HOUSE 1966	**A**
25	**The Egg in the Hole Book**	GOLDEN PRESS 1967	**B**
26	**Planes**	GOLDEN PRESS 1967	**A**
27	**Trains**	GOLDEN PRESS 1967	**A**
28	**Boats**	GOLDEN PRESS 1967	**A**
29	**Cars**	GOLDEN PRESS 1967	**A**

Hamlyn published two volumes in 1969:
Trains and Cars *and* Boats and Planes.
In 1985 they published all four in one volume.

30	**The Early Bird**	RANDOM HOUSE 1968	**A**
		COLLINS 1970	**A**
31	**What Do People Do All Day?**	RANDOM HOUSE 1968	**A**
		COLLINS 1969	**A**
32	**The Great Pie Robbery**	RANDOM HOUSE 1969	**A**
		COLLINS 1969	**A**
33	**The Supermarket Mystery**	RANDOM HOUSE 1969	**A**
		COLLINS 1969	**A**
34	**Great Big Schoolhouse**	RANDOM HOUSE 1969	**A**
		COLLINS 1969	**A**

35	**Great Big Air Book**	RANDOM HOUSE 1971	**A**
		COLLINS 1971	**A**
36	**ABC Word Book**	RANDOM HOUSE 1971	**A**
		COLLINS 1971	**A**
37	**Look and Learn Library** (*four volumes*):	GOLDEN PRESS 1971	**A**
	Best Stories Ever; Fun With Words;		**Each**
	Going Places; Things To Know.		
38	**Funniest Storybook Ever**	RANDOM HOUSE 1972	**A**
	Reissued in 1978 by both Random House and	COLLINS 1972	**A**
	Collins in two volumes: Little Bedtime		
	Book *and* Mr Fixit.		
39	**Nicky Goes to the Doctor**	GOLDEN PRESS 1972	**A**
		HAMLYN 1972	**A**
40	**Hop Aboard, Here We Go!**	RANDOM HOUSE 1972	**A**
		HAMLYN 1972	**A**
41	**Silly Stories**	GOLDEN PRESS 1973	**A**
		HAMLYN 1974	**A**
42	**Babykins and His Family**	GOLDEN PRESS 1973	**A**
		HAMLYN 1974	**A**
43	**Find Your ABCs**	RANDOM HOUSE 1973	**A**
44	**Please and Thank You Book**	RANDOM HOUSE 1973	**A**
45	**Best Rainy Day Book Ever**	RANDOM HOUSE 1974	**A**
		HAMLYN 1975	**A**
46	**European Word Book**	HAMLYN 1974	**A**
47	**Cars and Trucks and Things That Go**	GOLDEN PRESS 1974	**A**
		COLLINS 1974	**A**
48	**Great Steamboat Mystery**	RANDOM HOUSE 1975	**A**
		COLLINS 1976	**A**
49	**Animal Nursery Tales**	GOLDEN PRESS 1975	**A**
		COLLINS 1975	**A**
50	**Favorite Storybook**	RANDOM HOUSE 1976	**A**
		COLLINS 1976	**A**
51	**Busy Town, Busy People**	RANDOM HOUSE 1976	**A**
		COLLINS 1976	**A**

52	**Storytime**	COLLINS 1976	A
53	**Best Counting Book Ever**	RANDOM HOUSE 1976	A
		COLLINS 1977	A
54	**Busiest People Ever**	RANDOM HOUSE 1976	A
		COLLINS 1977	A
55	**Look-Look Books** (*ten volumes*): All Day Long; All Year Long; In My Town; Learn to Count; About Animals; At Work; My House; On The Farm; On Vacation; Short and Tall.	GOLDEN PRESS 1976	A
		HAMLYN 1977	A
			Each
56	**Early Words**	RANDOM HOUSE 1976	A
		COLLINS 1977	A
57	**Color Book**	RANDOM HOUSE 1976	A
		COLLINS 1977	A
58	**Laugh and Learn Library**	COLLINS 1976	A
59	**Picture Dictionary**	COLLINS 1976	A
60	**Teeny Tiny ABC**	GOLDEN PRESS 1976	A
		HAMLYN 1976	A
61	**Little ABC**	RANDOM HOUSE 1976	A
		COLLINS 1976	A
62	**Things to Know**	RANDOM HOUSE 1976	A
		COLLINS 1976	A
63	**Lowly Worm Story Book**	RANDOM HOUSE 1977	A
		COLLINS 1979	A
64	**Busy, Busy Word Book**	RANDOM HOUSE 1977	A
65	**Best Make-it Book Ever**	RANDOM HOUSE 1977	A
		COLLINS 1978	A
66	**Busy-Busy Counting Book**	COLLINS 1977	A
67	**Little Counting Book** *Same as 66.*	RANDOM HOUSE 1978	A
68	**Lowly Worm Sniffy Book**	RANDOM HOUSE 1978	A
69	**Postman Pig and His Busy Neighbors**	RANDOM HOUSE 1978	A
		COLLINS 1979	A

70	Toy Book	RANDOM HOUSE 1978	A
		COLLINS 1979	A
71	Stories to Color	RANDOM HOUSE 1978	A
		COLLINS 1979	A
72	Holiday Book	COLLINS 1979	A
73	Work and Play Book	COLLINS 1979	A
74	Mix or Match Storybook	RANDOM HOUSE 1979	A
		COLLINS 1980	A
75	Best First Book Ever	RANDOM HOUSE 1979	A
		COLLINS 1980	A
76	Huckle's Book	RANDOM HOUSE 1979	A
		COLLINS 1979	A
77	Busytown Pop-up Book	RANDOM HOUSE 1979	A
		COLLINS 1980	A
78	Can You Count?	COLLINS 1979	A
79	Lowly Worm Things on Wheels	COLLINS 1979	A
		RANDOM HOUSE 1980	A
80	Lowly Worm Where Does It Come from Book	COLLINS 1979	A
		RANDOM HOUSE 1980	A
81	Lowly Worm Tell-time Book	COLLINS 1979	A
		RANDOM HOUSE 1980	A
82	Peasant Pig and the Terrible Dragon	RANDOM HOUSE 1980	A
		COLLINS 1981	A
83	Lowly Worm Word Book	RANDOM HOUSE 1981	A
84	Christmas Mice	GOLDEN PRESS 1981	A
85	Best Christmas Book Ever	RANDOM HOUSE 1981	A
		COLLINS 1981	A
86	Busy Houses	RANDOM HOUSE 1981	A
		COLLINS 1982	A
87	Four Busy Word Books	RANDOM HOUSE 1982	A
88	Busytown Shape Book	COLLINS 1982	A
89	Sticker Books (*three volumes*): On Holiday; At School; I Can Count to Eleven.	COLLINS 1982	A Each

90	**Board Books** (*four volumes*): Colours; Words; My House; Things I Do.	COLLINS 1982	**A** **Each**
91	**Board Books** (*four volumes*): Old Mother Hubbard and Other Rhymes; This Little Pig Went to Market and Other Rhymes; One, Two, Buckle My Shoe and Other Rhymes; Little Miss Muffet and Other Rhymes.	HAMLYN 1983	**A** **Each**
92	**The Biggest Word Book Ever**	HAMLYN 1986	**A**
93	**The Busy Fun and Learn Book**	HAMLYN 1987	**A**
94	**The Best Ever Music Book**	RANDOM HOUSE 1987	**A**
		HAMLYN 1987	**A**
95	**Board Books** (*four volumes*): Going Places on the Water; Going Places in the Air; Going Places in the Car; Going Places with Goldbug.	COLLINS 1987	**A** **Each**

SENDAK, Maurice   *American. Born in New York, 1928*

A highly popular cult figure, and an avidly collected author and illustrator. Sendak has illustrated far more books than he has actually written, but it is these total creations listed below that have the greatest appeal. The early work is scarce, and prices can only go up.

1	**Kenny's Window**	HARPER 1956	**J**
2	**Very Far Away**	HARPER 1957	**I**
		WORLD'S WORK 1959	**G**
3	**The Acrobat**	PRIVATELY PRINTED 1959	**J**
4	**The Sign on Rosie's Door**	HARPER 1960	**H**
		BODLEY HEAD 1969	**D**
5	**The Nutshell Library** (*verse, 4 volumes*): Alligators All Around; Chicken Soup with Rice; One Was Johnny; Pierre: A Cautionary Tale.	HARPER 1962 COLLINS 1964	**B** **B** **Each**
6	**Where the Wild Things are**	HARPER 1963	**H**
		BODLEY HEAD 1967	**F**

7	**Higglety Pigglety Pop! or, There Must Be More to Life**	HARPER 1967 BODLEY HEAD 1969	**F** **E**
8	**In the Night Kitchen**	HARPER 1970 BODLEY HEAD 1971	**E** **E**
9	**The Magician: A Counting Book**	ROSENBACH US 1971	**E**
10	**Pictures**	HARPER 1971 BODLEY HEAD 1972	**F** **E**
11	**Really Rosie** (*play*) *Adaptation of 4 and 5.*	HARPER 1975	**D**
12	**Seven Little Monsters**	HARPER 1976 BODLEY HEAD 1977	**D** **C**
13	**Some Swell Pup; or, Are You Sure You Want a Dog?**	FARRAR STRAUS 1976 BODLEY HEAD 1976	**D** **C**
14	**Outside Over There**	HARPER 1981 BODLEY HEAD 1981	**C** **C**
15	**The Nutcracker**	HARPER 1984 BODLEY HEAD 1984	**C** **C**
16	**Posters**	HARPER 1987 BODLEY HEAD 1987	**C** **C**

Also of interest:
JEFFREY JON SMITH: **A Conversation with Maurice Sendak** (SMITH US 1975)
SELMA G. LANES: **The Art of Maurice Sendak** (ABRAMS 1980, BODLEY HEAD 1981)

SEUSS, Dr. *Pseudonym of Theodor Seuss Geisel*
American. Born in Massachusetts, 1904

As with Richard Scarry (the two have quite a lot in common), I am listing Dr. Seuss in as complete a form as possible – not because I think that collectors will want to gather them all, but because it is difficult to be selective – *you* can be that. Anyway, it would be rather a shame to omit any of Dr. Seuss's titles because of the delicious titles themselves, most of which are perfectly mad. This extraordinary writer has done more to foster literacy in children than most because he manages to combine lunacy with sanity, fun with learning, and quality with exuberant readability. He also has published under the pseudonym Theo le Sieg – I list these separately at the end. All of the following, unless otherwise stated, are wonderfully illustrated by the author.

1	And to Think That I Saw It on Mulberry Street	VANGUARD PRESS 1937 COUNTRY LIFE 1939	J I
2	The 500 Hats of Bartholomew Cubbins	VANGUARD PRESS 1938 OUP 1940	H G
3	The King's Stilts	RANDOM HOUSE 1939 HAMISH HAMILTON 1942	G D
4	Horton Hatches the Egg	RANDOM HOUSE 1940 HAMISH HAMILTON 1942	F D
5	McElligot's Pool	RANDOM HOUSE 1947 COLLINS 1975	D A
6	Thidwick, the Big-hearted Moose	RANDOM HOUSE 1948 COLLINS 1968	D A
7	Bartholomew and the Oobleck	RANDOM HOUSE 1949	C
8	If I Ran the Zoo	RANDOM HOUSE 1950	C
9	Scrambled Eggs Super!	RANDOM HOUSE 1953	C
10	Horton Hears a Who!	RANDOM HOUSE 1954 COLLINS 1976	C A
11	On Beyond Zebra	RANDOM HOUSE 1955	C
12	If I Ran the Circus	RANDOM HOUSE 1956 COLLINS 1969	C A
13	The Cat in the Hat	RANDOM HOUSE 1957 HUTCHINSON 1958	C B
14	How the Grinch Stole Christmas	RANDOM HOUSE 1957	C
15	The Cat in the Hat Comes Back!	RANDOM HOUSE 1958 COLLINS 1961	B A
16	Yertle the Turtle and Other Stories	RANDOM HOUSE 1958 COLLINS 1963	B A
17	Happy Birthday to You!	RANDOM HOUSE 1959	B
18	One Fish, Two Fish, Red Fish, Blue Fish	RANDOM HOUSE 1960 COLLINS 1962	B A
19	Green Eggs and Ham	RANDOM HOUSE 1960 COLLINS 1962	B A

20	The Sneetches and Other Stories	RANDOM HOUSE 1961	B
		COLLINS 1965	A
21	Sleep Book	RANDOM HOUSE 1962	B
		COLLINS 1964	A
22	Hop on Pop	RANDOM HOUSE 1963	B
		COLLINS 1964	A
23	ABC	RANDOM HOUSE 1963	B
		COLLINS 1964	A
24	The Cat in the Hat Dictionary, by the Cat Himself (*with Philip D. Eastman*)	RANDOM HOUSE 1964	B
25	Fox in Socks	RANDOM HOUSE 1965	A
		COLLINS 1966	A
26	I Had Trouble in Getting to Solla Sollew	RANDOM HOUSE 1965	A
		COLLINS 1967	A
27	The Cat in the Hat Songbook	RANDOM HOUSE 1967	A
28	The Foot Book	RANDOM HOUSE 1968	A
		COLLINS 1969	A
29	My Book About Me (*illus. Roy McKie*)	RANDOM HOUSE 1969	A
		COLLINS 1983	A
30	I Can Lick 30 Tigers Today and Other Stories	RANDOM HOUSE 1969	A
		COLLINS 1970	A
31	I Can Draw It Myself	RANDOM HOUSE 1970	A
32	Mr Brown Can Moo! Can You?	RANDOM HOUSE 1970	A
		COLLINS 1971	A
33	The Lorax	RANDOM HOUSE 1971	A
		COLLINS 1972	A
34	Marvin K. Mooney, Will You Please Go Now?	RANDOM HOUSE 1972	A
		COLLINS 1973	A
35	Did I Ever Tell You How Lucky You are?	RANDOM HOUSE 1973	A
		COLLINS 1974	A
36	The Shape of Me and Other Stuff	RANDOM HOUSE 1973	A
		COLLINS 1974	A

37	**There's a Wocket in My Pocket!**	RANDOM HOUSE 1974	A
		COLLINS 1975	A
38	**Great Day for Up!**	RANDOM HOUSE 1974	A
	(*illus. Quentin Blake*)	COLLINS 1975	A
39	**Oh, the Thinks You Can Think**	RANDOM HOUSE 1975	A
		COLLINS 1976	A
40	**The Cat's Quizzer**	RANDOM HOUSE 1976	A
		COLLINS 1977	A
41	**Hooper Humperdink...? Not Him!**	RANDOM HOUSE 1976	A
	(*illus. Charles Martin*)	COLLINS 1977	A
42	**I Can Read with My Eyes Shut!**	RANDOM HOUSE 1978	A
		COLLINS 1979	A
43	**Oh Say Can You Say?**	RANDOM HOUSE 1979	A
		COLLINS 1980	A
44	**Hunches in Bunches**	RANDOM HOUSE 1982	A
		COLLINS 1982	A
45	**Beginner Book Dictionary**	RANDOM HOUSE 1986	A
		COLLINS 1987	A

VERSE BY 'THEO LE SIEG':

1	**Ten Apples Up on Top**	RANDOM HOUSE 1961	B
	(*illus. Roy McKie*)	COLLINS 1963	A
2	**I Wish That I Had Duck Feet**	RANDOM HOUSE 1965	A
	(*illus. B. Tobey*)	COLLINS 1967	A
3	**Come Over to My House**	RANDOM HOUSE 1966	A
	(*illus. Richard Erdoes*)	COLLINS 1967	A
4	**The Eye Book**	RANDOM HOUSE 1968	A
	(*illus. Roy McKie*)	COLLINS 1969	A
5	**In a People House**	RANDOM HOUSE 1972	A
	(*illus. Roy McKie*)	COLLINS 1973	A
6	**The Many Mice of Mr Brice**	RANDOM HOUSE 1973	A
	(*illus. Roy McKie*)	COLLINS 1974	A
7	**Wacky Wednesday**	RANDOM HOUSE 1974	A
	(*illus. George Booth*)	COLLINS 1975	A

8	**Would You Rather be a Bullfrog?** (*illus. Roy McKie*)	RANDOM HOUSE 1975	A
		COLLINS 1976	A
9	**Please Try to Remember the First of Octember** (*illus. Arthur Cummings*)	RANDOM HOUSE 1977	A
		COLLINS 1978	A
10	**Maybe You Should Fly a Jet! Maybe You Should be a Vet!**	RANDOM HOUSE 1980	A
		COLLINS 1981	A
11	**The Tooth Book** (*illus. Roy McKie*)	RANDOM HOUSE 1981	A
		COLLINS 1982	A

SIMMONDS, Posy   *Born in England, 1945*

It's neck-sticking-out time: the wonderful Posy Simmonds has to date produced only one children's book, and it is a winner. In comic book form (*à la* Raymond Briggs), witty and enchanting. I hope it is the first of many.

1	**Fred**	CAPE 1987	B
		KNOPF 1987	B

SMITH, Dodie   *Born in Lancashire, 1896*

A popular playwright in her day, but for the purposes of this book she comes into her own for a very famous children's book (this fame, it must be admitted, almost wholly due to Walt Disney) written when the author was not much short of sixty. Dodie Smith has written only three books for children, and they are listed below.

1	**The Hundred and One Dalmatians**	HEINEMANN 1956	E
		VIKING PRESS 1957	C
2	**The Starlight Barking: More About the Hundred and One Dalmatians**	HEINEMANN 1967	B
		SIMON & SCHUSTER 1967	B
3	**The Midnight Kittens**	ALLEN 1978	A

STRANG, Herbert   *Pseudonym of George Herbert Ely Born in London, 1866. Died 1958 and C. James l'Estrange Born in London, 1867. Died 1947*

This unique collaboration between the above two men resulted in a huge outpouring of jolly readable, endlessly predictable and lovably old-fashioned material. If you go for Henty, you'll approve; if you like Westerman, you'll like 'Strang'. In addition to the deluge listed below, 'Strang' also produced a vast number of annuals as editor(s) only, all chock-a-block with stirring patriotic derring-do for all right-minded chaps.

1	**Tom Burnaby**	BLACKIE 1904	G
2	**Young Tom Burnaby** *Same as 1.*	STREET & SMITH US 1904	E
3	**Boys of the Light Brigade** *(illus. William Rainey)*	BLACKIE 1904	F
4	**The Light Brigade in Spain** *Same as 3.*	PUTNAM 1904	D
5	**Kobo** *(illus. William Rainey)*	BLACKIE 1904 PUTNAM 1905	E C
6	**Brown of Moukden** *(illus. William Rainey)*	BLACKIE 1905	E
7	**Jack Brown, the Hero** *Same as 6. The book was reissued by OUP in* *1923 as* Jack Brown in China.	STREET & SMITH US 1905	C
8	**The Adventures of Harry Rochester** *(illus. William Rainey)*	BLACKIE 1905 PUTNAM 1905	D C
9	**Jack Hardy** *(illus. William Rainey)*	HODDER & STOUGHTON 1906 BOBBS MERRILL 1907	D C
10	**One of Clive's Heroes** *(illus. William Rainey)*	HODDER & STOUGHTON 1906	D
11	**In Clive's Command** *Same as 10.*	BOBBS MERRILL 1906	C
12	**Samba** *(illus. William Rainey)*	HODDER & STOUGHTON 1906	D
13	**Fighting on the Congo** *Same as 12.*	BOBBS MERRILL 1906	C
14	**Rob the Ranger** *(illus. W.H. Margetson)*	HODDER & STOUGHTON 1907 BOBBS MERRILL 1907	C B

15	**With Drake on the Spanish Main**	HODDER & STOUGHTON	**C**
	(*illus. Archibald Webb*)	1907	
	The US edition omits the words With	BOBBS MERRILL 1909	**B**
	Drake.		
16	**King of the Air**	HODDER & STOUGHTON	**C**
	(*illus. W.E. Webster*)	1907	
		BOBBS MERRILL 1907	**B**
17	**On the Trail of the Arabs**	BOBBS MERRILL 1907	**C**
	(*illus. Charles Sheldon*)		
18	**Herbert Strang's Historical Series:**	HODDER & STOUGHTON	**B**
	With Marlborough to Malplaquet	1907–12	**Each**
	(*with Richard Stead*)		
	With the Black Prince		
	(*with Richard Stead*)		
	A Mariner of England		
	(*with Richard Stead*)		
	One of Rupert's Horse		
	(*with Richard Stead*)		
	Lion-Heart (*with Richard Stead*)		
	Claud the Archer (*with John Aston*)		
	In the New Forest (*with John Aston*)		
	Roger the Scout (*with George Lawrence*)		
	For the White Rose		
	(*with George Lawrence*)		
19	**Humphrey Bold**	HODDER & STOUGHTON	**C**
		1908	
		BOBBS MERRILL 1909	**B**
20	**Barclay of the Guides**	HODDER & STOUGHTON	**C**
	(*illus. H.W. Koekkoek*)	1908	
		DORAN 1909	**B**
21	**Lord of the Seas**	HODDER & STOUGHTON	**C**
	(*illus. C. Fleming Williams*)	1908	
		DORAN 1910	**B**
22	**Palm Tree Island**	HODDER & STOUGHTON	**C**
	(*illus. Archibald Webb & Alan Wright*)	1909	
		DORAN 1910	**B**
23	**Settlers and Scouts**	HODDER & STOUGHTON	**C**
	(*illus. T.C. Dugdale*)	1909	
		DORAN 1910	**B**

24	**Swift and Sure**	HODDER & STOUGHTON 1909	C
		DORAN 1910	B
25	**The Cruise of the Gyro-car** (*illus. A.C. Michael*)	HODDER & STOUGHTON 1910	C
26	**The Adventures of Dick Trevanion** (*illus. William Rainey*)	HODDER & STOUGHTON 1910	C
27	**Round the World in Seven Days** (*illus. A.C. Michael*)	HODDER & STOUGHTON 1910	C
		DORAN 1910	B
28	**The Flying Boat** (*illus. T.C. Dugdale*)	HODDER & STOUGHTON 1911	C
29	**The Air Scout** (*illus. W.R.S. Stott*)	HODDER & STOUGHTON 1911	C
30	**The Motor Scout** (*illus. Cyril Cuneo*)	HODDER & STOUGHTON 1912	C
31	**The Air Patrol** (*illus. Cyril Cuneo*)	HODDER & STOUGHTON 1912	C
32	**Cerdic the Saxon** (*illus. L.L. Weedon*)	HODDER & STOUGHTON 1913	C
33	**A Little Norman Maid**	HODDER & STOUGHTON 1913	C
34	**Sultan Jim, Empire Builder**	HODDER & STOUGHTON 1913	C
35	**A Gentleman-at-Arms**	HODDER & STOUGHTON 1914	C
36	**A Hero of Liège**	HODDER & STOUGHTON 1914	C
37	**Fighting with French**	HODDER & STOUGHTON 1915	C
38	**The Boy Who Would Not Learn**	OUP 1915	C
		OUP US 1921	B
39	**The Silver Shot**	OUP 1915	C
		OUP US 1921	B

40	In Trafalgar's Bay	OUP 1915	C
		OUP US 1921	B
41	Burton of the Flying Corps	HODDER & STOUGHTON 1916	C
42	Frank Forester	HODDER & STOUGHTON 1916	C
43	The Old Man of the Mountain (*illus. Rene Bull*)	HODDER & STOUGHTON 1916	C
44	Through the Enemy's Lines (*illus. H.E. Elcock*)	HODDER & STOUGHTON 1916	C
45	Carry On! (*illus. H.E. Elcock & H. Evison*)	HODDER & STOUGHTON 1917	C
46	With Haig on the Somme	OUP 1917	C
47	Steady, Boys, Steady	HODDER & STOUGHTON 1917	C
48	The Long Trail	OUP 1918	C
49	Tom Willoughby's Scouts	OUP 1919	C
50	The Blue Raider	OUP 1919	C
51	Bright Ideas (*illus. C.E. Brock*)	OUP 1920	C
52	No Man's Island (*illus. C.E. Brock*)	OUP 1921	C
53	The Cave in the Hills	OUP 1922	C
54	Bastable Cove	OUP 1922	C
55	Winning His Name (*illus. C.E. Brock*)	OUP 1922	C
56	Honour First (*illus. W.E. Wightman*)	OUP 1923	C
57	True as Steel (*illus. C.E. Brock*)	OUP 1923	C
58	A Thousand Miles an Hour	OUP 1924	C
59	The Heir of a Hundred Kings	OUP 1924	C

60 Young Jack	OUP 1924	**C**
61 Martin of Old London	OUP 1925	**C**
62 Olwyn's Secret	OUP 1925	**C**
63 Dan Bolton's Discovery	OUP 1926	**B**
64 Strang's Penny Books	OUP 1926–7	**B**

30 volumes comprising: Three Boys at the **Each**
Fair; Kitty's Kitten; The Cinema Dog;
Bill Sawyer's VC; The Game of
Brownies; Jenny's Ark; Baa-Baa and
the Wide World; Tom Leaves School;
The Mischief-making Magpie; A Ride
with Robin Hood; Pete's Elephant; Ten
Pounds Reward; Adolf's Dog; The
Adventures of a Penny Stamp; Don't be
Too Sure; Jack and Jocko; The Princess
and the Robbers; The Christmas Fairy;
The Seven Sons; The Red Candle; The
Miller's Daughter; The Grey Goose
Feathers; The Birthday Present; There
was a Little Pig; The Magic Smoke;
The Children of the Ferry; Sugar
Candy Town; Little Mr Pixie; The
Little Sea Horse; The Little Blue-Grey
Hare.

65 Lost in London	OUP 1927	**B**
66 The River Pirates	OUP 1927	**B**
67 The Riders	OUP 1928	**B**
68 On London River	OUP 1929	**B**
69 Ships and Their Story: Scouting Stories	OUP 1931	**B**
70 Dickon of the Chase	OUP 1931	**B**
71 A Servant of John Company	OUP 1932	**B**

STREATFEILD, Noel   *Born in Sussex, 1895*

Noel Streatfeild's first book is still loved by little girls everywhere, so brilliantly does it evoke the excitement and romance inherent in the greatest dream after pony-riding. And her second remains almost as popular – reputed to be Streatfeild's own personal favourite. Certainly her later work did not meet with the same critical acclaim, and is not so well loved, but there is a lot of goodness to be got out of much of it, and so below I list all the fiction, but omit her dozen or so non-fiction works.

1	**Ballet Shoes**	DENT 1936	**H**
	(*illus. Ruth Gervis*)	RANDOM HOUSE 1937	**E**
2	**Tennis Shoes**	DENT 1937	**E**
	(*illus. D.L. Mays*)	RANDOM HOUSE 1938	**C**
3	**The Circus is Coming**	DENT 1938	**D**
	(*illus. Steven Spurrier*)		
4	**Circus Shoes**	RANDOM HOUSE 1939	**C**
	Same as 3.		
5	**Dennis the Dragon**	DENT 1939	**C**
	(*illus. Ruth Gervis*)		
6	**The House in Cornwall**	DENT 1940	**C**
	(*illus. D.L. Mays*)		
7	**The Secret of the Lodge**	RANDOM HOUSE 1940	**B**
	Same as 6.		
8	**The Children of Primrose Lane**	DENT 1941	**B**
	(*illus. Marcia Lane Foster*)		
9	**The Stranger in Primrose Lane**	RANDOM HOUSE 1941	**B**
	Same as 8.		
10	**Harlequinade**	CHATTO & WINDUS 1943	**B**
	(*illus. Clarke Hutton*)		
11	**Curtain Up**	DENT 1944	**B**
	(*illus. D.L. Mays*)		
12	**Theater Shoes; or, Other People's Shoes**	RANDOM HOUSE 1945	**B**
	Same as 11.		
13	**Party Frock**	COLLINS 1946	**B**
	(*illus. Anna Zinkeisen*)		

14	**Party Shoes** *Same as 13.*	RANDOM HOUSE 1947	B
15	**The Painted Garden** *(illus. Ley Kenyon)*	COLLINS 1949	B
16	**Movie Shoes** *Same as 15.*	RANDOM HOUSE 1949	B
17	**Osbert** *(illus. Susanne Shuba)*	RAND McNALLY US 1950	B
18	**The Theater Cat** *(illus. Susanne Shuba)*	RAND McNALLY US 1951	B
19	**White Boots** *(illus. Milein Cosman)*	COLLINS 1951	B
20	**Skating Shoes** *Same as 19.*	RANDOM HOUSE 1951	B
21	**The Fearless Treasure** *(illus. Dorothy Braby)*	JOSEPH 1952	B
22	**The Bell Family** *(illus. Shirley Hughes)*	COLLINS 1954	B
23	**Family Shoes** *Same as 22.*	RANDOM HOUSE 1954	B
24	**The Grey Family** *(illus. Pat Marriott)*	HAMISH HAMILTON 1956	B
25	**Wintle's Wonders** *(illus. Richard Kennedy)*	COLLINS 1957	B
26	**Dancing Shoes** *Same as 25.*	RANDOM HOUSE 1958	B
27	**Bertram** *(illus. Margery Gill)*	HAMISH HAMILTON 1959	B
28	**New Town** *(illus. Shirley Hughes)*	COLLINS 1960	A
29	**New Shoes** *Same as 28.*	RANDOM HOUSE 1960	A
30	**Apple Bough** *(illus. Margery Gill)*	COLLINS 1962	A

31	**Traveling Shoes** *Same as 30.*	RANDOM HOUSE 1962	**A**
32	**Lisa Goes to Russia** (*illus. Geraldine Spence*)	COLLINS 1963	**A**
33	**The Children on the Top Floor** (*illus. Jillian Willett*)	COLLINS 1964 RANDOM HOUSE 1965	**A** **A**
34	**Let's Go Coaching** (*illus. Peter Warner*)	HAMISH HAMILTON 1965	**A**
35	**The Growing Summer** (*illus. Edward Ardizzone*)	COLLINS 1966	**C**
36	**The Magic Summer** *Same as 35.*	RANDOM HOUSE 1967	**B**
37	**Old Chairs to Mend** (*illus. Barry Wilkinson*)	HAMISH HAMILTON 1966	**A**
38	**Caldicott Place** (*illus. Betty Maxey*)	COLLINS 1967	**A**
39	**The Family at Caldicott Place** *Same as 38.*	RANDOM HOUSE 1968	**A**
40	**Gemma** (*illus. Betty Maxey*)	ARMADA 1968	**A**
41	**Gemma and Sisters** (*illus. Betty Maxey*)	ARMADA 1968	**A**
42	**The Barrow Lane Gang**	BBC 1968	**A**
43	**Gemma Alone**	ARMADA 1969	**A**
44	**Goodbye Gemma**	ARMADA 1969	**A**
45	**Thursday's Child** (*illus. Peggy Fortnum*)	COLLINS 1970 RANDOM HOUSE 1970	**A** **A**
46	**Ballet Shoes for Anna** (*illus. Mary Dinsdale*)	COLLINS 1972	**A**
47	**When the Siren Wailed** (*illus. Margery Gill*)	COLLINS 1974 RANDOM HOUSE 1977	**A** **A**
48	**Far to Go** (*illus. Charles Mozley*)	COLLINS 1976	**A**

| 49 | **Meet the Maitlands**
(*illus. Antony Maitland*) | ALLEN 1978 | B |
| 50 | **The Maitlands: All Change at Cuckly Place**
(*illus. Antony Maitland*) | ALLEN 1979 | B |

Also of interest:

BARBARA KER WILSON: **Noel Streatfeild** (BODLEY HEAD 1961, WALCK US 1964

ANGELA BULL: **Noel Streatfeild: A Biography** (COLLINS 1984)

SUTCLIFF, Rosemary   *Born in Surrey, 1920*

Certainly one of the most important living writers of children's fiction – in the realm of the historical novel she really is the doyenne. I say *children's* fiction, but Sutcliff is just as eagerly read and enjoyed by adults as she is by the younger people for whom the work was primarily intended. As if this were not accolade enough, her books are now edging into the interest of mainstream collectors of modern first editions – a rare situation shared only by the few, such as Leon Garfield. You will have gathered from the above that Rosemary Sutcliff is high-profile stuff, good, and eminently collectable; completists, therefore, might well be daunted – but, as may be seen below, the scope is wide.

1	**The Chronicles of Robin Hood** (*retelling*) (*illus. C. Walter Hodges*)	OUP 1950 OUP US 1978	C B
2	**The Queen Elizabeth Story** (*retelling*) (*illus. C. Walter Hodges*)	OUP 1950	C
3	**The Armourer's House** (*fiction*) (*illus. C. Walter Hodges*)	OUP 1951	F
4	**Brother Dusty-feet** (*fiction*) (*illus. C. Walter Hodges*)	OUP 1952	E
5	**Simon** (*fiction*) (*illus. Richard Kennedy*)	OUP 1953	E
6	**The Eagle of the Ninth** (*fiction*) (*illus. C. Walter Hodges*)	OUP 1954 WALCK 1961	E B
7	**Outcast** (*fiction*) (*illus. Richard Kennedy*)	OUP 1955 WALCK 1955	D C

8	**The Shield Ring** (*fiction*)	OUP 1956	D
	(*illus. C. Walter Hodges*)	WALCK 1962	C
9	**The Silver Branch** (*fiction*)	OUP 1957	D
	(*illus. Charles Keeping*)	WALCK 1959	C
10	**Warrior Scarlet** (*fiction*)	OUP 1958	D
	(*illus. Charles Keeping*)	WALCK 1958	C
11	**The Lantern Bearers** (*fiction*)	OUP 1959	D
	(*illus. Charles Keeping*)	WALCK 1959	C
12	**The Bridge Builders** (*fiction*)	BLACKWELL 1959	C
13	**Knight's Fee** (*fiction*)	OUP 1960	C
	(*illus. Charles Keeping*)	WALCK 1960	B
14	**Houses and History** (*non-fiction*)	BATSFORD 1960	C
	(*illus. William Stobbs*)		
15	**Dawn Wind** (*fiction*)	OUP 1961	C
	(*illus. Charles Keeping*)	WALCK 1962	B
16	**Beowulf** (*retelling*)	BODLEY HEAD 1961	C
	(*illus. Charles Keeping*)	DUTTON 1962	B
17	**The Hound of Ulster** (*legend*)	BODLEY HEAD 1963	B
	(*illus. Victor Ambrus*)	DUTTON 1963	B
18	**The Mark of the Horse Lord** (*fiction*)	OUP 1965	C
	(*illus. Charles Keeping*)		
19	**A Saxon Settler** (*non-fiction*)	OUP 1965	B
	(*illus. John Lawrence*)		
20	**Heroes and History** (*non-fiction*)	BATSFORD 1965	C
	(*illus. Charles Keeping*)	PUTNAM 1965	C
21	**The Chief's Daughter** (*fiction*)	HAMISH HAMILTON 1967	B
	(*illus. Victor Ambrus*)		
22	**The High Deeds of Finn MacCool**	BODLEY HEAD 1967	C
	(*retelling*) (*illus. Michael Charlton*)	DUTTON 1967	B
23	**A Circlet of Oak Leaves** (*fiction*)	HAMISH HAMILTON 1968	B
	(*illus. Victor Ambrus*)		
24	**The Witch's Brat** (*fiction*)	OUP 1970	B
	(*illus. Robert Micklewright*)	WALCK 1970	A

25	**The Truce of the Games** (*fiction*) (*illus. Victor Ambrus*)	HAMISH HAMILTON 1971	B
26	**Tristan and Iseult** (*retelling*) (*illus. Victor Ambrus*)	BODLEY HEAD 1971 DUTTON 1971	B A
27	**Heather, Oak, and Olive: Three Stories** (*illus. Victor Ambrus*) Contains 21 & 23 as well as A Crown of Wild Olive.	DUTTON 1972	B
28	**The Capricorn Bracelet** (*fiction*) (*illus. Charles Keeping*)	OUP 1973 WALCK 1973	C B
29	**The Changeling** (*fiction*) (*illus. Victor Ambrus*)	HAMISH HAMILTON 1974	B
30	**We Lived in Drumfyvie** (*fiction*) (*illus. Margaret Lyford-Pike*)	BLACKIE 1975	B
31	**Blood Feud** (*fiction*) (*illus. Charles Keeping*)	OUP 1977 DUTTON 1977	C B
32	**Shifting Sands** (*fiction*) (*illus. Laszlo Acs*)	HAMISH HAMILTON 1977	B
33	**Sun Horse, Moon Horse** (*fiction*) (*illus. Shirley Felts*)	BODLEY HEAD 1977 DUTTON 1978	B B
34	**Song for a Dark Queen** (*fiction*)	PELHAM 1978 CROWELL 1979	B B
35	**The Light Beyond the Forest: The Quest for the Holy Grail** (*non-fiction*) (*illus. Shirley Felts*)	BODLEY HEAD 1979 DUTTON 1980	B B
36	**Frontier Wolf** (*fiction*)	OUP 1980 DUTTON 1981	B B
37	**The Sword and the Circle: King Arthur and the Knights of the Round Table** (*retelling*) (*illus. Shirley Felts*)	BODLEY HEAD 1981 DUTTON 1981	B B
38	**Eagle's Egg** (*fiction*) (*illus. Victor Ambrus*)	HAMISH HAMILTON 1981	B

39	**The Road to Camlann: The Death of King Arthur** (*retelling*) (*illus. Shirley Felts*)	BODLEY HEAD 1981 DUTTON 1981	B B
40	**Bonny Dundee** (*non-fiction*)	BODLEY HEAD 1982 DUTTON 1982	B B
41	**The Roundabout Horse** (*fiction*) (*illus. Alan Marks*)	HAMISH HAMILTON 1986	B
42	**A Little Dog Like You** (*fiction*) (*illus. Jane Johnson*)	ORCHARD 1987	A

Also of interest:

ROSEMARY SUTCLIFF: **Blue Remembered Hills: A Recollection** (BODLEY HEAD 1983)

MARGARET MEEK: **Rosemary Sutcliff** (BODLEY HEAD 1962, WALCK US 1962)

SYMONDS, John   *Born in Britain, 1914*

As well as being an adult novelist and biographer of some repute, Symonds has written a number of very elegant, spare and quietly humorous books for children that today are little known and undervalued. Below is the complete listing.

1	**The Magic Currant Bun** (*illus. André François*)	LIPPINCOTT US 1952 FABER 1953	B C
2	**Travellers Three** (*illus. André François*)	LIPPINCOTT US 1953	C
3	**The Isle of Cats** (*illus. Gerard Hoffnung*)	LAURIE 1955	C
4	**Away to the Moon** (*illus. Pamela Bianco*)	LIPPINCOTT US 1956	B
5	**Lottie** (*illus. Edward Ardizzone*)	LANE 1957	D
6	**Elfrida and the Pig** (*illus. Edward Ardizzone*)	HARRAP 1959 WATTS 1960	D C
7	**Dapple Gray: The Story of a Rocking-horse** (*illus. James Boswell*)	HARRAP 1962	B

8	**The Story George Told Me**	HARRAP 1963	B
	(*illus. André François*)	PANTHEON 1964	B
9	**Tom and Tabby**	UNIVERSE US 1964	B
	(*illus. André François*)		
10	**Grodge-Cat and the Window Cleaner**	PANTHEON 1965	B
	(*illus. André François*)		
11	**The Stuffed Dog**	DENT 1967	C
	(*illus. Edward Ardizzone*)		
12	**Harold: The Story of a Friendship**	DENT 1973	C
	(*illus. Pauline Baynes*)		
13	**A Christmas Story**	WARREN HOUSE PRESS 1977	B

THURBER, James

American. Born in Ohio, 1894. Died 1961

One of the greatest humorists of all time – and far less known for his handful of children's books than for his masterpieces such as *My World – And Welcome To It* and *Men, Women and Dogs*. Of course, much of Thurber's 'adult' work may be enjoyed by children of a certain age, and although there is a certain crossing over in these two areas, the books listed below were actually written *expressly* for children.

1	**Many Moons**	HARCOURT BRACE 1943	F
	(*illus. Louis Slobodkin*)	HAMISH HAMILTON 1945	E
2	**The Great Quillow**	HARCOURT BRACE 1944	F
	(*illus. Doris Lee*)		
3	**The White Deer**	HARCOURT BRACE 1945	D
	(*illus. the author & Don Freeman*)	HAMISH HAMILTON 1946	D
4	**The 13 Clocks**	SIMON & SCHUSTER 1950	E
	(*illus. Marc Simont*)	HAMISH HAMILTON 1951	D
5	**The Wonderful O**	SIMON & SCHUSTER 1955	D
	(*illus. Marc Simont*)	HAMISH HAMILTON 1955	D

Also of interest:

CHARLES S. HOLMES: **The Clocks of Columbus: The Literary Career of James Thurber** (SECKER & WARBURG 1973, ATHENEUM US 1973)

TODD, Barbara Euphan

Born in Yorkshire, 1890. Died 1976

Creator of the most famous scarecrow in the world (possibly the *only* famous scarecrow in the world) rendered a household name by the really very amusing television series written by that formidably prolific (and good) duo, Keith Waterhouse and Willis Hall. The stories adapted from these scripts are published by Puffin, and it is apposite to mention that Barbara Euphan Todd's *Worzel Gummidge* was the very first Puffin ever published, in 1941.

1	**The 'Normous Saturday Fairy Book**	STANLEY PAUL 1924	C
	(*with Marjory Royce & Moira Meighn*)		
2	**The 'Normous Sunday Story Book**	STANLEY PAUL 1925	C
	(*with Marjory Royce & Moira Meighn*)		
3	**The Very Good Walkers**	METHUEN 1925	C
	(*with Marjory Royce*)		
	(*illus. H.R. Millar*)		

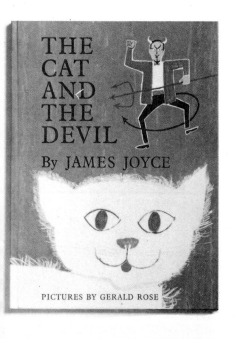

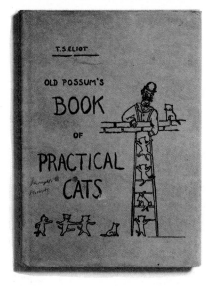

These authors are probably better known for such squibs as *Ulysses*, *The Waste Land*, *The Power and the Glory* and *Goldfinger*, but here they are in more uncharacteristic guise.

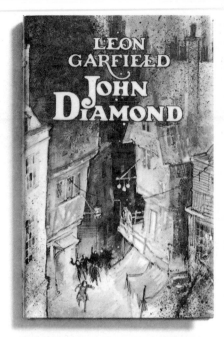

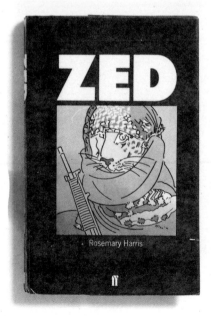

Leon Garfield's first book (1964) together with the 1980 *John Diamond*, both illustrated by Antony Maitland. Here too are a couple of representative works by Rosemary Harris and Peter Dickinson.

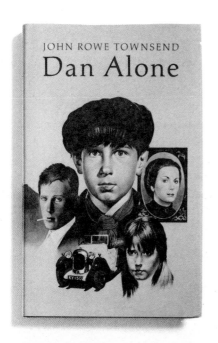

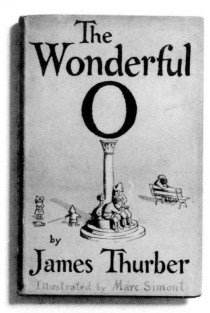

John Rowe Townsend's recent *Dan Alone*, together with a classic Thurber, a Treece, and a Trease.

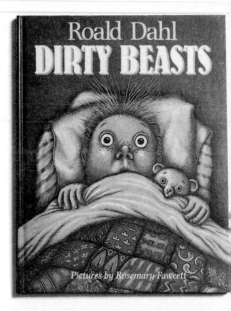

Four illustrated books with laminated boards – artwork by Quentin Blake, Rosemary Fawcett, Nicola Bayley, and Posy Simmonds with her first (and let us hope not her last) children's book.

4	**Mr Blossom's Shop**	NELSON 1929	D
5	**Happy Cottage** (*with Marjory Royce*)	COLLINS 1930	D
6	**South Country Secrets** (*as 'Euphan' with Klaxon*)	BURNS OATES 1935	D
7	**The Touchstone** (*with Klaxon*)	BURNS OATES 1935	D
8	**Worzel Gummidge; or, The** **Scarecrow of Scatterbrook** (*illus. Elizabeth Alldridge*)	BURNS OATES 1936	H
9	**Worzel Gummidge Again** (*illus. Elizabeth Alldridge*)	BURNS OATES 1937	E
10	**The Mystery Train**	UNIVERSITY OF LONDON 1937	D
11	**The Splendid Picnic**	UNIVERSITY OF LONDON 1937	D
12	**More About Worzel Gummidge**	BURNS OATES 1938	E
13	**Mr Dock's Garden** (*illus. Ruth Westcott*)	ARNOLD 1939	D
14	**Gertrude the Greedy Goose** (*illus. Benjamin Rabier*)	MULLER 1939	D
15	**The House That Ran Behind** (*with Esther Boumphrey*)	MULLER 1943	C
16	**Worzel Gummidge, the Scarecrow of** **Scatterbrook Farm** (*illus. Ursula Koering*) *Extracts from 8 & 9.*	PUTNAM US 1947	D
17	**Worzel Gummidge and Saucy Nancy** (*illus. Will Nickless*)	HOLLIS & CARTER 1947	D
18	**Worzel Gummidge Takes a Holiday** (*illus. Will Nickless*)	HOLLIS & CARTER 1949	D
19	**Aloysius Let Loose** (*with Klaxon*) (*illus. A.E. Batchelor*)	COLLINS 1950	C

20	**Earthy Mangold and Worzel Gummidge** (*illus. Jill Crockford*)	HOLLIS & CARTER 1954	**C**
21	**Worzel Gummidge and the Railway Scarecrows** (*illus. Jill Crockford*)	EVANS 1955	**B**
22	**Worzel Gummidge at the Circus** (*illus. Jill Crockford*)	EVANS 1956	**B**
23	**The Boy with the Green Thumb** (*illus. Charlotte Hough*)	HAMISH HAMILTON 1956	**B**
24	**The Wizard and the Unicorn** (*illus. Prudence Seward*)	HAMISH HAMILTON 1957	**B**
25	**Worzel Gummidge and the Treasure Ship** (*illus. Jill Crockford*)	EVANS 1958	**B**
26	**The Shop Around the Corner** (*illus. Olive Coughlan*)	HAMISH HAMILTON 1959	**B**
27	**Detective Worzel Gummidge** (*illus. Jill Crockford*)	EVANS 1963	**B**
28	**The Shop by the Sea** (*illus. Sarah Garland*)	HAMISH HAMILTON 1966	**B**
29	**The Clock Shop** (*illus. Jill Crockford*)	WORLD'S WORK 1967	**B**
30	**The Shop on Wheels** (*illus. Jill Crockford*)	WORLD'S WORK 1968	**B**
31	**The Box in the Attic** (*illus. Lynette Hemmant*)	WORLD'S WORK 1970	**B**
32	**The Wand from France** (*illus. Lynette Hemmant*)	WORLD'S WORK 1972	**B**

TOLKIEN, J.R.R. *British. Born South Africa, 1895. Died 1973*

Still a cult – although not quite such a *fetish* as he was in the 'sixties – and therefore sought-after, and expensive. Collectors of modern first editions have no especial interest in children's books *per se*, but still seek out (and pay high prices for) those primarily intended for children for the sake of completion: these are the chaps you are up against. But at least collectors of *just* the children's stuff do not have to cope with the endless annual stream of newly discovered and edited bits and bobs – they are almost never relevant to the true works for juveniles. Some people class *The Lord of the Rings* trilogy as a children's work, and some don't; I have included it in the list below on the grounds that even if all teenagers have not *read* the work, most have toted around the paperback for at least a year or two.

1   **The Hobbit** (*fiction*)   ALLEN & UNWIN 1937   **T**
     (*illus. the author*)   HOUGHTON MIFFLIN 1938   **R**

2   **Farmer Giles of Ham** (*fiction*)   ALLEN & UNWIN 1949   **G**
     (*illus. Pauline Baynes*)   HOUGHTON MIFFLIN 1950   **E**

3   **The Fellowship of the Ring** (*fiction*)   ALLEN & UNWIN 1954   **O**
                                  HOUGHTON MIFFLIN 1954   **L**

4   **The Two Towers** (*fiction*)   ALLEN & UNWIN 1954   **N**
                                  HOUGHTON MIFFLIN 1955   **K**

5   **The Return of the King** (*fiction*)   ALLEN & UNWIN 1955   **N**
     3, 4 & 5 form 'The Lord of the Rings'   HOUGHTON MIFFLIN 1956   **K**
     trilogy. A revised edition in three volumes was
     published by Allen & Unwin in 1966 and by
     Houghton Mifflin in 1967.

6   **The Adventures of Tom Bombadil**   ALLEN & UNWIN 1962   **F**
     and Other Verses from the Red   HOUGHTON MIFFLIN 1963   **D**
     Book
     (*illus. Pauline Baynes*)

7   **Smith of Wootton Major** (*fiction*)   ALLEN & UNWIN 1967   **E**
     (*illus. Pauline Baynes*)   HOUGHTON MIFFLIN 1967   **C**

8   **Bilbo's Last Song** (*verse*)   ALLEN & UNWIN 1974   **C**
     (*illus. Pauline Baynes*)   HOUGHTON MIFFLIN 1974   **C**

9   **The Father Christmas Letters** (*fiction*)   ALLEN & UNWIN 1976   **C**
     (*illus. the author*)   HOUGHTON MIFFLIN 1976   **B**

10   **Mr Bliss** (*fiction*)   ALLEN & UNWIN 1982   **B**
     (*illus. the author*)   HOUGHTON MIFFLIN 1983   **B**

Also of interest:

PAUL KOCHER: **Master of Middle-Earth: The Fiction of J.R.R.**
   Tolkien (HOUGHTON MIFFLIN 1972, THAMES & HUDSON 1973)

J.E.A. TYLER: **The New Tolkien Companion** (MACMILLAN 1979)
HUMPHREY CARPENTER: **J.R.R. Tolkien: A Biography** (ALLEN & UNWIN 1977,
  HOUGHTON MIFFLIN US 1977)
T.A. SHIPPEY: **The Road to Middle-Earth** (ALLEN & UNWIN 1982)

TOURTEL, Mary   *Born in Kent, 1874. Died 1948*

Creator of the most famous and most collected bear of all (yes, I *am* bearing in
mind Pooh and Paddington) and one of the most enduring comic icons ever.
Rupert becomes more and more popular, and has long been something of a
cult with adults as well as children, this being reflected in the scarcity of the
earlier titles, and the rising prices. Alfred Bestall took over the *Daily Express*
strip in 1935, due to Mary Tourtel's failing eyesight, and the ensuing thirty
years' worth of annuals are also collected – though not with such avidity as
those early little yellow books. Below is listed the entire output – all of them
illustrated by the author.

1	**A Horse Book**	RICHARDS 1901	**H**
		STOKES 1902	**E**
2	**The Three Little Foxes**	RICHARDS 1903	**H**
3	**The Adventures of Rupert the Little Lost Bear**	NELSON 1921	**N**
4	**The Little Bear and the Fairy Child**	NELSON 1921	**L**
5	**Margot the Midget; The Little Bear's Christmas**	NELSON 1922	**K**
6	**The Little Bear and the Ogres**	NELSON 1922	**K**
7	**Rupert Little Bear's Adventures 1:** Rupert and The Magic Toy Van; Rupert and The Princess; Rupert at School; Rupert and the Old Miser.	SAMPSON LOW 1924	**L**
8	**Rupert Little Bear's Adventures 2:** Rupert and the Magic Key; Rupert and the Brigands; Rupert and Reynard Fox; Rupert in Dreamland.	SAMPSON LOW 1924	**K**
9	**Rupert Little Bear's Adventures 3:** Rupert and the Robber Wolf; Rupert and the Dragon; Rupert and the Snowman; Rupert at the Seaside.	SAMPSON LOW 1925	**I**

10	**Rupert and the Enchanted Princess**	SAMPSON LOW 1928	H
11	**Rupert and the Black Dwarf**	SAMPSON LOW 1928	H
12	**Rupert and His Pet Monkey**	SAMPSON LOW 1928	H
13	**Rupert and His Friend Margot; Rupert, Margot and the Fairies**	SAMPSON LOW 1928	H
14	**Rupert in the Wood of Mystery**	SAMPSON LOW 1929	H
15	**Further Adventures of Rupert and His Pet Monkey; Rupert and the Stolen Apples**	SAMPSON LOW 1929	H
16	**Rupert and the Three Robbers**	SAMPSON LOW 1929	H
17	**Rupert, the Knight and the Lady; Rupert and the Wise Goat's Birthday Cake**	SAMPSON LOW 1929	H
18	**Rupert and the Circus Clown**	SAMPSON LOW 1929	H
19	**Rupert and the Magic Hat**	SAMPSON LOW 1929	H
20	**Daily Express Children's Annual** (*5 volumes*)	LANE 1930–34	F Each
21	**Rupert and the Little Prince**	SAMPSON LOW 1930	G
22	**Rupert and King Pippin**	SAMPSON LOW 1930	G
23	**Rupert and the Wilful Princess**	SAMPSON LOW 1930	G
24	**Rupert's Mysterious Flight**	SAMPSON LOW 1930	G
25	**Rupert in Trouble Again; Rupert and the Fancy Dress Party**	SAMPSON LOW 1930	G
26	**Rupert and the Wooden Soldiers; Rupert's Christmas Adventure**	SAMPSON LOW 1930	G
27	**Rupert and the Old Man of the Sea**	SAMPSON LOW 1931	G
28	**Rupert and Algy at Hawthorne Farm**	SAMPSON LOW 1931	G
29	**Monster Rupert** (7 *volumes*)	SAMPSON LOW 1931–50	H–D
30	**Rupert and the Magic Whistle**	SAMPSON LOW 1931	G
31	**Rupert Gets Stolen**	SAMPSON LOW 1931	G
32	**Rupert and the Wonderful Boots**	SAMPSON LOW 1931	G

33	Rupert and the Christmas Tree Fairies; Rupert and Bill Badger's Picnic Party	SAMPSON LOW 1931	G
34	Rupert and His Pet Monkey Again; Beppo Back with Rupert	SAMPSON LOW 1932	G
35	Rupert's Latest Adventure	SAMPSON LOW 1932	G
36	Rupert and Prince Humpty-Dumpty	SAMPSON LOW 1932	G
37	Rupert's Holiday Adventure; Rupert's Message to Father Christmas; Rupert's New Year's Eve Party	SAMPSON LOW 1932	G
38	Rupert's Christmas Tree; Rupert's Picnic Party	SAMPSON LOW 1932	G
39	Rupert, the Witch and Tabitha	SAMPSON LOW 1933	G
40	Rupert Goes Hiking	SAMPSON LOW 1933	G
41	Rupert and Willy Wispe	SAMPSON LOW 1933	G
42	Rupert, Margot and the Bandits	SAMPSON LOW 1933	G
43	Rupert and Bill Keep Shop; Rupert's Christmas Thrills	SAMPSON LOW 1933	G
44	Rupert and Algernon; Rupert and the White Dove	SAMPSON LOW 1934	G
45	Rupert and Dapple	SAMPSON LOW 1934	G
46	Rupert and Bill's Aeroplane Adventure	SAMPSON LOW 1934	G
47	Rupert and the Magician's Umbrella	SAMPSON LOW 1934	G
48	Rupert and Bill and the Pirates	SAMPSON LOW 1935	G
49	Rupert at the Seaside; Rupert and Bingo	SAMPSON LOW 1935	G
50	Rupert Gets Captured; Rupert and the Snow Babe's Christmas	SAMPSON LOW 1935	G
51	Rupert, the Manikin and the Black Knight	SAMPSON LOW 1935	G
52	Rupert and the Greedy Princess	SAMPSON LOW 1935	G

53	**Rupert and Bill's Seaside Holiday; Rupert and the Twin's Birthday Cake**	SAMPSON LOW 1936	G
54	**Rupert and Edward and the Circus**	SAMPSON LOW 1936	G
55	**The Rupert Story Book**	SAMPSON LOW 1938	F
56	**Rupert Little Bear: More Stories**	SAMPSON LOW 1939	E
57	**Rupert Again**	SAMPSON LOW 1940	E

Also of interest:

W.O.G. LOFTS & DEREK J. ADLEY: **The Rupert Index: A Bibliography of Rupert Bear** (PRIVATELY PRINTED, N.D.)

TOWNSEND, John Rowe   *Born in Yorkshire, 1922*

Some critics are of the opinion that Townsend's very considerable reputation is rather more considerable than he deserves, although his ardent supporters will, of course, have none of this. The truth is that one cannot lump all of Townsend's books together and pronounce the *oeuvre* either splendid or disappointing, because although I believe it to be true to say that he has never written a bad book, some do appear a little lightweight when set against the really good stuff, such as *The Intruder* – his highlight to date, and about as unjuvenile as a work for juveniles can be. Nonetheless, a highly collectable author – and one, I think, that one can go on collecting as each year throws up its new offerings. I rather like the recent Viking Kestrel stuff, although they have their detractors; the wit, lightness and accomplishment see them through.

1	**Gumble's Yard** (*illus. Dick Hart*)	HUTCHINSON 1961	G
2	**Hell's Edge**	HUTCHINSON 1963	F
		LOTHROP 1969	C
3	**Widdershins Crescent** *This was published in 1967 by Lippincott US as* Goodbye to the Jungle, *and again by Puffin in 1981 as* Goodbye to Gumble's Yard.	HUTCHINSON 1965	F
4	**The Hallersage Sound**	HUTCHINSON 1966	E

5	**Pirate's Island**	OUP 1968	**D**
	(*illus. Douglas Hall*)	LIPPINCOTT 1968	**C**
6	**The Intruder**	OUP 1969	**D**
	(*illus. Graham Humphreys*)	LIPPINCOTT 1970	**C**
7	**Trouble in the Jungle**	LIPPINCOTT 1969	**B**
	Same as 1.		
8	**Goodnight, Prof, Love**	OUP 1970	**C**
	(*illus. Peter Farmer*)		
9	**Goodnight, Prof, Dear**	LIPPINCOTT 1971	**B**
	Same as 8.		
10	**The Summer People**	OUP 1972	**C**
	(*illus. Robert Micklewright*)	LIPPINCOTT 1972	**B**
11	**A Wish for Wings**	HEINEMANN 1972	**C**
	(*illus. Philip Gough*)		
12	**Forest of the Night**	OUP 1974	**C**
		LIPPINCOTT 1975	**B**
13	**Noah's Castle**	OUP 1975	**C**
		LIPPINCOTT 1976	**B**
14	**Top of the World**	OUP 1976	**C**
	(*illus. Nikki Jones*)	LIPPINCOTT 1977	**B**
15	**The Xanadu Manuscript**	OUP 1977	**C**
	(*illus. Paul Ritchie*)		
16	**The Visitors**	LIPPINCOTT 1977	**B**
	Same as 15.		
17	**King Creature, Come**	OUP 1980	**B**
18	**The Creatures**	LIPPINCOTT 1980	**B**
	Same as 17.		
19	**The Islanders**	OUP 1981	**B**
		LIPPINCOTT 1981	**B**
20	**Clever Dick**	OUP 1982	**B**
21	**A Foreign Affair**	KESTREL 1982	**B**
22	**Kate and the Revolution**	LIPPINCOTT 1983	**B**
	Same as 21.		

23	**Dan Alone**	KESTREL 1983	**B**
		HARPER & ROW 1983	**B**
24	**Cloudy-bright**	KESTREL 1984	**B**
		LIPPINCOTT 1984	**B**
25	**Tom Tiddler's Ground**	VIKING KESTREL 1985	**B**
	(*illus. Marke Peppe*)	HARPER & ROW 1986	**B**
26	**The Persuading Stick**	VIKING KESTREL 1986	**B**
		LOTHROP 1987	**B**
27	**Rob's Place**	VIKING KESTREL 1987	**B**

Also of interest:

JOHN ROWE TOWNSEND: **Written for Children: An Outline of English Children's Literature** (MILLER 1965, LOTHROP US 1967. *Revised ed:* KESTREL 1974, LIPPINCOTT US 1975)

JOHN ROWE TOWNSEND: **A Sense of Story: Essays on Contemporary Writers for Children** (LONGMAN 1971, LIPPINCOTT US 1971. *Revised ed. as* **A Sounding of Storytellers: New and Revised Essays on Contemporary Writers for Children** – KESTREL 1979, LIPPINCOTT US 1979)

JOHN ROWE TOWNSEND: **25 Years of Children's Books** (NBL 1977)

TRAVERS, P.L.　　　　　　　　　*British. Born in Australia, 1906*

Just as Jeeves is *the* gentleman's gentleman, so Mary Poppins is *the* nanny – ask any child. Wonderful (in every sense) since her inception over fifty years ago and rendered utterly immortal by the first-rate Walt Disney film, this flying paragon with the most covetable carpet bag in the world is here to stay – and, as the latest Poppins adventure was published as recently as 1982 (after a thirty-year gap), we may even hope to see another new work, because at the age of 82 Pamela Lyndon Travers is still alive and kicking. Below is listed all her work for children.

1	**Mary Poppins**	HOWE 1934	**I**
	(*illus. Mary Shepard*)	REYNAL 1934	**G**
2	**Mary Poppins Comes Back**	DICKSON & THOMPSON 1935	**G**
	(*illus. Mary Shepard*)	REYNAL 1935	**E**
3	**Happy Ever After**	PRIVATELY PRINTED 1940	**H**
	(*illus. Mary Shepard*)		

4	**I Go by Sea, I Go by Land**	DAVIES 1941	**E**
	(*illus. Gertrude Hermes*)	HARPER 1941	**C**
5	**Mary Poppins Opens the Door**	REYNAL 1943	**E**
	(*illus. Mary Shepard & Agnes Sims*)	DAVIES 1944	**C**
6	**Mary Poppins in the Park**	DAVIES 1952	**D**
	(*illus. Mary Shepard*)	HARCOURT BRACE 1952	**C**
7	**The Fox at the Manger**	NORTON 1962	**B**
	(*illus. Thomas Bewick*)	COLLINS 1963	**B**
8	**Mary Poppins from A to Z**	HARCOURT BRACE 1962	**C**
	(*illus. Mary Shepard*)	COLLINS 1963	**C**
9	**Friend Monkey**	HARCOURT BRACE 1971	**B**
		COLLINS 1972	**B**
10	**About the Sleeping Beauty**	McGRAW HILL 1975	**C**
	(*illus. Charles Keeping*)	COLLINS 1977	**C**
11	**Mary Poppins in the Kitchen:**	HARCOURT BRACE 1975	**B**
	A Cookery Book with a Story	COLLINS 1977	**B**
	(*with Maurice Moore-Betty*)		
	(*illus. Mary Shepard*)		
12	**Two Pairs of Shoes** (*folk tales*)	VIKING PRESS 1980	**B**
	(*illus. Leo & Diane Dillon*)		
13	**Mary Poppins in Cherry Tree Lane**	COLLINS 1982	**B**
	(*illus. Mary Shepard*)	DELACORTE 1982	**B**

TREASE, Geoffrey   *Born in Nottingham, 1909*

Although not hugely collected, Trease remains one of the true long-term professional exponents of the well-crafted adventure story with the authentic historical setting – indeed, he was one of its earliest exponents. What might be of even more interest today are his five 'Banner' novels concerning a grammar school that is also a *day* school: singular, if not unique.

Trease published a good many non-fiction works for children (largely concerning kings and queens, though one is a biography of D.H. Lawrence) as well as many fiction and non-fiction works for adults, and also plays. Below is listed all the children's fiction.

1	**Bows Against the Barons**	LAWRENCE 1934	**C**
	(*illus. Michael Boland*)	INTERNATIONAL 1934	**B**

2   **Comrades for the Charter**   LAWRENCE 1934   C
    (*illus. Michael Boland*)

3   **The Call to Arms**   LAWRENCE 1935   C

4   **Missing from Home**   LAWRENCE & WISHART   C
    (*illus. Scott*)   1936

5   **Red Comet**   LAWRENCE 1937   C
    (*illus. Fred Ellis*)
    Preceded by an edition published in Moscow –
    Trease was quite a Leftie – by the Cooperative
    Publishing of Foreign Workers, 1936.

6   **The Christmas Holiday Mystery**   BLACK 1937   C
    (*illus. Alfred Sindall*)

7   **Mystery on the Moors**   BLACK 1937   C
    (*illus. Alfred Sindall*)

8   **Detectives of the Dales**   BLACK 1938   C
    (*illus. A.C.H. Gorham*)

9   **In the Land of the Mogul**   BLACKWELL 1938   C
    (*illus. J.C.B. Knight*)

10 **North Sea Spy**   FORE 1939   C

11 **Cue for Treason**   BLACKWELL 1940   C
    (*illus. Beatrice Goldsmith*)   VANGUARD 1941   B

12 **Running Deer**   HARRAP 1941   B
    (*illus. W. Lindsay Cable*)

13 **The Grey Adventurer**   BLACKWELL 1942   B
    (*illus. Beatrice Goldsmith*)

14 **Black Night, Red Morning**   BLACKWELL 1944   B
    (*illus. Donia Nachsen*)

15 **Army without Banners**   FORE 1945   C

16 **Trumpets in the West**   BLACKWELL 1947   B
    (*illus. Alan Blyth*)   HARCOURT BRACE 1947   B

17 **Silver Guard**   BLACKWELL 1948   B
    (*illus. Alan Blyth*)

18 **The Hills of Varna**   MACMILLAN 1948   B
    (*illus. Treyer Evans*)

19	**Shadow of the Hawk** *Same as 18.*	HARCOURT BRACE 1949	B
20	**The Mystery of Moorside Farm** *(illus. Alan Blyth)*	BLACKWELL 1949	B
21	**No Boats on Bannermere** *(illus. Richard Kennedy)*	HEINEMANN 1949 NORTON 1965	C B
22	**The Secret Fiord** *(illus. H.M. Brock)*	MACMILLAN 1949 HARCOURT BRACE 1950	C B
23	**Under Black Banner** *(illus. Richard Kennedy)*	HEINEMANN 1950	C
24	**The Crown of Violet** *(illus. C. Walter Hodges)*	MACMILLAN 1952	B
25	**Web of Traitors** *Same as 24.*	VANGUARD PRESS 1952	B
26	**The Barons' Hostage** *(illus. Alan Jessett)*	PHOENIX HOUSE 1952	B
27	**Black Banner Players** *(illus. Richard Kennedy)*	HEINEMANN 1952	C
28	**The New House at Hardale**	LUTTERWORTH PRESS 1953	B
29	**The Silken Secret** *(illus. Alan Jessett)*	BLACKWELL 1953 VANGUARD PRESS 1954	B B
30	**Black Banner Abroad**	HEINEMANN 1954 WARNE 1955	C C
31	**The Fair Flower of Danger**	BLACKWELL 1955	B
32	**Word to Caesar** *(illus. Geoffrey Whittam)*	MACMILLAN 1956	B
33	**Message to Hadrian** *Same as 32.*	VANGUARD PRESS 1956	B
34	**The Gates of Bannerdale**	HEINEMANN 1956 WARNE 1957	C C
35	**Mist Over Athelney** *(illus. R.S. Sherriffs & J.L. Stockle)*	MACMILLAN 1958	B

36	**Escape to King Alfred** *Same as 35.*	VANGUARD PRESS 1958	**B**
37	**The Maythorn Story** (*illus. Robert Hodgson*)	HEINEMANN 1960	**B**
38	**Thunder of Valmy** (*illus. John S. Goodall*)	MACMILLAN 1960	**B**
39	**Victory at Valmy** *Same as 38.*	VANGUARD PRESS 1961	**B**
40	**Change at Maythorn** (*illus. Robert Hodgson*)	HEINEMANN 1962	**B**
41	**Follow My Black Plume** (*illus. Brian Wildsmith*)	MACMILLAN 1963 VANGUARD PRESS 1963	**C** **B**
42	**A Thousand for Sicily** (*illus. Brian Wildsmith*)	MACMILLAN 1964 VANGUARD PRESS 1964	**C** **B**
43	**The Dutch are Coming** (*illus. Lynette Hemmant*)	HAMISH HAMILTON 1965	**B**
44	**Bent is the Bow** (*illus. Charles Keeping*)	NELSON 1965 NELSON US 1967	**C** **B**
45	**The Red Towers of Granada** (*illus. Charles Keeping*)	MACMILLAN 1966 VANGUARD PRESS 1967	**C** **B**
46	**The White Nights of St Petersburg** (*illus. William Stobbs*)	MACMILLAN 1967 VANGUARD PRESS 1967	**B** **B**
47	**The Runaway Serf** (*illus. Mary Russon*)	HAMISH HAMILTON 1968	**B**
48	**A Masque for the Queen** (*illus. Krystyna Turska*)	HAMISH HAMILTON 1970	**B**
49	**Horsemen on the Hills**	MACMILLAN 1971	**B**
50	**A Ship to Rome** (*illus. Leslie Atkinson*)	HEINEMANN 1972	**B**
51	**A Voice in the Night** (*illus. Sara Silcock*)	HEINEMANN 1973	**B**
52	**Popinjay Stairs**	MACMILLAN 1973	**B**
53	**The Chocolate Boy** (*illus. David Walker*)	HEINEMANN 1975	**B**

54	**The Iron Tsar**	MACMILLAN 1975	**B**
55	**When the Drums Beat**	HEINEMANN 1976	**B**
	(*illus. Janet Marsh*)		
56	**Violet for Bonaparte**	MACMILLAN 1976	**B**
57	**The Seas of Morning**	PUFFIN 1976	**B**
	(*illus. David Smee*)		
58	**The Spy Catchers**	HAMISH HAMILTON 1976	**B**
	(*illus. Geoffrey Bargery*)		
59	**The Field of the Forty Footsteps**	MACMILLAN 1977	**B**
60	**The Claws of the Eagle**	HEINEMANN 1977	**B**
	(*illus. Ionicus*)		
61	**Mandeville**	MACMILLAN 1980	**A**
62	**A Wood by Moonlight and Other Stories**	CHATTO & WINDUS 1981	**A**
63	**The Running of the Deer**	HAMISH HAMILTON 1982	**A**
	(*illus. Maureen Bradley*)		
64	**Saraband for Shadows**	MACMILLAN 1982	**A**
65	**The Cormorant Venture**	MACMILLAN 1984	**A**
66	**Tomorrow is a Stranger**	HEINEMANN 1987	**A**

Also of interest:
MARGARET MEEK: **Geoffrey Trease** (BODLEY HEAD 1960, WALCK US 1964)

TREECE, Henry   *Born in Staffordshire, 1911. Died 1966*

Treece was known in the 1940s primarily as a poet – reacting against the
Auden, Spender, MacNeice camp, although published by T.S. Eliot at
Faber. In the 1950s he turned to both adult and children's fiction and – as
will be seen from the ensuing list – became extremely prolific in the field of
reasonably straightforward adventure and historical novels. He is not, I
think, *seriously* collected, but will be sought out by enthusiasts of boys' books,
and those who appreciate uncomplicated entertainment.

| 1 | **Legions of the Eagle** | LANE 1954 | **C** |
| | (*illus. Christine Price*) | | |

2	**The Eagles Have Flown** (*illus. Christine Price*)	LANE 1954	B
3	**Desperate Journey** (*illus. Richard Kennedy*)	FABER 1954	B
4	**Ask for King Billy** (*illus. Richard Kennedy*)	FABER 1955	B
5	**Viking's Dawn** (*illus. Christine Price*)	LANE 1955 / CRITERION 1956	B / A
6	**Hounds of the King** (*illus. Christine Price*)	LANE 1955	B
7	**Men of the Hills** (*illus. Christine Price*)	LANE 1957 / CRITERION 1958	B / A
8	**The Road to Miklagard** (*illus. Christine Price*)	LANE 1957 / CRITERION 1957	B / A
9	**Hunter Hunted** (*illus. Richard Kennedy*)	FABER 1957	B
10	**Don't Expect Any Mercy!**	FABER 1958	B
11	**The Children's Crusade** (*illus. Christine Price*)	BODLEY HEAD 1958	B
12	**Perilous Pilgrimage** Same as 11.	CRITERION 1959	A
13	**The Return of Robinson Crusoe** (*illus. Will Nickless*)	HULTON PRESS 1958	C
14	**The Further Adventures of Robinson Crusoe** Same as 13.	CRITERION 1958	B
15	**The Bombard** (*illus. Christine Price*)	BODLEY HEAD 1959	B
16	**Ride to Danger** Same as 15.	CRITERION 1959	A
17	**Wickham and the Armada** (*illus. Hookway Cowles*)	HULTON PRESS 1959	B
18	**Castles and Kings** (*non-fiction*) (*illus. C. Walter Hodges*)	BATSFORD 1959 / CRITERION 1960	C / B

19	**Viking's Sunset** (*illus. Christine Price*) *5, 8 & 19 form a trilogy.*	BODLEY HEAD 1960 CRITERION 1961	**B** **A**
20	**Red Settlement**	BODLEY HEAD 1960	**B**
21	**The True Book About Castles** (*non-fiction*) (*illus. G.H. Channing*)	MULLER 1960	**A**
22	**The Jet Beads** (*illus. W.A. Sillince*)	BROCKHAMPTON PRESS 1961	**B**
23	**The Golden One** (*illus. William Stobbs*)	BODLEY HEAD 1961 CRITERION 1962	**B** **A**
24	**Man with a Sword** (*illus. William Stobbs*)	BODLEY HEAD 1962 PANTHEON 1964	**B** **A**
25	**War Dog** (*illus. Roger Payne*)	BROCKHAMPTON PRESS 1962 CRITERION 1963	**B** **A**
26	**Horned Helmet** (*illus. Charles Keeping*)	BROCKHAMPTON PRESS 1963 CRITERION 1963	**B** **A**
27	**Know About the Crusades** (*non-fiction*) *The American edition omits the word 'know' from the title.*	BLACKIE 1963 DUFOUR 1966	**A** **A**
28	**Fighting Men: How Men Have Fought Through the Ages** (*non-fiction*) (*with Ewart Oakeshott*)	BROCKHAMPTON PRESS 1963 PUTNAM 1965	**A** **A**
29	**The Burning of Njal** (*retelling*) (*illus. Bernard Blatch*)	BODLEY HEAD 1963 CRITERION 1964	**A** **A**
30	**The Last of the Vikings** (*illus. Charles Keeping*)	BROCKHAMPTON PRESS 1964	**C**
31	**The Last Viking** *Same as 30.*	PANTHEON 1966	**B**
32	**Hounds of the King, with Two Radio Plays** (*illus. Stuart Tresilian*) *Includes* Harold Godwinson *and* William, Duke of Normandy.	LONGMAN 1965	**B**

33	**The Bronze Sword** (*illus. Mary Russon*)	HAMISH HAMILTON 1965	**A**
34	**The Centurion** *Augmented edition of 33.*	MEREDITH PRESS US 1967	**A**
35	**Splintered Sword** (*illus. Charles Keeping*) *26, 30 & 35 form a trilogy.*	BROCKHAMPTON PRESS 1965 DUELL 1966	**C** **B**
36	**Killer in Dark Glasses**	FABER 1965	**A**
37	**Bang, You're Dead!**	FABER 1966	**A**
38	**The Queen's Brooch**	HAMISH HAMILTON 1966 PUTNAM 1967	**A** **A**
39	**Swords from the North** (*illus. Charles Keeping*)	FABER 1967 PANTHEON 1967	**B** **A**
40	**The Windswept City** (*illus. Faith Jaques*)	HAMISH HAMILTON 1967 MEREDITH PRESS 1968	**A** **A**
41	**Vinland the Good** (*illus. William Stobbs*)	BODLEY HEAD 1967	**A**
42	**Westward to Vinland** *Same as 41.*	PHILLIPS US 1967	**A**
43	**The Dream-Time** (*illus. Charles Keeping*)	BROCKHAMPTON PRESS 1967 MEREDITH PRESS 1968	**B** **A**
44	**The Invaders: Three Stories** (*illus. Charles Keeping*)	BROCKHAMPTON PRESS 1972 CROWELL 1972	**B** **A**

Also of interest:

MARGERY FISHER: **Henry Treece** (*included in* Three Bodley Head Monographs, BODLEY HEAD 1969)

UTTLEY, Alison

Full name Alice Jane Uttley
Born in Derbyshire, 1884. Died 1976

Best known as the creator of Little Grey Rabbit and Sam Pig – as well as for a clutch of much-loved country books for adults – Alison Uttley (or Alice Jane, as she was christened) is sometimes rather unfairly seen to be the poor man's Beatrix Potter. The books should be viewed in their own right – very charming evocations of animal and country life, immediately attractive to young (and not-so-young) children. I think it is true to say that even the best of the artwork does not compare with Beatrix Potter, though.

Below are listed all the works for children. Fine copies, it almost goes without saying, are damnably elusive.

1	**The Squirrel, the Hare and the Little Grey Rabbit** (*illus. Margaret Tempest*)	HEINEMANN 1929	G
2	**How Little Grey Rabbit Got Back Her Tail** (*illus. Margaret Tempest*)	HEINEMANN 1930	F
3	**The Great Adventure of Hare** (*illus. Margaret Tempest*)	HEINEMANN 1931	F
4	**Moonshine and Magic** (*illus. Will Townsend*)	FABER 1932	E
5	**The Story of Fuzzypeg the Hedgehog** (*illus. Margaret Tempest*)	HEINEMANN 1932	E
6	**Squirrel Goes Skating** (*illus. Margaret Tempest*)	COLLINS 1934	E
7	**Wise Owl's Story** (*illus. Margaret Tempest*)	COLLINS 1935	E
8	**The Adventures of Peter and Judy in Bunnyland** (*illus. L. Young*)	COLLINS 1935	E
9	**Candlelight Tales** (*illus. Elinor Bellingham-Smith*)	FABER 1936	E
10	**Little Grey Rabbit's Party** (*illus. Margaret Tempest*)	COLLINS 1936	F
11	**The Knot Squirrel Tied** (*illus. Margaret Tempest*)	COLLINS 1937	E

12	**The Adventures of No Ordinary Rabbit** (*illus. Alec Buckels*)	FABER 1937	**E**
13	**Mustard, Pepper and Salt** (*illus. Gwen Raverat*)	FABER 1938	**G**
14	**Fuzzypeg Goes to School** (*illus. Margaret Tempest*)	COLLINS 1938	**E**
15	**A Traveller in Time**	FABER 1939 PUTNAM 1940	**D** **C**
16	**Tales of the Four Pigs and Brock the Badger** (*illus. Alec Buckels*)	FABER 1939	**D**
17	**Little Grey Rabbit's Christmas** (*illus. Margaret Tempest*)	COLLINS 1939	**E**
18	**Moldy Warp, the Mole** (*illus. Margaret Tempest*)	COLLINS 1940	**D**
19	**The Adventures of Sam Pig** (*illus. Francis Gower*)	FABER 1940	**E**
20	**Sam Pig Goes to Market** (*illus. A.E. Kennedy*)	FABER 1941	**D**
21	**Six Tales of Brock the Badger** (*illus. Alec Buckels & Francis Gower*)	FABER 1941	**D**
22	**Six Tales of Sam Pig** (*illus. Alec Buckels & Francis Gower*)	FABER 1941	**D**
23	**Six Tales of the Four Pigs** (*illus. Alec Buckels*)	FABER 1941	**D**
24	**Ten Tales of Tim Rabbit** (*illus. Alec Buckels & Francis Gower*)	FABER 1941	**D**
25	**Hare Joins the Home Guard** (*illus. Margaret Tempest*)	COLLINS 1942	**D**
26	**Little Grey Rabbit's Washing-day** (*illus. Margaret Tempest*)	COLLINS 1942	**D**
27	**Nine Starlight Tales** (*illus. Irene Hawkins*)	FABER 1942	**D**

28	**Sam Pig and Sally** (*illus. A.E. Kennedy*)	FABER 1943	D
29	**Cuckoo Cherry-Tree** (*illus. Irene Hawkins*)	FABER 1943	C
30	**Sam Pig at the Circus** (*illus. A.E. Kennedy*)	FABER 1943	C
31	**Water-rat's Picnic** (*illus. Margaret Tempest*)	COLLINS 1943	C
32	**Little Grey Rabbit's Birthday** (*illus. Margaret Tempest*)	COLLINS 1944	D
33	**The Spice Woman's Basket and Other Tales** (*illus. Irene Hawkins*)	FABER 1944	C
34	**Mrs Nimble and Mr Bumble** (*illus. Horace Knowles*)	JAMES 1944	C
35	**Some Moonshine Tales** (*illus. Sarah Nechamkin*)	FABER 1945	C
36	**The Adventures of Tim Rabbit** (*illus. A.E. Kennedy*)	FABER 1945	C
37	**The Weather Cock and Other Stories** (*illus. Nancy Innes*)	FABER 1945	C
38	**The Speckledy Hen** (*illus. Margaret Tempest*)	FABER 1946	C
39	**Little Grey Rabbit to the Rescue** (*play*) (*illus. Margaret Tempest*)	COLLINS 1946	E
40	**The Washerwoman's Child: A Play on the Life and Stories of Hans Christian Andersen** (*illus. Irene Hawkins*)	FABER 1946	C
41	**Little Grey Rabbit and the Weasels** (*illus. Margaret Tempest*)	COLLINS 1947	D
42	**Grey Rabbit and the Wandering Hedgehog** (*illus. Margaret Tempest*)	COLLINS 1948	D
43	**John Barleycorn: Twelve Tales of Fairy and Magic** (*illus. Philip Hepworth*)	FABER 1948	C

44	**Sam Pig in Trouble** (*illus. A.E. Kennedy*)	FABER 1948	**C**
45	**The Cobbler's Shop and Other Stories** (*illus. Irene Hawkins*)	FABER 1950	**C**
46	**MacDuff** (*illus. A.E. Kennedy*)	FABER 1950	**C**
47	**Little Grey Rabbit Makes Lace** (*illus. Margaret Tempest*)	COLLINS 1950	**D**
48	**The Little Brown Mouse Books** (*12 volumes, all illus. Katherine Wigglesworth*):	HEINEMANN 1950–7	**B** **Each**

Snug and Serena Meet a Queen
Snug and Serena Pick Cowslips
Going to the Fair
Toad's Castle
Mrs Mouse Spring-cleans
Christmas at the Rose and Crown
The Gypsy Hedgehogs
Snug and the Chimney-sweeper
The Mouse Telegrams
The Flower Show
Snug and the Silver Spoon
Mr Stoat Walks In

49	**Yours Ever, Sam Pig** (*illus. A.E. Kennedy*)	FABER 1951	**C**
50	**Hare and the Easter Eggs** (*illus. Margaret Tempest*)	COLLINS 1952	**C**
51	**Little Grey Rabbit Goes to Sea** (*illus. Margaret Tempest*)	COLLINS 1954	**C**
52	**Little Red Fox and the Wicked Uncle** (*illus. Katherine Wigglesworth*)	HEINEMANN 1954 BOBBS MERRILL 1962	**C** **B**
53	**Sam Pig and the Singing Gate** (*illus. A.E. Kennedy*)	FABER 1955	**C**
54	**Hare and Guy Fawkes** (*illus. Margaret Tempest*)	COLLINS 1956	**C**

55	**Little Red Fox and Cinderella** (*illus. Katherine Wigglesworth*)	HEINEMANN 1956	C
56	**Magic in My Pocket: A Selection of Tales** (*illus. Judith Brook*)	PUFFIN 1957	B
57	**Little Grey Rabbit's Paint-box** (*illus. Margaret Tempest*)	COLLINS 1958	C
58	**Little Grey Rabbit and the Magic Moon** (*illus. Katherine Wigglesworth*)	HEINEMANN 1958	C
59	**Snug and Serena Count Twelve** (*illus. Katherine Wigglesworth*)	HEINEMANN 1959 BOBBS MERRILL 1962	C B
60	**Tim Rabbit and Company** (*illus. A.E. Kennedy*)	FABER 1959	C
61	**Sam Pig Goes to the Seaside: Sixteen Stories** (*illus. A.E. Kennedy*)	FABER 1960	C
62	**Grey Rabbit Finds a Shoe** (*illus. Margaret Tempest*)	COLLINS 1960	C
63	**John at the Old Farm** (*illus. Jennifer Miles*)	HEINEMANN 1960	B
64	**Grey Rabbit and the Circus** (*illus. Margaret Tempest*)	COLLINS 1961	C
65	**Snug and Serena Go to Town** (*illus. Katherine Wigglesworth*)	HEINEMANN 1961 BOBBS MERRILL 1963	B B
66	**Three Little Grey Rabbit Plays:** *Comprises*: Grey Rabbit's Hospital; The Robber; A Christmas Story.	HEINEMANN 1961	C
67	**Little Red Fox and the Unicorn** (*illus. Katherine Wigglesworth*)	HEINEMANN 1962	B
68	**The Little Knife Who Did All the Work: Twelve Tales of Magic** (*illus. Pauline Baynes*)	FABER 1962	C
69	**Grey Rabbit's May Day** (*illus. Margaret Tempest*)	COLLINS 1963	C
70	**Tim Rabbit's Dozen** (*illus. Shirley Hughes*)	FABER 1964	B

71	**Hare Goes Shopping** (*illus. Margaret Tempest*)	COLLINS 1965	C
72	**The Sam Pig Storybook** (*illus. Cecil Leslie*)	FABER 1965	B
73	**The Mouse, the Rabbit and the Little White Hen** (*illus. Jennie Corbett*)	HEINEMANN 1966	B
74	**Enchantment** (*illus. Jennie Corbett*)	HEINEMANN 1966	B
75	**Little Grey Rabbit's Pancake Day** (*illus. Margaret Tempest*)	COLLINS 1967	B
76	**The Little Red Fox and the Big Tree** (*illus. Jennie Corbett*)	HEINEMANN 1968	B
77	**Little Grey Rabbit Goes to the North Pole** (*illus. Katherine Wigglesworth*)	COLLINS 1970	B
78	**Lavender Shoes: Eight Tales of Enchantment** (*illus. Janina Ede*)	FABER 1970	B
79	**The Brown Mouse Book: Magical Tales of Two Little Mice** (*illus. Katherine Wigglesworth*)	HEINEMANN 1971	B
80	**Fuzzypeg's Brother** (*illus. Katherine Wigglesworth*)	HEINEMANN 1971	B
81	**Little Grey Rabbit's Spring Cleaning Party** (*illus. Katherine Wigglesworth*)	COLLINS 1972	B
82	**Little Grey Rabbit and the Snow-Baby** (*illus. Katherine Wigglesworth*)	COLLINS 1973	B
83	**Fairy Tales** (*illus. Ann Strugnell*)	FABER 1975	B
84	**Hare and the Rainbow** (*illus. Katherine Wigglesworth*)	COLLINS 1975	B
85	**Stories for Christmas** (*illus. Gavin Rowe*)	FABER 1977	B
86	**From Spring to Spring: Stories of the Four Seasons** (*illus. Shirley Hughes*)	FABER 1978	B

WALSH, Jill Paton   *Born in London, 1937*

An important, highly respected and – more to the point – jolly *good* writer, whose work continues to improve and develop. She pulls off that rare thing – books that are primarily aimed at what may loosely be termed 'adolescents', and yet neither wallow in all the attendant problems nor condescend; moreover, they may also be appreciated by younger children and, of course, adults. Collectable and – wouldn't you know it? – collected.

1	**Hengest's Tale**	MACMILLAN 1966	E
	(*illus. Janet Margrie*)	ST MARTIN'S PRESS 1966	C
2	**The Dolphin Crossing**	MACMILLAN 1967	D
		ST MARTIN'S PRESS 1967	B
3	**Wordhoard: Anglo-Saxon Stories**	MACMILLAN 1969	C
	(*with Kevin Crossley-Holland*)	FARRAR STRAUS 1969	B
4	**Fireweed**	MACMILLAN 1969	C
		FARRAR STRAUS 1970	B
5	**Goldengrove**	MACMILLAN 1972	C
		FARRAR STRAUS 1972	B
6	**Toolmaker**	HEINEMANN 1973	C
	(*illus. Jeroo Roy*)	SEABURY PRESS 1974	B
7	**The Dawnstone**	HAMISH HAMILTON 1973	C
	(*illus. Mary Dinsdale*)		
8	**The Emperor's Winding Sheet**	MACMILLAN 1974	C
		FARRAR STRAUS 1974	B
9	**The Butty Boy**	MACMILLAN 1975	C
	(*illus. Juliette Palmer*)		
10	**The Huffler**	FARRAR STRAUS 1975	B
	Same as 9.		
11	**The Island Sunrise: Prehistoric**	DEUTSCH 1975	C
	Britain (*non-fiction*)	SEABURY PRESS 1976	C
12	**Unleaving**	MACMILLAN 1976	C
		FARRAR STRAUS 1976	B
13	**Crossing to Salamis**	HEINEMANN 1977	C
	(*illus. David Smee*)		

14	**The Walls of Athens** (*illus. David Smee*)	HEINEMANN 1977	C
15	**Persian Gold** (*illus. David Smee*) *13, 14 & 15 form a trilogy.*	HEINEMANN 1978	C
16	**Children of the Fox** *Contains 13, 14 & 15.*	FARRAR STRAUS 1978	B
17	**A Chance Child**	MACMILLAN 1978 FARRAR STRAUS 1978	B B
18	**The Green Book** (*illus. Joanna Stubbs*)	MACMILLAN 1981 FARRAR STRAUS 1982	B B
19	**Babylon** (*illus. Jenny Northway*)	DEUTSCH 1982	B
20	**A Parcel of Patterns**	KESTREL 1983 FARRAR STRAUS 1984	B B
21	**Lost and Found** (*illus. Mary Rayner*)	DEUTSCH 1984	B
22	**Gaffer Samson's Luck** (*illus. Brock Cole*)	FARRAR STRAUS 1984 VIKING KESTREL 1985	B B

WESTERMAN, Percy

Born in Hampshire, 1876. Died 1959

The reason I am listing *all* of Westerman's spiffing yarns is because I reason that a collector would either be not at all interested in acquiring any (in which case, skip) or else would love to have them *all*. These books for chaps of the right sort (plenty of pluck, gallons of grit) tend to grab a fellow like that. During the 1930s, Westerman was regarded by boys as just a very short step below God, and constantly outsold all his rivals. A revival of such enthusiasm seems timely.

1	**A Lad of Grit** (*illus. E.S. Hodgson*)	BLACKIE 1908	F
2	**The Winning of Golden Spurs**	NISBET 1911	E
3	**The Young Cavalier** (*illus. Gordon Browne*)	PEARSON 1911	E
4	**The Quest of the 'Golden Hope'** (*illus. Frank Wiles*)	BLACKIE 1911	E

5   **The Flying Submarine**   NISBET 1912   **D**

6   **Captured at Tripoli**   BLACKIE 1912   **D**
    (*illus. Charles Seldon*)

7   **The Sea Monarch**   BLACK 1912   **D**
    (*illus. E.S. Hodgson*)

8   **The Scouts of Seal Island**   BLACK 1913   **D**
    (*illus. Ernest Prater*)

9   **The Rival Submarines**   PARTRIDGE 1913   **D**
    (*illus. C. Fleming Williams*)

10 **The Stolen Cruiser**   JARROLDS 1913   **D**

11 **When East Meets West**   BLACKIE 1913   **D**
    (*illus. C.M. Padday*)

12 **Under King Henry's Banners**   PILGRIM PRESS 1913   **D**
    (*illus. John Campbell*)

13 **The Sea-girt Fortress**   BLACKIE 1914   **C**
    (*illus. W.E. Wigfull*)

14 **The Sea Scouts of the 'Petrel'**   BLACK 1914   **C**
    (*illus. Ernest Prater*)

15 **The Log of a Snob**   CHAPMAN & HALL 1914   **C**
    (*illus. W.E. Wigfull*)

16 **'Gainst the Might of Spain**   PILGRIM PRESS 1914   **C**
    (*illus. Savile Lumley*)

17 **Building the Empire**   JARROLDS 1914   **C**

18 **The Dreadnought of the Air**   PARTRIDGE 1914   **C**

19 **The Dispatch-riders**   BLACKIE 1915   **C**

20 **The Fight for Constantinople**   BLACKIE 1915   **C**

21 **The Nameless Island**   PARTRIDGE 1915   **C**

22 **A Sub of the RNR**   PARTRIDGE 1915   **C**

23 **Rounding Up the Raider**   BLACKIE 1916   **C**
    (*illus. E.S. Hodgson*)

24 **The Secret Battleplane**   BLACKIE 1916   **C**

25 **The Treasures of the 'San Philipo'** RTS 1916   **C**

26	A Watch-dog of the North Sea	PARTRIDGE 1916	C
27	Deeds of Pluck and Daring in the Great War	BLACKIE 1917	C
28	To the Fore with the Tanks! (*illus. Dudley Tennant*)	PARTRIDGE 1917	C
29	Under the White Ensign	BLACKIE 1917	C
30	The Fritzstrafers	PARTRIDGE 1918	C
31	Billy Barcroft R.N.A.S.	PARTRIDGE 1918	C
32	A Lively Bit of the Front (*illus. Wal Paget*)	BLACKIE 1918	C
33	The Secret Channel and Other Stories	BLACK 1918 MACMILLAN US 1919	C C
34	The Submarine Hunters	BLACKIE 1918	C
35	A Sub and a Submarine	BLACKIE 1918	C
36	With Beatty Off Jutland	BLACKIE 1918	C
37	Wilmshurst of the Frontier Force	PARTRIDGE 1919	C
38	Winning His Wings (*illus. E.S. Hodgson*)	BLACKIE 1919	C
39	The Thick of the Fray at Zeebruge, April 1918 (*illus. W.E. Wigfull*)	BLACKIE 1919	C
40	'Midst Arctic Perils	PEARSON 1919	C
41	The Airship 'Golden Hind'	PARTRIDGE 1920	C
42	The Mystery Ship	PARTRIDGE 1920	C
43	The Salving of the 'Fusi Yama' (*illus. E.S. Hodgson*)	BLACKIE 1920	C
44	Sea Scouts All (*illus. Charles Pears*)	BLACKIE 1920	C
45	Sea Scouts Abroad (*illus. Charles Pears*)	BLACKIE 1921	C
46	The Third Officer (*illus. E.S. Hodgson*)	BLACKIE 1921	C

47 **Sea Scouts Up-channel**   BLACKIE 1922   **C**
   (*illus. C.M. Padday*)

48 **The Wireless Officer**   BLACKIE 1922   **C**
   (*illus. W.E. Wigfull*)

49 **The War of the Wireless Waves**   OUP 1923   **C**
   (*illus. W.E. Wightman*)

50 **The Pirate Submarine**   NISBET 1923   **C**

51 **A Cadet of the Mercantile Marine**   BLACKIE 1923   **C**
   (*illus. W.E. Wigfull*)

52 **Clipped Wings**   BLACKIE 1923   **C**
   (*illus. E.S. Hodgson*)

53 **The Mystery of Stockmere School**   PARTRIDGE 1923   **C**

54 **Sinclair's Luck**   PARTRIDGE 1923   **C**

55 **Captain Cain**   NISBET 1924   **B**

56 **The Good Ship 'Golden Effort'**   BLACKIE 1924   **B**
   (*illus. W.E. Wigfull*)

57 **The Treasure of the Sacred Lake**   PEARSON 1924   **B**

58 **Unconquered Wings**   BLACKIE 1924   **B**
   (*illus. E.S. Hodgson*)

59 **Clinton's Quest**   PEARSON 1925   **B**
   (*illus. R.B. Ogle*)

60 **East in the 'Golden Gain'**   BLACKIE 1925   **C**
   (*illus. Rowland Hilder*)

61 **The Boys of the 'Puffin'**   PARTRIDGE 1925   **B**
   (*illus. G.W. Goss*)

62 **The Buccaneers of Boya**   BLACKIE 1925   **B**
   (*illus. William Rainey*)

63 **The Sea Scouts of the 'Kestrel'**   SEELEY 1925   **B**

64 **Annesley's Double**   BLACK 1926   **B**
                                 MACMILLAN US 1926   **B**

65 **King of Kilba**   WARD LOCK 1926   **B**

66 **The Luck of the 'Golden Dawn'**   BLACKIE 1926   **C**
   (*illus. Rowland Hilder*)

67	**The Riddle of the Air** (*illus. Rowland Hilder*)	BLACKIE 1926	C
68	**Tireless Wings**	BLACKIE 1926	B
69	**The Terror of the Seas**	WARD LOCK 1927	B
70	**Mystery Island**	OUP 1927	B
71	**Captain Blundell's Treasure** (*illus. J. Cameron*)	BLACKIE 1927	B
72	**Chums of the 'Golden Vanity'** (*illus. Rowland Hilder*)	BLACKIE 1927	C
73	**In the Clutches of the Dyaks** (*illus. F. Marston*)	PARTRIDGE 1927	B
74	**The Junior Cadet** (*illus. Rowland Hilder*)	BLACKIE 1928	C
75	**On the Wings of the Wind** (*illus. W.E. Wigfull*)	BLACKIE 1928	B
76	**A Shanghai Adventure** (*illus. Leo Bates*)	BLACKIE 1928	B
77	**Pat Stobart in the 'Golden Dawn'** (*illus. Rowland Hilder*)	BLACKIE 1929	C
78	**Rivals of the Reef** (*illus. Kenneth Inns*)	BLACKIE 1929	B
79	**Captain Starlight** (*illus. W.E. Wigfull*)	BLACKIE 1929	B
80	**Captain Sang**	BLACKIE 1930	B
81	**Leslie Dexter, Cadet**	BLACKIE 1930	B
82	**A Mystery of the Broads** (*illus. E.A. Cox*)	BLACKIE 1930	B
83	**The Secret of the Plateau** (*illus. W.E. Wigfull*)	BLACKIE 1931	B
84	**The Senior Cadet** (*illus. Rowland Hilder*)	BLACKIE 1931	C
85	**In Defiance of the Ban** (*illus. E.S. Hodgson*)	BLACKIE 1931	B

86	**All Hands to the Boats!** (*illus. Rowland Hilder*)	BLACKIE 1932	C
87	**The Amir's Baby** (*illus. W.E. Wigfull*)	BLACKIE 1932	B
88	**Captain Fosdyke's Gold** (*illus. E.S. Hodgson*)	BLACKIE 1932	B
89	**King for a Month** (*illus. Comerford Watson*)	BLACKIE 1933	B
90	**Rocks Ahead!** (*illus. D.L. Mays*)	BLACKIE 1933	B
91	**The White Arab** (*illus. Henry Coller*)	BLACKIE 1933	B
92	**The Disappearing Dhow** (*illus. D.L. Mays*)	BLACKIE 1933	B
93	**Chasing the 'Pleiad'**	BLACKIE 1933	B
94	**Tales of the Sea** (*with others*) (*illus. Terence Cuneo*)	TUCK 1933	B
95	**The Westlow Talisman** (*illus. W.E. Wigfull*)	BLACKIE 1934	B
96	**Andy-all-Alone** (*illus. D.L. Mays*)	BLACKIE 1934	B
97	**The Black Hawk** (*illus. Rowland Hilder*)	BLACKIE 1934	C
98	**Standish of the Air Police**	BLACKIE 1935	B
99	**The Red Pirate** (*illus. Rowland Hilder*)	BLACKIE 1935	C
100	**Sleuths of the Air** (*illus. Comerford Watson*)	BLACKIE 1935	B
101	**On Board the 'Golden Effort'**	BLACKIE 1935	B
102	**The Call of the Sea** (*illus. D.L. Mays*)	BLACKIE 1935	B
103	**Captain Flick** (*illus. E.S. Hodgson*)	BLACKIE 1936	B

104 **His First Ship**   BLACKIE 1936   B

105 **Midshipman Raxworthy**   BLACKIE 1936   B

106 **Ringed by Fire**   BLACKIE 1936   B

107 **Winged Might**   BLACKIE 1937   B

108 **Under Fire in Spain**   BLACKIE 1937   B
     (*illus. Ernest Prater*)

109 **The Last of the Buccaneers**   BLACKIE 1937   B

110 **Haunted Harbour**   BLACKIE 1937   B
     (*illus. John de Walton*)

111 **His Unfinished Voyage**   BLACKIE 1937   B
     (*illus. D.L. Mays*)

112 **Cadet Alan Carr**   BLACKIE 1938   B
     (*illus. D.L. Mays*)

113 **Midshipman Webb's Treasure**   BLACKIE 1938   B
     (*illus. D.L. Mays*)

114 **Standish Gets His Man**   BLACKIE 1938   B
     (*illus. W.E. Wigfull*)

115 **Sea Scouts Alert!**   BLACKIE 1938   B

116 **Standish Loses His Man**   BLACKIE 1939   B
     (*illus. W.E. Wigfull*)

117 **In Eastern Seas**   BLACKIE 1939   B

118 **The Bulldog Breed**   BLACKIE 1939   B
     (*illus. E. Boye Uden*)

119 **At Grips with the Swastika**   BLACKIE 1940   B
     (*illus. Leo Bates*)

120 **Eagles' Talons**   BLACKIE 1940   B

121 **In Dangerous Waters**   BLACKIE 1940   B

122 **When the Allies Swept the Seas**   BLACKIE 1940   B
     (*illus. J.C.B. Knight*)

123 **Standish Pulls It Off**   BLACKIE 1940   B

124 **The War – and Alan Carr**   BLACKIE 1940   B
     (*illus. E. Boye Uden*)

125 **War Cargo**   BLACKIE 1941   **B**

126 **Sea Scouts at Dunkirk**   BLACKIE 1941   **B**

127 **Standish Holds On**   BLACKIE 1941   **B**

128 **Fighting for Freedom**   BLACKIE 1941   **B**

129 **Alan Carr in the Near East**   BLACKIE 1942   **B**

130 **Destroyer's Luck**   BLACKIE 1942   **B**

131 **On Guard for England**   BLACKIE 1942   **B**
  (*illus. J.C.B. Knight*)

132 **Secret Flight**   BLACKIE 1942   **B**

133 **With the Commandoes**   BLACKIE 1943   **B**
  (*illus. S. Van Abbe*)

134 **Sub-lieutenant John Cloche**   BLACKIE 1943   **B**
  (*illus. H. Pym*)

135 **Alan Carr in Command**   BLACKIE 1943   **B**
  (*illus. Terence Cuneo*)

136 **Alan Carr in the Arctic**   BLACKIE 1943   **B**
  (*illus. E. Boye Uden*)

137 **Combined Operations**   BLACKIE 1944   **B**
  (*illus. S. Van Abbe*)

138 **Engage the Enemy Closely**   BLACKIE 1944   **B**
  (*illus. Terence Cuneo*)

139 **Secret Convoy**   BLACKIE 1944   **B**
  (*illus. Terence Cuneo*)

140 **One of the Many**   BLACKIE 1945   **B**
  (*illus. Ellis Silas*)

141 **Operations Successfully Executed**   BLACKIE 1945   **B**
  (*illus. S. Drigin*)

142 **By Luck and Pluck**   BLACKIE 1946   **B**
  (*illus. Terence Cuneo*)

143 **Return to Base**   BLACKIE 1946   **B**
  (*illus. Leslie Wilcox*)

144 **Squadron Leader**   BLACKIE 1946   **B**
  (*illus. Terence Cuneo*)

145 **Unfettered Night**
 (*illus. S. Jezzard*)   BLACKIE 1947   **B**

146 **Trapped in the Jungle**
 (*illus. A.S. Forrest*)   BLACKIE 1947   **B**

147 **The Phantom Submarine**
 (*illus. J.C.B. Knight*)   BLACKIE 1947   **B**

148 **The 'Golden Gleaner'**
 (*illus. M. Mackinlay*)   BLACKIE 1948   **B**

149 **First Over**
 (*illus. Ellis Silas*)   BLACKIE 1948   **B**

150 **Mystery of the Key**
 (*illus. Ellis Silas*)   BLACKIE 1948   **B**

151 **Missing Believed Lost**
 (*illus. Will Nickless*)   BLACKIE 1949   **B**

152 **Contraband**
 (*illus. A. Barclay*)   BLACKIE 1949   **B**

153 **Beyond the Burma Road**
 (*illus. Victor Bertoglio*)   BLACKIE 1949   **B**

154 **Sabarinda Island**
 (*illus. A. Barclay*)   BLACKIE 1950   **A**

155 **Mystery of Nix Hall**
 (*illus. D.C. Eyles*)   BLACKIE 1950   **A**

156 **By Sea and Air**   BLACKIE 1950   **A**

157 **Desolation Island**
 (*illus. W. Gale*)   BLACKIE 1950   **A**

158 **Held to Ransom**
 (*illus. Ellis Silas*)   BLACKIE 1951   **A**

159 **The Isle of Mystery**
 (*illus. Philip*)   BLACKIE 1951   **A**

160 **Working Their Passage**
 (*illus. Ellis Silas*)   BLACKIE 1951   **A**

161 **Sabotage!**
 (*illus. Ellis Silas*)   BLACKIE 1952   **A**

162 Round the World in the 'Golden Gleaner' (*illus. Jack Matthew*)	BLACKIE 1952	A
163 Dangerous Cargo (*illus. W. Gale*)	BLACKIE 1952	A
164 Bob Strickland's Log (*illus. Jack Matthew*)	BLACKIE 1953	A
165 The Missing Diplomat (*illus. R.G. Campbell*)	BLACKIE 1953	A
166 Rolling Down to Rio (*illus. R.G. Campbell*)	BLACKIE 1953	A
167 Wrested from the Deep (*illus. Robert Johnston*)	BLACKIE 1954	A
168 A Midshipman of the Fleet (*illus. P.A. Jobson*)	BLACKIE 1954	A
169 The Ju-Ju Hand	BLACKIE 1954	A
170 The Dark Scout (*illus. Victor Bertoglio*)	BLACKIE 1954	A
171 Daventry's Quest (*illus. P.A. Jobson*)	BLACKIE 1955	A
172 The Lure of the Lagoon (*illus. E. Kearon*)	BLACKIE 1955	A
173 Held in the Frozen North (*illus. Edward Osmond*)	BLACKIE 1956	A
174 The Mystery of the 'Sempione' (*illus. P.B. Batchelor*)	BLACKIE 1957	A
175 Jack Craddock's Commission (*illus. Edward Osmond*)	BLACKIE 1958	A
176 Mistaken Identity (*illus. Robert Johnston*)	BLACKIE 1959	A

WHITE, E.B.　　　　　　　　　*American. Born in New York, 1899*

A very stylish writer indeed, known chiefly for his long association with the *New Yorker*, and his collaboration with fellow contributor James Thurber (*Is*

Sex Necessary? or, Why You Feel the Way You Do – Harper 1929, Heinemann 1930).
White has written only three children's books – *Charlotte's Web* is quite rightly
regarded as a modern classic, though his first has pretty strong claims in that
direction too.

1	**Stuart Little**	HARPER 1945	**G**
	(*illus. Garth Williams*)	HAMISH HAMILTON 1946	**F**
2	**Charlotte's Web**	HARPER 1952	**G**
	(*illus. Garth Williams*)	HAMISH HAMILTON 1952	**F**
3	**The Trumpet of the Swan**	HARPER 1970	**C**
	(*illus. Edward Frascino*)	HAMISH HAMILTON 1970	**C**

Also of interest:
EDWARD C. SAMPSON: **E.B. White** (TWAYNE US 1974)

WHITE, T.H.   *British. Born in India, 1906. Died 1964*

The majority of White's books may be enjoyed by adults and children alike,
and the classification of the books below as those 'intended' for children is
largely arbitrary – although few would argue that it is these Arthurian tales
that they love best. The classic and wonderful *The Sword in the Stone* is much
preferable to the really rather radically altered version *The Once and Future King*
– though collectors will, of course, want both.

1	**The Sword in the Stone**	COLLINS 1938	**N**
	(*illus. the author*)	PUTNAM 1939	**K**
2	**The Witch in the Wood**	PUTNAM 1939	**K**
	(*illus. the author*)	COLLINS 1940	**J**
3	**The Ill-made Knight**	PUTNAM 1940	**J**
	(*illus. the author*)	COLLINS 1941	**I**
4	**Mistress Masham's Repose**	PUTNAM 1946	**E**
	(*illus. Fritz Eichenberg*)	CAPE 1947	**D**
5	**The Master: An Adventure Story**	CAPE 1957	**D**
		PUTNAM 1957	**C**
6	**The Once and Future King**	COLLINS 1958	**D**
	This contains revised editions of 1, 2 (retitled	PUTNAM 1958	**D**
	The Queen of Air and Darkness) *& 3.*		

7   **The Book of Merlyn: The**   UNIVERSITY OF TEXAS   **C**
    Unpublished Conclusion to The   1977
    Once And Future King   COLLINS 1978   **C**
    (*illus. Trevor Stubley*)

Also of interest:

SYLVIA TOWNSEND WARNER: **T.H. White: A Biography** (CAPE/CHATTO & WINDUS 1967, VIKING PRESS US 1978)

WILDER, Laura Ingalls   *American. Born in Wisconsin, 1867. Died 1957*

Little House on the Prairie remains a favourite – as much in Britain as in America – and we should be grateful that Laura Ingalls Wilder's daughter's eternal nagging finally resolved her to commence the saga, at the age of 65. Good cowboy books are hard to find.

1   **Little House in the Big Woods**   HARPER 1932   **G**
    (*illus. Helen Sewell*)   METHUEN 1956   **C**

2   **Farmer Boy**   HARPER 1933   **F**
    (*illus. Helen Sewell*)   LUTTERWORTH PRESS   **C**
                                           1965

3   **Little House on the Prairie**   HARPER 1935   **G**
    (*illus. Helen Sewell*)   METHUEN 1957   **C**

4   **On the Banks of Plum Creek**   HARPER 1937   **E**
    (*illus. Helen Sewell & Mildred Boyle*) METHUEN 1958   **C**

5   **By the Shores of Silver Lake**   HARPER 1939   **D**
    (*illus. Helen Sewell & Mildred Boyle*) LUTTERWORTH PRESS   **B**
                                           1961

6   **The Long Winter**   HARPER 1940   **C**
    (*illus. Helen Sewell & Mildred Boyle*) LUTTERWORTH PRESS   **B**
                                           1962

7   **Little Town on the Prairie**   HARPER 1941   **D**
    (*illus. Helen Sewell & Mildred Boyle*) LUTTERWORTH PRESS   **C**
                                           1963

8   **These Happy Golden Years**   HARPER 1943   **C**
    (*illus. Helen Sewell & Mildred Boyle*) LUTTERWORTH PRESS   **B**
                                           1964

9	**The First Four Years**	HARPER 1971	C
	(*illus. Garth Williams*)	LUTTERWORTH PRESS	C
		1973	

WILLANS, Geoffrey   *Born in England, 1911. Died 1958*

One of the great unsung heroes – it is often forgotten that Ronald Searle's illustrations for the Molesworth books (first-class though they are) were just that: illustrations to complement the inimitable words of Willans, the sole begetter of the sublime Nigel and his bro – to say nothing of fotherington-tomas ('Hullo cloud, hullo sky'), Molesworth's grate friend Peason, and Grabber (head of school, captain of games, and winner of Mrs Joyful prize for rafia work). The first in the series, *Down with Skool!*, was worked up from some *Punch* pieces based (we trust not *too* literally) upon Willans' experiences as a prep school master; between October and December 1953, the book sold over 50,000 copies. Alas, Willans died before the fourth and last in the series saw print – but Molesworth lives for ever!

1	**Down With Skool!**	PARRISH 1953	C
	(*illus. Ronald Searle*)	VANGUARD PRESS 1954	B
2	**How to be Topp**	PARRISH 1954	C
	(*illus. Ronald Searle*)	VANGUARD PRESS 1954	B
3	**Whizz for Atomms**	PARRISH 1956	B
	(*illus. Ronald Searle*)		
4	**Molesworth's Guide to the Atommic Age**	VANGUARD PRESS 1957	B
	Same as 3.		
5	**Back in the Jug Agane**	PARRISH 1959	B
	(*illus. Ronald Searle*)	VANGUARD PRESS 1960	B
	The American edition has the word		
	'Molesworth' preceding the title.		

WILLARD, Barbara   *Born in Sussex, 1909*

A prolific writer of children's fiction, who had published more than a dozen adult novels before she adopted the genre at all. The historical fiction (and in particular the 'Mantlemass' sequence) is generally more successful than the contemporary stuff, but I give a complete listing here as some may perceive Barbara Willard to provide a relatively little plundered haul for collectors.

1	**Snail and the Pennithornes** (*illus. Geoffrey Fletcher*)	EPWORTH PRESS 1957	C
2	**Snail and the Pennithornes Next Time** (*illus. Geoffrey Fletcher*)	EPWORTH PRESS 1958	C
3	**Son of Charlemagne** (*illus. Emil Weiss*)	DOUBLEDAY 1959 HEINEMANN 1960	B B
4	**The House with Roots** (*illus. Robert Hodgson*)	CONSTABLE 1959 WATTS 1960	B B
5	**Snail and the Pennithornes and the Princess** (*illus. Geoffrey Fletcher*)	EPWORTH PRESS 1960	B
6	**The Dippers and Jo** (*illus. Jean Harper*)	HAMISH HAMILTON 1960	B
7	**Eight for a Secret** (*illus. Lewis Hart*)	CONSTABLE 1960 WATTS 1961	B B
8	**The Penny Pony** (*illus. Juliette Palmer*)	HAMISH HAMILTON 1961	B
9	**If All the Swords in England** (*illus. Robert M. Sax*)	DOUBLEDAY 1961 BURNS OATES 1961	B B
10	**Stop the Train!** (*illus. Jean Harper*)	HAMISH HAMILTON 1961	B
11	**The Summer with Spike** (*illus. Anne Linton*)	CONSTABLE 1961 WATTS 1962	B B
12	**Duck on a Pond** (*illus. Mary Rose Hardy*)	CONSTABLE 1962 WATTS 1962	B B
13	**Hetty** (*illus. Pamela Mara*)	CONSTABLE 1962 HARCOURT BRACE 1963	B B
14	**Augustine Came to Kent** (*illus. Hans Guggenheim*)	DOUBLEDAY 1963 WORLD'S WORK 1964	B C
15	**The Battle of Wednesday Week** (*illus. Douglas Hall*)	CONSTABLE 1963	B
16	**Storm from the West** Same as 15.	HARCOURT BRACE 1964	B

17	**The Dippers and the High-flying Kite** (*illus. Maureen Eckersley*)	HAMISH HAMILTON 1963	B
18	**The Suddenly Gang** (*illus. Lynne Hemmant*)	HAMISH HAMILTON 1963	B
19	**The Pram Race** (*illus. Constance Marshall*)	HAMISH HAMILTON 1964	B
20	**A Dog and a Half** (*illus. Jane Paton*)	HAMISH HAMILTON 1964 NELSON 1971	B B
21	**Three and One to Carry** (*illus. Douglas Hall*)	CONSTABLE 1964 HARCOURT BRACE 1965	B B
22	**The Wild Idea** (*illus. Douglas Bissett*)	HAMISH HAMILTON 1965	B
23	**Charity at Home** (*illus. Douglas Hall*)	CONSTABLE 1965 HARCOURT BRACE 1966	B B
24	**Surprise Island** (*illus. Jane Paton*)	HAMISH HAMILTON 1966 MEREDITH PRESS 1969	B B
25	**The Richleighs of Tantamount** (*illus. C. Walter Hodges*)	CONSTABLE 1966 HARCOURT BRACE 1967	B B
26	**The Grove of Green Holly** (*illus. Gareth Floyd*)	CONSTABLE 1967	B
27	**Flight to the Forest** *Same as 26.*	DOUBLEDAY 1967	B
28	**The Pet Club** (*illus. Lynne Hemmant*)	HAMISH HAMILTON 1967	B
29	**To London! To London!** (*illus. Antony Maitland*)	LONGMAN 1968 WEYBRIGHT & TALLEY 1968	C B
30	**Hurrah For Rosie!** (*illus. Gareth Floyd*)	HUTCHINSON 1968	B
31	**Royal Rosie** (*illus. Gareth Floyd*)	HUTCHINSON 1968	B
32	**The Family Tower**	CONSTABLE 1968 HARCOURT BRACE 1968	B B

33	**The Toppling Towers**	LONGMAN 1969	**B**
		HARCOURT BRACE 1969	**B**
34	**The Pocket Mouse**	HAMISH HAMILTON 1969	**B**
	(*illus. Mary Russon*)	KNOPF 1969	**B**
35	**Junior Motorist: The Driver's**	COLLINS 1969	**B**
	Apprentice (*non-fiction*)		
	(*with Frances Howell*) (*illus. Ionicus*)		
36	**Chichester and Lewes** (*non-fiction*)	LONGMAN 1970	**B**
	(*illus. Graham Humphreys*)		

Numbers 37–44 comprise the 'Mantlemass' *saga:*

37	**The Lark and the Laurel**	LONGMAN 1970	**C**
	(*illus. Gareth Floyd*)	HARCOURT BRACE 1970	**B**
38	**The Sprig of Broom**	LONGMAN 1971	**C**
	(*illus. Paul Shardlow*)	DUTTON 1972	**B**
39	**A Cold Wind Blowing**	LONGMAN 1972	**B**
		DUTTON 1973	**B**
40	**The Iron Lily**	LONGMAN 1973	**B**
		DUTTON 1974	**B**
41	**Harrow and Harvest**	KESTREL 1974	**B**
		DUTTON 1975	**B**
42	**The Miller's Boy**	KESTREL 1976	**B**
	(*illus. Gareth Floyd*)	DUTTON 1976	**B**
43	**The Eldest Son**	KESTREL 1977	**B**
44	**A Flight of Swans**	KESTREL 1980	**B**
	This concludes the Mantlemass saga.		
45	**Priscilla Pentecost**	HAMISH HAMILTON 1970	**B**
	(*illus. Doreen Roberts*)		
46	**The Reindeer Slippers**	HAMISH HAMILTON 1970	**B**
	(*illus. Tessa Jordan*)		
47	**The Dragon Box**	HAMISH HAMILTON 1972	**B**
	(*illus. Tessa Jordan*)		
48	**Jubilee!**	HEINEMANN 1973	**B**
	(*illus. Hilary Abrahams*)		

49	**Bridesmaid**	HAMISH HAMILTON 1976	**B**
	(*illus. Jane Paton*)		
50	**The Country Maid**	HAMISH HAMILTON 1978	**B**
		GREENWILLOW 1980	**A**
51	**The Gardener's Grandchildren**	KESTREL 1978	**B**
	(*illus. Gordon King*)	McGRAW HILL 1979	**A**
52	**Spell Me a Witch**	HAMISH HAMILTON 1979	**B**
	(*illus. Phillida Gili*)	HARCOURT BRACE 1981	**A**
53	**The Keys of Mantlemass** (*stories*)	KESTREL 1981	**B**
54	**Summer Season**	MACRAE 1981	**A**
55	**Famous Rowena Lamont**	HARDY 1983	**A**
56	**The Queen of the Pharisees' Children**	MACRAE 1983	**A**
57	**Smiley Tiger**	MACRAE 1984	**A**
58	**Ned Only**	MACRAE 1985	**A**

WILLIAMSON, Henry
Born in Dorset, 1895. Died 1977

Another author who did not expressly intend any of his work to be for the children's market, and yet although his two best known works may be re-read and appreciated by anyone of any age at all, it is likely that they were first encountered fairly early on in one's reading life: in this sense, they have become 'children's books'. I list below those few works in Williamson's large *oeuvre* which are similarly classified.

1	**Tarka the Otter, Being His Joyful Water-life and Death in the Country of the Two Rivers**	PUTNAM 1927	**G**
		DUTTON 1928	**D**
2	**Salar the Salmon**	FABER 1935	**F**
		LITTLE BROWN 1936	**D**
3	**Scribbling Lark**	FABER 1949	**D**
4	**The Henry Williamson Animal Saga** (*stories*)	MACDONALD 1960	**C**
5	**The Scandaroon**	MACDONALD 1972	**B**
	(*illus. Ken Lilly*)	SATURDAY REVIEW PRESS 1973	**B**

Also of interest:

ED. BROCARD SEWELL: **Henry Williamson: The Man, the Writings**
  (TABB HOUSE 1980)

DANIEL FARSON: **An Appreciation of Henry Williamson** (JOSEPH 1982)

WODEHOUSE, P.G.   *Born in Surrey, 1881. Died 1975*

Now of course any child worth his or her salt is reading any Wodehouse available at as early an age as possible – swaddling clothes onwards, I should say. However, Wodehouse did start off writing specifically for public school boys, somewhat in the way of Frank Richards, but with very much more rounded characters and subtler wit. I list these below – the high prices reflecting the truth that Plum is one of the most collected authors of all, and these books represent his very earliest work.

1	**The Pothunters**	BLACK 1902	**P**
	(*illus. R. Noel Pocock*)	MACMILLAN US 1924	**G**
	This is Wodehouse's first book.		
2	**A Prefect's Uncle**	BLACK 1903	**O**
	(*illus. R. Noel Pocock*)	MACMILLAN US 1924	**G**
3	**Tales of St Austin's** (*stories*)	BLACK 1903	**O**
	(*illus. T.M.R. Whitwell, R. Noel Pocock & E.F. Skinner*)	MACMILLAN US 1923	**G**
4	**The Gold Bat**	BLACK 1904	**O**
	(*illus. T.M.R. Whitwell*)	MACMILLAN US 1923	**G**
5	**William Tell Told Again** (*retelling*)	BLACK 1904	**L**
	(*illus. Philip Dadd*)		
6	**The Head of Kay's**	BLACK 1905	**O**
	(*illus. T.M.R. Whitwell*)	MACMILLAN US 1922	**G**
7	**The White Feather**	BLACK 1907	**O**
	(*illus. W. Townend*)	MACMILLAN US 1922	**G**
8	**Mike**	BLACK 1909	**O**
	(*illus. T.M.R. Whitwell*)	MACMILLAN US 1924	**G**
	The second part of this novel was reissued as Enter Psmith *by Black in 1935. The whole novel was then rewritten and reissued in two volumes:* Mike at Wrykn *and* Mike and Psmith *(Jenkins 1953).*		

Also of interest:

RICHARD USBORNE: **Wodehouse at Work** (JENKINS 1961. *Revised ed. as*
Wodehouse at Work to the End BARRIE & JENKINS 1977)

DAVID A. JASEN: **A Bibliography and Reader's Guide to the First Editions
of P.G. Wodehouse** (BARRIE & JENKINS 1971, *revised ed.* GREENHILL 1986)

JOSEPH CONNOLLY: **P.G. Wodehouse: An Illustrated Biography** (ORBIS 1979,
new ed. as **P.G. Wodehouse** THAMES & HUDSON 1987)

ED. JAMES A. HEINEMAN & DONALD R. BENSON: **P.G. Wodehouse: A Centenary
Celebration 1881–1981** (PIERPONT MORGAN LIBRARY 1981)

FRANCES DONALDSON: **P.G. Wodehouse: The Authorized Biography**
(WEIDENFELD & NICOLSON 1982)

INDEX OF ILLUSTRATORS

Abbey, J. 52, 53, 167
Abrahams, Hilary 99, 233, 328
Acs, Laszlo 28, 203, 281
Adams, Adrienne 130
Adamson, George 158, 160
Adshead, Mary 223
Ahlberg, Janet 17, 18, 19, 20
Aldridge, Alan 16
Allamand, Pascale 41
Alldridge, Elizabeth 289
Almond, W. Douglas 196
Ambrus, Victor 111, 192, 201, 280, 281
Amstutz, André 18, 19
Appleton, Honor C. 90
Archer, Janet 233
Archer, Peter 97
Ardizzone, Edward 88, 114, 119, 181, 186, 232, 245–8, 259, 278, 282, 283
Armitage, David 233
Arnold, James 159
Astrop, John 89
Atkinson Jacqueline 182
Atkinson, Leslie 231, 301
Aveten, John 115
Ayer, Jacqueline 114

Bacon, H. L. 197, 227
Bagnold, Enid 31
Banberry, Fred 61, 62, 131
Barclay, A. 321
Bargery, Geoffrey 302
Barker, Alan 233
Barker Carol 98, 131
Bartlett, Maurice 181
Barton, Byron 156
Baskin, Leonard 159
Batchelor, A. E. 289
Batchelor, P. B. 322
Bates, Leo 197, 317, 319
Baumer, Lewis 220, 221
Bayley, Nicola 16, 156, 204
Baynes, John 136
Baynes, Pauline 131, 147, 186, 224, 283, 291, 310
Baynton, Martin 157
Bedford, F. D. 37
Beitz, Geoffrey 47
Bellingham-Smith, Elinor 306
Benatar, Molly 227
Benda, Wladyslaw T. 236
Bennett, Jill 94, 102, 147, 183
Benson, Patrick 204
Bentley, Nicholas 44, 112, 123
Berbeck, Frank 38
Berg, Bjorn 243
Berridge, Celia 99–101
Bertoglio, Victor 321, 322
Bianco, Pamela 282
Birch, Linda 183
Biro, Val 182
Bissett, Douglas 327
Blackwood, Basil 43, 44
Blake, Quentin, 22–4, 102, 103, 155–7, 160, 246, 269
Blampied, E. 66
Blanc, Martine 93
Blatch, Bernard 304
Blegvad, Erik 223

Blyth, Alan 299, 300
Boland, Michael 298, 299
Bold 109
Booth, George 269
Boston, Peter 64
Boswell, James 282
Boye Uden, E. 319, 320
Boyle, Mildred, 324
Braby, Dorothy 277
Bradley, Maureen 302
Bragg, Michael 127, 183
Brandt, R. A. 158
Brazil, Amy 65
Brazil, Angela 65
Brier, E. 198
Briggs, Raymond 202, 248
Briggs, Winifred 75
Brisley, Nina K. 68, 73, 226, 227
Brock, C. E. 115, 221, 274
Brock, H. M. 206, 211, 300
Brook, George 56
Brook, Judith 310
Brooker, Christopher 201
Brown, Marc 111
Browne, Gordon 196, 199, 220, 221, 313
Browne, Nina 226
Bruce, Joyce 217, 218
Brundage, Frances 219
Brundage, Will 219
Brunsman, James 185
Bryan, James 131
Buchanan, Lilian 54
Buckels, Alec 307
Bull, Rene 274
Bullen, Anne 217
Burkert, Nancy Ekholm 102, 165
Burningham, John 120
Byrnes, Lynne 131

Cable, W. Lindsay 58, 68, 299
Cadby, Carine 104
Cadby, Will 104
Caldwell, Doreen 47, 89
Cameron, J. 317
Campbell, Aileen 224
Campbell, Jennifer 17
Campbell, John 66, 210, 314
Campbell, R. G. 322
Carey, Joanna 47, 48
Carter, Helen 244
Cattaneo, Tony 62
Chadwick, Oliver 46, 48
Chaffin, Donald 102
Chalmers, Mary 155
Chamberlain, Margaret 94, 127
Channing, G. H. 304
Chapman, C. H. 255, 256
Charlton, George 157
Charlton, Michael 280
Chesterman, Hugh 115, 116
Clark, Mary Cowles 38
Clarke, Bridget 94
Claus, M. A. 207
Claus, W. A. 207
Claveloux, Nicole 157
Claverie, Jean 111
Cloke, R. 228
Cober, Alan 111, 125

Cole, Babette 23, 161
Cole, Brock 313
Collard, Derek 224, 233
Coller, Henry 67, 197, 198, 318
Cook, Anyon 53
Cooley, V. 198
Cope, Jane 27
Corbett, Jennie 88, 89, 311
Cory, Fanny 38
Cosman, Milein 277
Cottam, Martin 127
Coughlan, Olive 290
Cousins, Derek 160, 161
Cowles, Hookway 303
Cox, E. A. 317
Craig, Frank 184
Craig, Helen 224
Craigie, Dorothy 137
Crockford, Jill 290
Crossley-Holland, Kevin 312
Cummings, Arthur 270
Cuneo, Cyrus 195, 196, 273
Cuneo, Terence 167, 318, 320
Cutler, Dudley 245

Dalby, C. Reginald 29, 30
Dalton, Ann 189
Davies, Jo 183
Davies, Joyce 52
De Walton, John 319
De Wilde, Dick 217
Denny, Antony 257
Denslow, W. W. 38
Dewar Mills, J. 67, 68
Dillon, Diane 298
Dillon, Leo 298
Dinsdale, Mary 203, 278, 312
Dixon, A. A. 194, 209, 210, 225, 226
Dobson, M. 116
Dodd, Philip 331
Downes, Gerry 99
Drigin, S. 320
Drummond, V. H. 91
Duchesne, James 201
Duchesne, Janet 27, 201, 202
Dudley, Ambrose 221
Dugdale, T. C. 199, 272, 273
Dunlop, Gilbert 53, 54
Durden, James 225

Earnshaw, H. C. 225, 226
Eckersley, Maureen 91, 326
Ede, Janina 92, 311
Edwards, Gunvor 30, 46
Edwards, Peter 30
Eichenberg, Fritz 157, 323
Einzig, Susan 232
Elcock, H. E. 274
Ellis, Fred 299
Emett, Rowland 109
Englander, Alice 48, 183
Enright, Elizabeth 112, 113
Erdoes, Richard 269
Esor 61
Estes, Eleanor 114
Evans, C. R. 45
Evans, J. D. 230
Evans, Treyer 53, 54, 66, 299
Evison, H. 274

Ewan, Frances 195
Eyles, D. C. 321

Farjeon, Joan Jefferson 118
Farmer, Peter 296
Fawcett, Rosemary 103
Fawley, Audrey 231
Felts, Shirley 88, 281, 282
Fiammenghi, Gioia 62
Firth, Barbara 204
Fisk, Nicholas 203
Fleming Williams, C. 272, 314
Fletcher, Geoffrey 325, 326
Floyd, Gareth 91, 92, 111, 188,
    247, 248, 327, 328
Ford, Henry 97
Foreman, Michael 111, 127, 129
Forrest, A. S. 32
Fortnum, Peggy 44, 60–62, 91,
    119, 124, 258, 278
Foyster, G. B. 225
François, André 282, 283
Frascino, Edward 323
Fraser, Betty 21
Freeman, Don 284
Freshman, Shelley 224
Froud, Brian 224
Fukazawa, Kuniro 88

Gale, W. 321, 322
Ganly, Helen 233
Garland, Sarah 290
Garnett, Eve 159
Garside, John 115
Garraty, Gail 185
Geary, Clifford 148
Geldart, William 124
Gentleman, David 156
Gervis, Ruth 276
Gibbs, George 207
Gibson, Colin 182
Gilbert, Yvonne 17, 76
Gili, Phillida 37, 48, 329
Gill, Margery 45, 64, 92, 93,
    136, 137, 201, 202, 277, 278
Gill, McDonald 115
Giovanetti 181
Glegg, Creina 131
Goddard, David 16
Goldsmith, Beatrice 299
Gollins, David 123
Goodall, John S. 301
Gooderman, H. 167
Goodman, M. 219
Goodwin, Philip R. 191
Gordon, Margaret 45–47, 92,
    94
Gorham, A. C. H. 299
Goss, G. W. 316
Goss, John 208
Gough, Philip 119, 296
Gower, Frances 307
Grahame, Elspeth 136
Gray, Reg 46
Gri 257–259
Groves, Diana 182
Gruelle, Justin 139, 140
Gruelle, Worth 139, 140
Guggenheim, Hans 326
Guthrie, Robin 115

Haas, Irene 113
Hales, Robert 46, 98, 111

Hall, Douglas 296, 326, 327
Hardy, Mary Rose 326
Hardy, Paul 194
Harper, Jean 326
Hart, Dick 21, 28, 246, 295
Hart, Lewis 326
Hawes, Meredith W. 119
Hawkins, Irene 109, 110, 258,
    307–309
Hawkins, Sheila 224
Hays, Ethel 140
Heade 228
Heale, Jonathan 204
Heap, Jonathan 94
Heath Robinson, T. 225
Heath Robinson, W. 159, 160,
    205
Hedderwick, Mairi 131
Hellard, Susan 183
Helweg, Hans 61–63
Hemmant, Lynette 91, 192, 290,
    301, 326, 327
Hemming, Caroline 64
Henry, Thomas 95–97
Hepwroth, Philip 309
Hickling, P. B. 67, 226
Hickson, Joan 99, 100, 123
Hilder, Rowland 316–318
Hiley, F. E. 67, 198
Hoban, Lilian 153–155
Hodges, C. Walter 135, 200,
    201, 279, 280, 300, 303, 327
Hodges, Edgar 47
Hodgson, E. S., 313–318
Hodgson, Jim 61
Hodgson, Robert 45, 301
Hofbauer, Imre 45
Hoffnung, Gerard 282
Honey, Elizabeth 204
Honeysett, Martin 183
Hope, Robert 195
Hopper, John 140
Horder, Margaret 228, 229
Horrell, C. 210
Hough, Charlotte 290
Howard, Norman 167
Hughes, David 160
Hughes, Shirley 40, 91, 92, 94,
    200, 202, 259, 277, 311, 312
Humphreys, Graham 296, 328
Hunt, James 46
Hutchins, Laurence 162, 163
Hutton, Clarke 276

Innes, Nancy 258, 308
Inns, Kenneth 317
Ionicus 30, 302, 328

Jackson, Helen 220
Jacques, Robin 21, 91, 92
Jaques, Faith 19, 28, 93, 98,
    126, 237, 305
Jellicoe, John 193
Jessett, Alan 300
Jezzard, S. 321
Jobson, P. A. 322
Johnson, Jane 282
Johnston, Robert 322
Jones, David 115
Jones, Harold 109, 189
Jones, Laurian 31
Jones, Lyn 27
Jones, Nikki 296

Jordan, Tessa 328
Julian-Ottie, Vanessa 63

Kakimoto, Kozo 88
Kallin, Tasha 122
Kastner, Erich 176
Kay, B. 230
Kay, Bruno 56, 57
Kaye, Margaret 257, 258
Kazuko 183
Kealey, E. J. 227
Kearon, E. 322
Keeping, Charles 27, 41, 89,
    127, 128, 247, 280, 281, 298,
    301, 304, 305
Kemp, Pamela 230
Kemp-Walsh, Lucy 219, 220
Kennedy, A. E. 307–310
Kennedy, Paul 110
Kennedy, Richard 92, 135, 181,
    182, 218, 247, 277, 279, 300,
    303
Kenney, John 29, 30
Kenyon, Ley 277
Kettlewell, Doritie 122
Kiddell-Monroe, Joan 223, 247
King, Gordon 329
Kipling, Rudyard 184
Knight, Anne 93
Knight, David 119
Knight, J. C. B. 299, 319–321
Knowles, Horace 308
Koekkoek, H. W. 272
Koering, Ursula 289
Kopper, Lisa 89
Krush, Beth 113
Krush, Joe 113

Lamb, Lynton 200, 201, 246
Lambert, Saul 125
Lambert, Thelma 175
Land, Jessie 52
Lane Foster, Marcia 200, 276
Lathrop, Dorothy P. 104,
    109–110
Lawrence, John 16, 18, 28, 125,
    189, 233, 248, 280
Lawson, Robert 118
Le Cain, Errol 92, 147
Lee, Doris 284
Lee, Stephen 16
Leigh, Howard 166, 167
Leighton, Clare 117
Lenski, Lois 190
Leslie, Cecil 311
Lewitt-Him, George 258
Lilly, Ken 329
Lilly, Kenneth 204
Lindsay, Alan 123
Linton, Anne 202, 326
Littlejohns, J. 115
Livingston Bull, Charles 184,
    191
Lloyd, R. J. 159
Lloyd, Stanley 58
Lockwood Kipling, J. 184
Lumley, Savile 314
Lyford-Pike, Margaret 281

Macdonald, R. J., 253–255
Macey, Barry 63
MacGregor, Sheila 136
MacIntyre, J. 319

INDEX OF ILLUSTRATORS

MacKenzie 244
MacKinlay, M. 68, 321
Maitland, Antony 29, 120, 125–127, 157, 188, 232, 279, 327
Margetson, W. H., 195, 271
Margrie, Janet 312
Marks, Alan 282
Marriott, Pat 21–24, 277
Marsh, Janet 302
Marshall, Constance 192, 259, 327
Marshall, James 156
Marston, F. 317
Martin, Charles 269
Martinez, Mina 233
Matthew, Jack 322
Maxey, Betty 278
May, J. A. 199
Mays 82, 83
Mays, D. L. 68, 276, 318, 319
Mazure, 83, 84
McArthur, Molly 116
McCully, Emily 156
McDonald, Jill 98, 160, 161
McGavin, Hilda 52
McGrath, Edward 136
McKee, David 63
McKie, Roy 268–270
McNaughton, Colin 19, 20, 156, 247
Medley, Robert 123
Melnyczuk, Peter 233
Mendoza 168
Meredith, Norman 53
Merrill, Frank 235
Meyerheim, F. 227
Meyer, Renate 92
Michael, A. C. 273
Micklewright, Robert 280, 296
Miles, Jennifer 44, 310
Millar, H. R. 184, 220–222, 284
Miller, Jon 192
Milligan, Spike 205
Mitrokhin, Dmitri 244
Moorsom, F. 65
Morgan, Ike 38
Morton-Sale, Isobel 118, 119
Morton-Sale, John 118
Mounsey, R. K. 220
Mountfort, Irene 118
Mozley, Charles 217, 278
Mozley, Juliet 188
Mulford, Stockton 235
Murch, Frank 235
Murphy, Jill 2
Murray, Webster 230

Nachsen, Donia 299
Nadejen, Theodore 109
Naish, Roger 118
Nankivell, Selma 88
Narraway, Will 167
Nechamkin, Sarah 248, 308
Neild, Julie 230
Neill, John R. 38, 39
Neilson, M. D. 229
Nelson, Edmund 118, 119
Newsham, Ian 111, 182, 183
Nickless, Will 218, 289, 303, 321
Nicolle, Jack 167
Nightingale, C. T. 109
Northway, Jenny 313

Oakenshott, Ewart 304
Ogle, R. B. 316
Oldham, F. 67
Orton Jones, Elizabeth 119
Osmond, Edward 322
Overnell, E. A. 225
Owens, Majorie 122

Padday, C. M. 314, 316
Paget, Wal 197, 209
Pailthorpe, Doris 116
Palmer, Juliette 312
Pannett, Juliet 44
Parkins, David 182, 189
Paton, Jane 119, 246, 327, 328
Payne, Roger 54, 304
Pears, Charles 315
Pearse, S. B. 117, 118, 151
Peddie, Tom 210
Peirce, Waldo 223
Pendle, Alexy 41, 98, 99
Pene Du Bois, William 102
Peppe, Mark 182, 297
Petherick, Rosa 226
Philip 321
Pieńkowski, Jan 21, 23, 222
Piffard, Harold 194, 195
Pizer, Abigail 183
Pocock, R. Noel 330
Pollard, Michael 189
Porter, Gene Stratton 236
Porter, Sue 111
Praeger, S. Rosamund 220
Prater, Ernest 314, 319
Price, Christine 302–304
Price, Janet 192
Primrose, Jean 131
Prout, Victor 225
Pryse, Spencer 222
Pym, H. 320

Rabier, Benjamin 289
Rackham, Arthur 37
Rainey, William 193, 195, 196
Ransome, Arthur 244, 245
Raverat, Gwendolen 117, 307
Rawlins, Janet 124, 203
Rayner, Mary 182, 183, 313
Relf, Douglas 170, 171
Ribbons, Ian 135
Richards, Eugenie 116
Richardson, Frederick 38
Riddell, Chris 159
Ridley, Trevor 125
Ritchie, Paul 296
Robb, Brian 222
Robbins, Ruth 185
Roberts, Doreen 92, 328
Roberts, Lunt 97
Robertson, Graham 136
Robinson, Charles 84
Rocker, Fermin 27
Rodber, Julia 174
Rodwell, Jenny 248
Rogers, Kate 48
Rose, Gerald 158, 161, 175
Rosoman, Leonard 145
Ross, Diana 257–259
Rothenstein, William Michael 115
Rountree, Harry 221
Rowan, Evadne 245
Rowe, Gavin 312

Rowles, Daphne 60
Roy, Jeroo 131, 312
Rush, Peter 192
Russell Flint, W. 117
Russon, Mary 202, 301, 305, 327

Saida 206
Saintsbury, Dana 130
Salmon, Balliol 66
Sanders, Beryl 61
Sanders, Toffee 88, 89
Sax, Robert M. 326
Schindelman, Joseph 102
Schoenherr, John 165
Schreiter, Rick 157
Scott 299
Scott, David 156
Scott, W. R. S. 195
Scruton, Clive 156
Searle, Ronald 325
Seldon, Charles 314
Selig, Sylvie 156
Sendak, Maurice 165
Sergeant, John 233
Seward, Prudence 99, 201, 259, 290
Sewell, Helen 118, 324
Sewell, John 175
Shardlow, Paul 328
Sharpe, Caroline 47, 233
Sharrocks, Burgess 57, 58
Shedden, Dinah 48
Sheldon, Charles 194, 272
Shepard, Ernest H. 119, 206
Shepard, Mary 207, 297, 298
Shepperson, Claude 220
Sherriffs, R. S. 300
Shuba, Susanne 277
Silas, Ellis 320, 321
Silcock, Sara 301
Sillince, W. A. 304
Simont, Marc 284
Sims, Agnes 298
Sindall, Alfred 166, 167, 299
Skinner, E. F. 320
Slade, Irene 48
Slobodkin, Louis 113, 114, 283
Smee, David 111, 302, 312, 313
Smith, Mary 230
Smith, May 117
Smith, Wendy 182
Smithson Broadbent, W. 67
Soper, Eileen A. 53, 55, 56
Soper, G. 195
Speed, Lancelot 195
Spence, Geraldine 160, 246, 278
Spurrier, Steven 135, 200, 276
Stacey, W. S. 194–196
Stanley, Diana 223
Stanwell Smith, Juliet 131
Stead, Leslie, 167–174
Stecher, William 235
Steele, Lorna R. 135
Stetson Crawford, E. 236
Stevenson, Hugh 119
Stobbs, William 99, 201, 280, 301, 304, 305
Stockle, J. L. 300
Stott, W. R. S. 196, 197, 273
Stowell, Gordon 119
Strugnell, Ann 93, 131, 311
Stubbs, Joanna 94, 203, 313

Stubley, Trevor 47, 203, 217, 323
Suba, Susanne 114
Sutcliffe, John E. 197
Swiderska, Barbara 247

Taber, I. W. 184
Taft Dixon, Rachel 140
Tarrant, Margaret 116
Tarrant, Percy 226, 227
Taylor, J. B. 85
Taylor, Leigh 85
Tealby, Norman 117
Tempest, Margaret 306–311
Tenison, N. 195
Tennant, Dudley 315
Thayer, Lee 236
Theobald, Tessa 201
Thompson, Sheila M. 118
Thorne, Jenny 93
Thorneycroft, Rosalind 116, 117
Thorpe, Barry 48
Thurber, James 284
Tobey, B. 269
Tod, R. 194
Tolkein, J. R. R. 291
Tout, Ann 45, 46
Townend, W. 330
Townsend, Will 116, 306
Tozer, Katharine 118
Tresilian, Stuart 52–54, 167, 168, 304
Trotter, Stuart 100
Troughton, Joanna 224, 248
Trowski, Albin 129
Turska, Krystyna 28, 203, 204, 224, 246, 247, 301
Turvey, R. M. 230
Tyas, Martin 167

Uderzo, Albert 132–134
Unwin, Nora S. 222
Upsdale-Jones, Clare 47

Valpy, Judith 45, 48
Van Abbe, S. 320
Van Beek, Harmsen 59
Veevers, Isobel 54
Verney, John 28
Visscher, Peter 204
Voter, Thomas 148

Wade Walker, Roger 62, 63
Wain, Louis 222
Walford, P. 211
Walker, David 301
Walsh, David 218
Walt Disney Studio 102
Warner, Peter 202, 278
Watkin, Isabel 221
Watkins-Pitchford, D. J. 200, 201
Watson, A. H. 109
Watson, Clixby 91
Watson, Comerford 318
Webb, Archibald 211, 272
Webb, Clifford 244
Webster, W. E. 272
Weedon, L. L. 273
Wegner, Fritz 19, 20, 98, 125–127, 160, 203
Wehr, Julian 139
Weiss, Emil 326

Wells, Robin Jane 91
Westcott, Ruth 118, 289
Wheeler, Dorothy M. 52, 53
Whistler, Rex 109
White, Freire 121
White, T. H. 323
Whiting, F. 195
Whittam, Geoffrey 300
Whitwell, T. M. R. 330
Whydale, E. Herbert 117
Wigful, W. E. 314–319
Wigglesworth, Katherine 309–312
Wightman, W. E. 67, 274, 316
Wijngaard, Juan 147, 148, 197
Wilcox, Leslie 320
Wildsmith, Brian 301
Wiles, Frank 66, 67, 313
Wilkinson, Barry 62, 278
Willett, Jillian 278
Williams, Adrian 16
Williams, Garth 154, 165, 323, 324
Williams, Kathleen 232
Williams, Pat 45
Willis, Charles 68
Wilson, E. 52
Wilson, Marice 99, 247
Wilson, Oscar 195
Wilson, Ratcliffe 167
Wolpe, Berthold 110
Wood, Elsie 222, 226
Wood, Ivor 46, 61, 62
Wood, Leslie 61, 91, 202, 258, 259
Wright, Alan 272
Wright, Joe 18

Young, L. 306

Zemach, Margot 165
Zinkeison, Anna 276

ACKNOWLEDGEMENTS

My thanks are due to dedicated collector of children's books, Sarah Jardine-Willoughby, for her advice and assistance, as well as to Chris Mason, the principal librarian at Wandsworth Town Hall, for allowing me access to their fine collection of children's books.

Gratitude is also due to the following publishers for permission to reproduce dust-wrapper designs and illustrations:

Gillian Avery, *The Greatest Gresham* (Collins, 1962). Blackie and Son Ltd: A. Brazil, *The Fortunes of Philippa, The Nicest Girl in the School, A Pair of School-girls*; Mrs H. Cradock, *Josephine's Christmas Party*; B. Marchant, *Sylvia's Secret*; H. Strang, *Kobo*; Percy F. Westerman, *Combined Operations*. The Bodley Head Ltd: L.M. Boston, *The Stones of Green Knowe*; M. Sendak, *Fly by Night, Higgelty Piggelty Pop*; R. Sutcliff, *The Light Beyond the Forest, The Road to Camlan, The Sword and the Circle*. Curtis Brown: A.A. Milne, *Winnie the Pooh, The House at Pooh Corner*. Jonathan Cape Ltd: R. Adams, *Tyger Voyage* (illustrated by N. Bayley); J. Aiken, *Go Saddle the Sea* (illustrated by Pat Marriott); Q. Blake, *Quentin Blake's Nursery Rhyme Book*; R. Dahl, *Dirty Beasts, The Witches* (illustrated by Q. Blake); I. Fleming, *Chitty-Chitty-Bang-Bang* (illustrated by J. Burningham); H. Lofting, *Doctor Dolittle and the Green Canary, Gub Gub's Book*; A. Ransome, *Pigeon Post*; P. Simmonds, *Fred*. Century Hutchinson Publishing Ltd: A. Prøysen, *Little Old Mrs Pepperpot* (1959); P.G. Wodehouse, *The Pothunters* (1902), *A Prefect's Uncle* (1903), *Tales of St Austins* (1903), *The Gold Bat* (1904), *The Head of Kays* (1905), *The White Feather* (1907), *Mike* (1909), *Mike at Wrykyn* (1953), *Mike and Psmith* (1953). Chatto & Windus: G. Trease, *A Word by Moonlight* (1981). Rex Collings Ltd: R. Adams, *Watership Down*. William Collins & Co Ltd: M. Bond, *A Bear Called Paddington*; A. Buckeridge, *Jennings' Little Hut, Jennings Goes to School, Jennings Follows a Clue, Jennings and Darbishire, Jennings' Diary, According to Jennings*; A. Garner, *Elidor, The Weirdstone of Brisingamen, The Moon of Gomrath*; C.S. Lewis, *The Lion, the Witch and the Wardrobe, Prince Caspian*; Dr. Seuss, *Fox in Socks*; P.L. Travers, *Mary Poppins*. Dent Children's Books: M. Norton, *The Borrowers, The Borrowers Afield, The Borrowers Afloat, The Borrowers Aloft*. By permission of Gerald Duckworth & Co Ltd: H. Belloc, *New Cautionary Tales*. Express Newspapers plc: M. Tourtel, *Rupert in Dreamland, Rupert and the Enchanted Princess*. Eyre & Spottiswoode: B.B., *The Little Grey Men*; G. Greene, *The Little Steamroller*; M. Peak, *Titus Groan, Gormenghast, Titus Alone*. Reprinted by permission of Faber and Faber Ltd: jacket designs from T.S. Eliot, *Old Possum's Book of Practical Cats*; jacket design for *Zed* by R. Harris; Ted Hughes, *The Earth-owl and Other Moon-people, How the Whale Became, Meet My Folks!*; J. Joyce, *The Cat and the Devil*. Victor Gollancz Ltd: P. Dickinson, *Healer* (jacket illustration by Alun Hood); U. le Guin, *The Wizard of Earthsea, The Tombs of Atuan, The Farthest Shore* (jacket illustrations by Barbara Kaiser). Elaine Greene Ltd: Theo Le Sieg, *The Many Mice of Mr. Brice*, illustration by Roy McKie (Collins, Copyright 1973 under the International Union for the Protection of Literary and Artistic works). Hamish Hamilton: J. Gardam, *Bilgewater*; W. Mayne, *Earthfasts, The Battlefield, It*; R. Briggs, *The Snowman*; J. Thurber, *The Wonderful O*. Hamlyn: R. Crompton, *William the Explorer* (Newnes, 1960). Harrap: M. Bond, *Here Comes Thursday*. William Heinemann Ltd: P. Lively, *The Ghost of Thomas Kempe*; J. and A. Ahlberg, *The Jolly Postman*; E. Hill, *Spot's Hospital Visit*; J. Pieńkowski, *Haunted House*; M. Sendak, *Very Far Away*; Rev W. Awdry, the 26 titles in the *Tank Engine* series. Hodder & Stoughton: Captain W.E. Johns, *Biggles Goes Home*. H. Treece, *The Horned Helmet*. Justin Knowles Publishing Group: L.F. Baum, *The Wonderful Wizard of Oz*. Macmillan Publishers Ltd: R. Godden, *The Dark Horse*; R. Kipling, *Captains Courageous, Just So Stories*; D. Wynne Jones, *Charmed Life, Dogsbody*. Julia Macrae Books: B. Willard, *The Queen of the Pharisees' Children*. Methuen: D. Bruna, *B is for Bear*. Orchard Books: J. Pieńkowski, *Little Monsters*. Oxford University Press: W. Mayne, *A Grass Rope*. Reproduced by permission of Penguin Books Ltd: L. Garfield, *Jack Holborn* (Kestrel Books, 1967), *The Strange Affair of Adelaide Harris* (Kestrel Books, 1974), *John Diamond* (Kestrel Books, 1981); K. Hale, *Orlando's Evening Out* (Puffin Books, 1941), *Orlando's Home Life* (Penguin, 1942); R. Jarrell, *Animal Family* (Kestrel Books, 1976); C. King, *Stig of the Dump* (Kestrel Books, 1980); J. Murphy, *The Worst Witch* (Kestrel Books, 1988), *The Worst Witch Strikes Again* (Kestrel Books, 1988); M. Norton, *The Borrowers Avenged* (Kestrel Books, 1982); B. Potter, *The Tale of the Flopsy Bunnies* © Frederick Warne & Co., 1909, *The Tale of Mrs. Tittlemouse* © Frederick Warne & Co., 1910, *The Story of a Fierce Bad Rabbit* © Frederick Warne & Co., 1906, *The Tale of the Pie and the Patty Pan* © Frederick Warne & Co., 1905, *The Tale of Ginger and Pickles* © Frederick Warne & Co., 1909, *The Tale of Timmy Tiptoes* © Frederick Warne & Co., 1911, *The Tale of Peter Rabbit* © Frederick Warne & Co., 1911, *The Tailor of Gloucester* © Frederick Warne & Co., 1903; J. Rowe Townsend, *Dan Alone* (Kestrel Books, 1983). Pilot: Hergé, *Destination Moon* (Methuen, 1959), *Explorers on the Moon* (Methuen, 1959). Quiller Press Limited: F. Richards, *Billy Bunter's Postal Order, Lord Billy Bunter*. Tessa Sayle Agency: C. Willans and R. Searle, *Down with Skool, How to be Topp, Whizz for Atomms, Back in the Jug Agane*. Taylor Vinters: H. Pardoe, *Bunkle Breaks Away* (Routledge, 1945). Unwin Hyman: R. Dahl, *Charlie and the Chocolate Factory*; J.R.R. Tolkien, *The Adventures of Tom Bombadil*.